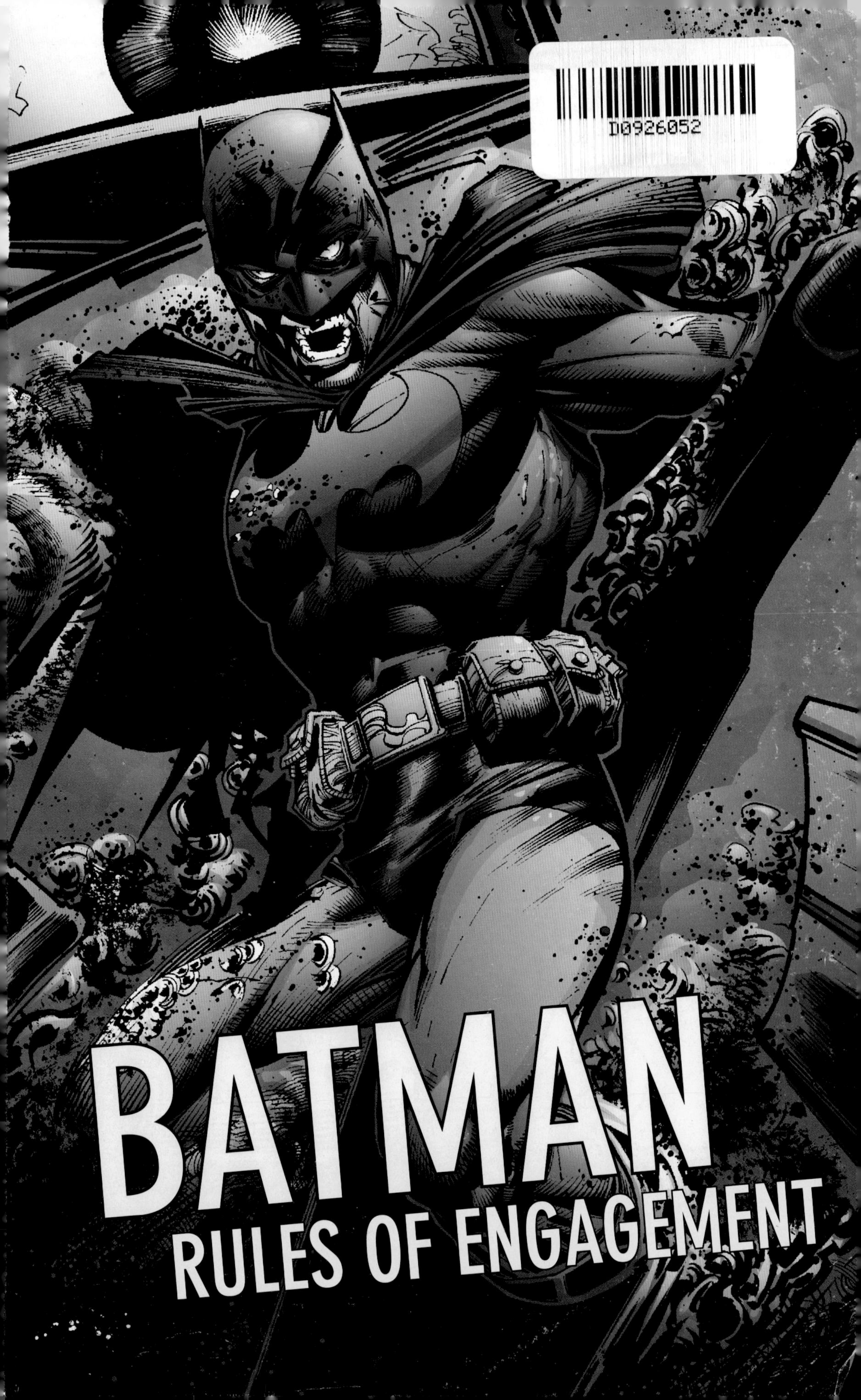
BATMAN
RULES OF ENGAGEMENT

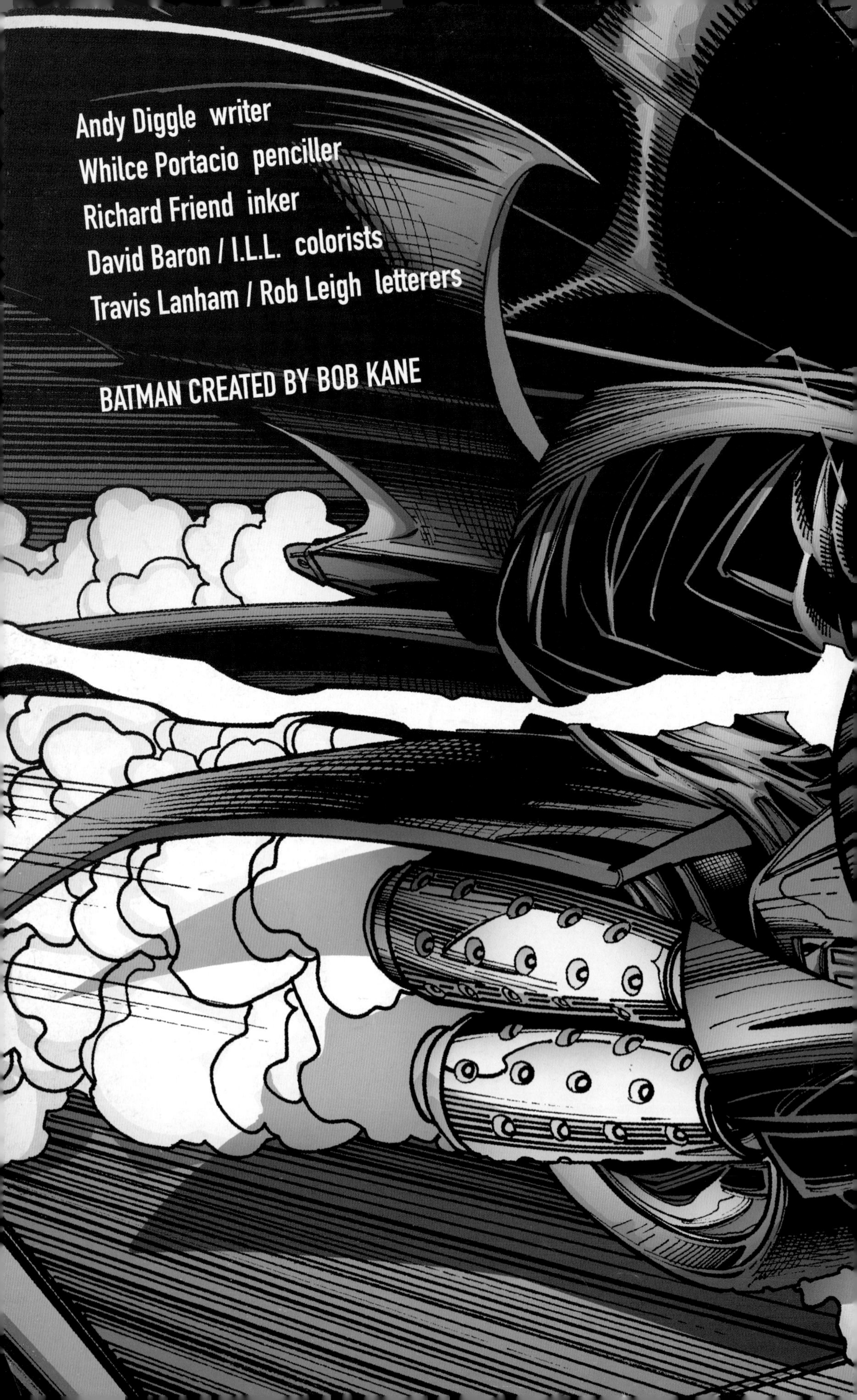

Andy Diggle writer
Whilce Portacio penciller
Richard Friend inker
David Baron / I.L.L. colorists
Travis Lanham / Rob Leigh letterers

BATMAN CREATED BY BOB KANE

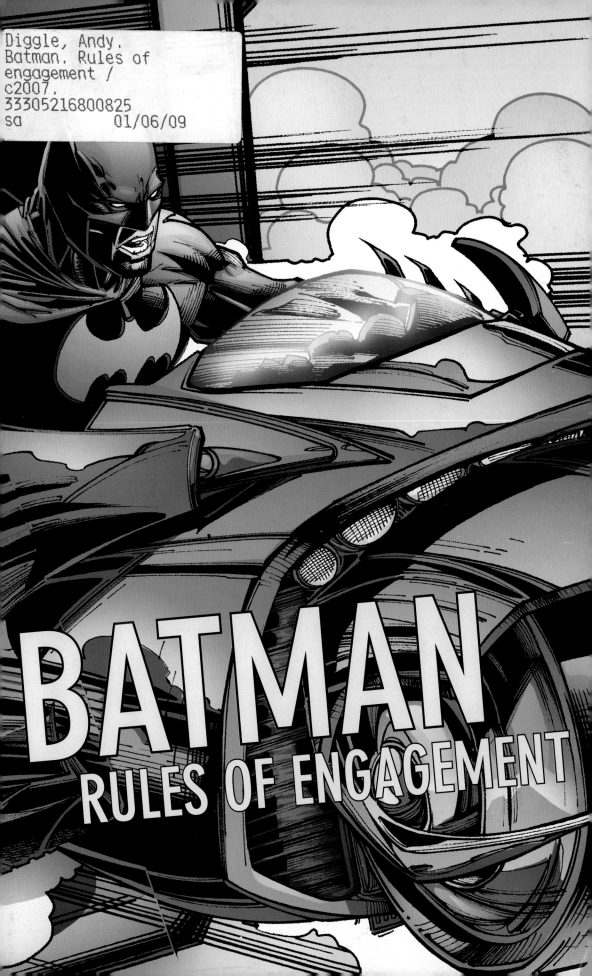

BATMAN
RULES OF ENGAGEMENT

Cover art by Whilce Portacio and Richard Friend.

BATMAN: RULES OF ENGAGEMENT
Published by DC Comics. Cover and compilation copyright © 2007 DC Comics. All Rights Reserved. Originally published in single magazine form in BATMAN CONFIDENTIAL #1-6. Copyright © 2007 DC Comics. All Rights Reserved. All characters, their distinctive likenesses and related elements featured in this publication are trademarks of DC Comics. The stories, characters and incidents featured in this publication are entirely fictional. DC Comics does not read or accept unsolicited submissions of ideas, stories or artwork. DC Comics, 1700 Broadway, New York, NY 10019. A Warner Bros. Entertainment Company. Printed in China. First Printing. HC ISBN: 1-4012-1481-9. HC ISBN 13: 978-1-4012-1481-4. SC ISBN: 1-4012-1706-0. SC ISBN 13: 978-1-4012-1706-8.

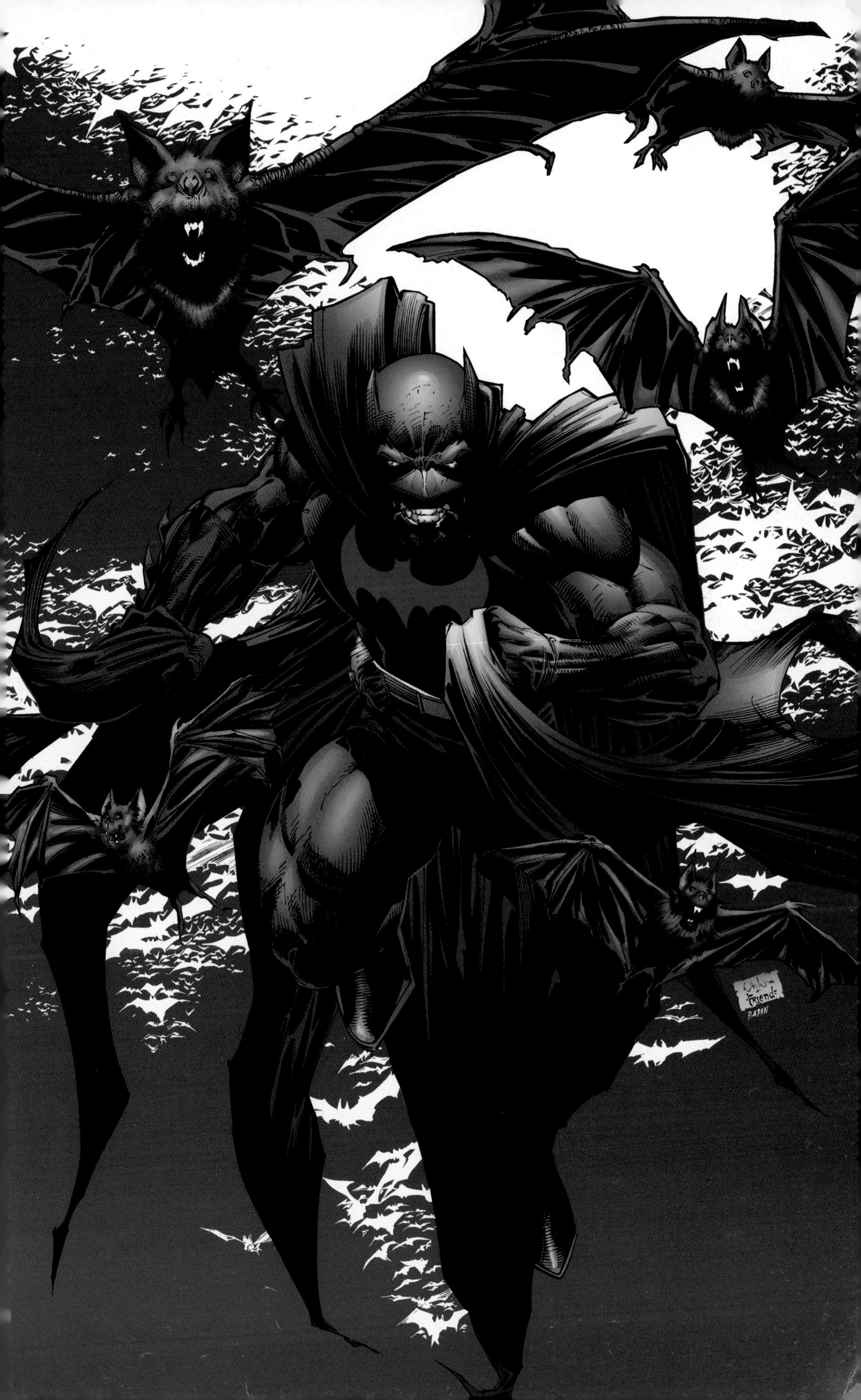

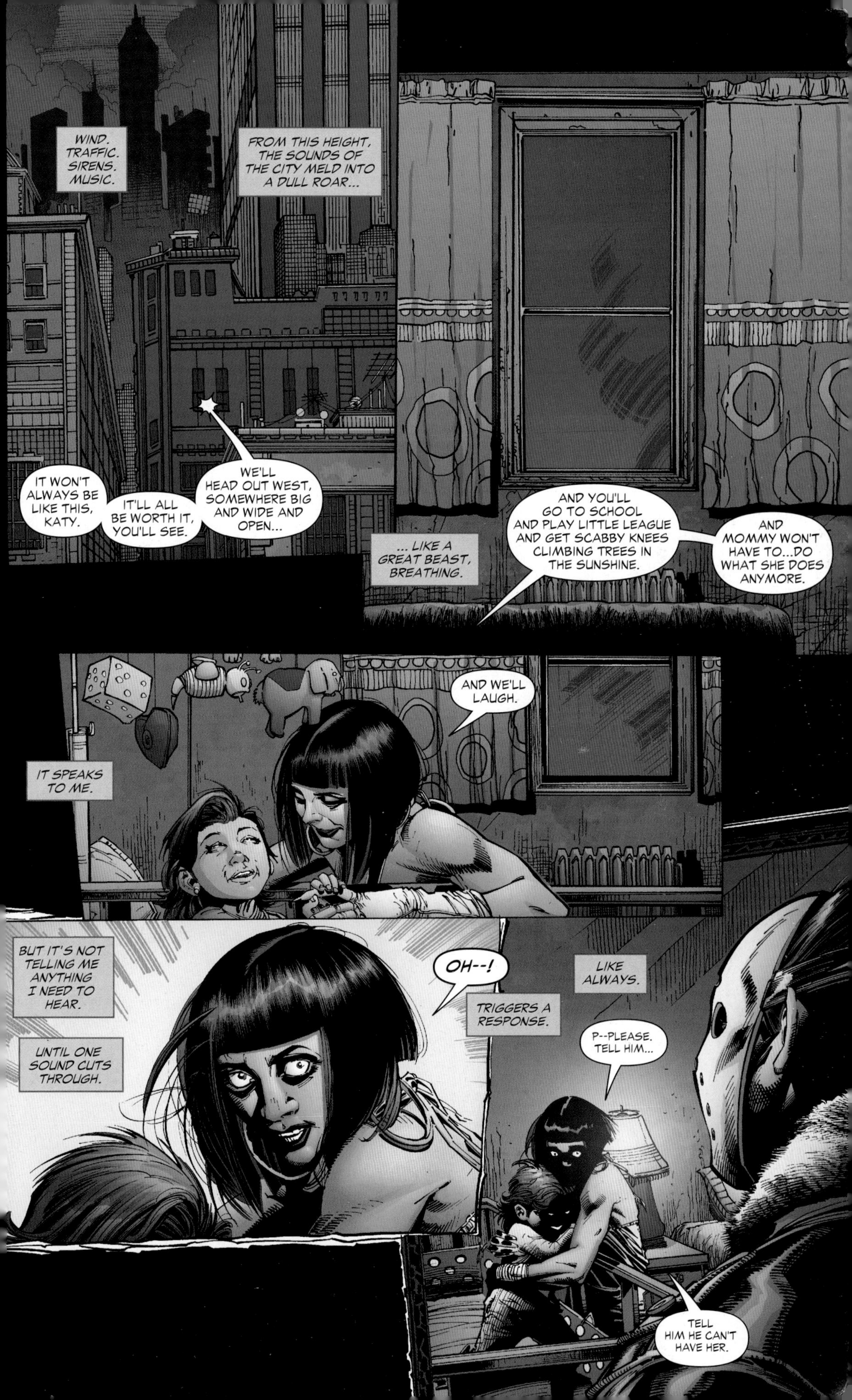
WIND. TRAFFIC. SIRENS. MUSIC.
FROM THIS HEIGHT, THE SOUNDS OF THE CITY MELD INTO A DULL ROAR...
IT WON'T ALWAYS BE LIKE THIS, KATY.
IT'LL ALL BE WORTH IT, YOU'LL SEE.
WE'LL HEAD OUT WEST, SOMEWHERE BIG AND WIDE AND OPEN...
... LIKE A GREAT BEAST, BREATHING.
AND YOU'LL GO TO SCHOOL AND PLAY LITTLE LEAGUE AND GET SCABBY KNEES CLIMBING TREES IN THE SUNSHINE.
AND MOMMY WON'T HAVE TO...DO WHAT SHE DOES ANYMORE.
AND WE'LL LAUGH.
IT SPEAKS TO ME.
BUT IT'S NOT TELLING ME ANYTHING I NEED TO HEAR.
UNTIL ONE SOUND CUTS THROUGH.
OH--!
TRIGGERS A RESPONSE.
LIKE ALWAYS.
P--PLEASE. TELL HIM...
TELL HIM HE CAN'T HAVE HER.

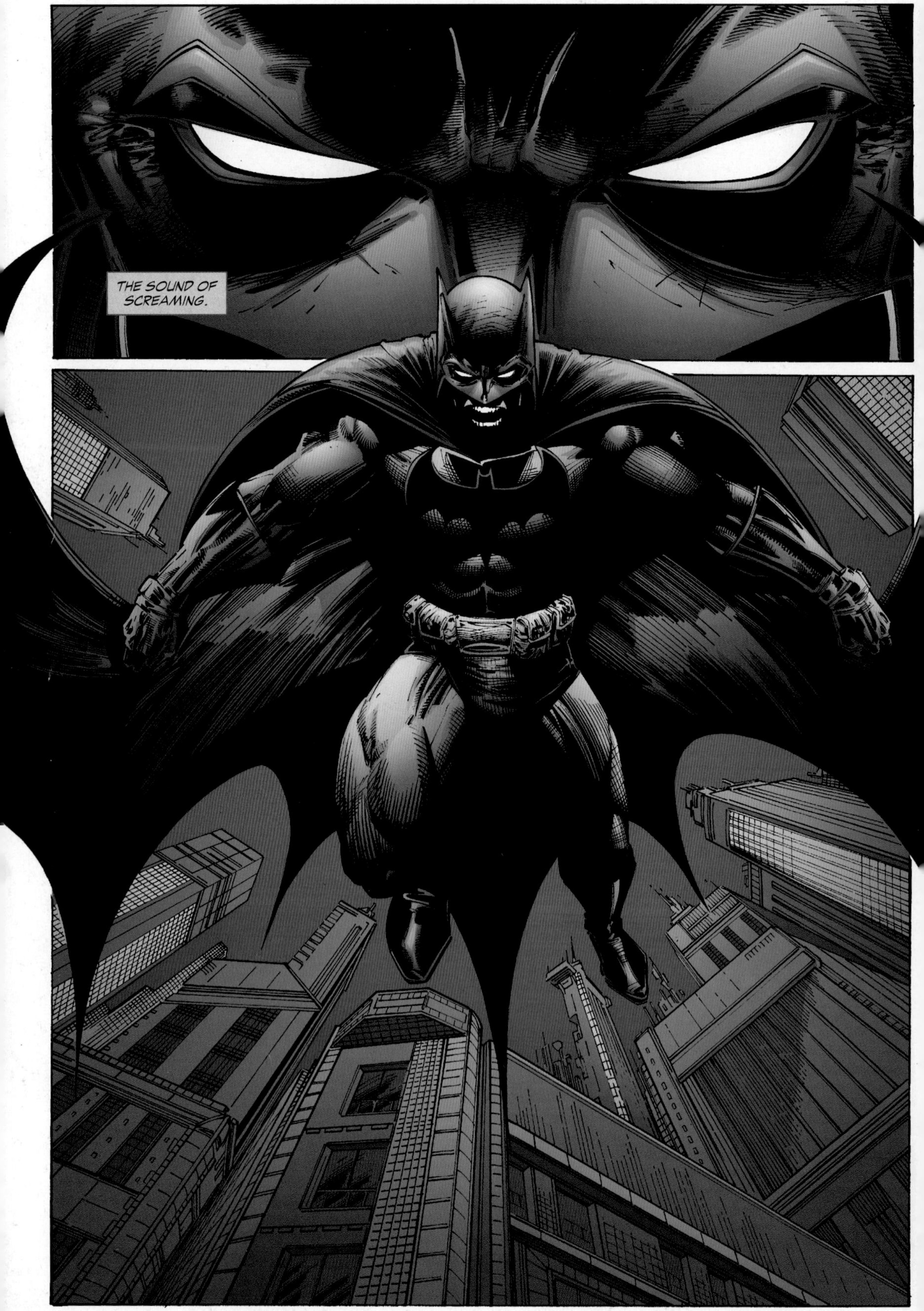
THE SOUND OF SCREAMING.

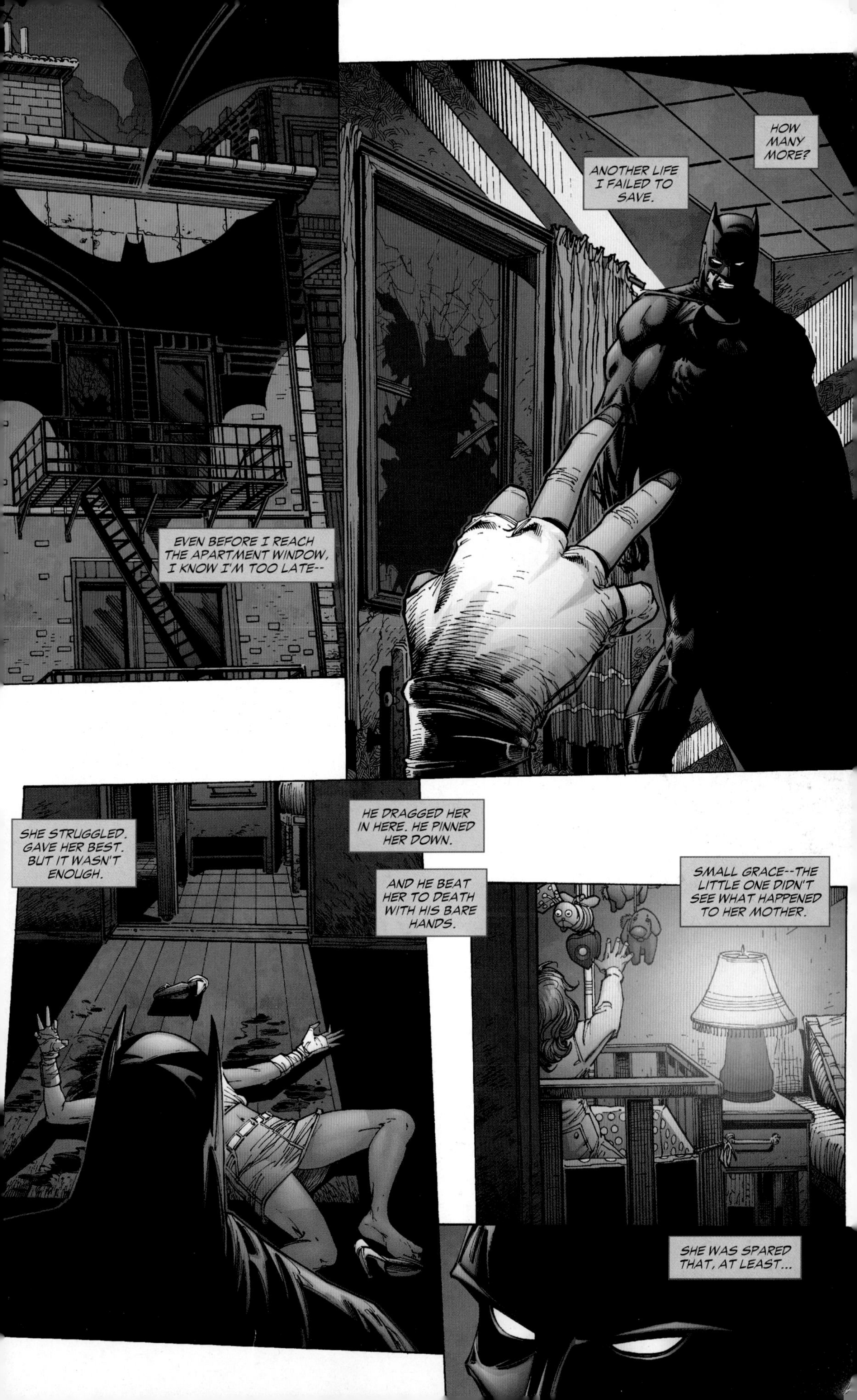
EVEN BEFORE I REACH THE APARTMENT WINDOW, I KNOW I'M TOO LATE--
ANOTHER LIFE I FAILED TO SAVE.
HOW MANY MORE?
SHE STRUGGLED. GAVE HER BEST. BUT IT WASN'T ENOUGH.
HE DRAGGED HER IN HERE. HE PINNED HER DOWN.
AND HE BEAT HER TO DEATH WITH HIS BARE HANDS.
SMALL GRACE--THE LITTLE ONE DIDN'T SEE WHAT HAPPENED TO HER MOTHER.
SHE WAS SPARED THAT, AT LEAST...

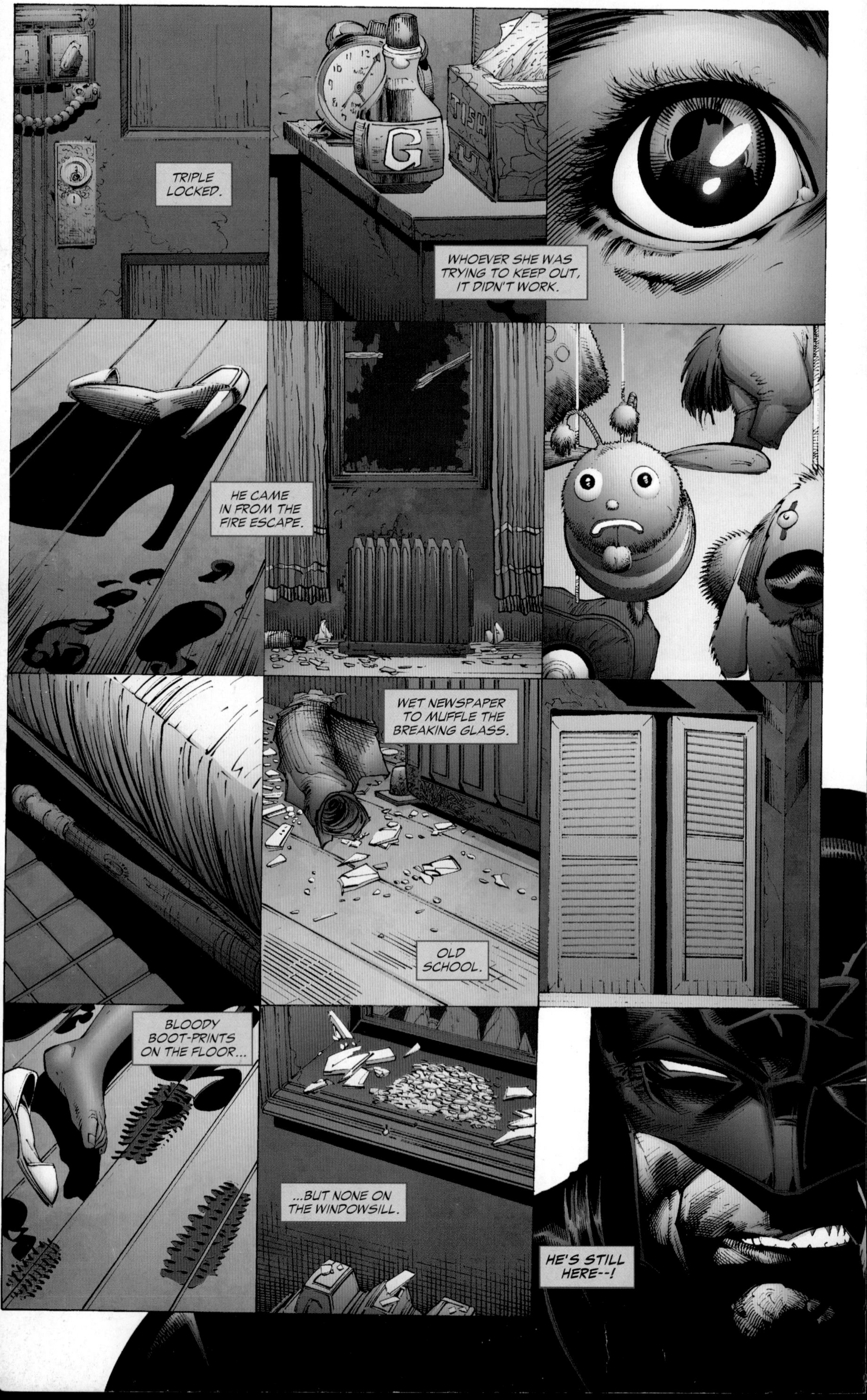
TRIPLE LOCKED.
WHOEVER SHE WAS TRYING TO KEEP OUT, IT DIDN'T WORK.
HE CAME IN FROM THE FIRE ESCAPE.
WET NEWSPAPER TO MUFFLE THE BREAKING GLASS.
OLD SCHOOL.
BLOODY BOOT-PRINTS ON THE FLOOR...
...BUT NONE ON THE WINDOWSILL.
HE'S STILL HERE--!

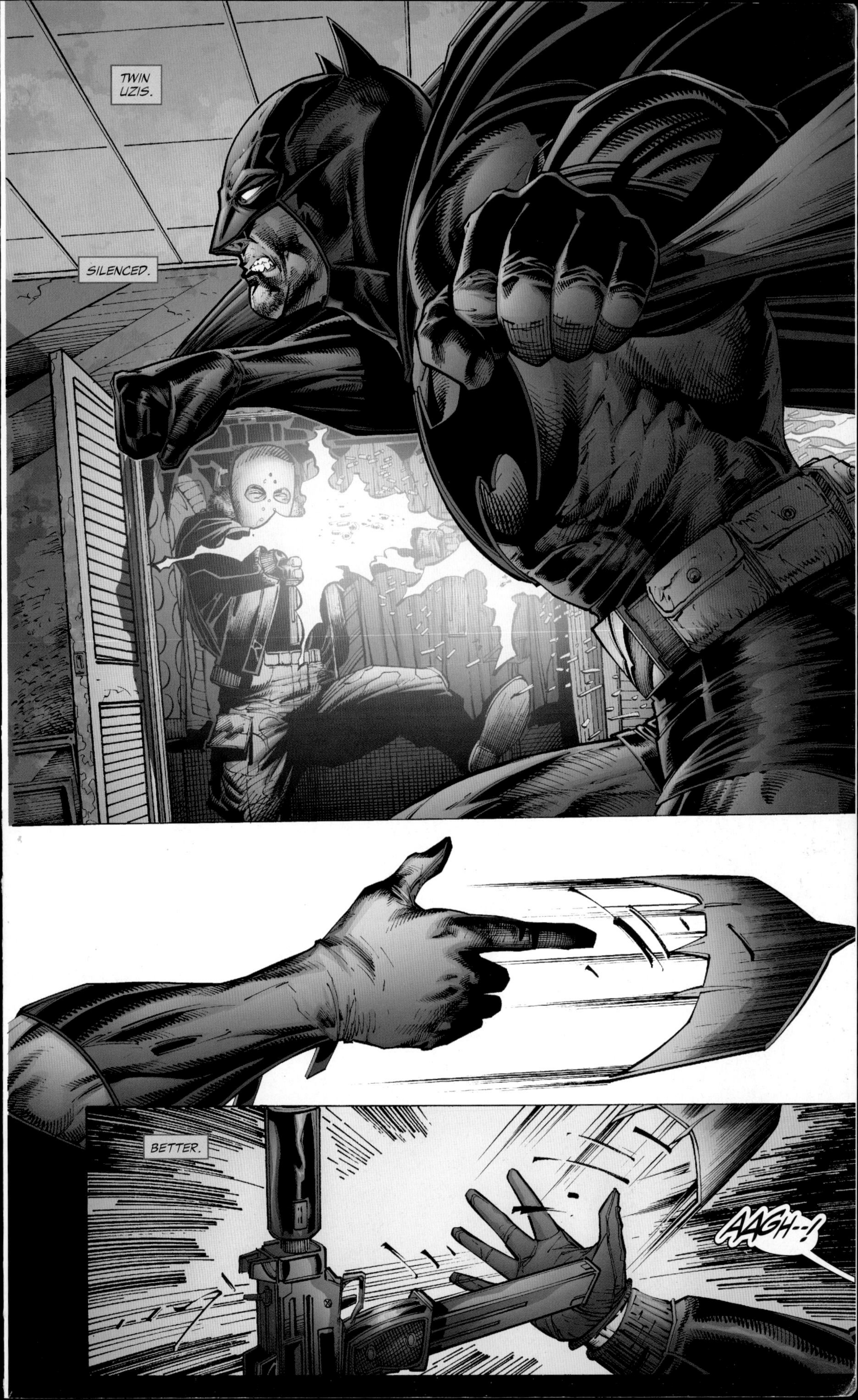
TWIN UZIS.
SILENCED.
BETTER.
AAGH--!

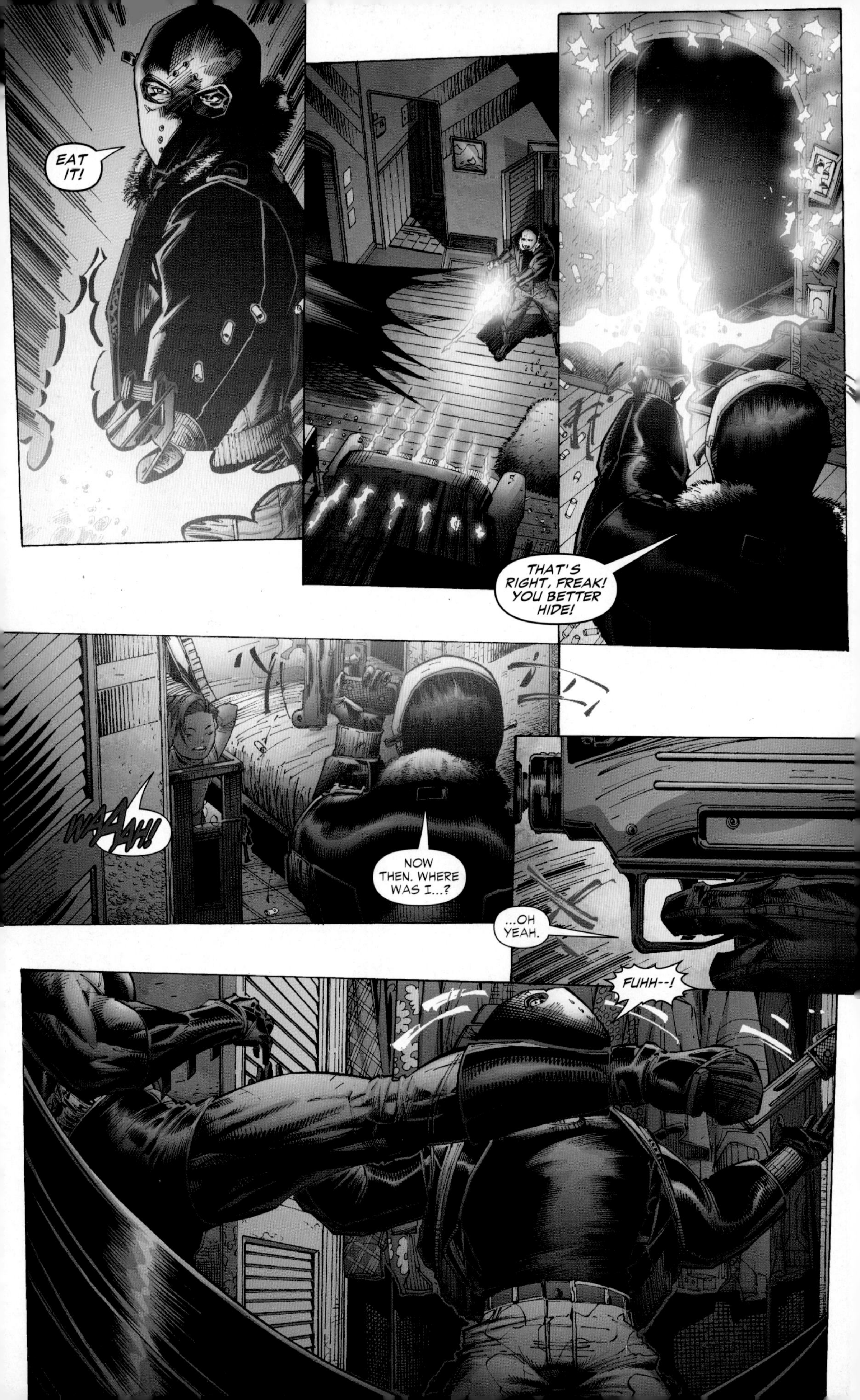
EAT IT!
THAT'S RIGHT, FREAK! YOU BETTER HIDE!
WAAAAH!
NOW THEN. WHERE WAS I...?
...OH YEAH.
FUHH--!

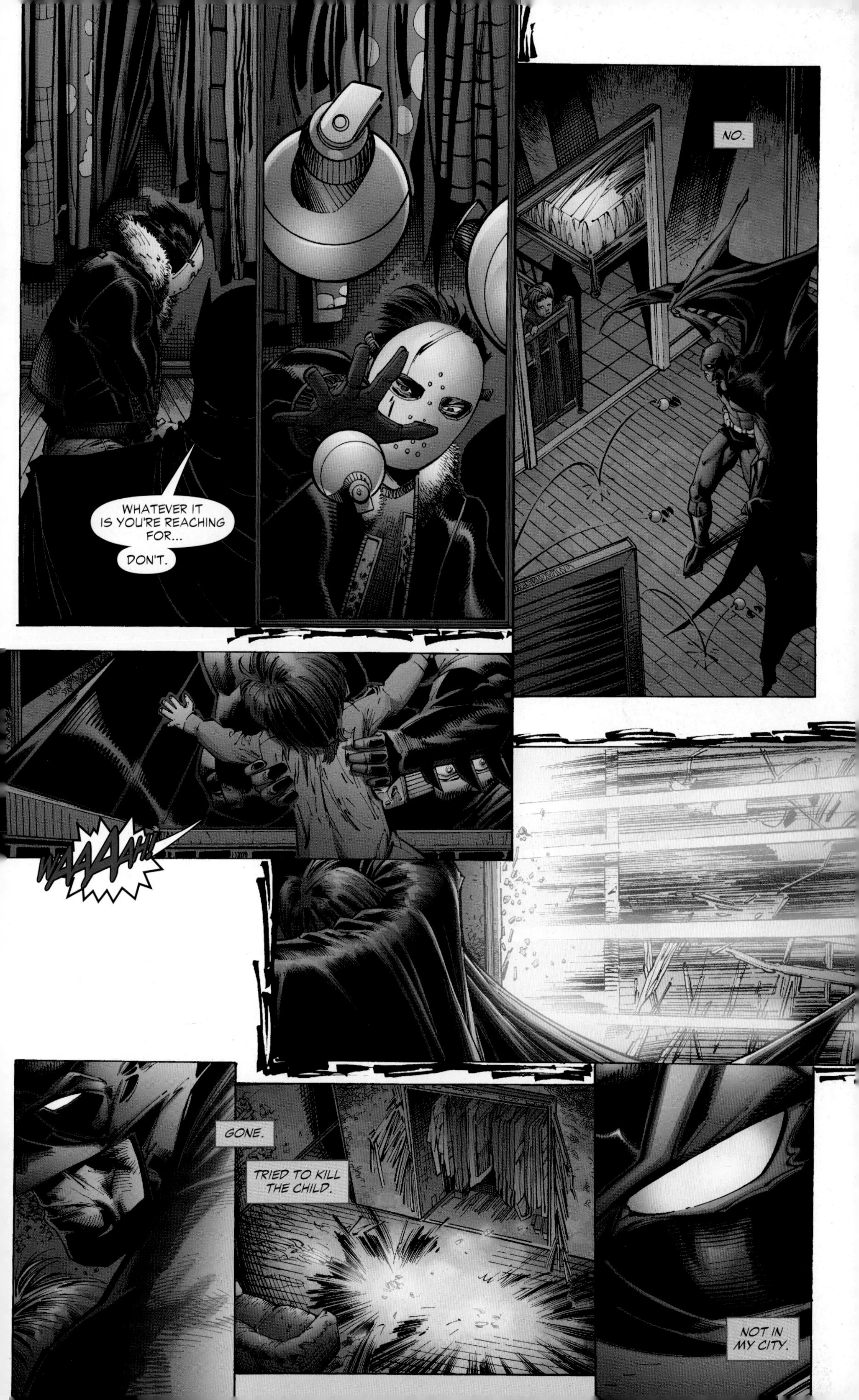
NO.
WHATEVER IT IS YOU'RE REACHING FOR...
DON'T.
WAAAAH!
GONE.
TRIED TO KILL THE CHILD.
NOT IN MY CITY.

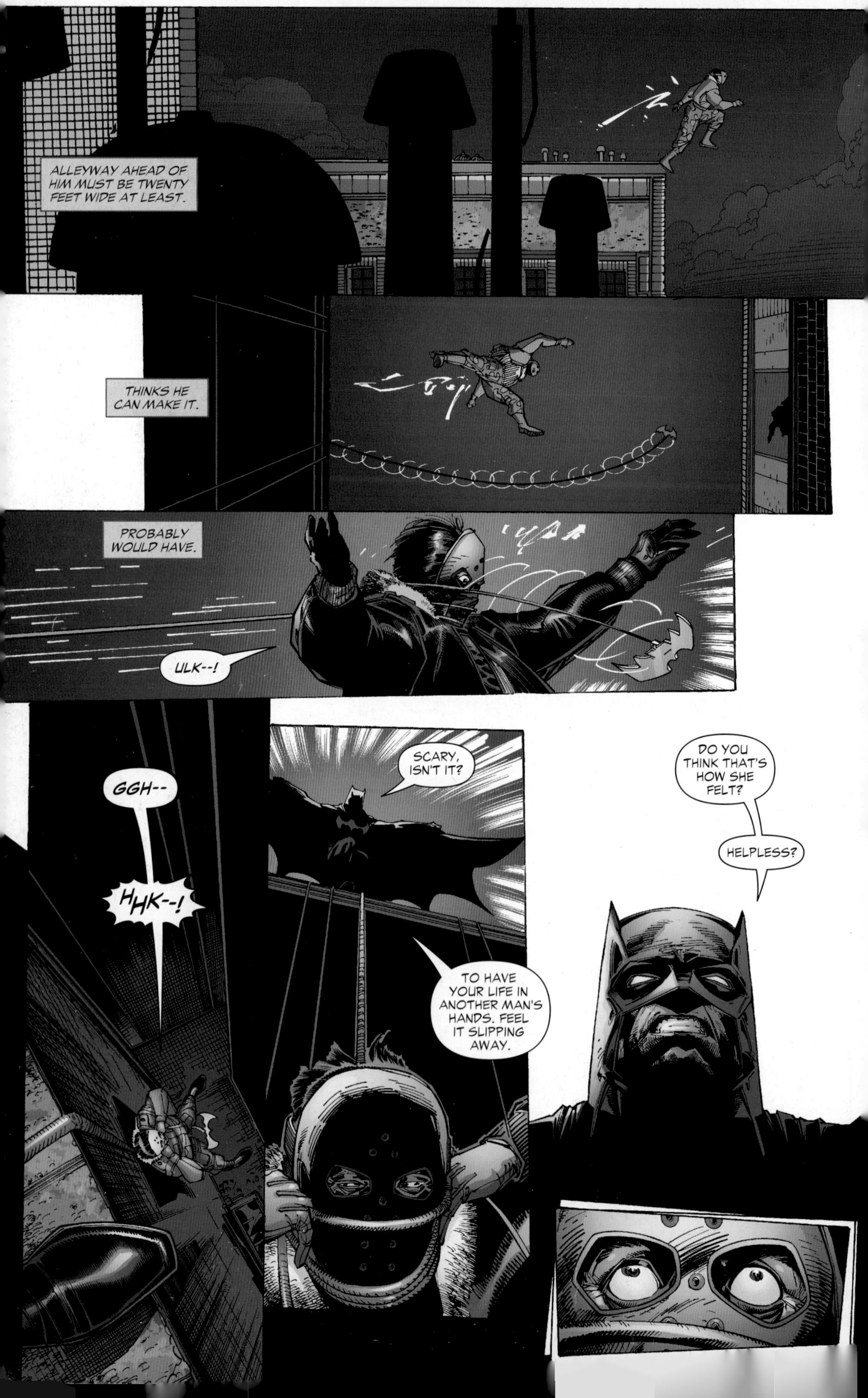

ALLEYWAY AHEAD OF HIM MUST BE TWENTY FEET WIDE AT LEAST.
THINKS HE CAN MAKE IT.
PROBABLY WOULD HAVE.
ULK--!
GGH--
HHK--!
SCARY, ISN'T IT?
TO HAVE YOUR LIFE IN ANOTHER MAN'S HANDS. FEEL IT SLIPPING AWAY.
DO YOU THINK THAT'S HOW SHE FELT?
HELPLESS?

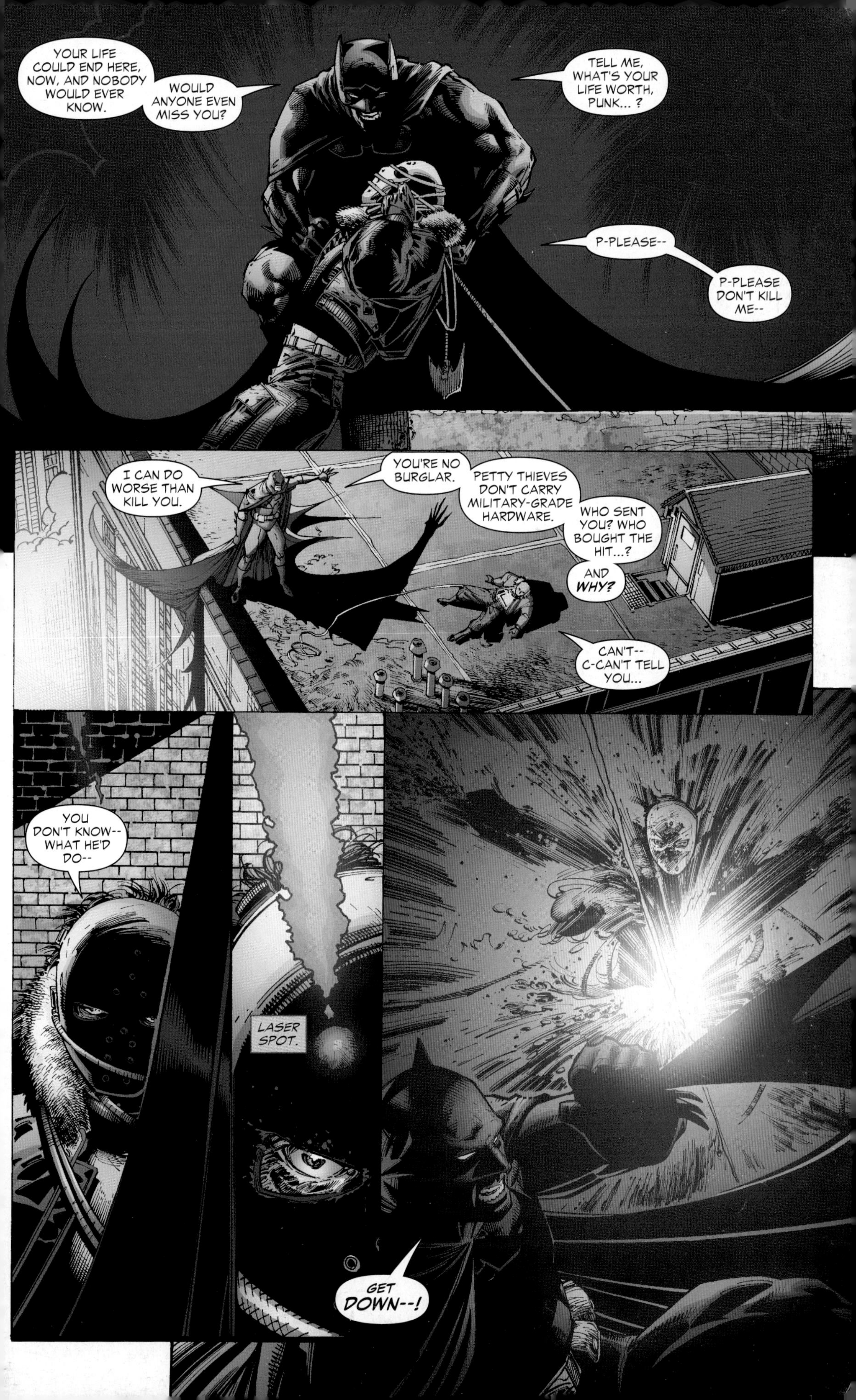
YOUR LIFE COULD END HERE, NOW, AND NOBODY WOULD EVER KNOW.
WOULD ANYONE EVEN MISS YOU?
TELL ME, WHAT'S YOUR LIFE WORTH, PUNK... ?
P-PLEASE--
P-PLEASE DON'T KILL ME--
I CAN DO WORSE THAN KILL YOU.
YOU'RE NO BURGLAR.
PETTY THIEVES DON'T CARRY MILITARY-GRADE HARDWARE.
WHO SENT YOU? WHO BOUGHT THE HIT...?
AND *WHY?*
CAN'T-- C-CAN'T TELL YOU...
YOU DON'T KNOW-- WHAT HE'D DO--
LASER SPOT.
GET *DOWN--!*

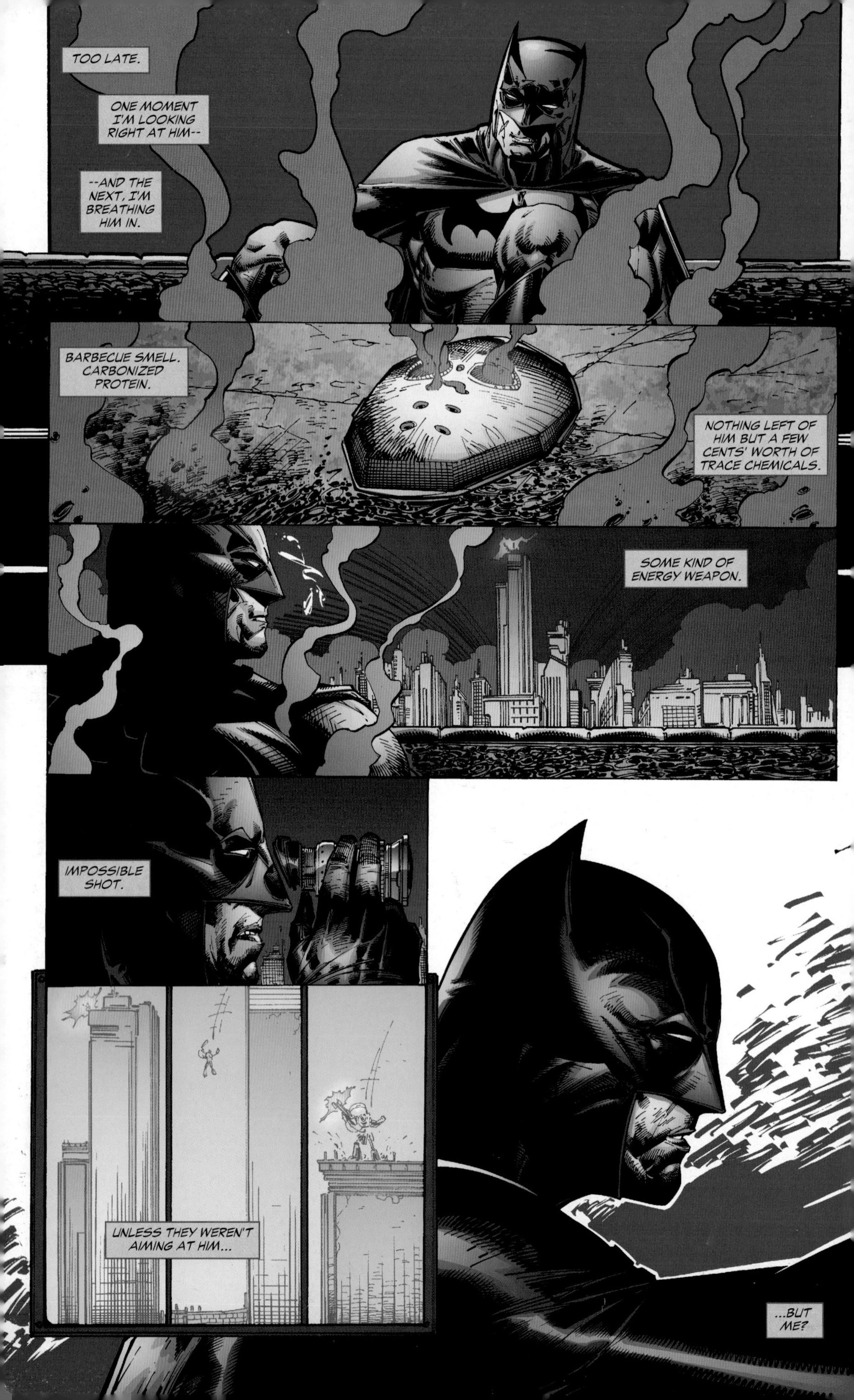
TOO LATE.
ONE MOMENT I'M LOOKING RIGHT AT HIM--
--AND THE NEXT, I'M BREATHING HIM IN.
BARBECUE SMELL. CARBONIZED PROTEIN.
NOTHING LEFT OF HIM BUT A FEW CENTS' WORTH OF TRACE CHEMICALS.
SOME KIND OF ENERGY WEAPON.
IMPOSSIBLE SHOT.
UNLESS THEY WEREN'T AIMING AT HIM...
...BUT ME?

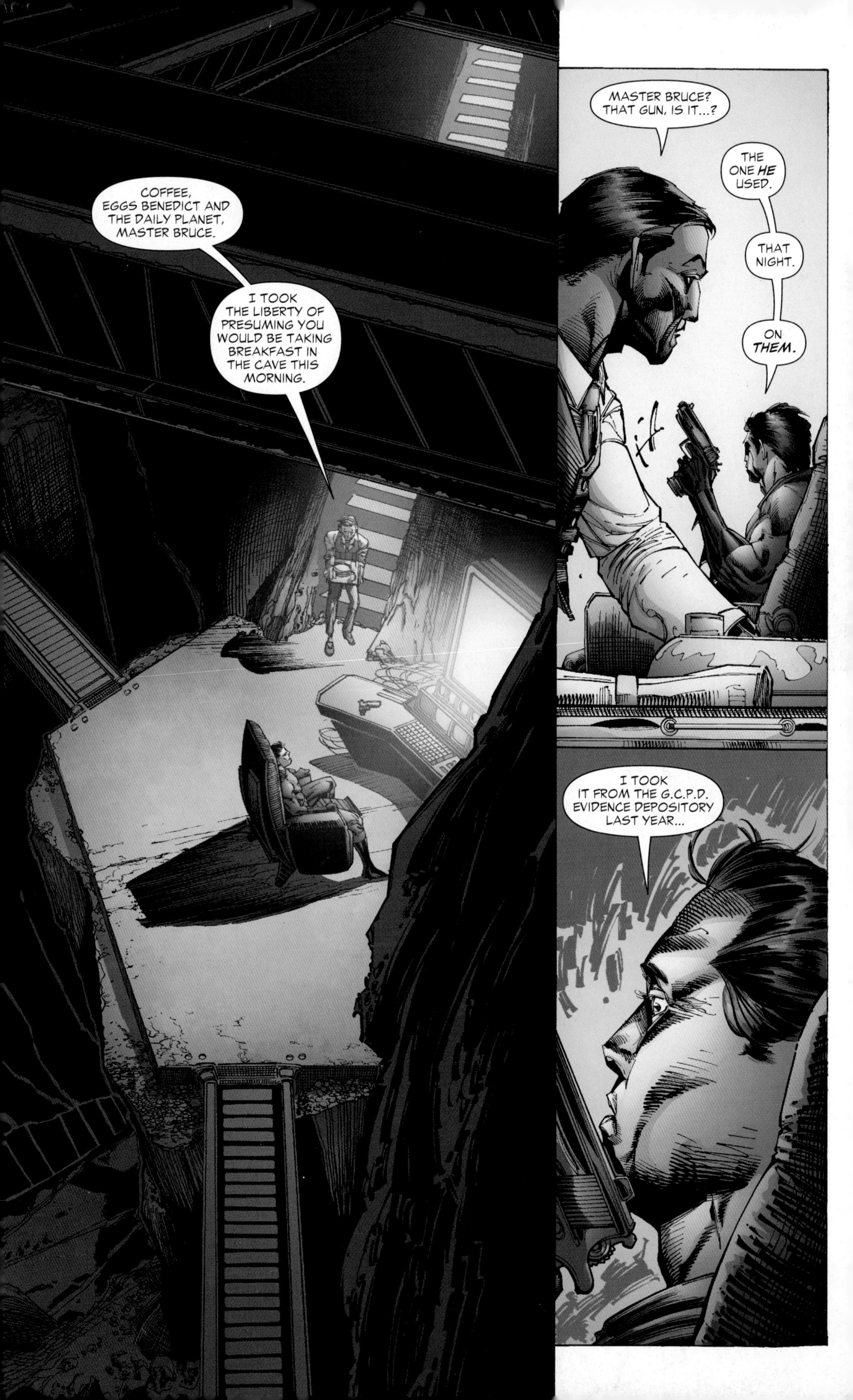
COFFEE, EGGS BENEDICT AND THE DAILY PLANET, MASTER BRUCE.
I TOOK THE LIBERTY OF PRESUMING YOU WOULD BE TAKING BREAKFAST IN THE CAVE THIS MORNING.
MASTER BRUCE? THAT GUN, IS IT...?
THE ONE HE USED.
THAT NIGHT.
ON THEM.
I TOOK IT FROM THE G.C.P.D. EVIDENCE DEPOSITORY LAST YEAR...

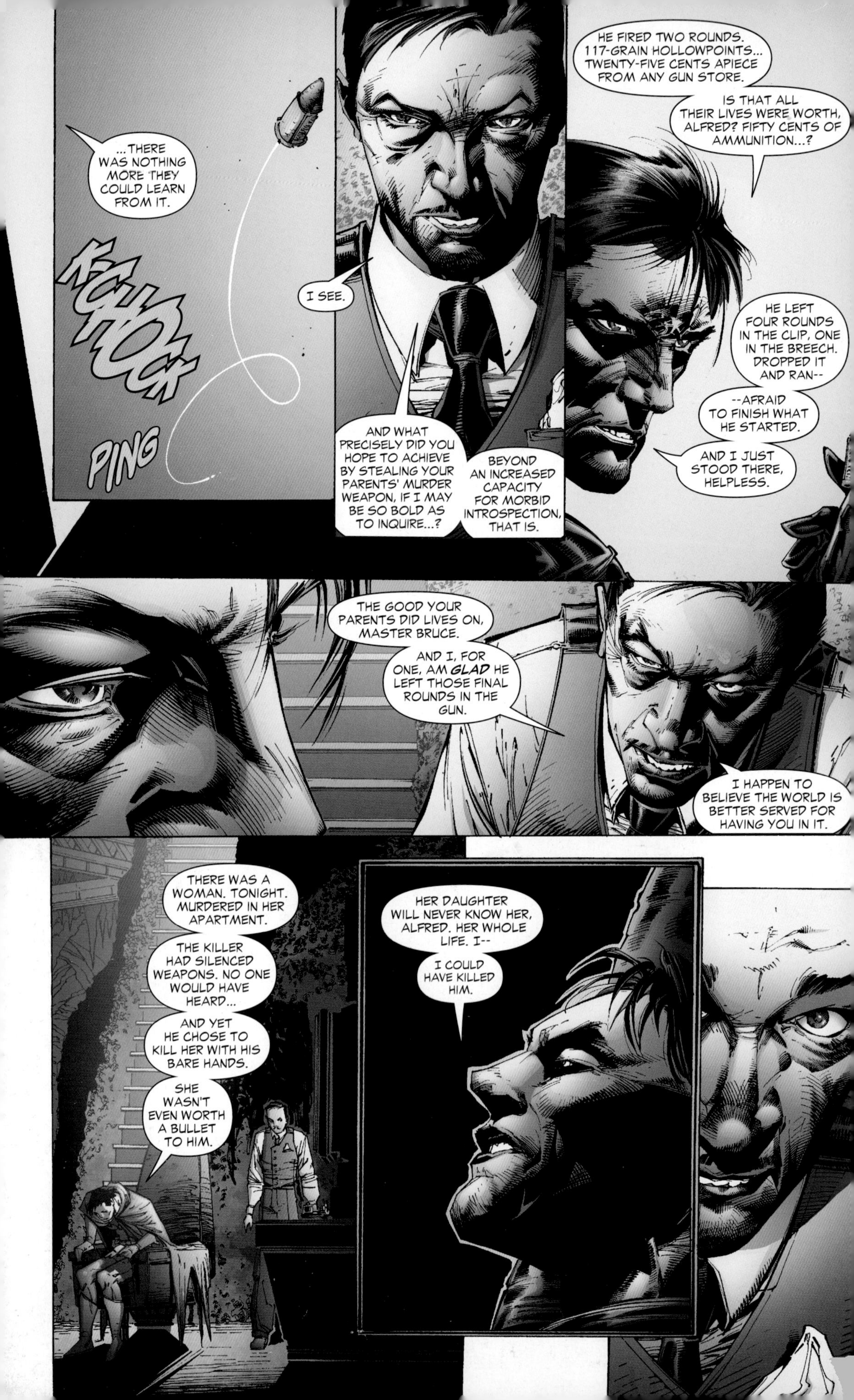
...THERE WAS NOTHING MORE THEY COULD LEARN FROM IT.
K-CHOCK
PING
I SEE.
AND WHAT PRECISELY DID YOU HOPE TO ACHIEVE BY STEALING YOUR PARENTS' MURDER WEAPON, IF I MAY BE SO BOLD AS TO INQUIRE...?
BEYOND AN INCREASED CAPACITY FOR MORBID INTROSPECTION, THAT IS.
HE FIRED TWO ROUNDS. 117-GRAIN HOLLOWPOINTS... TWENTY-FIVE CENTS APIECE FROM ANY GUN STORE.
IS THAT ALL THEIR LIVES WERE WORTH, ALFRED? FIFTY CENTS OF AMMUNITION...?
HE LEFT FOUR ROUNDS IN THE CLIP, ONE IN THE BREECH. DROPPED IT AND RAN--
--AFRAID TO FINISH WHAT HE STARTED.
AND I JUST STOOD THERE, HELPLESS.
THE GOOD YOUR PARENTS DID LIVES ON, MASTER BRUCE.
AND I, FOR ONE, AM *GLAD* HE LEFT THOSE FINAL ROUNDS IN THE GUN.
I HAPPEN TO BELIEVE THE WORLD IS BETTER SERVED FOR HAVING YOU IN IT.
THERE WAS A WOMAN. TONIGHT. MURDERED IN HER APARTMENT.
THE KILLER HAD SILENCED WEAPONS. NO ONE WOULD HAVE HEARD...
AND YET HE CHOSE TO KILL HER WITH HIS BARE HANDS.
SHE WASN'T EVEN WORTH A BULLET TO HIM.
HER DAUGHTER WILL NEVER KNOW HER, ALFRED. HER WHOLE LIFE. I--
I COULD HAVE KILLED HIM.

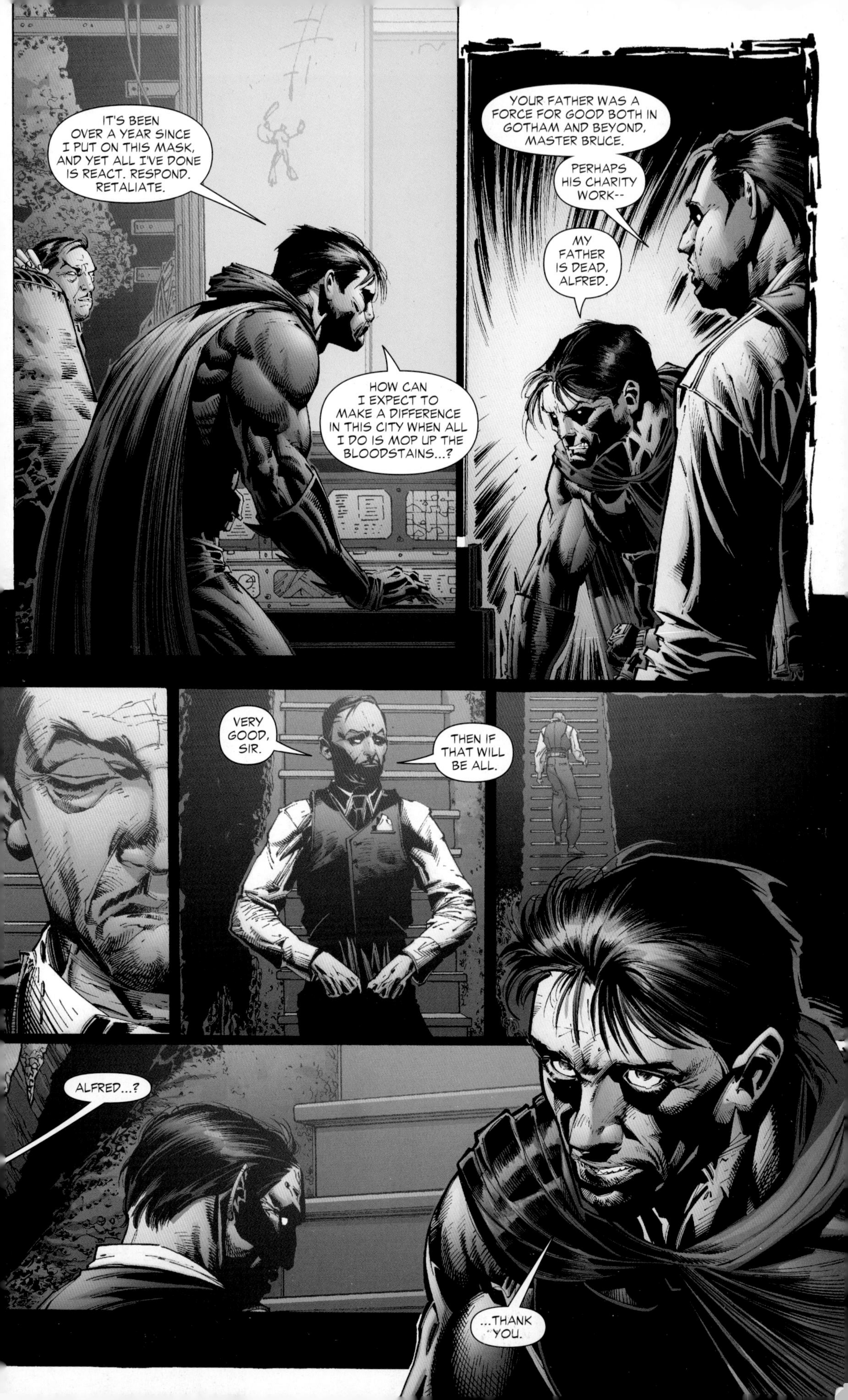
IT'S BEEN OVER A YEAR SINCE I PUT ON THIS MASK, AND YET ALL I'VE DONE IS REACT. RESPOND. RETALIATE.
HOW CAN I EXPECT TO MAKE A DIFFERENCE IN THIS CITY WHEN ALL I DO IS MOP UP THE BLOODSTAINS...?
YOUR FATHER WAS A FORCE FOR GOOD BOTH IN GOTHAM AND BEYOND, MASTER BRUCE.
PERHAPS HIS CHARITY WORK--
MY FATHER IS DEAD, ALFRED.
VERY GOOD, SIR.
THEN IF THAT WILL BE ALL.
ALFRED...?
...THANK YOU.

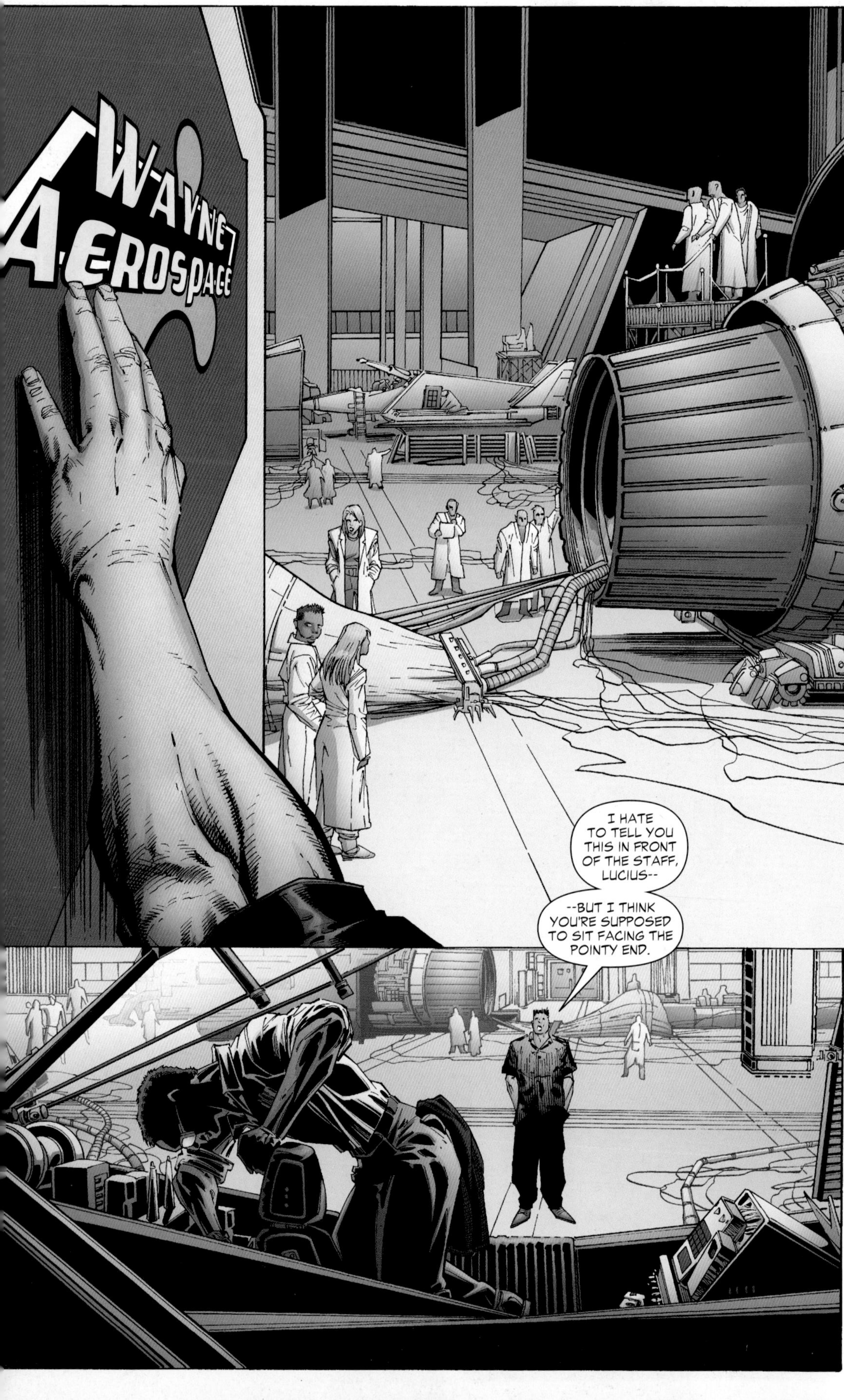
WAYNE AEROSPACE
I HATE TO TELL YOU THIS IN FRONT OF THE STAFF, LUCIUS--
--BUT I THINK YOU'RE SUPPOSED TO SIT FACING THE POINTY END.

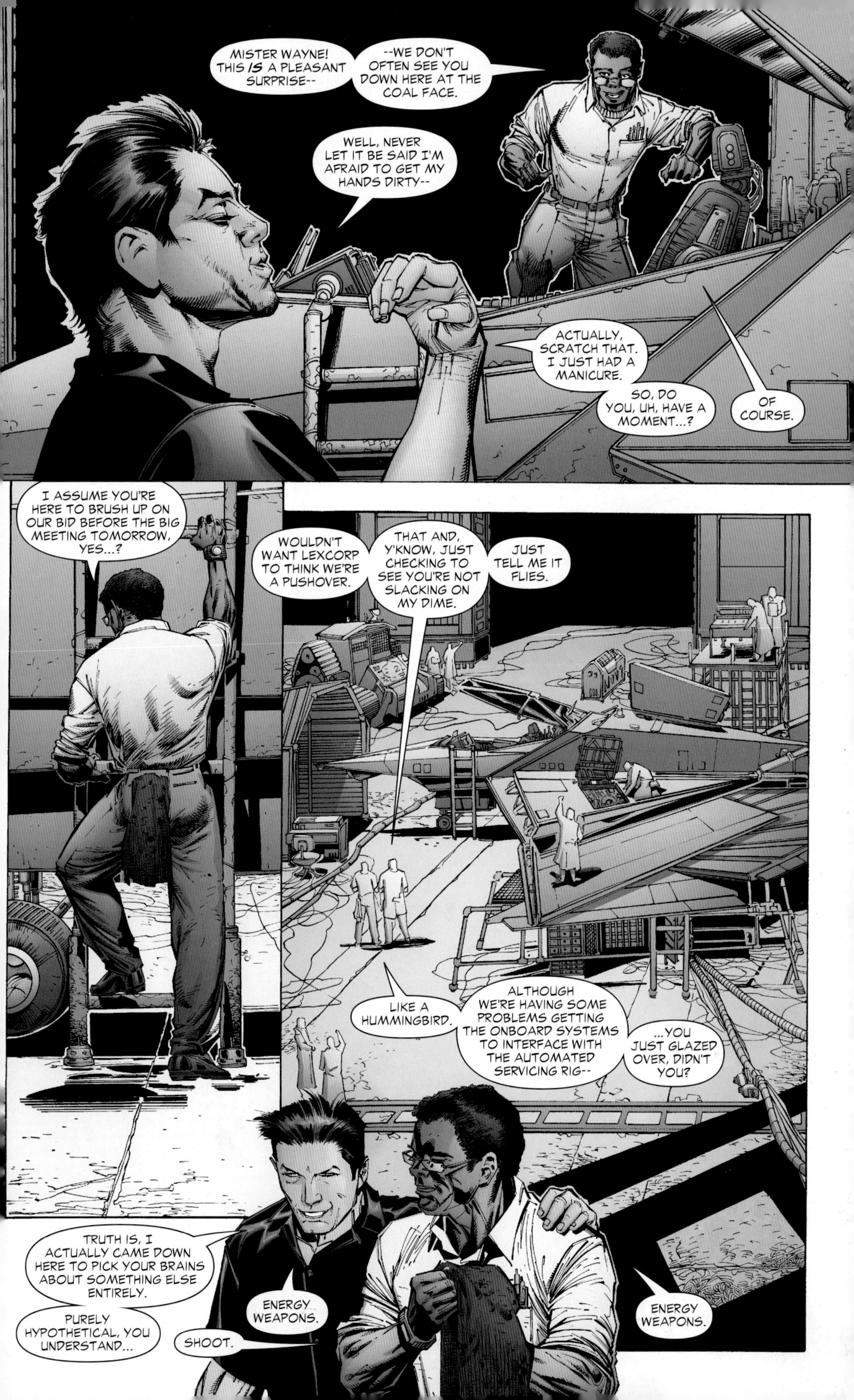
MISTER WAYNE! THIS *IS* A PLEASANT SURPRISE--
--WE DON'T OFTEN SEE YOU DOWN HERE AT THE COAL FACE.
WELL, NEVER LET IT BE SAID I'M AFRAID TO GET MY HANDS DIRTY--
ACTUALLY, SCRATCH THAT. I JUST HAD A MANICURE.
SO, DO YOU, UH, HAVE A MOMENT...?
OF COURSE.
I ASSUME YOU'RE HERE TO BRUSH UP ON OUR BID BEFORE THE BIG MEETING TOMORROW, YES...?
WOULDN'T WANT LEXCORP TO THINK WE'RE A PUSHOVER.
THAT AND, Y'KNOW, JUST CHECKING TO SEE YOU'RE NOT SLACKING ON MY DIME.
JUST TELL ME IT FLIES.
LIKE A HUMMINGBIRD.
ALTHOUGH WE'RE HAVING SOME PROBLEMS GETTING THE ONBOARD SYSTEMS TO INTERFACE WITH THE AUTOMATED SERVICING RIG--
...YOU JUST GLAZED OVER, DIDN'T YOU?
TRUTH IS, I ACTUALLY CAME DOWN HERE TO PICK YOUR BRAINS ABOUT SOMETHING ELSE ENTIRELY.
PURELY HYPOTHETICAL, YOU UNDERSTAND...
SHOOT.
ENERGY WEAPONS.
ENERGY WEAPONS.

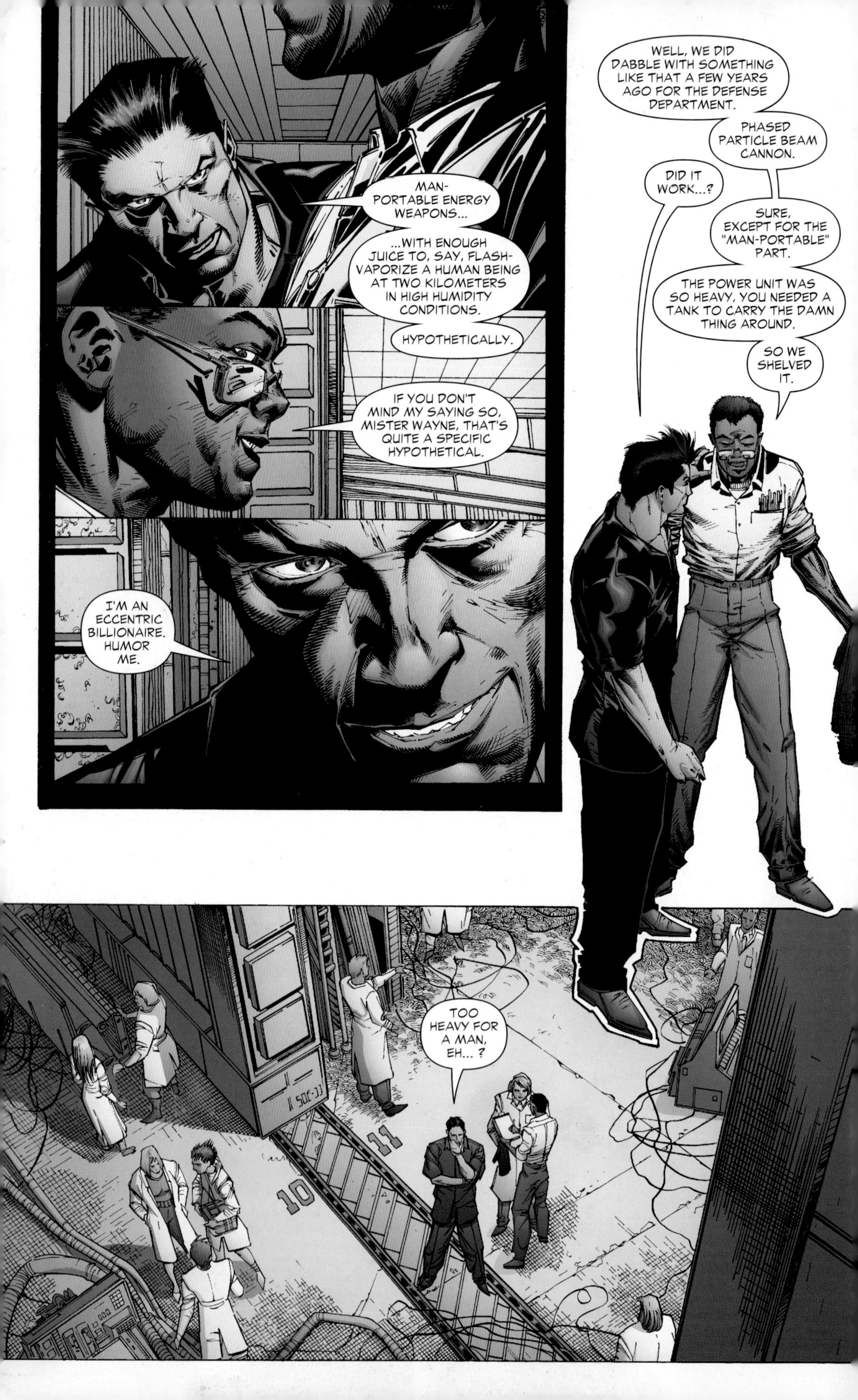
MAN-PORTABLE ENERGY WEAPONS...
...WITH ENOUGH JUICE TO, SAY, FLASH-VAPORIZE A HUMAN BEING AT TWO KILOMETERS IN HIGH HUMIDITY CONDITIONS.
HYPOTHETICALLY.
IF YOU DON'T MIND MY SAYING SO, MISTER WAYNE, THAT'S QUITE A SPECIFIC HYPOTHETICAL.
I'M AN ECCENTRIC BILLIONAIRE. HUMOR ME.
WELL, WE DID DABBLE WITH SOMETHING LIKE THAT A FEW YEARS AGO FOR THE DEFENSE DEPARTMENT.
PHASED PARTICLE BEAM CANNON.
DID IT WORK...?
SURE, EXCEPT FOR THE "MAN-PORTABLE" PART.
THE POWER UNIT WAS SO HEAVY, YOU NEEDED A TANK TO CARRY THE DAMN THING AROUND.
SO WE SHELVED IT.
TOO HEAVY FOR A MAN, EH... ?
10
11

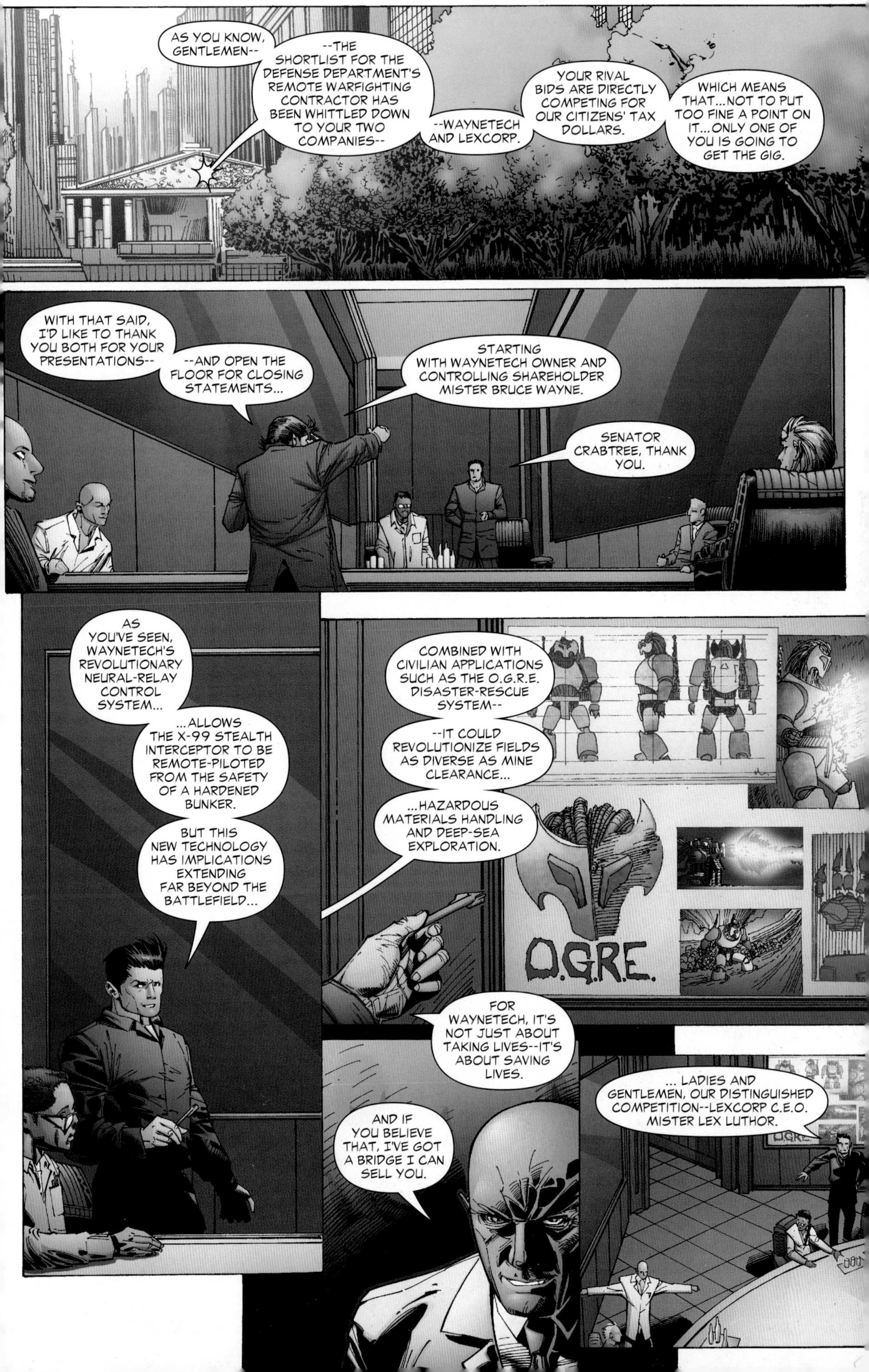
AS YOU KNOW, GENTLEMEN--
--THE SHORTLIST FOR THE DEFENSE DEPARTMENT'S REMOTE WARFIGHTING CONTRACTOR HAS BEEN WHITTLED DOWN TO YOUR TWO COMPANIES--
--WAYNETECH AND LEXCORP.
YOUR RIVAL BIDS ARE DIRECTLY COMPETING FOR OUR CITIZENS' TAX DOLLARS.
WHICH MEANS THAT...NOT TO PUT TOO FINE A POINT ON IT...ONLY ONE OF YOU IS GOING TO GET THE GIG.
WITH THAT SAID, I'D LIKE TO THANK YOU BOTH FOR YOUR PRESENTATIONS--
--AND OPEN THE FLOOR FOR CLOSING STATEMENTS...
STARTING WITH WAYNETECH OWNER AND CONTROLLING SHAREHOLDER MISTER BRUCE WAYNE.
SENATOR CRABTREE, THANK YOU.
AS YOU'VE SEEN, WAYNETECH'S REVOLUTIONARY NEURAL-RELAY CONTROL SYSTEM...
...ALLOWS THE X-99 STEALTH INTERCEPTOR TO BE REMOTE-PILOTED FROM THE SAFETY OF A HARDENED BUNKER.
BUT THIS NEW TECHNOLOGY HAS IMPLICATIONS EXTENDING FAR BEYOND THE BATTLEFIELD...
COMBINED WITH CIVILIAN APPLICATIONS SUCH AS THE O.G.R.E. DISASTER-RESCUE SYSTEM--
--IT COULD REVOLUTIONIZE FIELDS AS DIVERSE AS MINE CLEARANCE...
...HAZARDOUS MATERIALS HANDLING AND DEEP-SEA EXPLORATION.
O.G.R.E.
FOR WAYNETECH, IT'S NOT JUST ABOUT TAKING LIVES--IT'S ABOUT SAVING LIVES.
AND IF YOU BELIEVE THAT, I'VE GOT A BRIDGE I CAN SELL YOU.
... LADIES AND GENTLEMEN, OUR DISTINGUISHED COMPETITION--LEXCORP C.E.O. MISTER LEX LUTHOR.

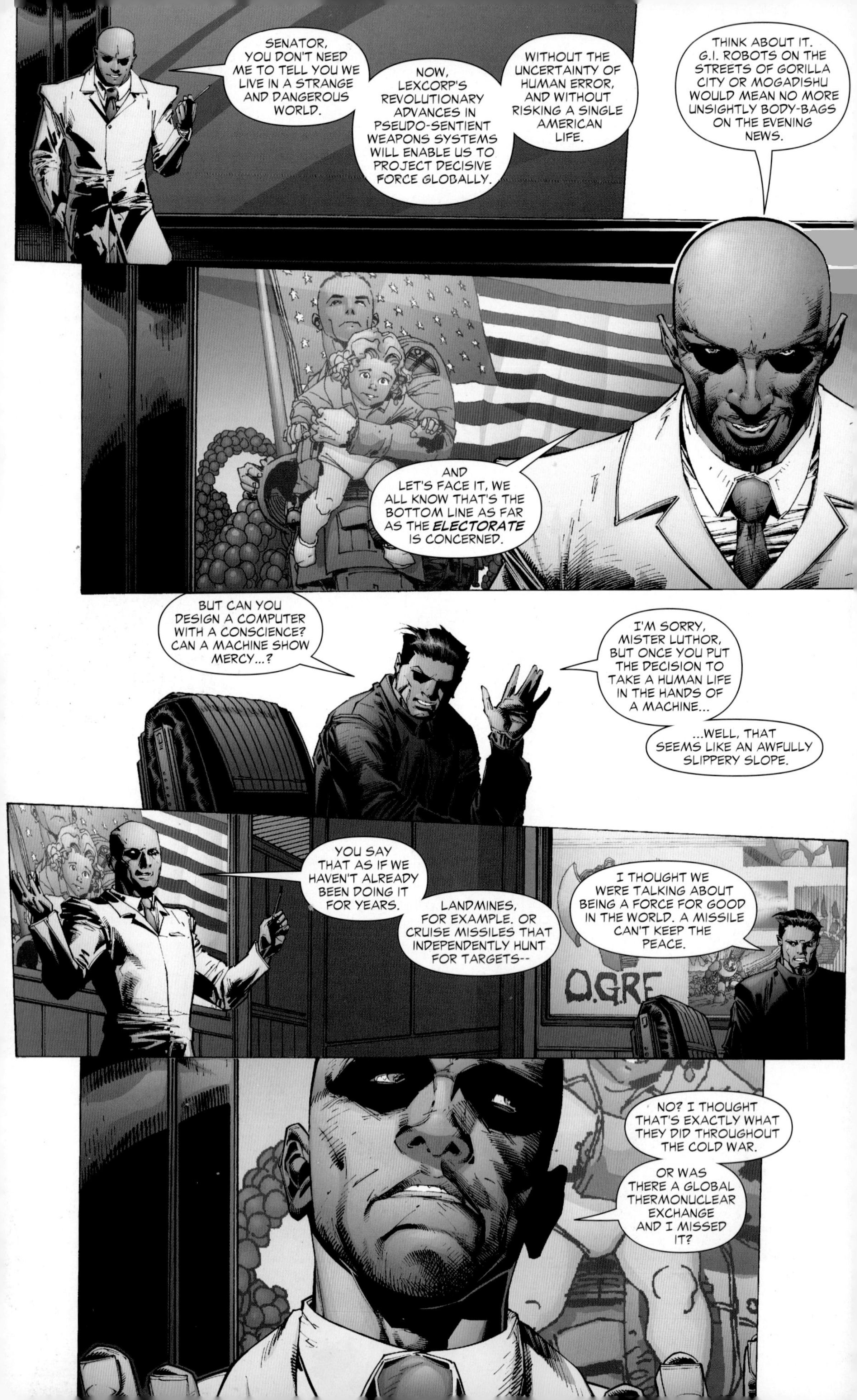
SENATOR, YOU DON'T NEED ME TO TELL YOU WE LIVE IN A STRANGE AND DANGEROUS WORLD.
NOW, LEXCORP'S REVOLUTIONARY ADVANCES IN PSEUDO-SENTIENT WEAPONS SYSTEMS WILL ENABLE US TO PROJECT DECISIVE FORCE GLOBALLY.
WITHOUT THE UNCERTAINTY OF HUMAN ERROR, AND WITHOUT RISKING A SINGLE AMERICAN LIFE.
THINK ABOUT IT. G.I. ROBOTS ON THE STREETS OF GORILLA CITY OR MOGADISHU WOULD MEAN NO MORE UNSIGHTLY BODY-BAGS ON THE EVENING NEWS.
AND LET'S FACE IT, WE ALL KNOW THAT'S THE BOTTOM LINE AS FAR AS THE *ELECTORATE* IS CONCERNED.
BUT CAN YOU DESIGN A COMPUTER WITH A CONSCIENCE? CAN A MACHINE SHOW MERCY...?
I'M SORRY, MISTER LUTHOR, BUT ONCE YOU PUT THE DECISION TO TAKE A HUMAN LIFE IN THE HANDS OF A MACHINE...
...WELL, THAT SEEMS LIKE AN AWFULLY SLIPPERY SLOPE.
YOU SAY THAT AS IF WE HAVEN'T ALREADY BEEN DOING IT FOR YEARS.
LANDMINES, FOR EXAMPLE. OR CRUISE MISSILES THAT INDEPENDENTLY HUNT FOR TARGETS--
I THOUGHT WE WERE TALKING ABOUT BEING A FORCE FOR GOOD IN THE WORLD. A MISSILE CAN'T KEEP THE PEACE.
O.G.R.E
NO? I THOUGHT THAT'S EXACTLY WHAT THEY DID THROUGHOUT THE COLD WAR.
OR WAS THERE A GLOBAL THERMONUCLEAR EXCHANGE AND I MISSED IT?

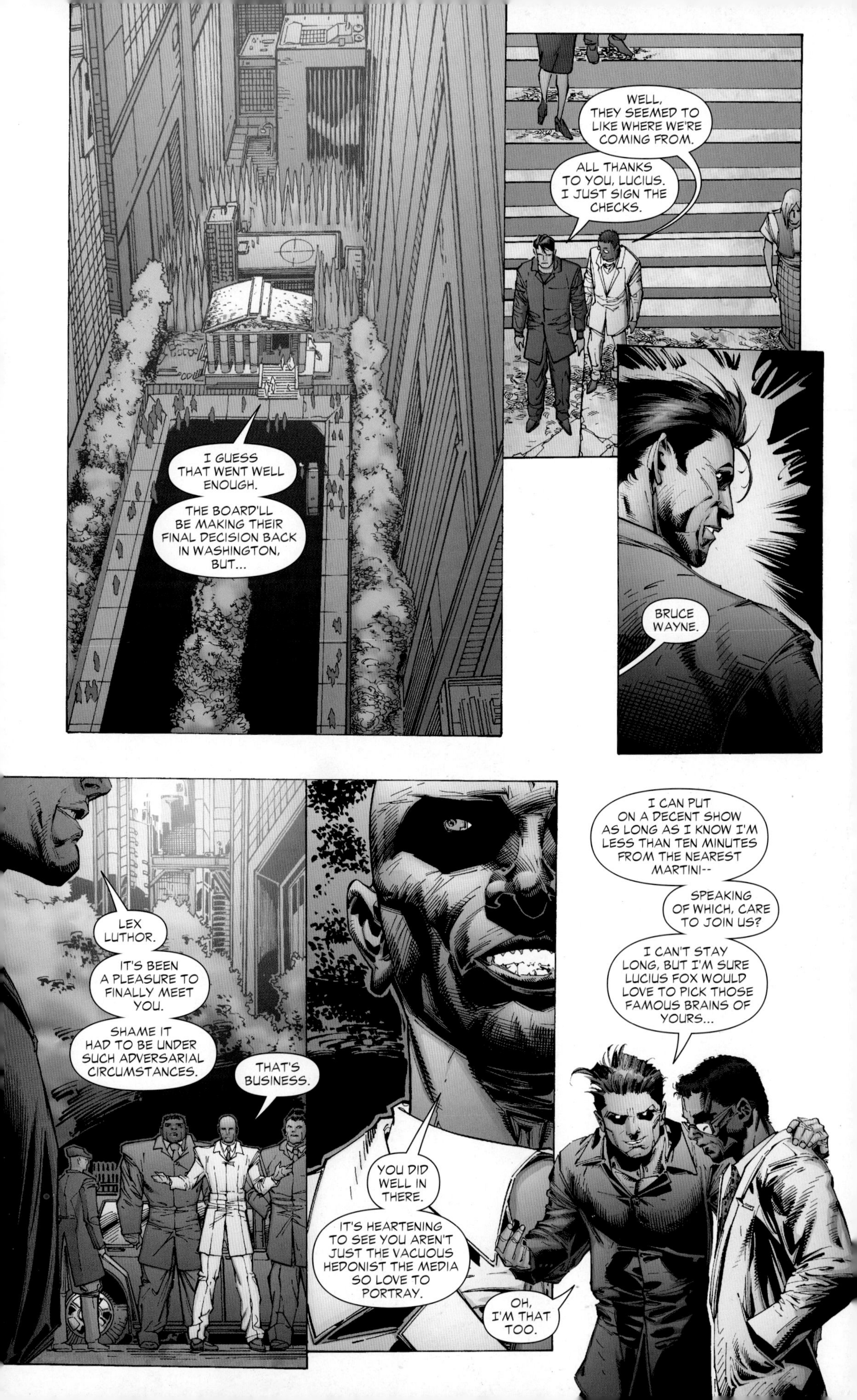
I GUESS THAT WENT WELL ENOUGH.
THE BOARD'LL BE MAKING THEIR FINAL DECISION BACK IN WASHINGTON, BUT...
WELL, THEY SEEMED TO LIKE WHERE WE'RE COMING FROM.
ALL THANKS TO YOU, LUCIUS. I JUST SIGN THE CHECKS.
BRUCE WAYNE.
LEX LUTHOR.
IT'S BEEN A PLEASURE TO FINALLY MEET YOU.
SHAME IT HAD TO BE UNDER SUCH ADVERSARIAL CIRCUMSTANCES.
THAT'S BUSINESS.
YOU DID WELL IN THERE.
IT'S HEARTENING TO SEE YOU AREN'T JUST THE VACUOUS HEDONIST THE MEDIA SO LOVE TO PORTRAY.
OH, I'M THAT TOO.
I CAN PUT ON A DECENT SHOW AS LONG AS I KNOW I'M LESS THAN TEN MINUTES FROM THE NEAREST MARTINI--
SPEAKING OF WHICH, CARE TO JOIN US?
I CAN'T STAY LONG, BUT I'M SURE LUCIUS FOX WOULD LOVE TO PICK THOSE FAMOUS BRAINS OF YOURS...

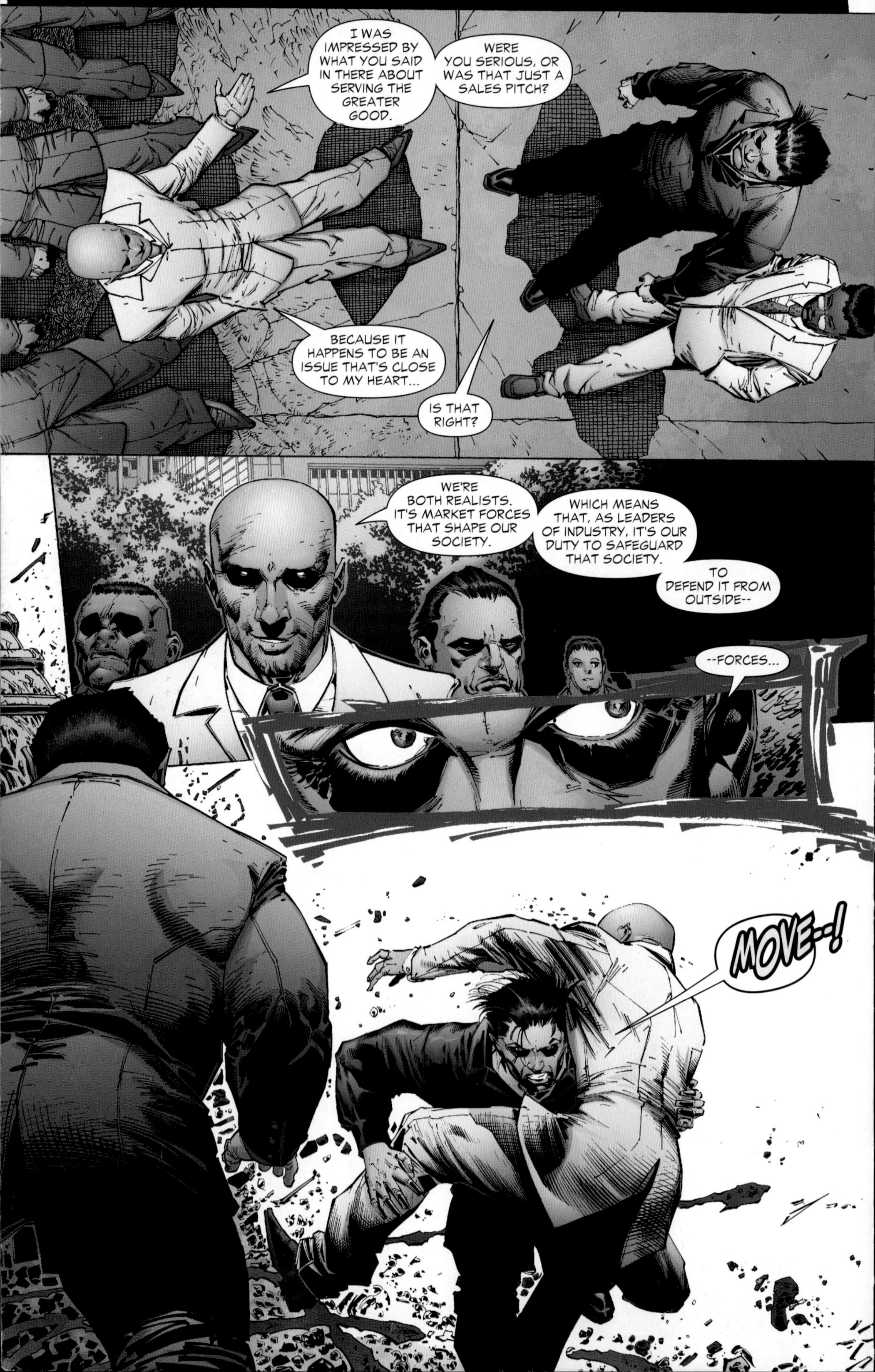
I WAS IMPRESSED BY WHAT YOU SAID IN THERE ABOUT SERVING THE GREATER GOOD.
WERE YOU SERIOUS, OR WAS THAT JUST A SALES PITCH?
BECAUSE IT HAPPENS TO BE AN ISSUE THAT'S CLOSE TO MY HEART...
IS THAT RIGHT?
WE'RE BOTH REALISTS. IT'S MARKET FORCES THAT SHAPE OUR SOCIETY.
WHICH MEANS THAT, AS LEADERS OF INDUSTRY, IT'S OUR DUTY TO SAFEGUARD THAT SOCIETY.
TO DEFEND IT FROM OUTSIDE--
--FORCES...
MOVE--!

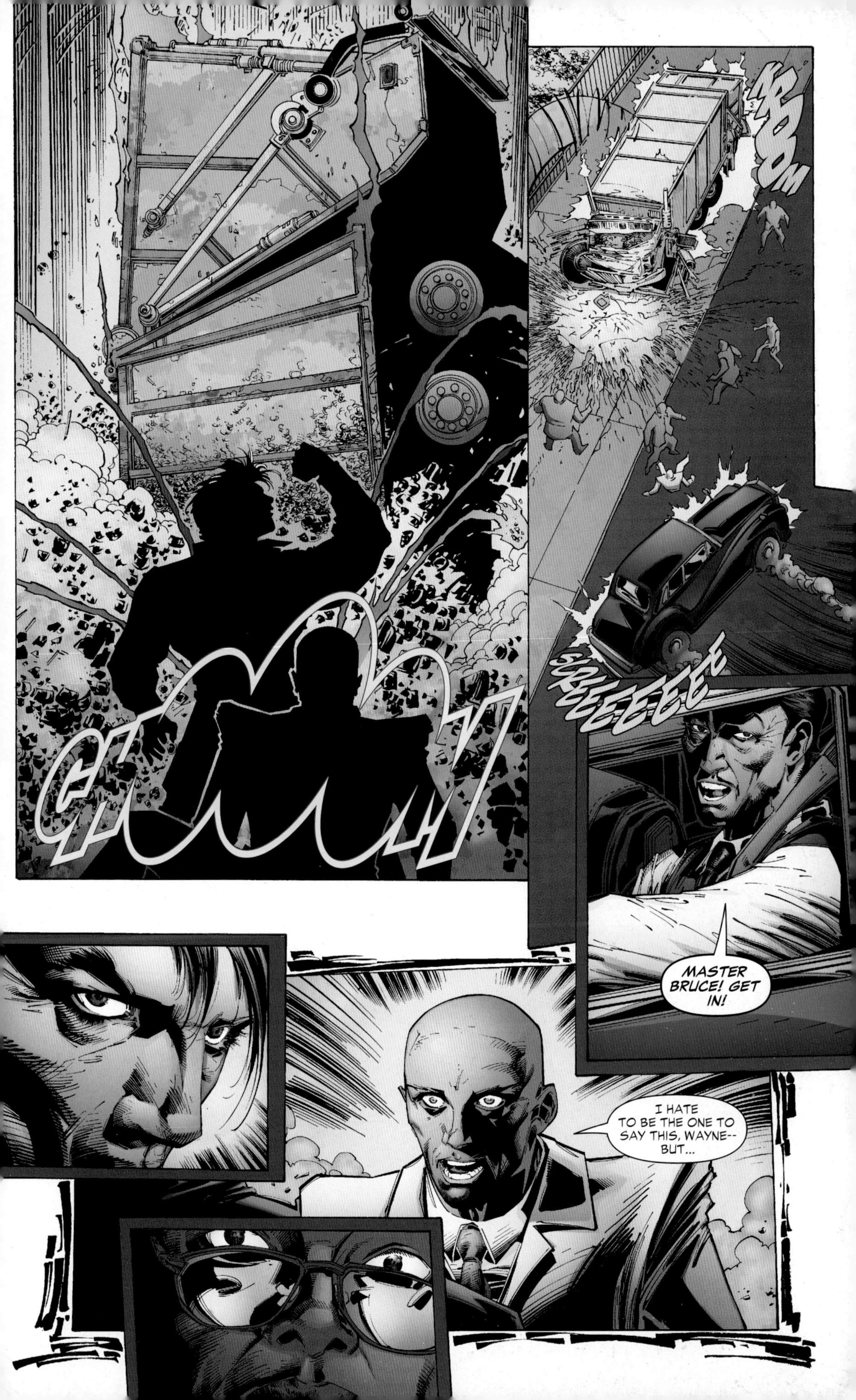
MASTER BRUCE! GET IN!
I HATE TO BE THE ONE TO SAY THIS, WAYNE-- BUT...

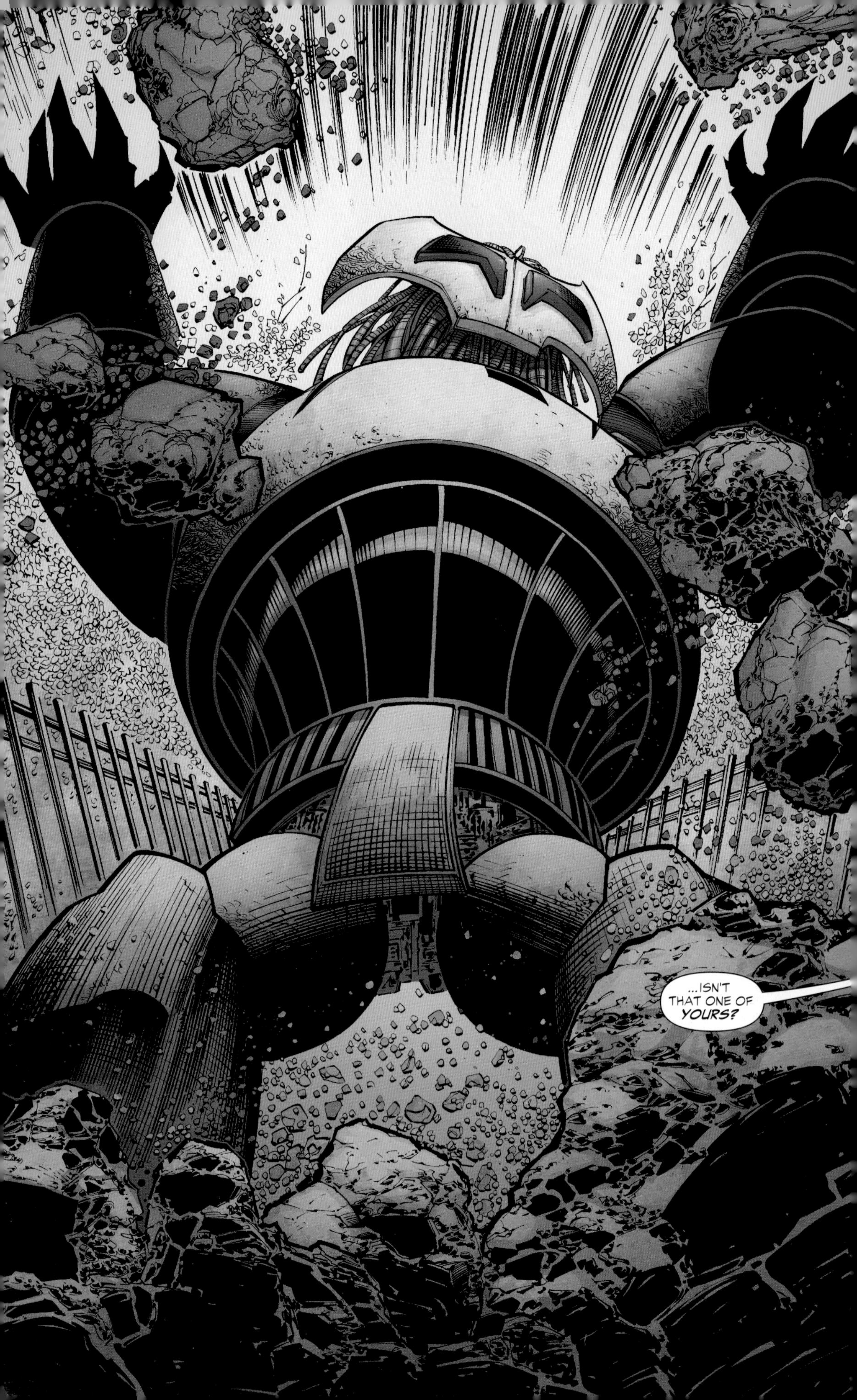
...ISN'T THAT ONE OF YOURS?

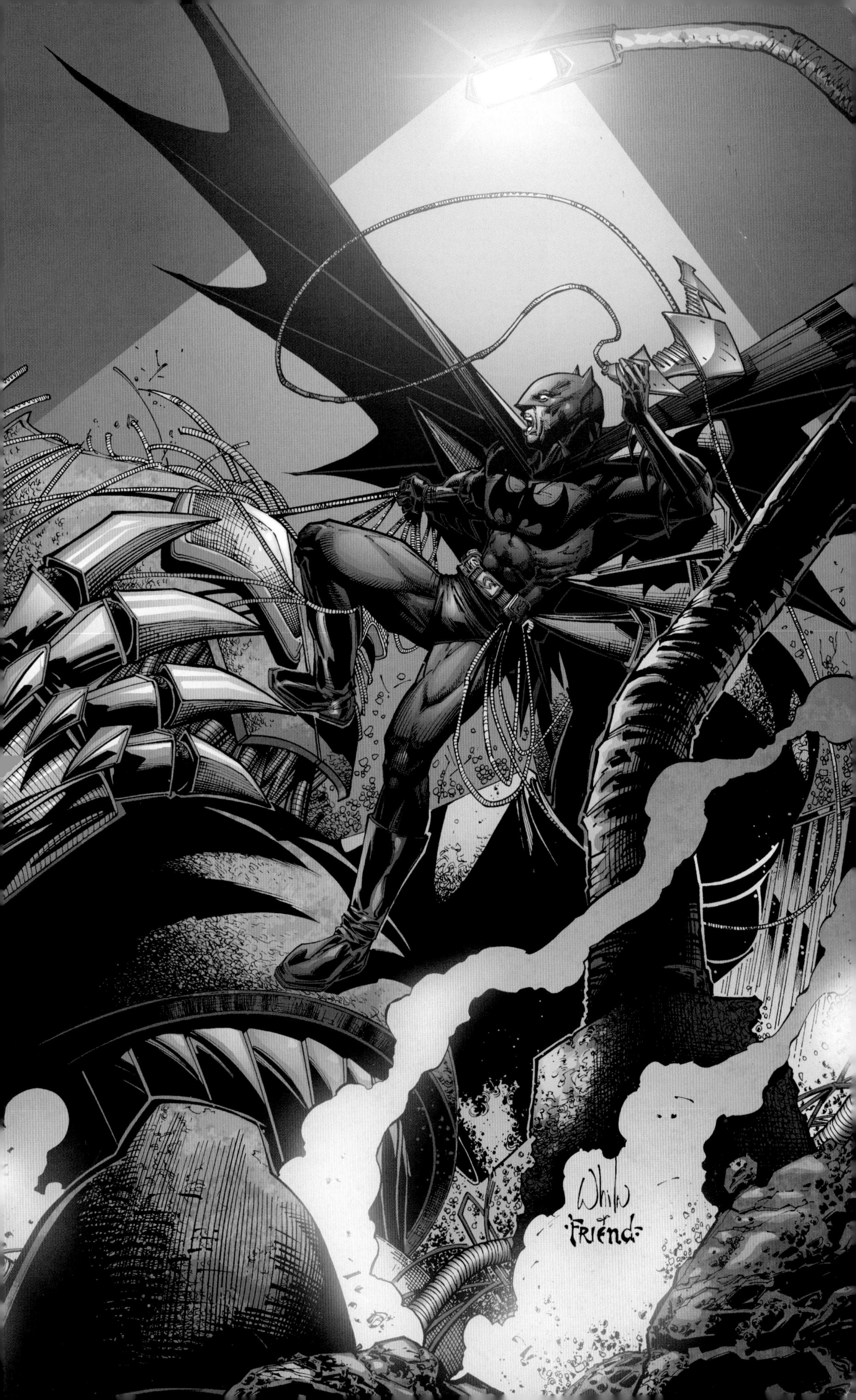
Whilce
·FRIEND·

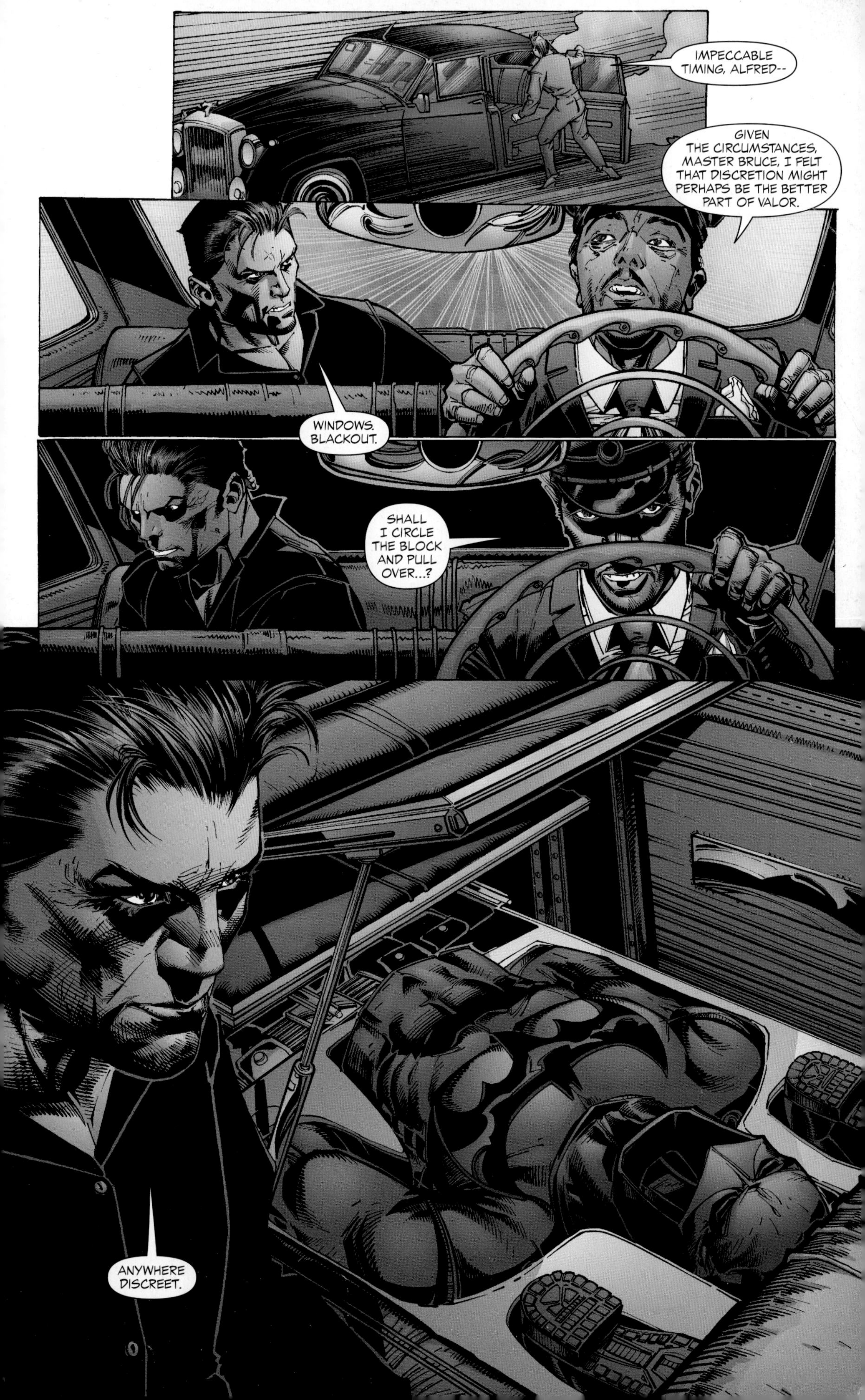
IMPECCABLE TIMING, ALFRED--
GIVEN THE CIRCUMSTANCES, MASTER BRUCE, I FELT THAT DISCRETION MIGHT PERHAPS BE THE BETTER PART OF VALOR.
WINDOWS. BLACKOUT.
SHALL I CIRCLE THE BLOCK AND PULL OVER...?
ANYWHERE DISCREET.

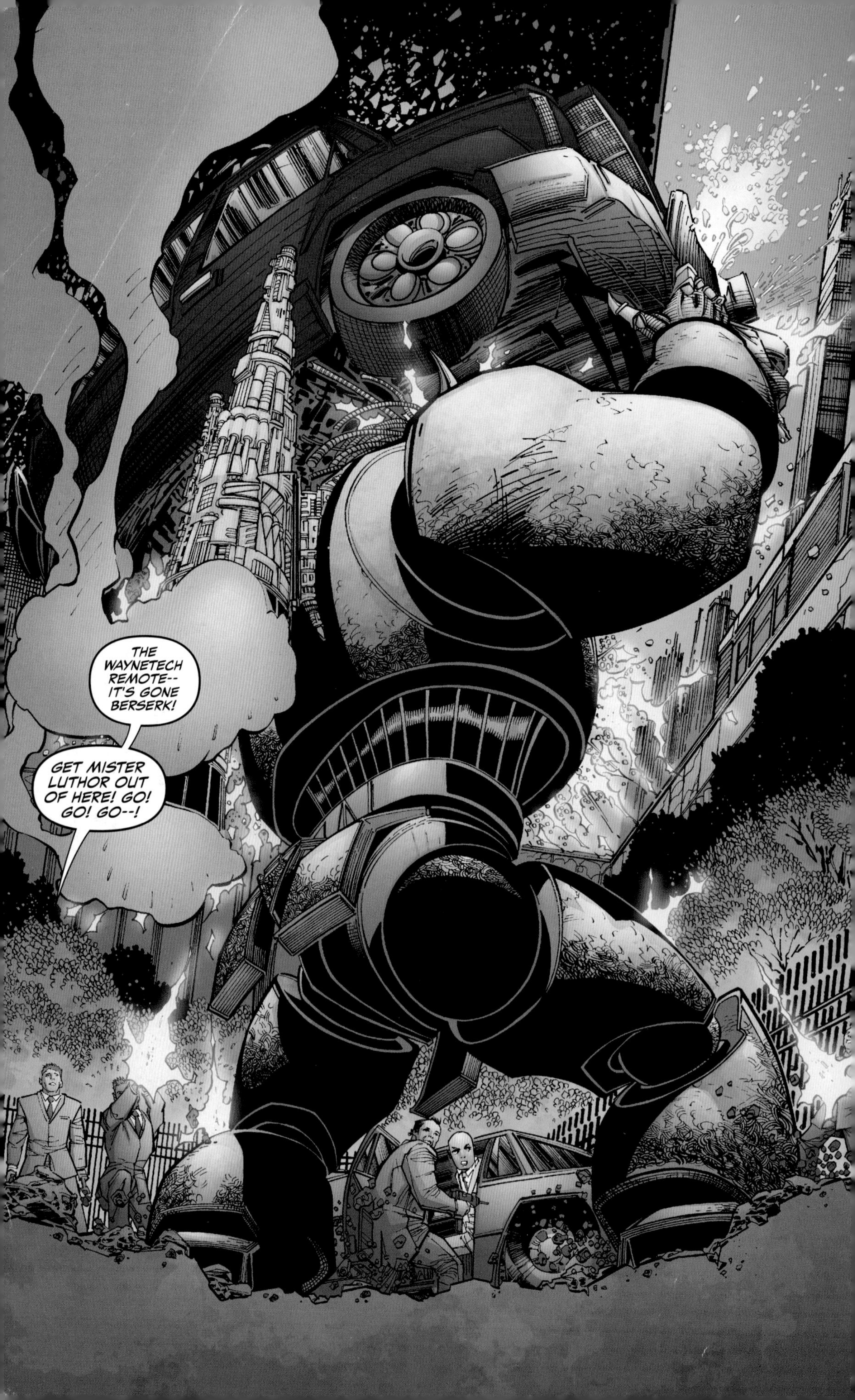
THE WAYNETECH REMOTE-- IT'S GONE BERSERK!
GET MISTER LUTHOR OUT OF HERE! GO! GO! GO--!

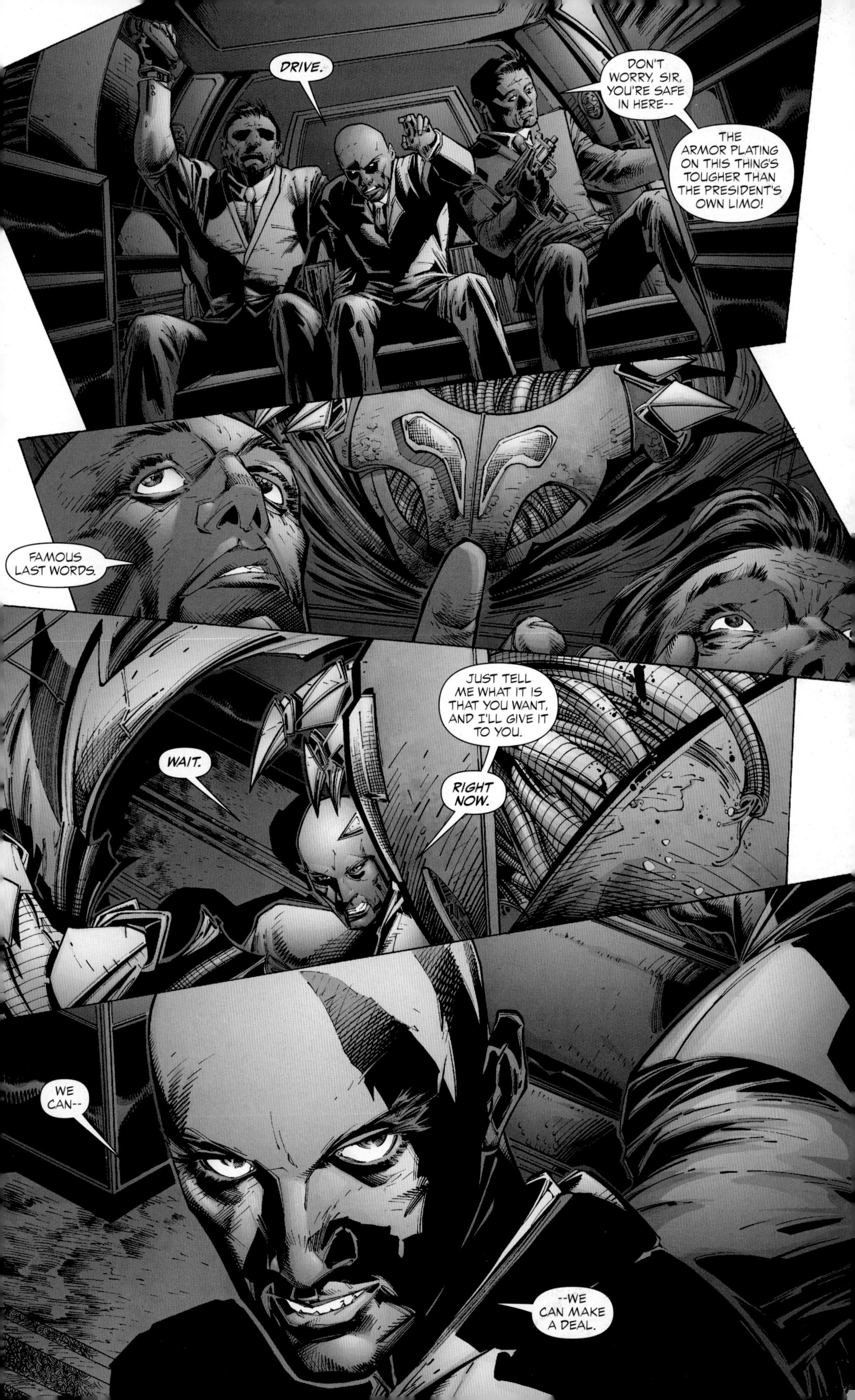
DRIVE.
DON'T WORRY, SIR, YOU'RE SAFE IN HERE--
THE ARMOR PLATING ON THIS THING'S TOUGHER THAN THE PRESIDENT'S OWN LIMO!
FAMOUS LAST WORDS.
WAIT.
JUST TELL ME WHAT IT IS THAT YOU WANT, AND I'LL GIVE IT TO YOU.
RIGHT NOW.
WE CAN--
--WE CAN MAKE A DEAL.

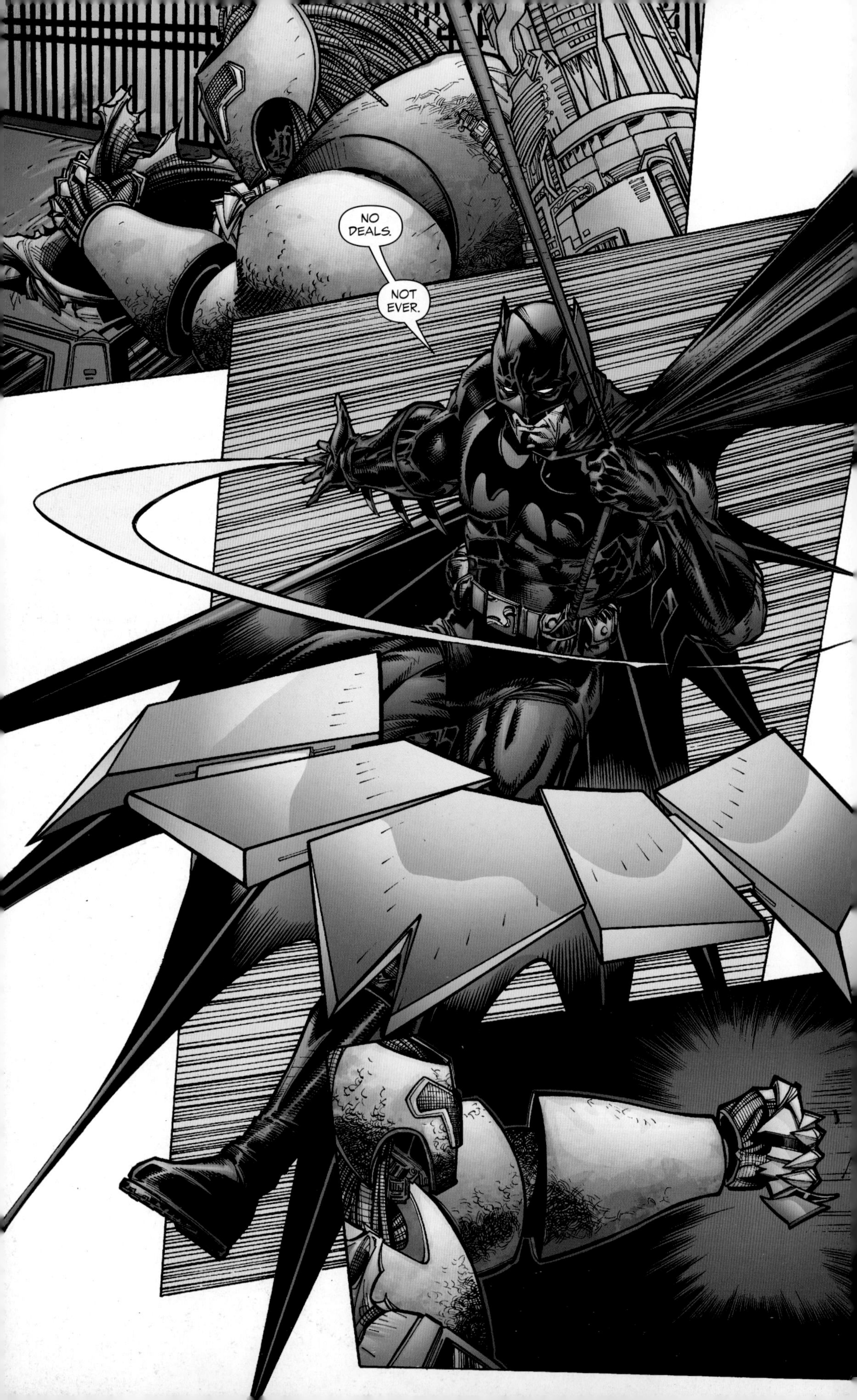
NO DEALS.
NOT EVER.

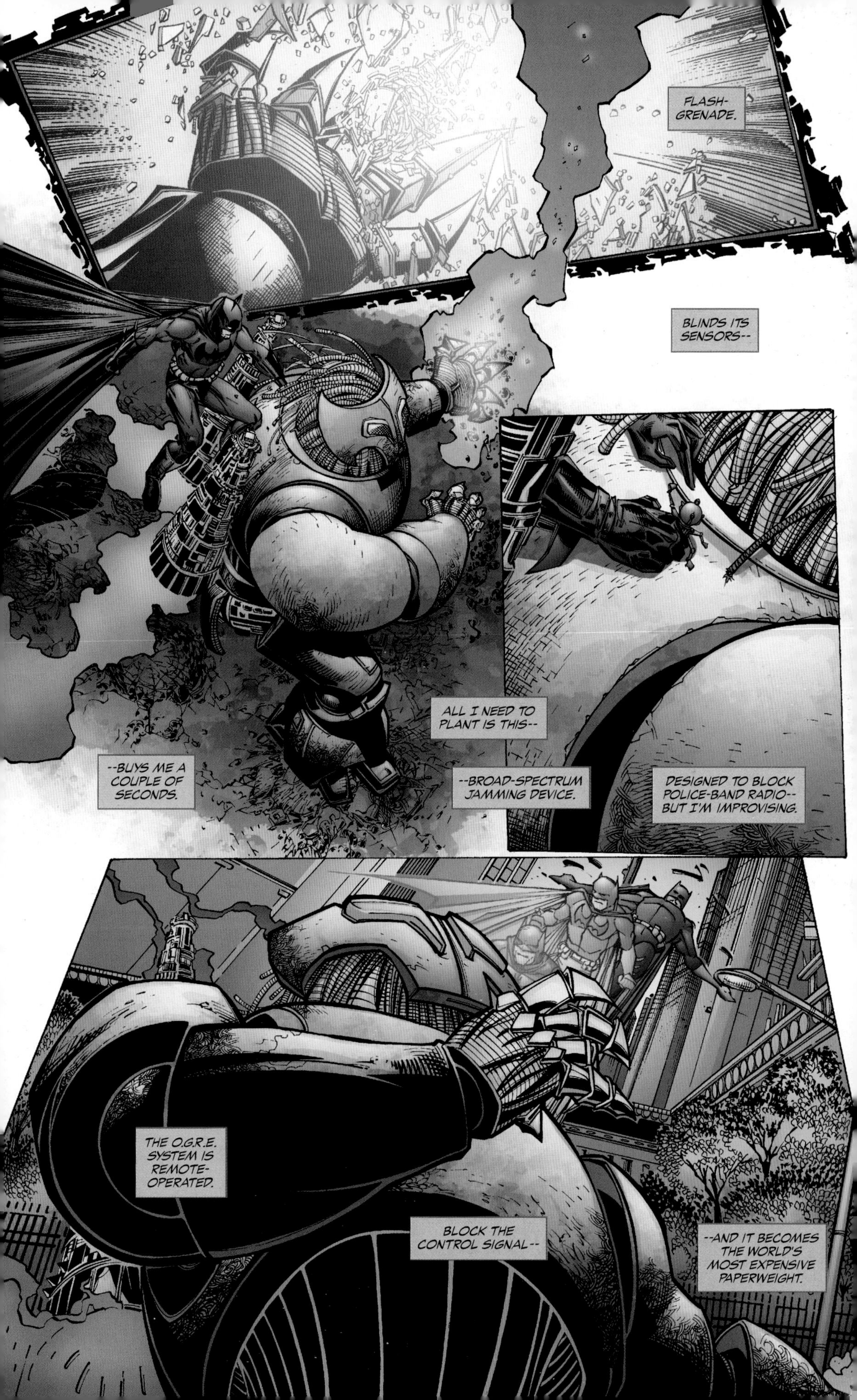
FLASH-GRENADE.
BLINDS ITS SENSORS--
--BUYS ME A COUPLE OF SECONDS.
ALL I NEED TO PLANT IS THIS--
--BROAD-SPECTRUM JAMMING DEVICE.
DESIGNED TO BLOCK POLICE-BAND RADIO--BUT I'M IMPROVISING.
THE O.G.R.E. SYSTEM IS REMOTE-OPERATED.
BLOCK THE CONTROL SIGNAL--
--AND IT BECOMES THE WORLD'S MOST EXPENSIVE PAPERWEIGHT.

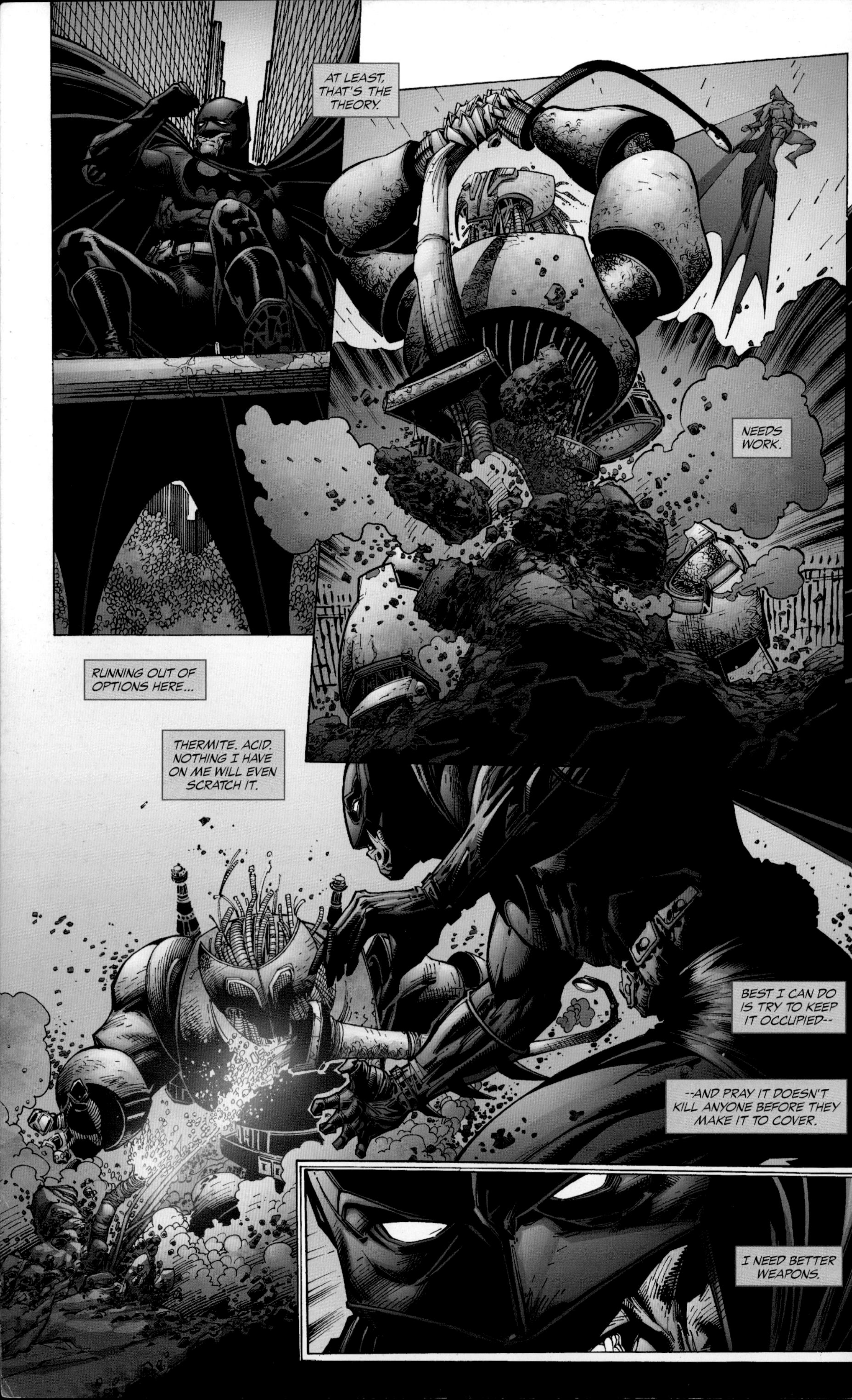
AT LEAST, THAT'S THE THEORY.
NEEDS WORK.
RUNNING OUT OF OPTIONS HERE...
THERMITE. ACID. NOTHING I HAVE ON ME WILL EVEN SCRATCH IT.
BEST I CAN DO IS TRY TO KEEP IT OCCUPIED--
--AND PRAY IT DOESN'T KILL ANYONE BEFORE THEY MAKE IT TO COVER.
I NEED BETTER WEAPONS.

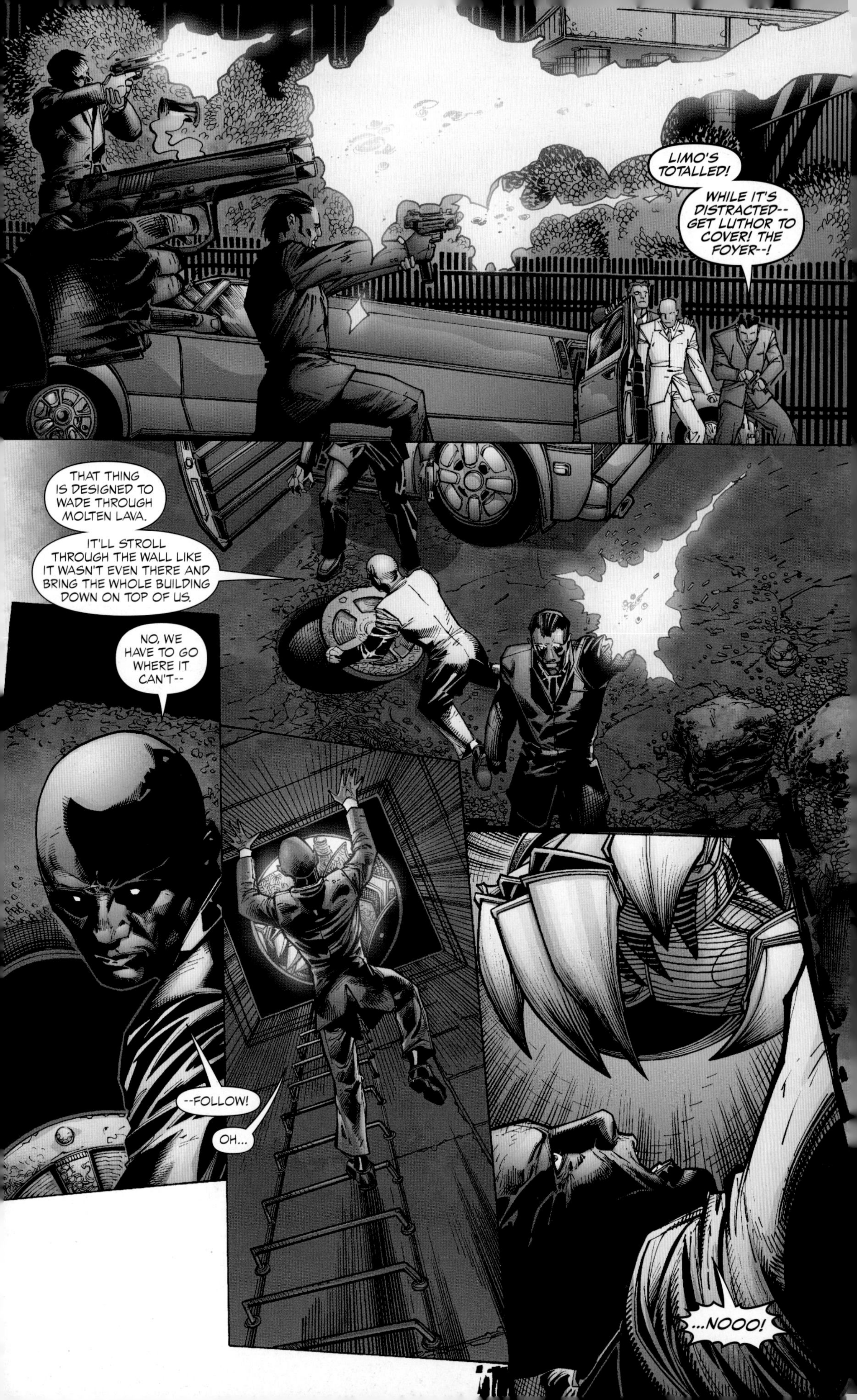
LIMO'S TOTALLED!
WHILE IT'S DISTRACTED--GET LUTHOR TO COVER! THE FOYER--!
THAT THING IS DESIGNED TO WADE THROUGH MOLTEN LAVA.
IT'LL STROLL THROUGH THE WALL LIKE IT WASN'T EVEN THERE AND BRING THE WHOLE BUILDING DOWN ON TOP OF US.
NO, WE HAVE TO GO WHERE IT CAN'T--
--FOLLOW!
OH...
...NOOO!

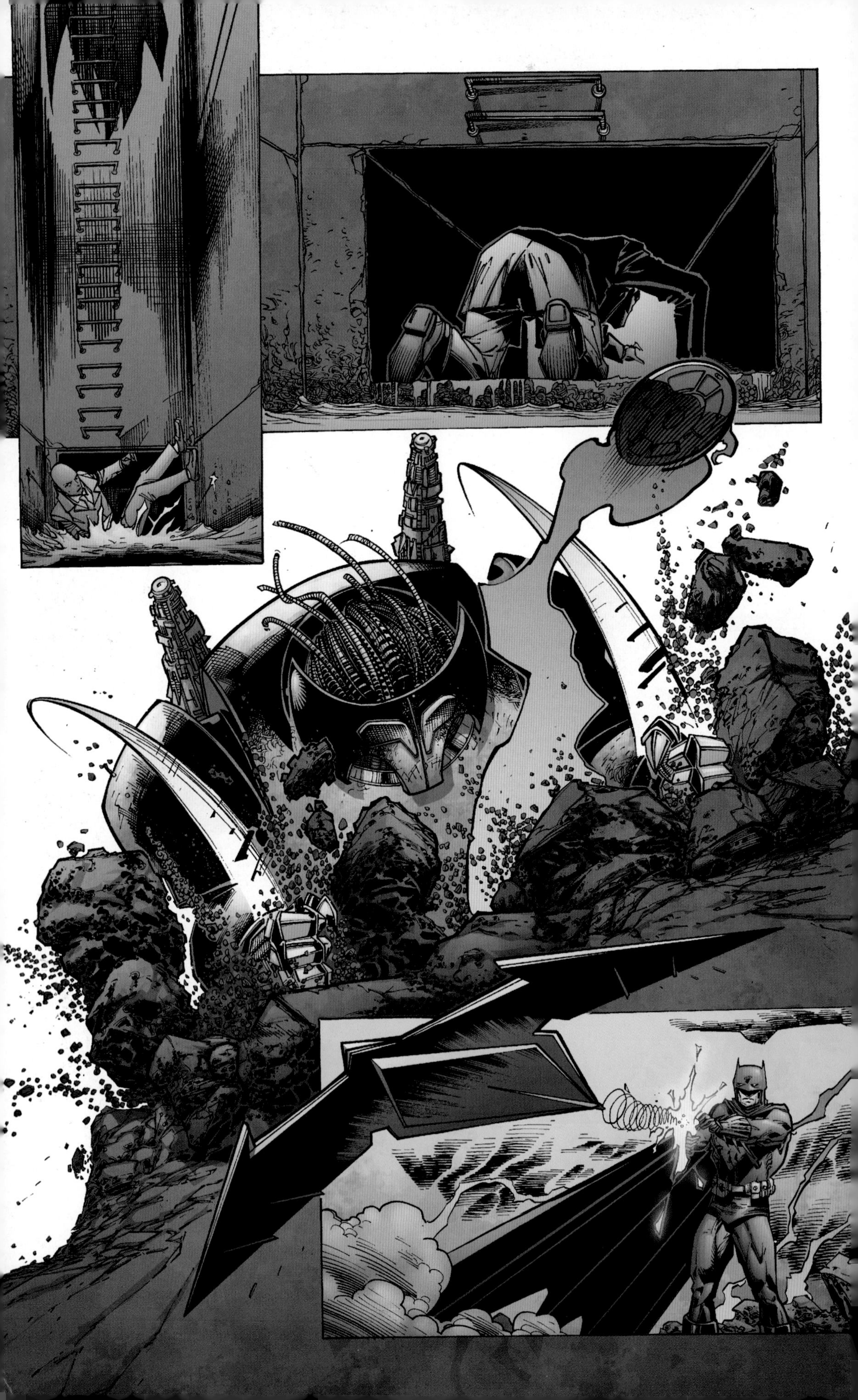

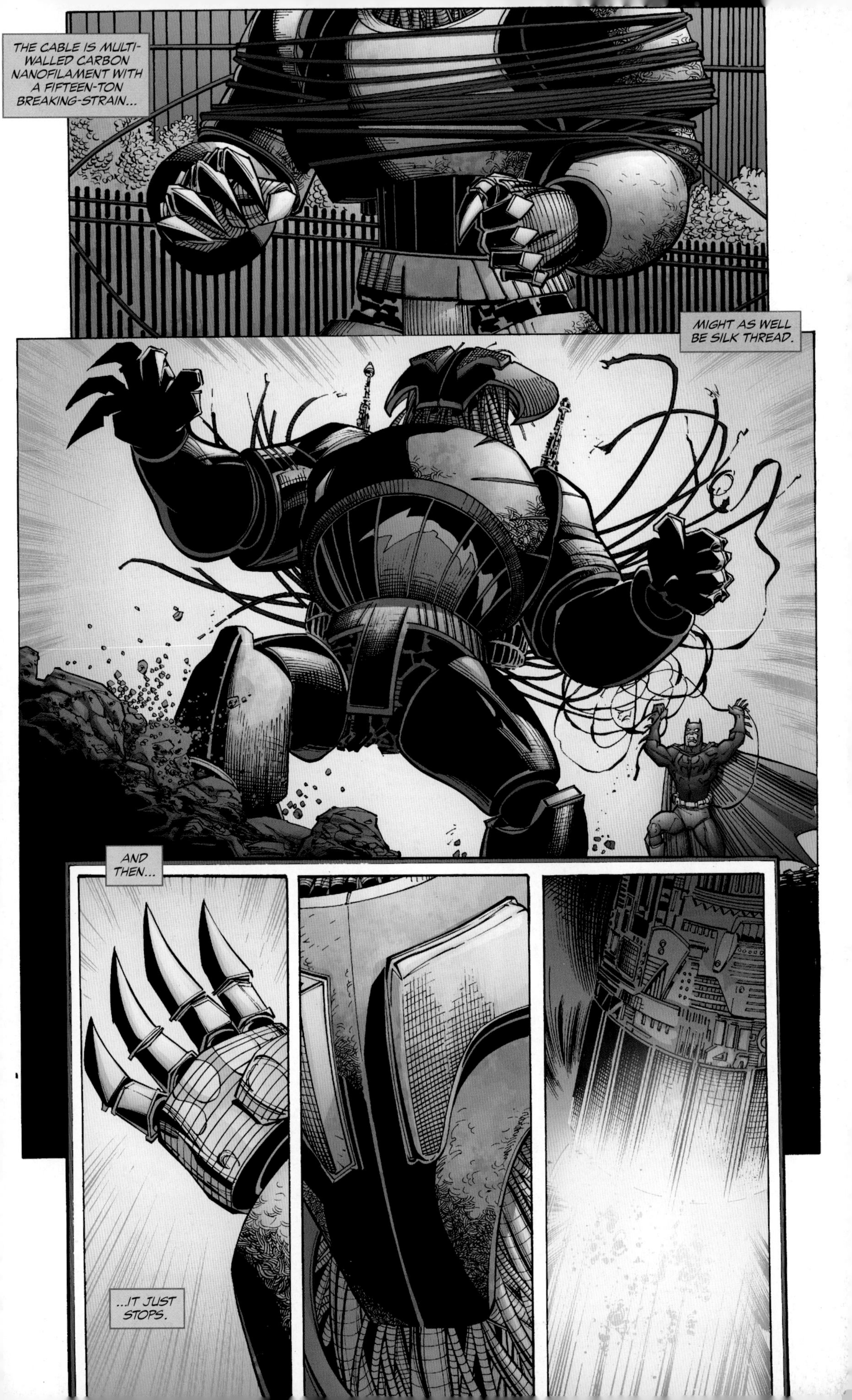
THE CABLE IS MULTI-WALLED CARBON NANOFILAMENT WITH A FIFTEEN-TON BREAKING-STRAIN...
MIGHT AS WELL BE SILK THREAD.
AND THEN...
...IT JUST STOPS.

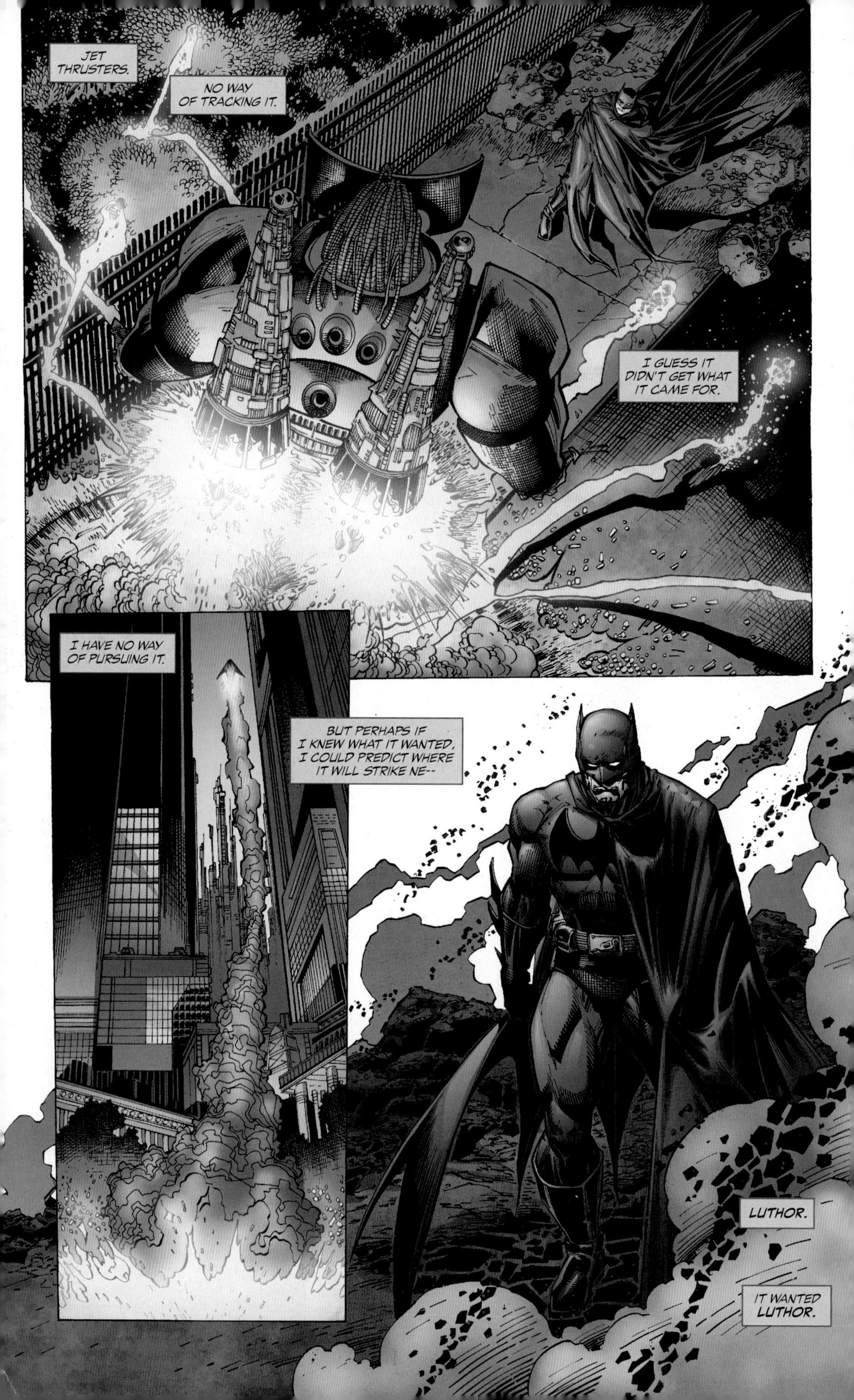

JET THRUSTERS.
NO WAY OF TRACKING IT.
I GUESS IT DIDN'T GET WHAT IT CAME FOR.
I HAVE NO WAY OF PURSUING IT.
BUT PERHAPS IF I KNEW WHAT IT WANTED, I COULD PREDICT WHERE IT WILL STRIKE NE--
LUTHOR.
IT WANTED LUTHOR.

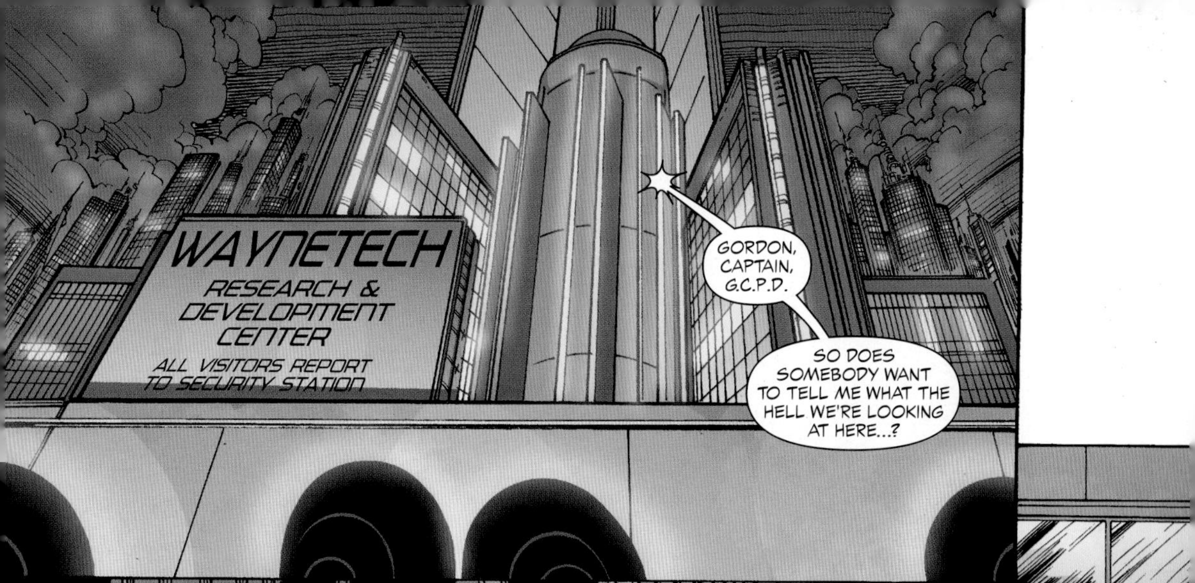
WAYNETECH
RESEARCH & DEVELOPMENT CENTER
ALL VISITORS REPORT TO SECURITY STATION
GORDON, CAPTAIN, G.C.P.D.
SO DOES SOMEBODY WANT TO TELL ME WHAT THE HELL WE'RE LOOKING AT HERE...?

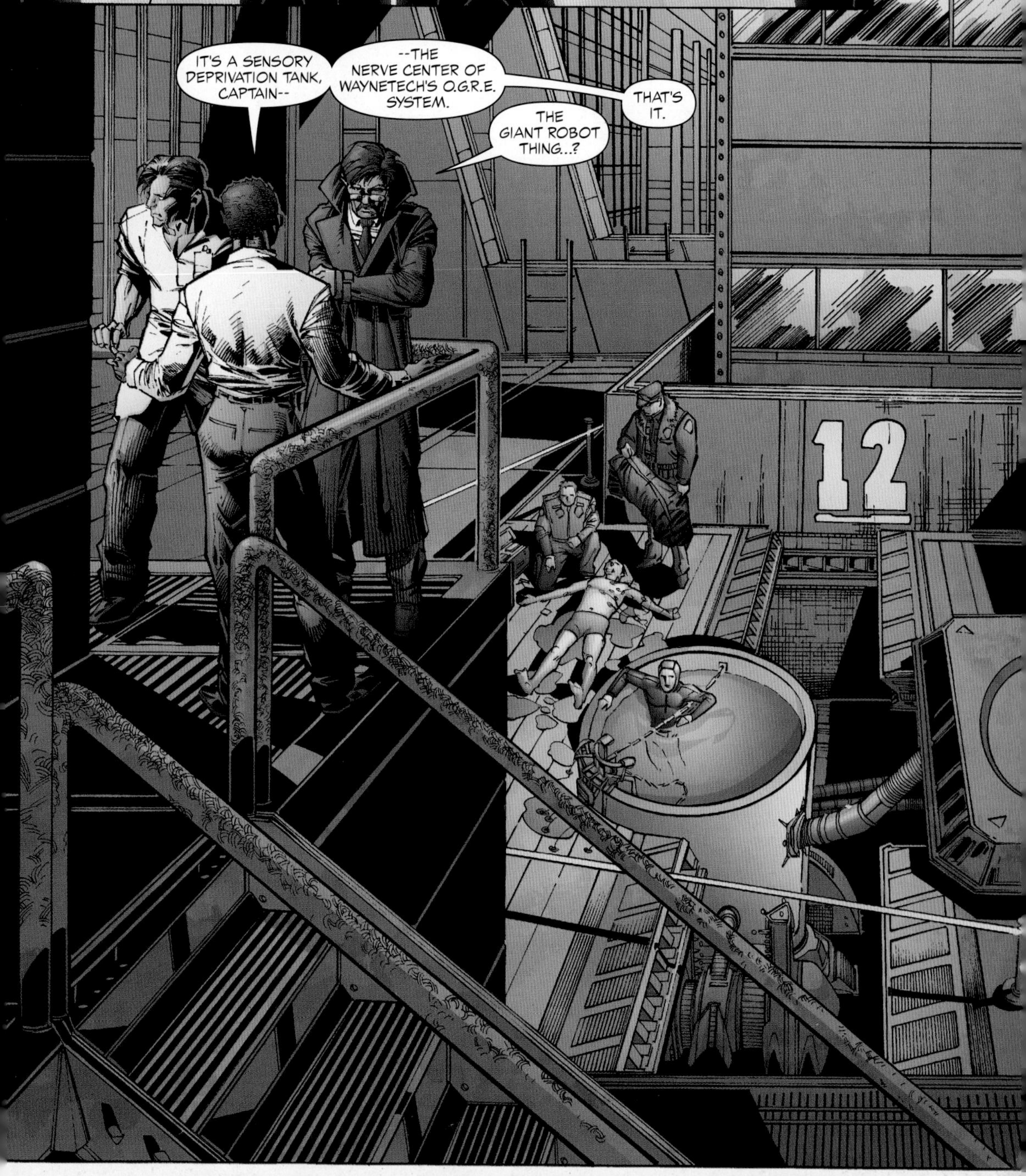
IT'S A SENSORY DEPRIVATION TANK, CAPTAIN--
--THE NERVE CENTER OF WAYNETECH'S O.G.R.E. SYSTEM.
THE GIANT ROBOT THING...?
THAT'S IT.
12

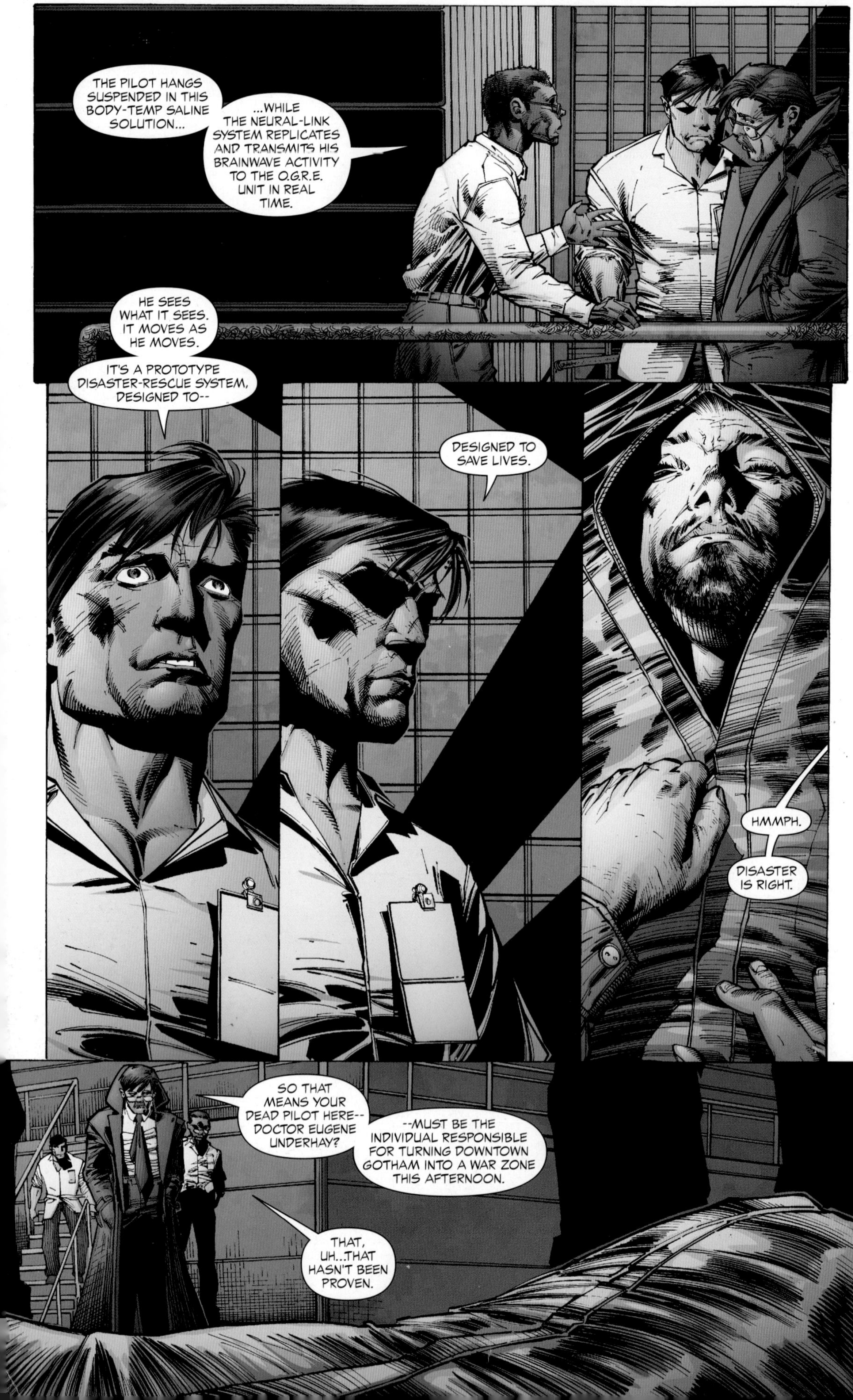
THE PILOT HANGS SUSPENDED IN THIS BODY-TEMP SALINE SOLUTION...
...WHILE THE NEURAL-LINK SYSTEM REPLICATES AND TRANSMITS HIS BRAINWAVE ACTIVITY TO THE O.G.R.E. UNIT IN REAL TIME.
HE SEES WHAT IT SEES. IT MOVES AS HE MOVES.
IT'S A PROTOTYPE DISASTER-RESCUE SYSTEM, DESIGNED TO--
DESIGNED TO SAVE LIVES.
HMMPH.
DISASTER IS RIGHT.
SO THAT MEANS YOUR DEAD PILOT HERE-- DOCTOR EUGENE UNDERHAY?
--MUST BE THE INDIVIDUAL RESPONSIBLE FOR TURNING DOWNTOWN GOTHAM INTO A WAR ZONE THIS AFTERNOON.
THAT, UH...THAT HASN'T BEEN PROVEN.

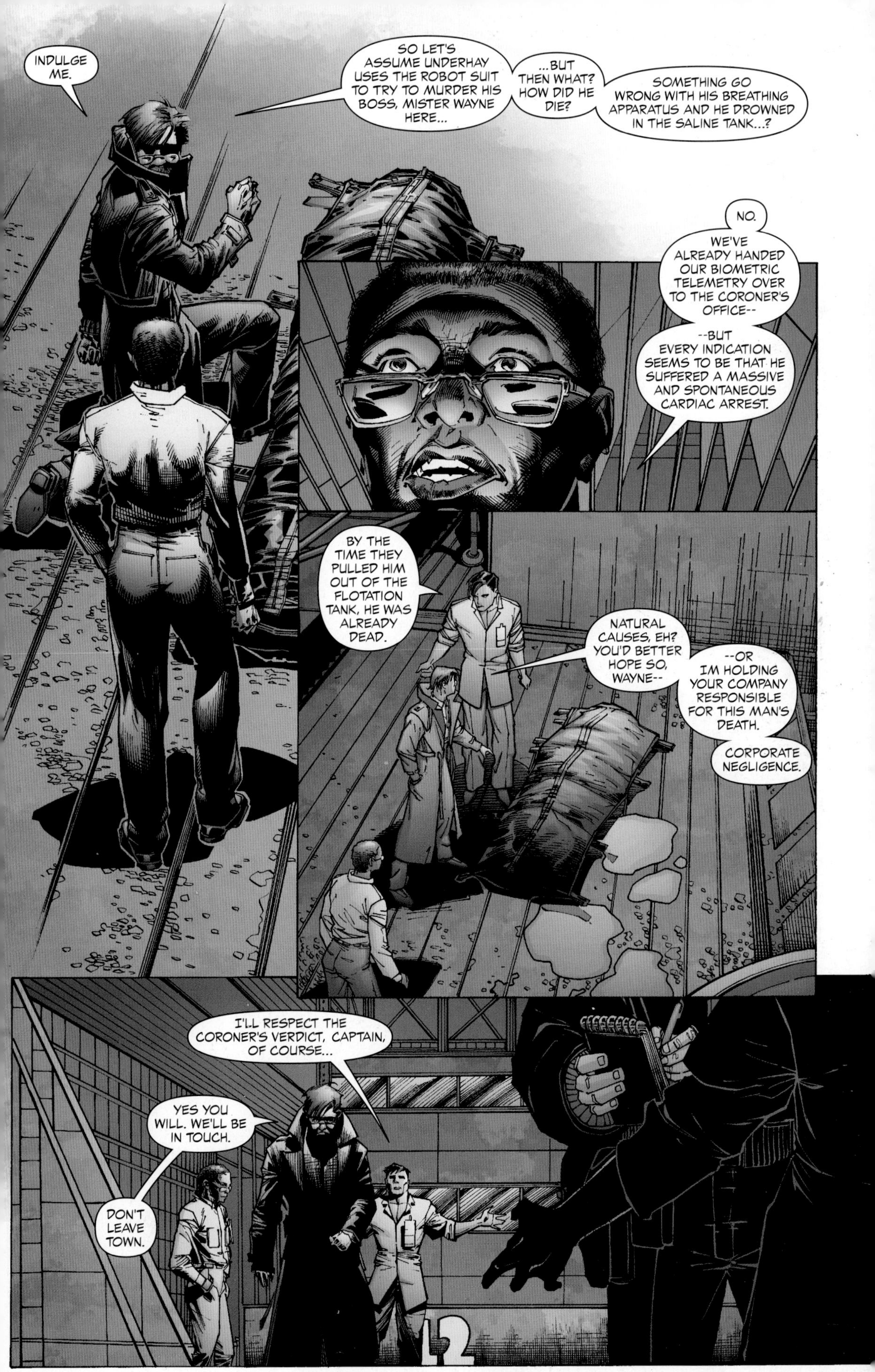
INDULGE ME.
SO LET'S ASSUME UNDERHAY USES THE ROBOT SUIT TO TRY TO MURDER HIS BOSS, MISTER WAYNE HERE...
...BUT THEN WHAT? HOW DID HE DIE?
SOMETHING GO WRONG WITH HIS BREATHING APPARATUS AND HE DROWNED IN THE SALINE TANK...?
NO.
WE'VE ALREADY HANDED OUR BIOMETRIC TELEMETRY OVER TO THE CORONER'S OFFICE--
--BUT EVERY INDICATION SEEMS TO BE THAT HE SUFFERED A MASSIVE AND SPONTANEOUS CARDIAC ARREST.
BY THE TIME THEY PULLED HIM OUT OF THE FLOTATION TANK, HE WAS ALREADY DEAD.
NATURAL CAUSES, EH? YOU'D BETTER HOPE SO, WAYNE--
--OR IM HOLDING YOUR COMPANY RESPONSIBLE FOR THIS MAN'S DEATH.
CORPORATE NEGLIGENCE.
I'LL RESPECT THE CORONER'S VERDICT, CAPTAIN, OF COURSE...
YES YOU WILL. WE'LL BE IN TOUCH.
DON'T LEAVE TOWN.
12

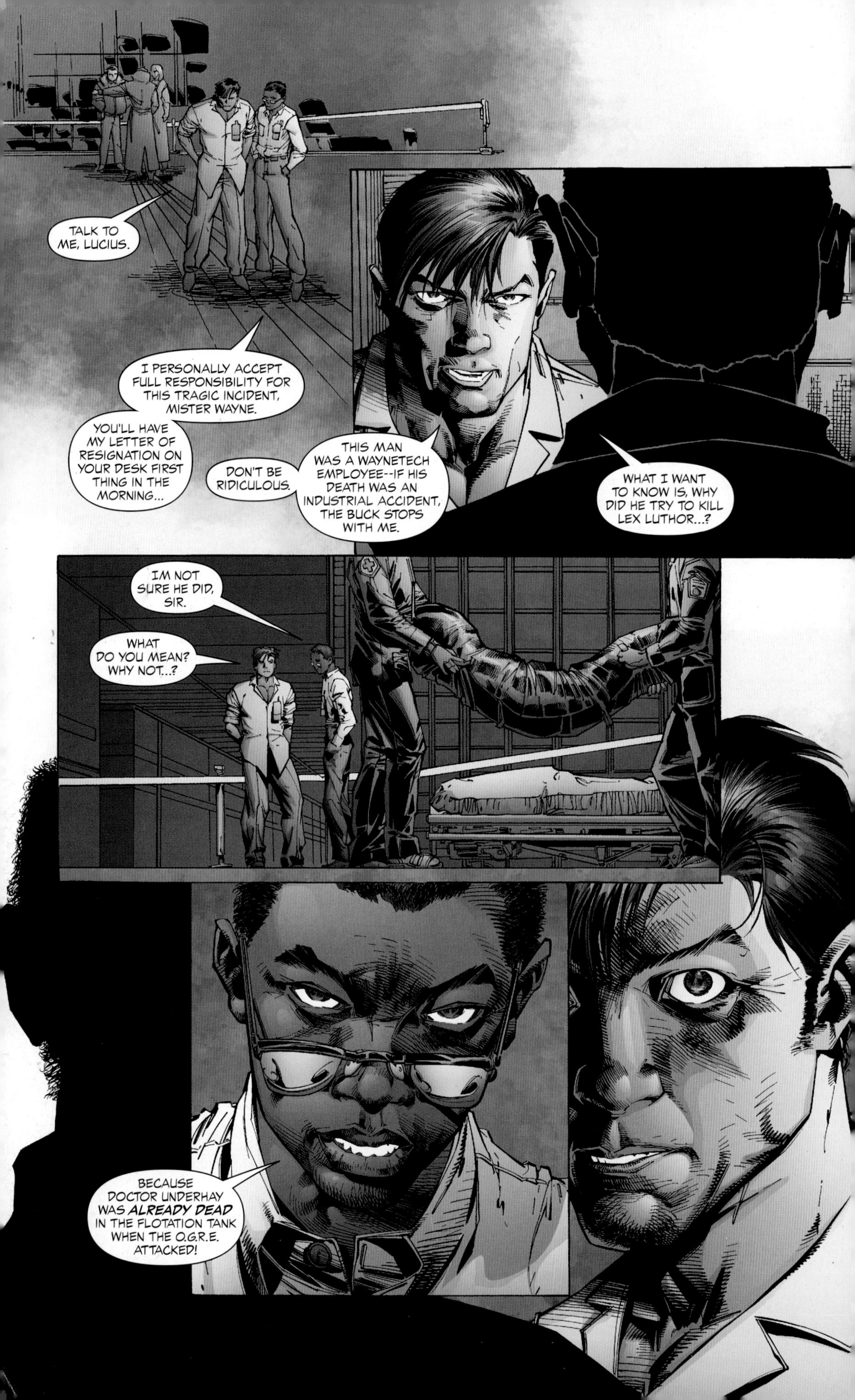
TALK TO ME, LUCIUS.
I PERSONALLY ACCEPT FULL RESPONSIBILITY FOR THIS TRAGIC INCIDENT, MISTER WAYNE.
YOU'LL HAVE MY LETTER OF RESIGNATION ON YOUR DESK FIRST THING IN THE MORNING...
DON'T BE RIDICULOUS.
THIS MAN WAS A WAYNETECH EMPLOYEE--IF HIS DEATH WAS AN INDUSTRIAL ACCIDENT, THE BUCK STOPS WITH ME.
WHAT I WANT TO KNOW IS, WHY DID HE TRY TO KILL LEX LUTHOR...?
IM NOT SURE HE DID, SIR.
WHAT DO YOU MEAN? WHY NOT...?
BECAUSE DOCTOR UNDERHAY WAS ***ALREADY DEAD*** IN THE FLOTATION TANK WHEN THE O.G.R.E. ATTACKED!

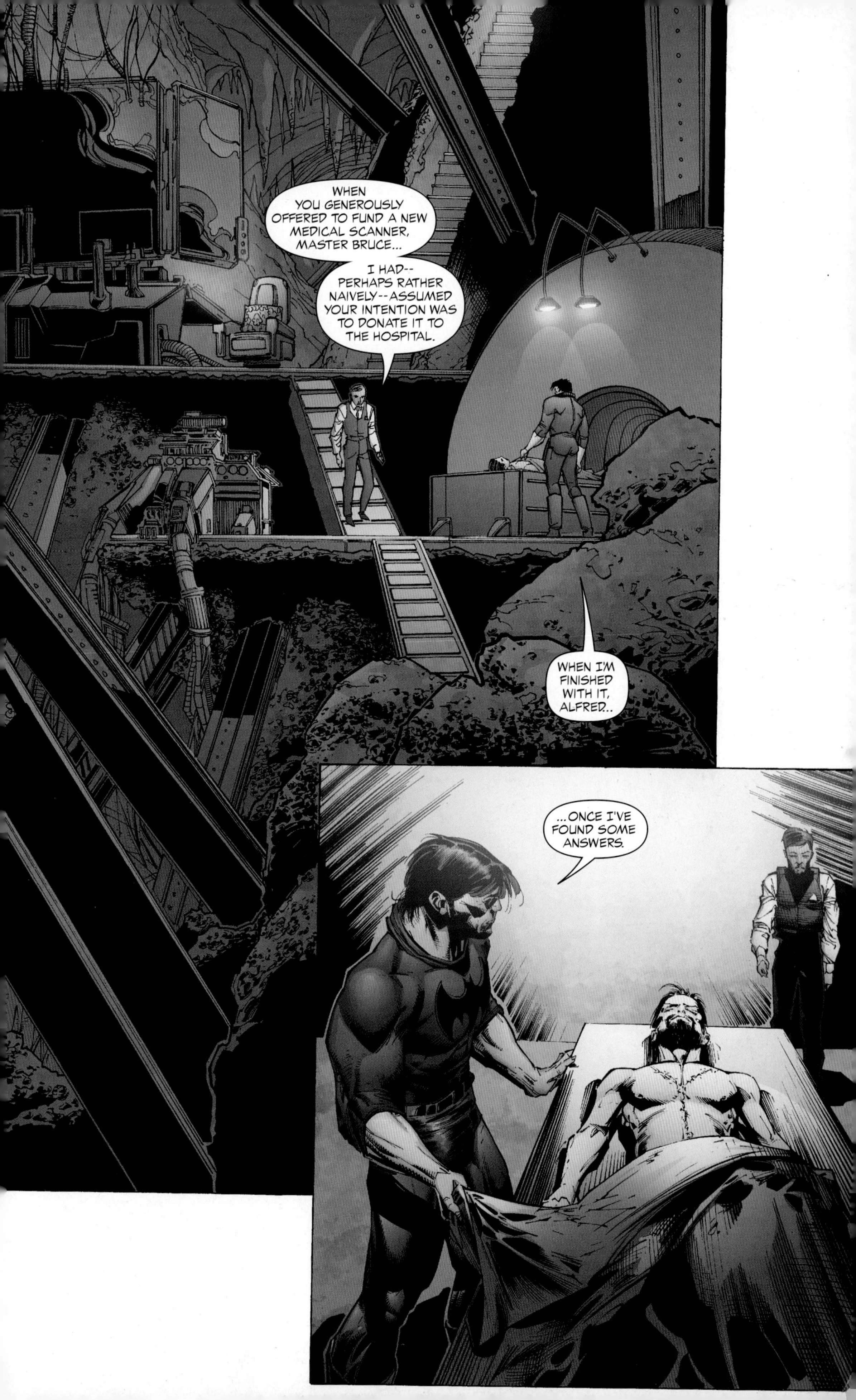
WHEN YOU GENEROUSLY OFFERED TO FUND A NEW MEDICAL SCANNER, MASTER BRUCE...
I HAD-- PERHAPS RATHER NAIVELY--ASSUMED YOUR INTENTION WAS TO DONATE IT TO THE HOSPITAL.
WHEN I'M FINISHED WITH IT, ALFRED..
...ONCE I'VE FOUND SOME ANSWERS.

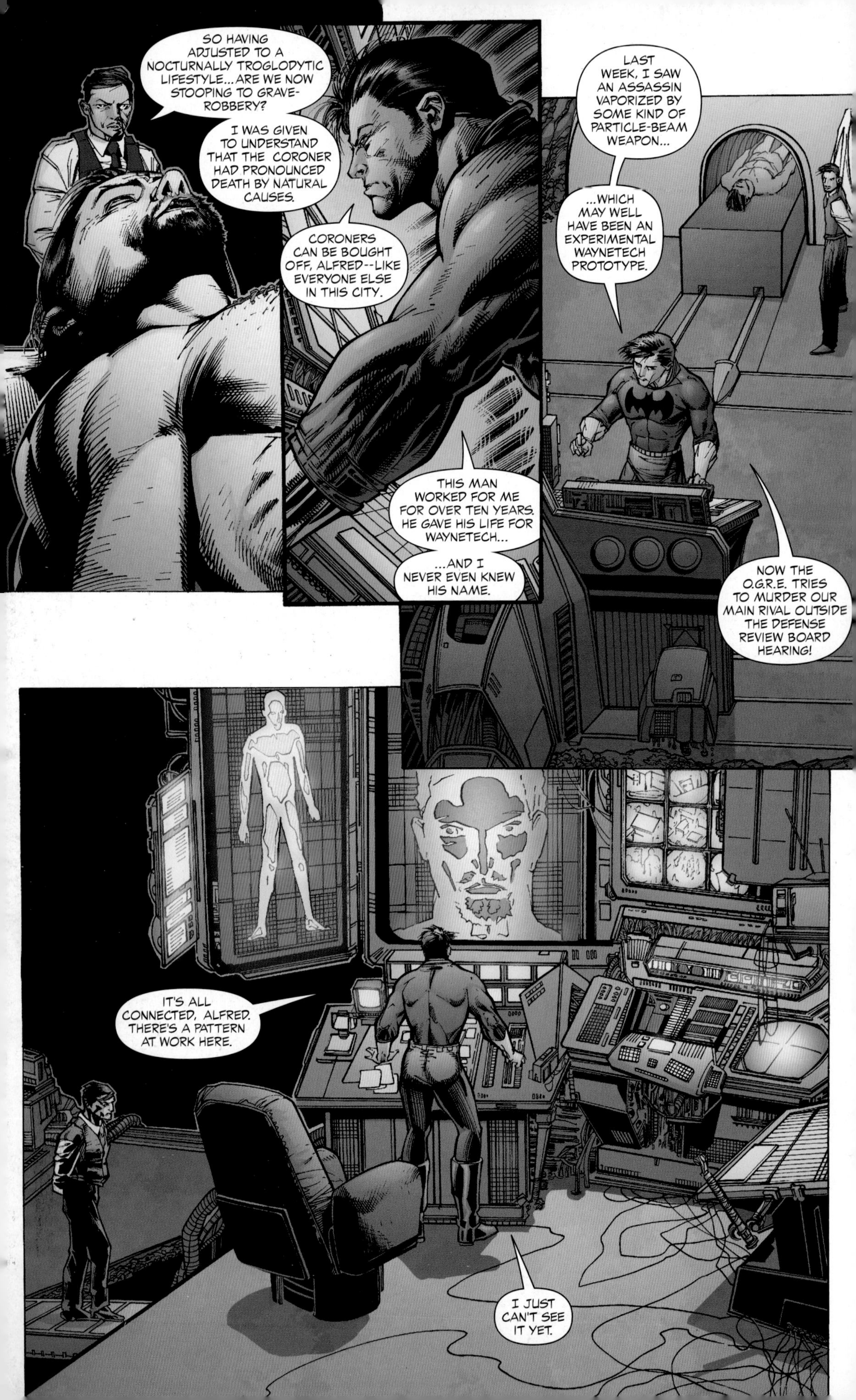
SO HAVING ADJUSTED TO A NOCTURNALLY TROGLODYTIC LIFESTYLE... ARE WE NOW STOOPING TO GRAVE-ROBBERY?
I WAS GIVEN TO UNDERSTAND THAT THE CORONER HAD PRONOUNCED DEATH BY NATURAL CAUSES.
CORONERS CAN BE BOUGHT OFF, ALFRED--LIKE EVERYONE ELSE IN THIS CITY.
THIS MAN WORKED FOR ME FOR OVER TEN YEARS. HE GAVE HIS LIFE FOR WAYNETECH...
...AND I NEVER EVEN KNEW HIS NAME.
LAST WEEK, I SAW AN ASSASSIN VAPORIZED BY SOME KIND OF PARTICLE-BEAM WEAPON...
...WHICH MAY WELL HAVE BEEN AN EXPERIMENTAL WAYNETECH PROTOTYPE.
NOW THE O.G.R.E. TRIES TO MURDER OUR MAIN RIVAL OUTSIDE THE DEFENSE REVIEW BOARD HEARING!
IT'S ALL CONNECTED, ALFRED. THERE'S A PATTERN AT WORK HERE.
I JUST CAN'T SEE IT YET.

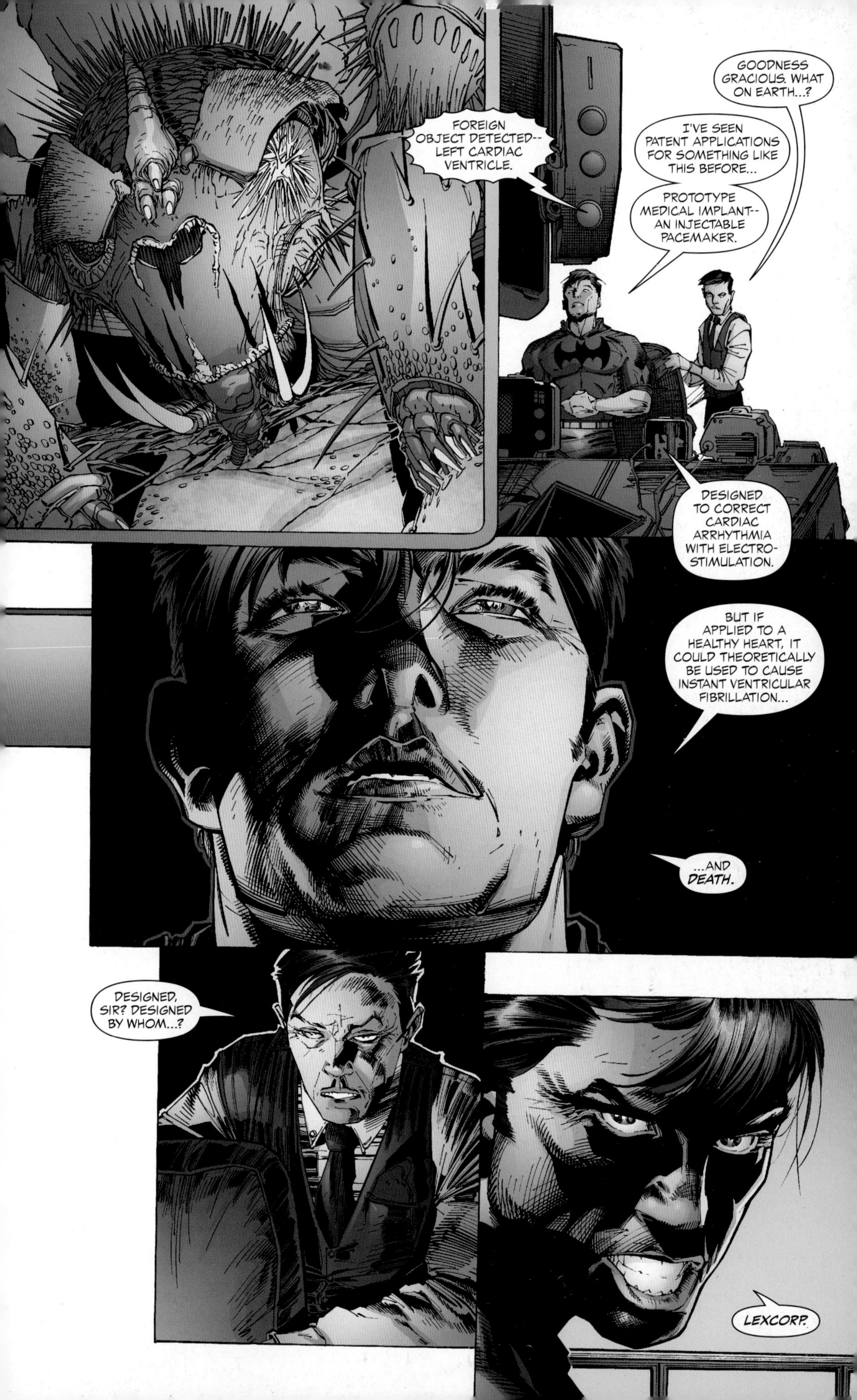

FOREIGN OBJECT DETECTED--LEFT CARDIAC VENTRICLE.
GOODNESS GRACIOUS. WHAT ON EARTH...?
I'VE SEEN PATENT APPLICATIONS FOR SOMETHING LIKE THIS BEFORE...
PROTOTYPE MEDICAL IMPLANT--AN INJECTABLE PACEMAKER.
DESIGNED TO CORRECT CARDIAC ARRHYTHMIA WITH ELECTRO-STIMULATION.
BUT IF APPLIED TO A HEALTHY HEART, IT COULD THEORETICALLY BE USED TO CAUSE INSTANT VENTRICULAR FIBRILLATION...
...AND DEATH.
DESIGNED, SIR? DESIGNED BY WHOM...?
LEXCORP.

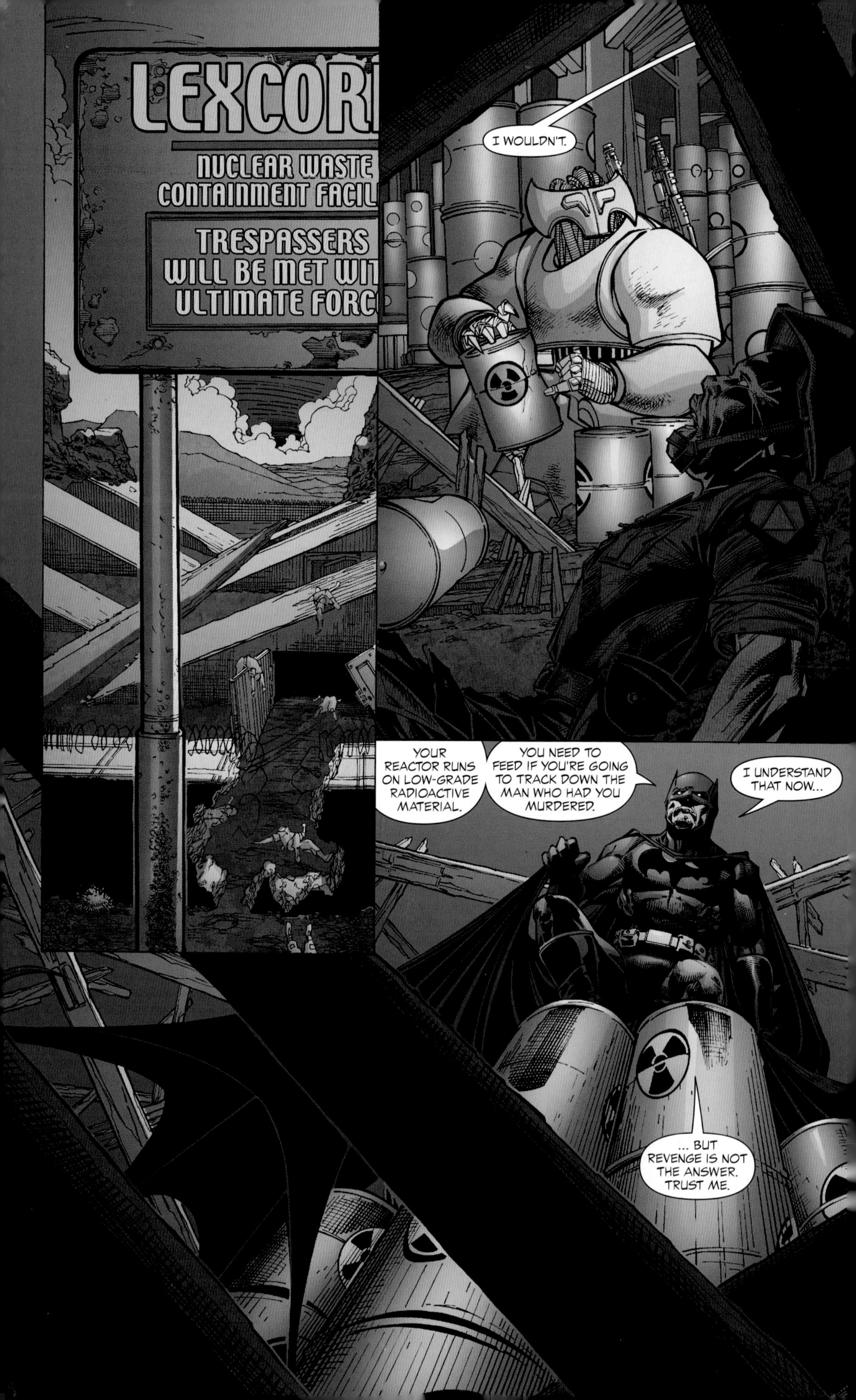
LEXCORP
NUCLEAR WASTE
CONTAINMENT FACIL
TRESPASSERS
WILL BE MET WIT
ULTIMATE FORC
I WOULDN'T.
YOUR REACTOR RUNS ON LOW-GRADE RADIOACTIVE MATERIAL.
YOU NEED TO FEED IF YOU'RE GOING TO TRACK DOWN THE MAN WHO HAD YOU MURDERED.
I UNDERSTAND THAT NOW...
... BUT REVENGE IS NOT THE ANSWER. TRUST ME.

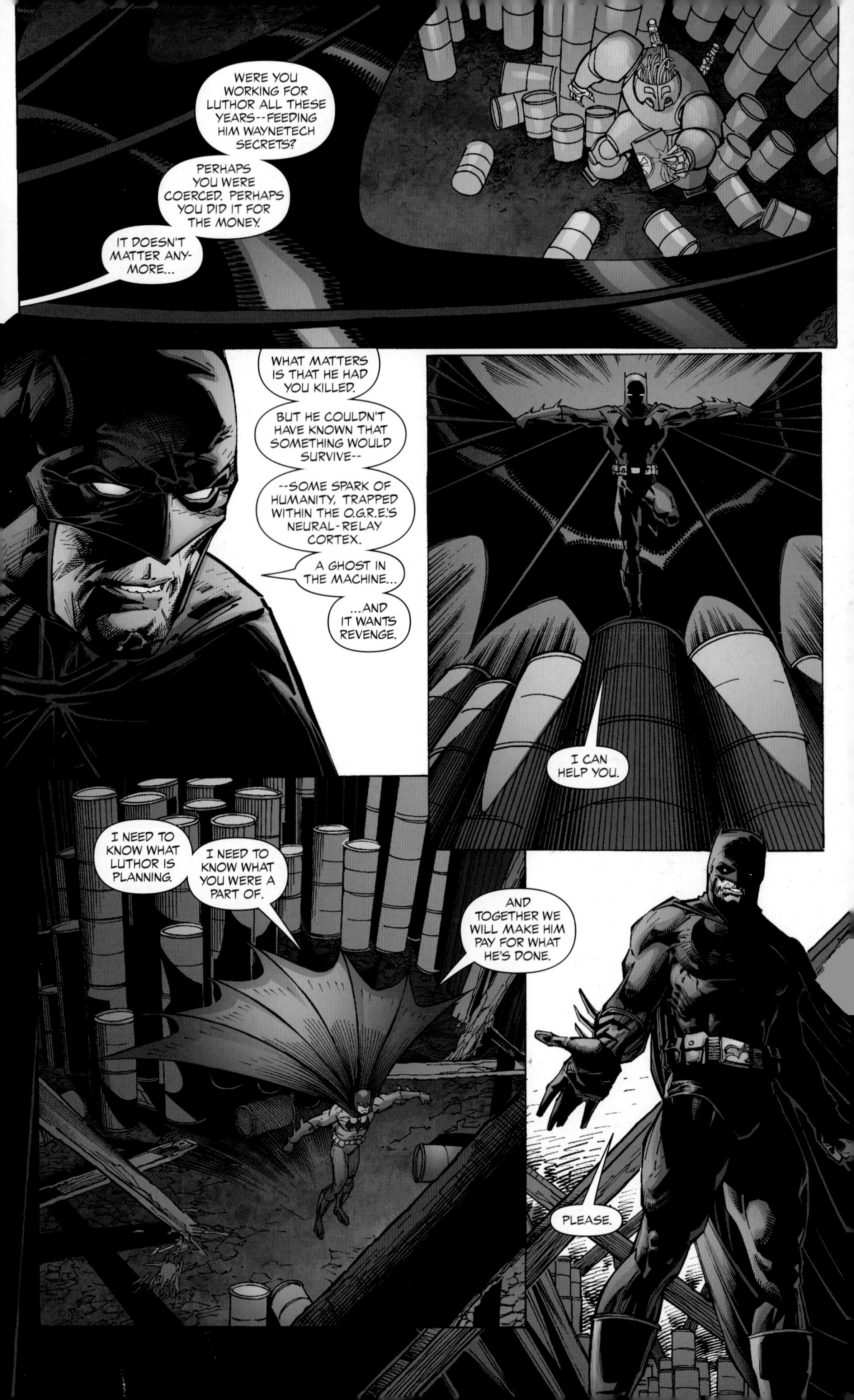
WERE YOU WORKING FOR LUTHOR ALL THESE YEARS--FEEDING HIM WAYNETECH SECRETS?
PERHAPS YOU WERE COERCED. PERHAPS YOU DID IT FOR THE MONEY.
IT DOESN'T MATTER ANY-MORE...
WHAT MATTERS IS THAT HE HAD YOU KILLED.
BUT HE COULDN'T HAVE KNOWN THAT SOMETHING WOULD SURVIVE--
--SOME SPARK OF HUMANITY, TRAPPED WITHIN THE O.G.R.E.'S NEURAL-RELAY CORTEX.
A GHOST IN THE MACHINE...
...AND IT WANTS REVENGE.
I CAN HELP YOU.
I NEED TO KNOW WHAT LUTHOR IS PLANNING.
I NEED TO KNOW WHAT YOU WERE A PART OF.
AND TOGETHER WE WILL MAKE HIM PAY FOR WHAT HE'S DONE.
PLEASE.

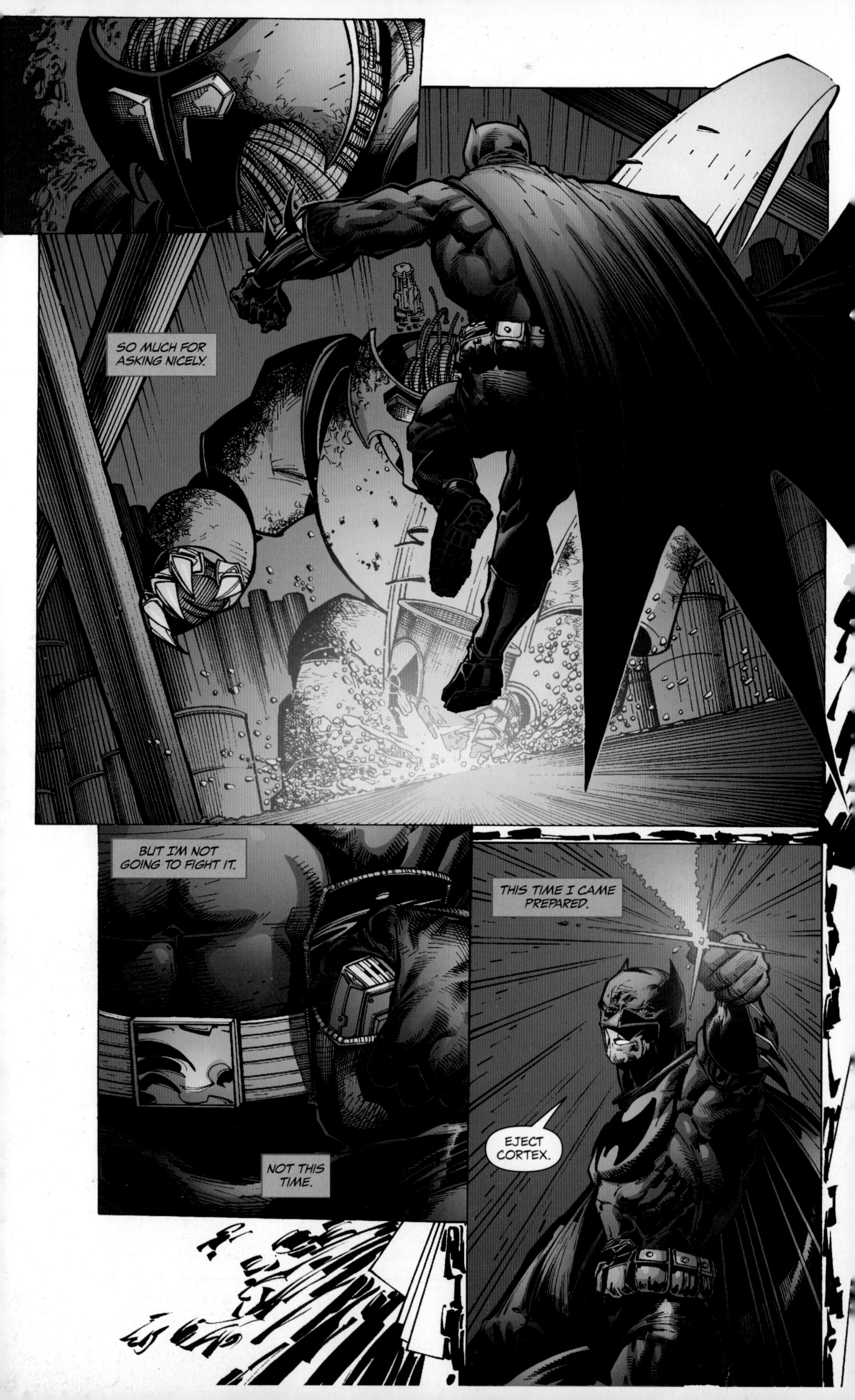
SO MUCH FOR ASKING NICELY.
BUT I'M NOT GOING TO FIGHT IT.
NOT THIS TIME.
THIS TIME I CAME PREPARED.
EJECT CORTEX.

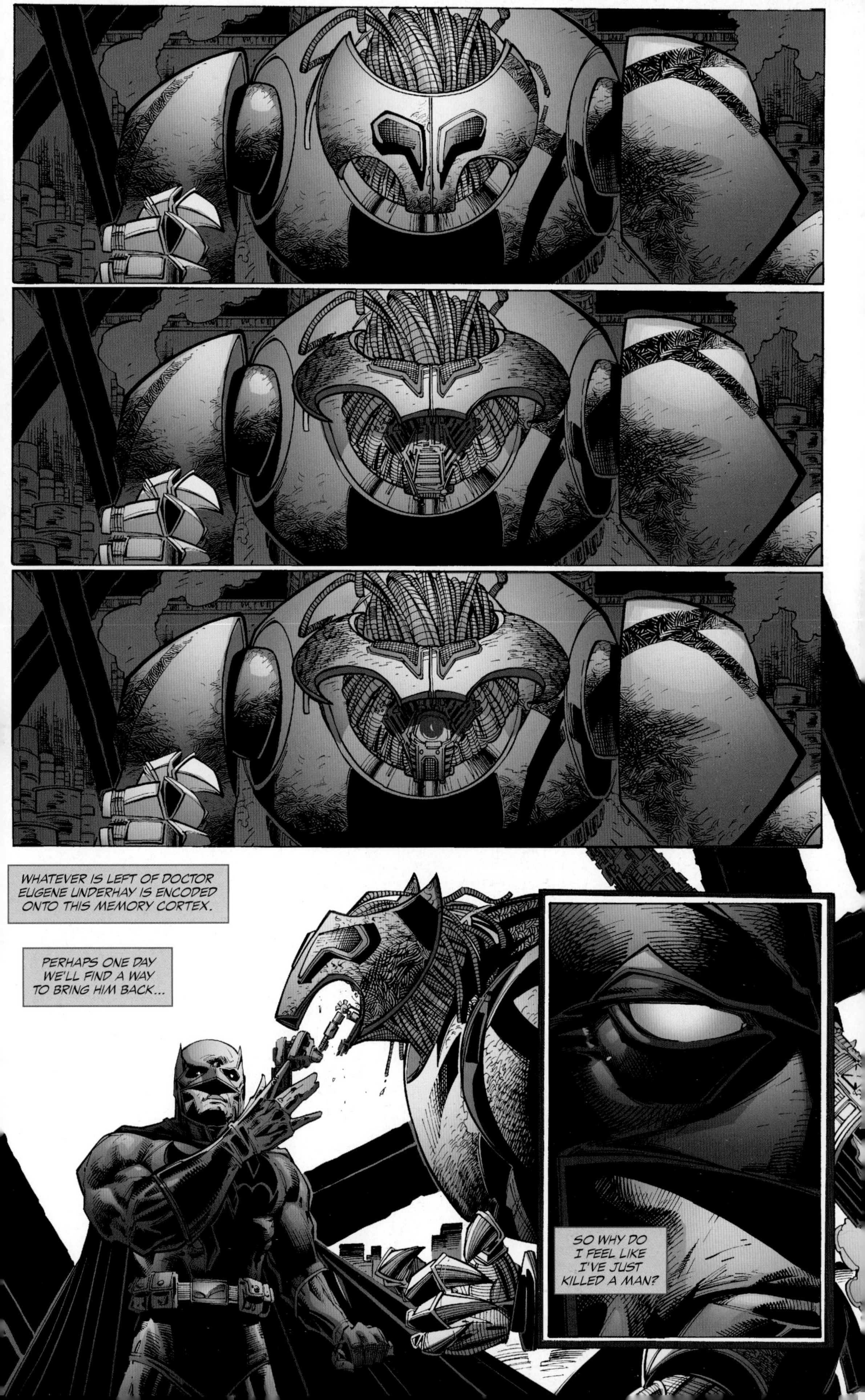

WHATEVER IS LEFT OF DOCTOR EUGENE UNDERHAY IS ENCODED ONTO THIS MEMORY CORTEX.
PERHAPS ONE DAY WE'LL FIND A WAY TO BRING HIM BACK...
SO WHY DO I FEEL LIKE I'VE JUST KILLED A MAN?

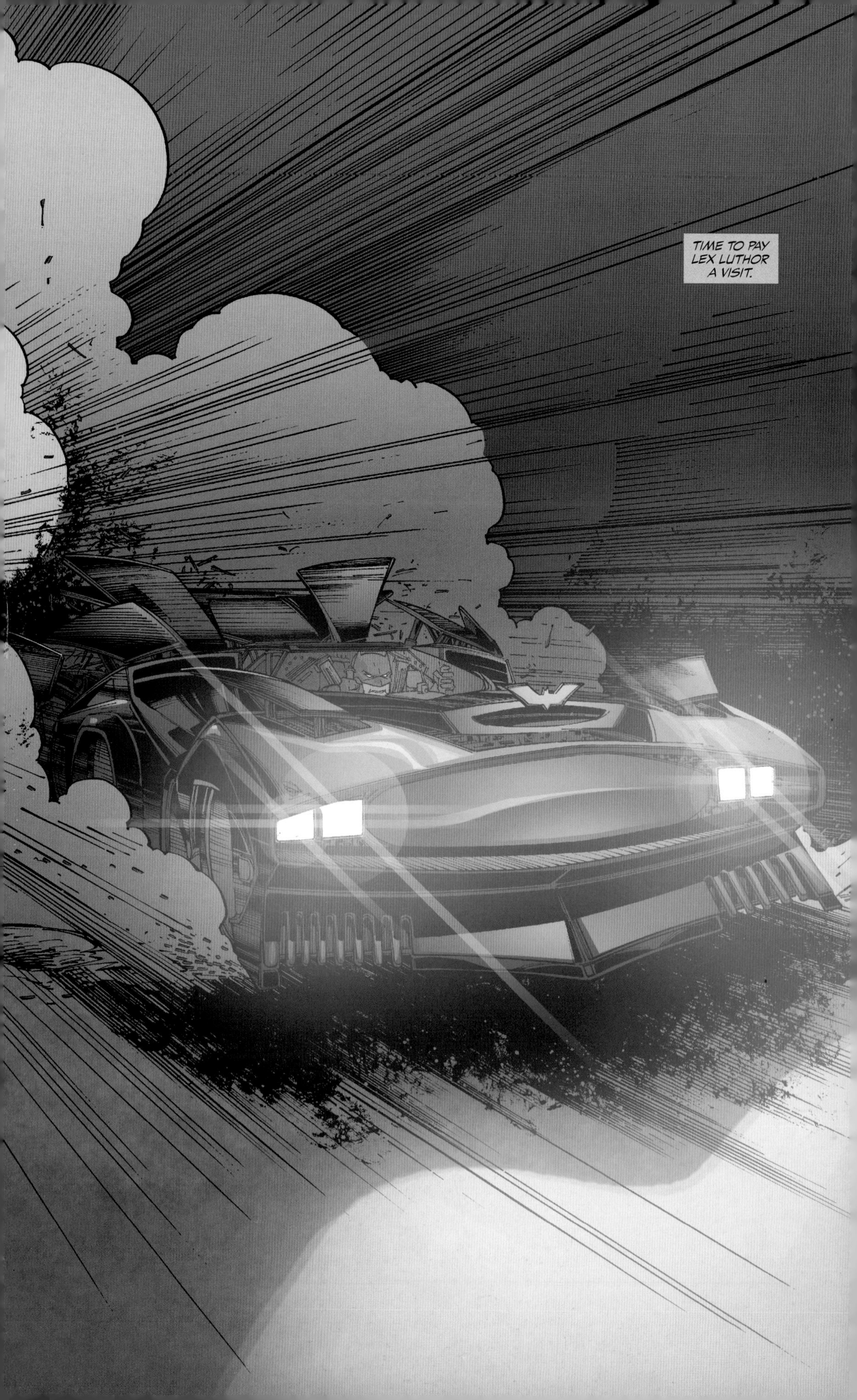
TIME TO PAY LEX LUTHOR A VISIT.

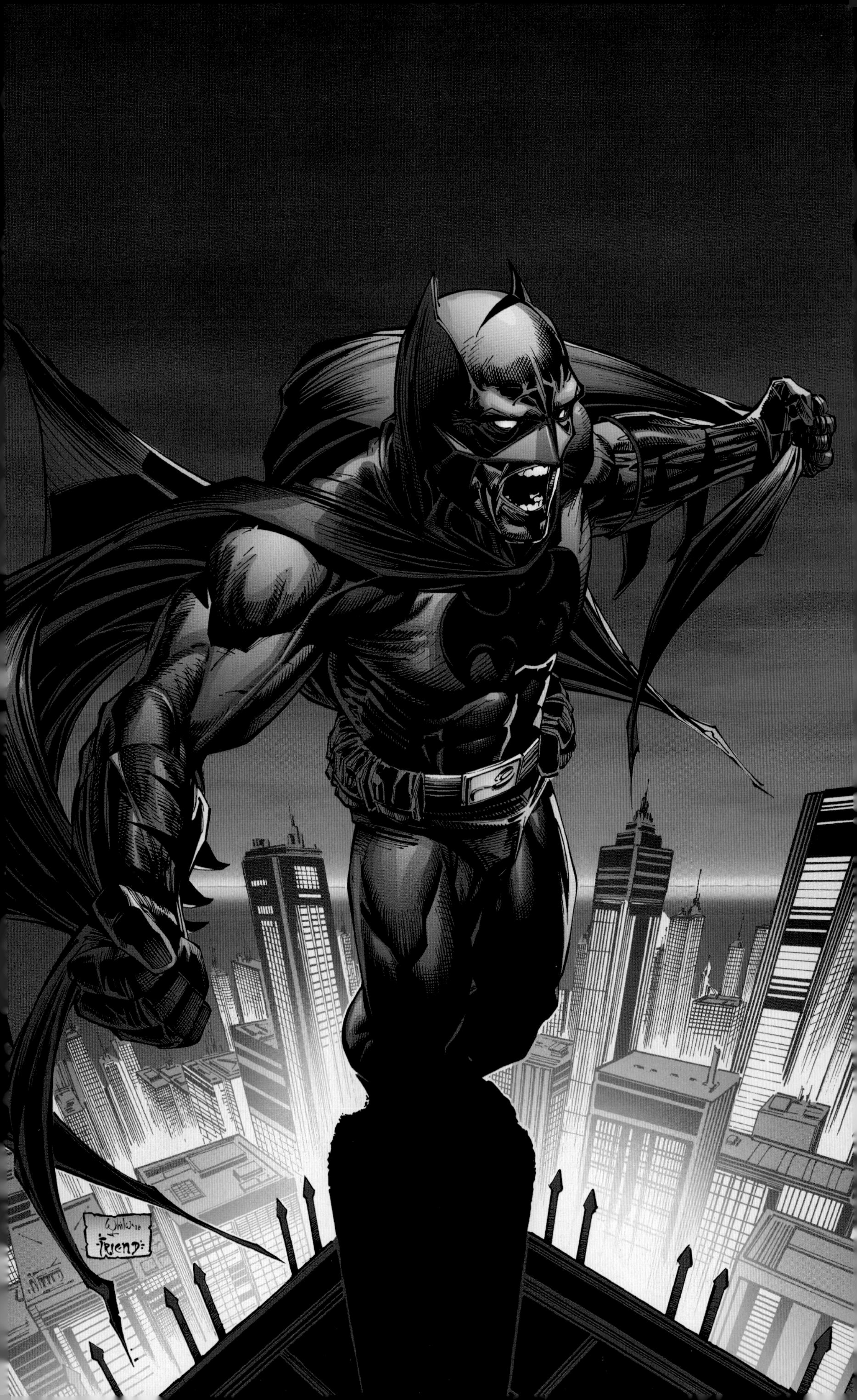

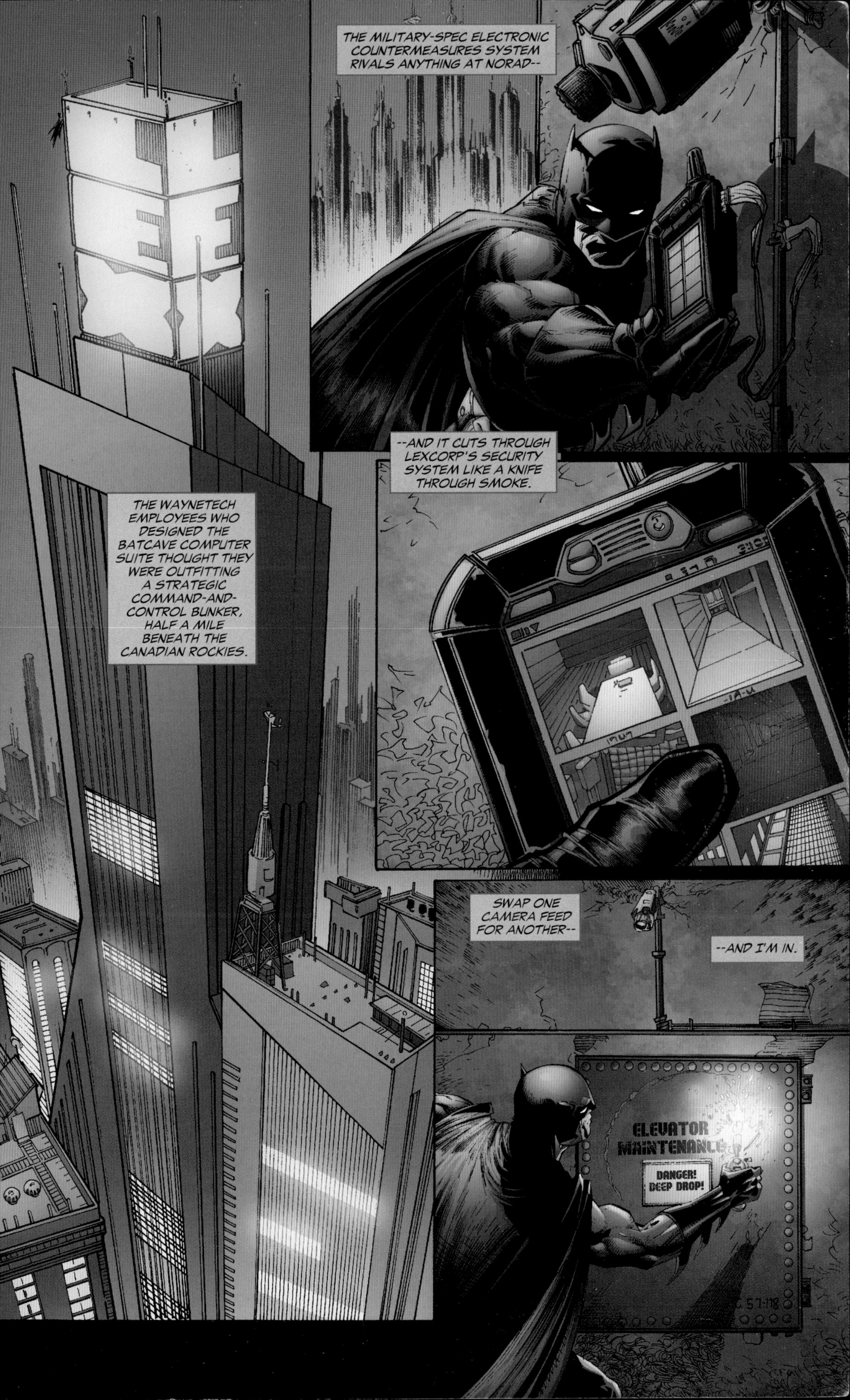
THE MILITARY-SPEC ELECTRONIC COUNTERMEASURES SYSTEM RIVALS ANYTHING AT NORAD--
THE WAYNETECH EMPLOYEES WHO DESIGNED THE BATCAVE COMPUTER SUITE THOUGHT THEY WERE OUTFITTING A STRATEGIC COMMAND-AND-CONTROL BUNKER, HALF A MILE BENEATH THE CANADIAN ROCKIES.
--AND IT CUTS THROUGH LEXCORP'S SECURITY SYSTEM LIKE A KNIFE THROUGH SMOKE.
SWAP ONE CAMERA FEED FOR ANOTHER--
--AND I'M IN.
ELEVATOR MAINTENANCE
DANGER! DEEP DROP!

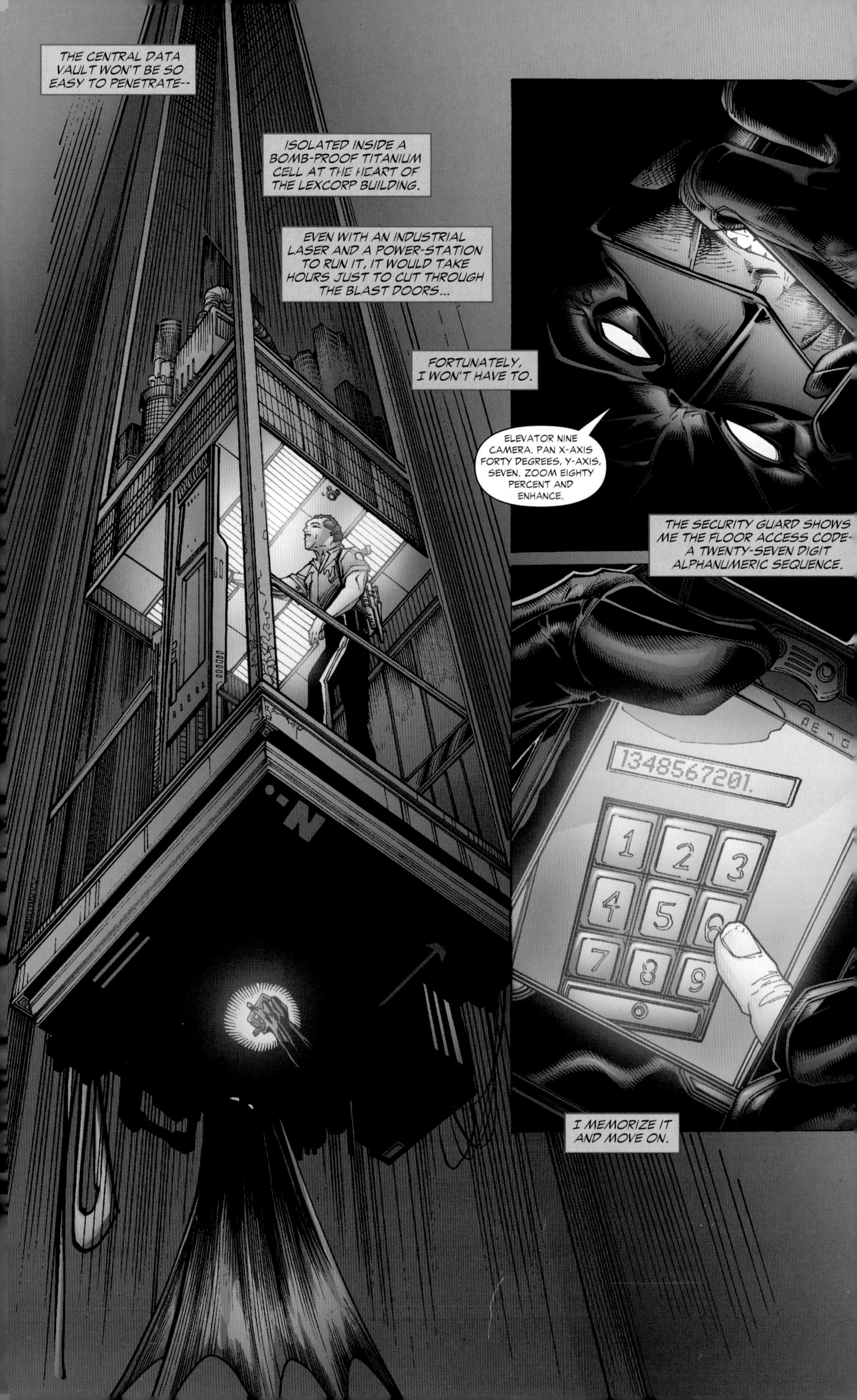

THE CENTRAL DATA VAULT WON'T BE SO EASY TO PENETRATE--
ISOLATED INSIDE A BOMB-PROOF TITANIUM CELL AT THE HEART OF THE LEXCORP BUILDING.
EVEN WITH AN INDUSTRIAL LASER AND A POWER-STATION TO RUN IT, IT WOULD TAKE HOURS JUST TO CUT THROUGH THE BLAST DOORS...
FORTUNATELY, I WON'T HAVE TO.
ELEVATOR NINE CAMERA. PAN X-AXIS FORTY DEGREES, Y-AXIS, SEVEN. ZOOM EIGHTY PERCENT AND ENHANCE.
THE SECURITY GUARD SHOWS ME THE FLOOR ACCESS CODE-A TWENTY-SEVEN DIGIT ALPHANUMERIC SEQUENCE.
1348567201.
1 2 3
4 5 6
7 8 9
I MEMORIZE IT AND MOVE ON.

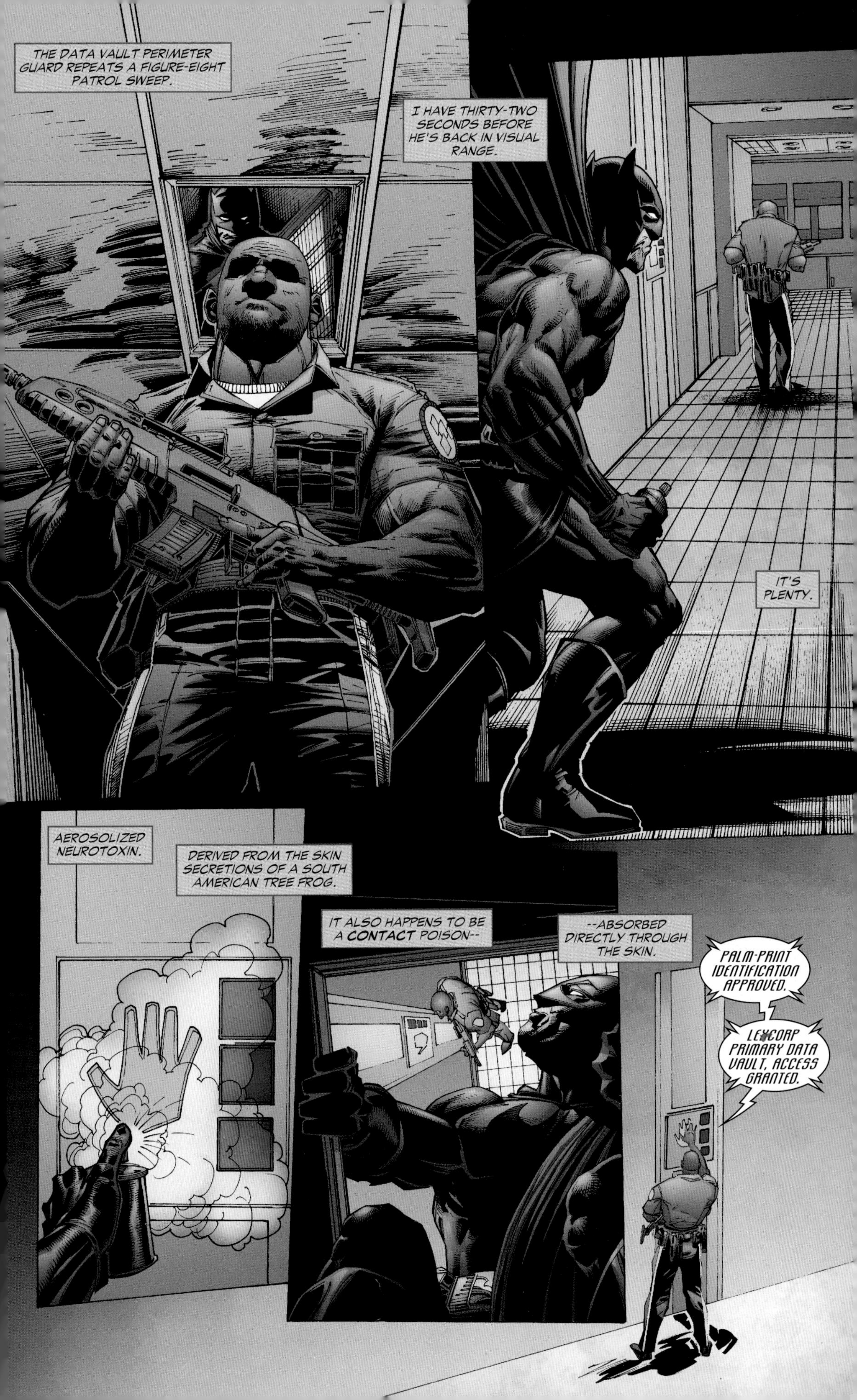
THE DATA VAULT PERIMETER GUARD REPEATS A FIGURE-EIGHT PATROL SWEEP.
I HAVE THIRTY-TWO SECONDS BEFORE HE'S BACK IN VISUAL RANGE.
IT'S PLENTY.
AEROSOLIZED NEUROTOXIN.
DERIVED FROM THE SKIN SECRETIONS OF A SOUTH AMERICAN TREE FROG.
IT ALSO HAPPENS TO BE A CONTACT POISON--
--ABSORBED DIRECTLY THROUGH THE SKIN.
PALM-PRINT IDENTIFICATION APPROVED.
LEXCORP PRIMARY DATA VAULT, ACCESS GRANTED.

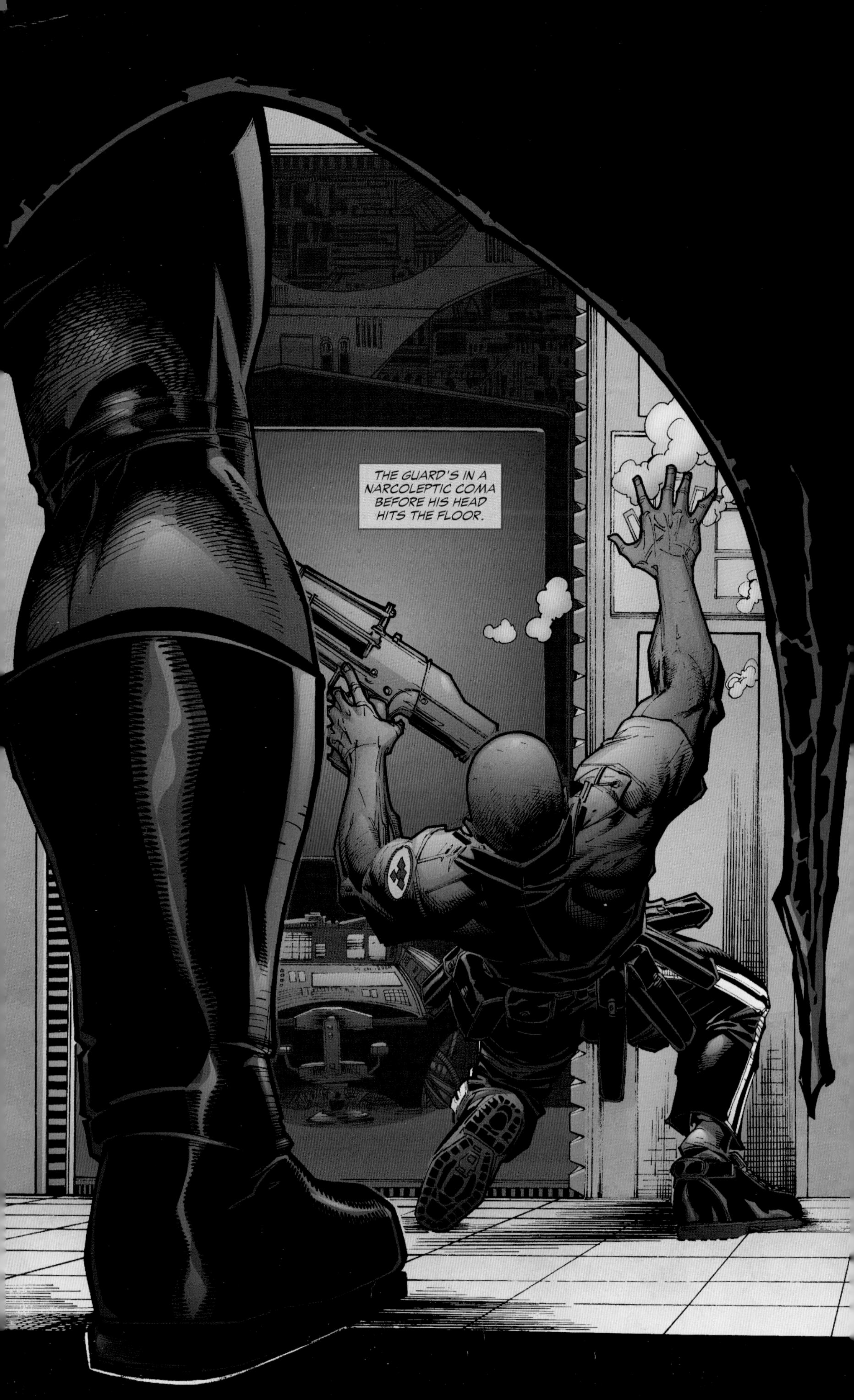
THE GUARD'S IN A NARCOLEPTIC COMA BEFORE HIS HEAD HITS THE FLOOR.

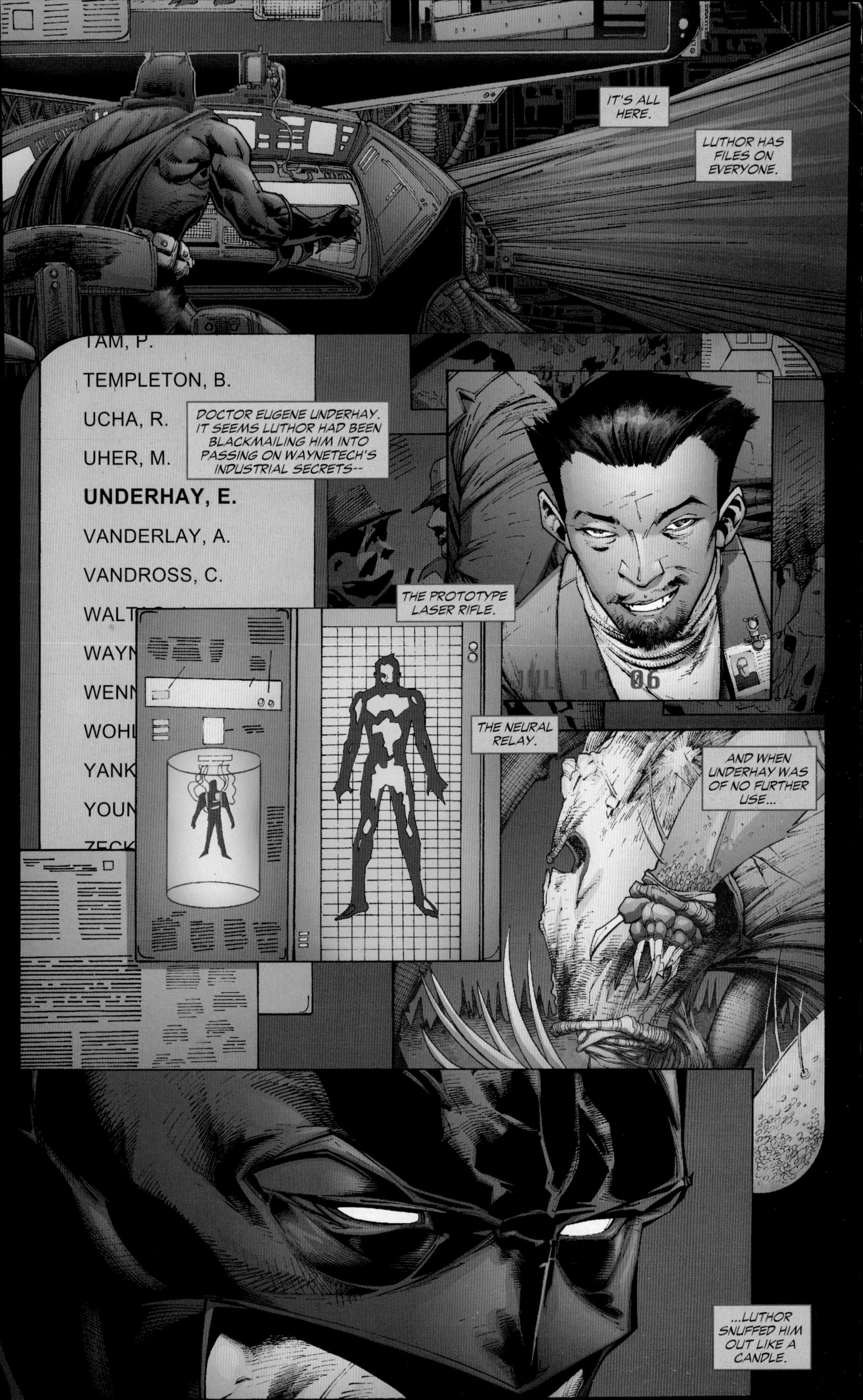
IT'S ALL HERE.
LUTHOR HAS FILES ON EVERYONE.
TEMPLETON, B.
UCHA, R.
UHER, M.
UNDERHAY, E.
VANDERLAY, A.
VANDROSS, C.
DOCTOR EUGENE UNDERHAY. IT SEEMS LUTHOR HAD BEEN BLACKMAILING HIM INTO PASSING ON WAYNETECH'S INDUSTRIAL SECRETS--
THE PROTOTYPE LASER RIFLE.
THE NEURAL RELAY.
AND WHEN UNDERHAY WAS OF NO FURTHER USE...
...LUTHOR SNUFFED HIM OUT LIKE A CANDLE.

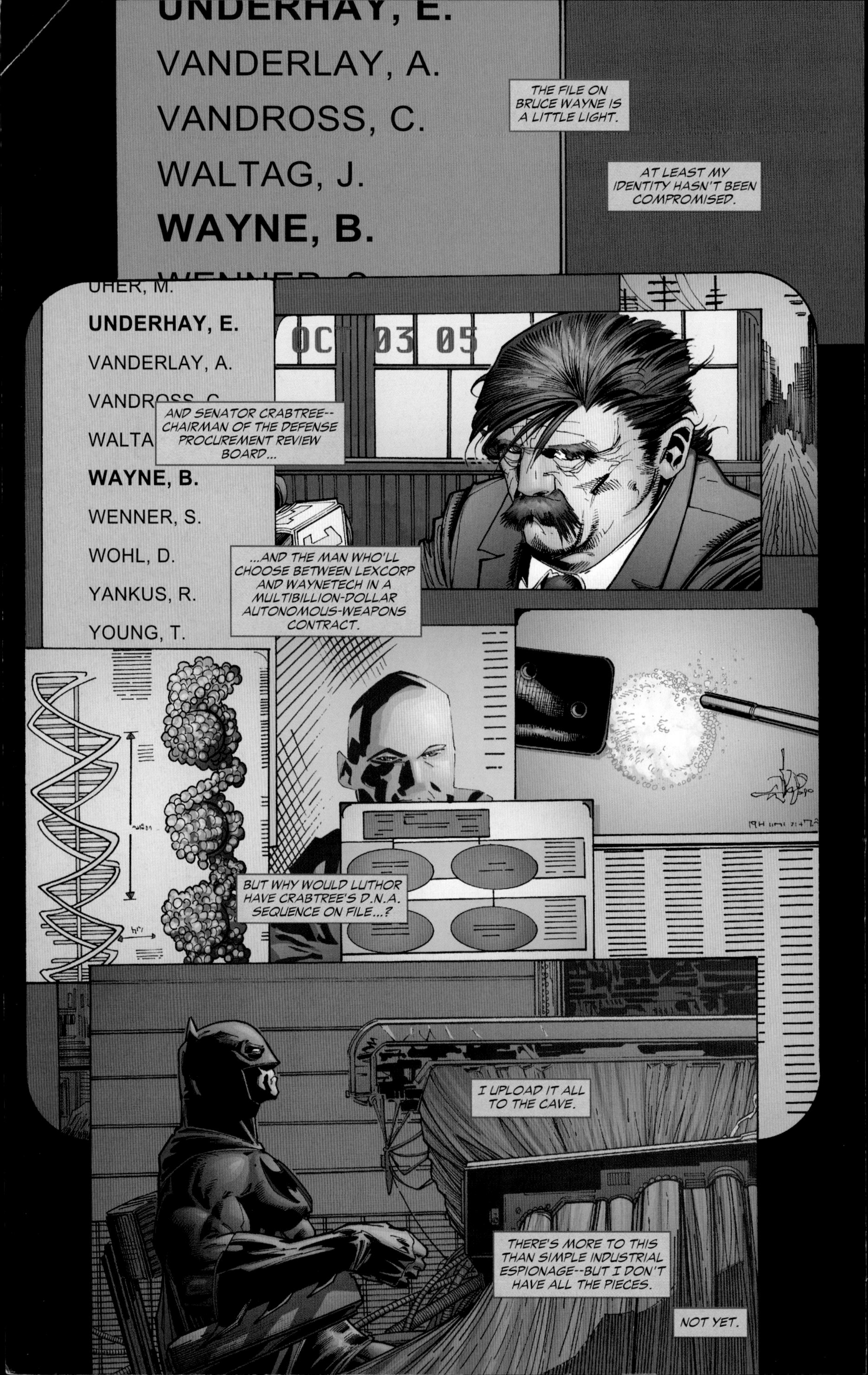
UNDERHAY, E.
VANDERLAY, A.
VANDROSS, C.
WALTAG, J.
WAYNE, B.
THE FILE ON BRUCE WAYNE IS A LITTLE LIGHT.
AT LEAST MY IDENTITY HASN'T BEEN COMPROMISED.
UHER, M.
UNDERHAY, E.
VANDERLAY, A.
WAYNE, B.
WENNER, S.
WOHL, D.
YANKUS, R.
YOUNG, T.
OCT 03 05
AND SENATOR CRABTREE--CHAIRMAN OF THE DEFENSE PROCUREMENT REVIEW BOARD...
...AND THE MAN WHO'LL CHOOSE BETWEEN LEXCORP AND WAYNETECH IN A MULTIBILLION-DOLLAR AUTONOMOUS-WEAPONS CONTRACT.
BUT WHY WOULD LUTHOR HAVE CRABTREE'S D.N.A. SEQUENCE ON FILE...?
I UPLOAD IT ALL TO THE CAVE.
THERE'S MORE TO THIS THAN SIMPLE INDUSTRIAL ESPIONAGE--BUT I DON'T HAVE ALL THE PIECES.
NOT YET.

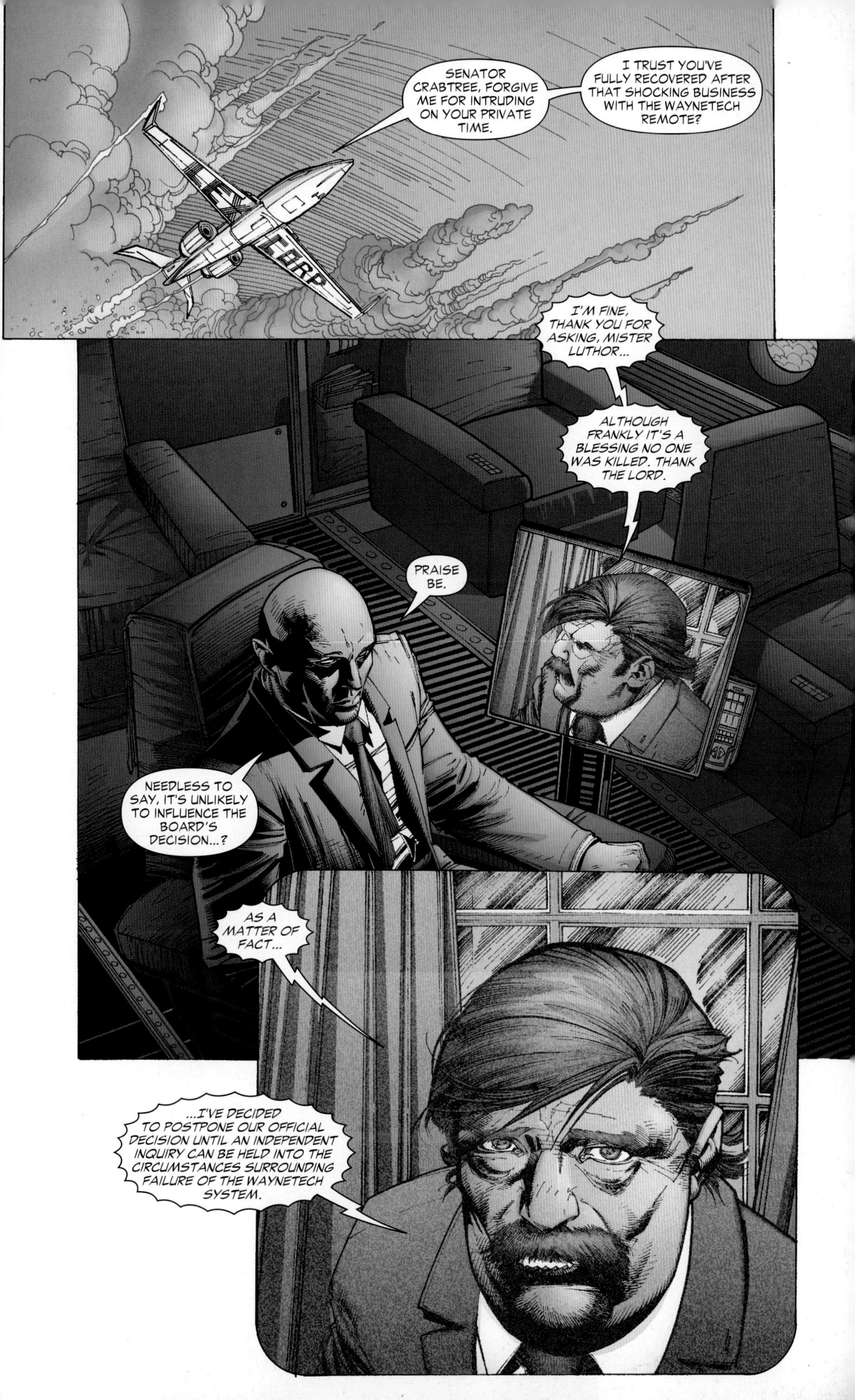
SENATOR CRABTREE, FORGIVE ME FOR INTRUDING ON YOUR PRIVATE TIME.
I TRUST YOU'VE FULLY RECOVERED AFTER THAT SHOCKING BUSINESS WITH THE WAYNETECH REMOTE?
LEX CORP
I'M FINE, THANK YOU FOR ASKING, MISTER LUTHOR...
ALTHOUGH FRANKLY IT'S A BLESSING NO ONE WAS KILLED. THANK THE LORD.
PRAISE BE.
NEEDLESS TO SAY, IT'S UNLIKELY TO INFLUENCE THE BOARD'S DECISION...?
AS A MATTER OF FACT...
...I'VE DECIDED TO POSTPONE OUR OFFICIAL DECISION UNTIL AN INDEPENDENT INQUIRY CAN BE HELD INTO THE CIRCUMSTANCES SURROUNDING FAILURE OF THE WAYNETECH SYSTEM.

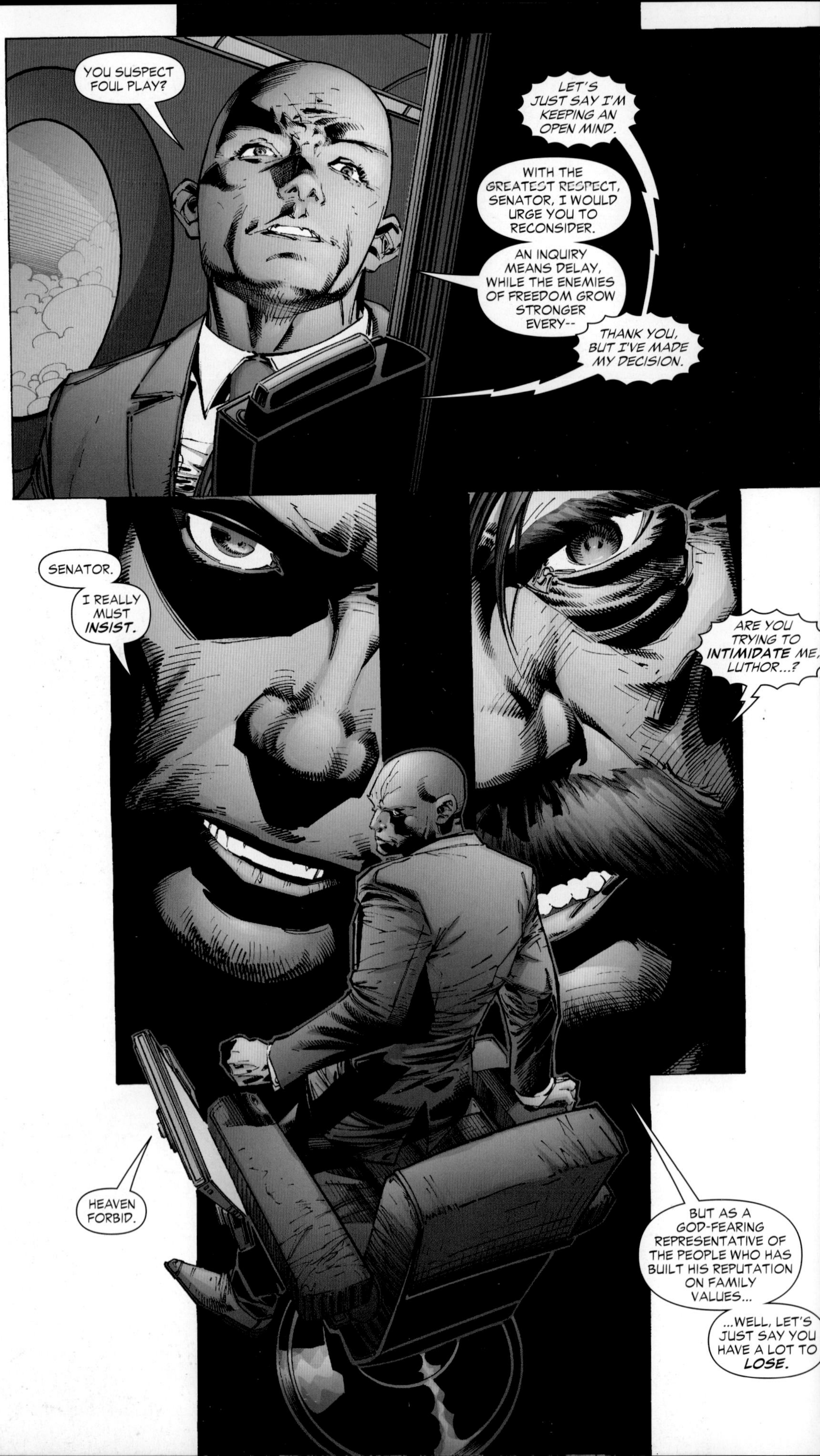
YOU SUSPECT FOUL PLAY?
LET'S JUST SAY I'M KEEPING AN OPEN MIND.
WITH THE GREATEST RESPECT, SENATOR, I WOULD URGE YOU TO RECONSIDER.
AN INQUIRY MEANS DELAY, WHILE THE ENEMIES OF FREEDOM GROW STRONGER EVERY--
THANK YOU, BUT I'VE MADE MY DECISION.
SENATOR.
I REALLY MUST *INSIST.*
ARE YOU TRYING TO *INTIMIDATE* ME, LUTHOR...?
HEAVEN FORBID.
BUT AS A GOD-FEARING REPRESENTATIVE OF THE PEOPLE WHO HAS BUILT HIS REPUTATION ON FAMILY VALUES...
...WELL, LET'S JUST SAY YOU HAVE A LOT TO *LOSE.*

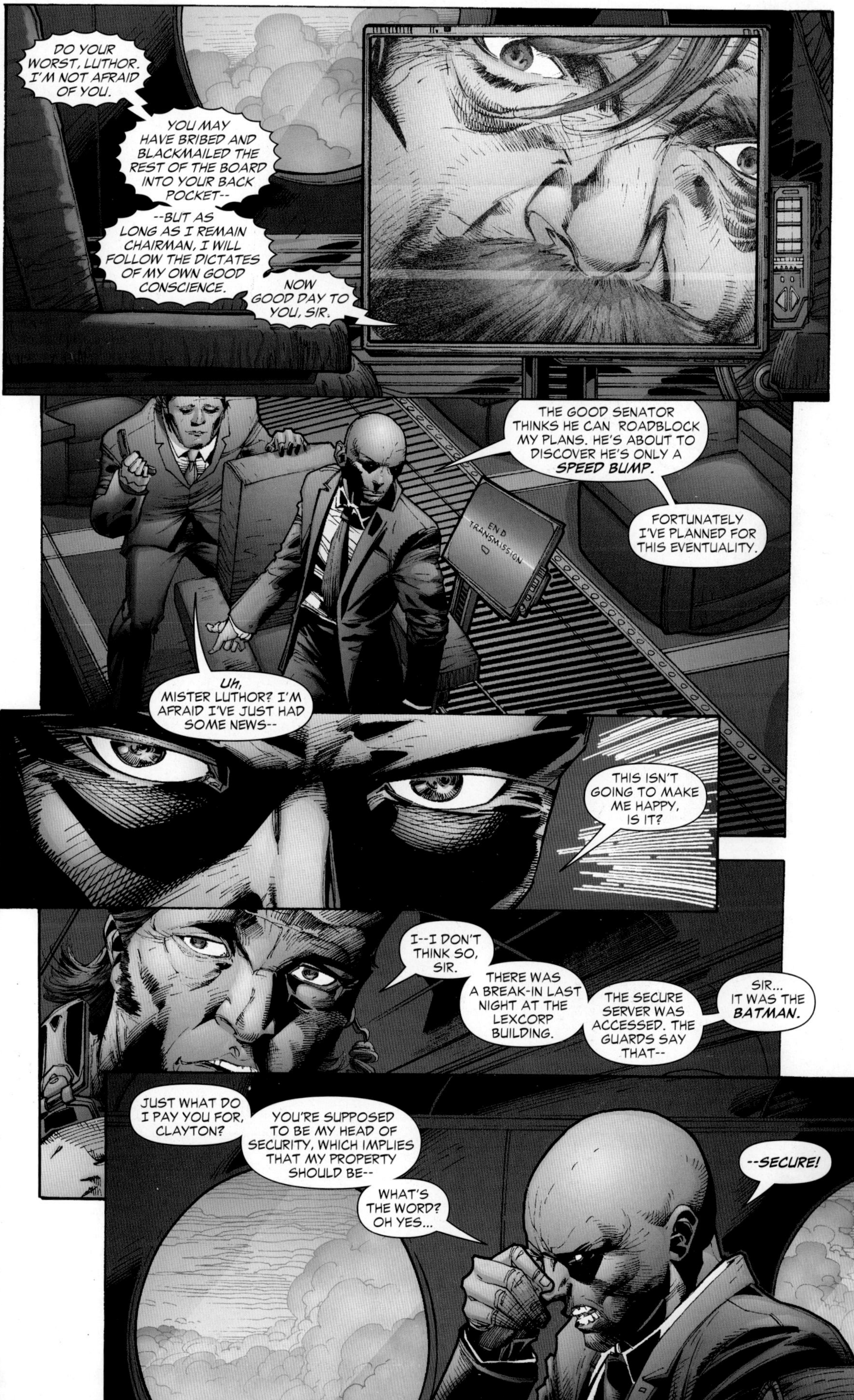
DO YOUR WORST, LUTHOR. I'M NOT AFRAID OF YOU.
YOU MAY HAVE BRIBED AND BLACKMAILED THE REST OF THE BOARD INTO YOUR BACK POCKET--
--BUT AS LONG AS I REMAIN CHAIRMAN, I WILL FOLLOW THE DICTATES OF MY OWN GOOD CONSCIENCE.
NOW GOOD DAY TO YOU, SIR.
THE GOOD SENATOR THINKS HE CAN ROADBLOCK MY PLANS. HE'S ABOUT TO DISCOVER HE'S ONLY A SPEED BUMP.
FORTUNATELY I'VE PLANNED FOR THIS EVENTUALITY.
END TRANSMISSION
Uh, MISTER LUTHOR? I'M AFRAID I'VE JUST HAD SOME NEWS--
THIS ISN'T GOING TO MAKE ME HAPPY, IS IT?
I--I DON'T THINK SO, SIR.
THERE WAS A BREAK-IN LAST NIGHT AT THE LEXCORP BUILDING.
THE SECURE SERVER WAS ACCESSED. THE GUARDS SAY THAT--
SIR... IT WAS THE BATMAN.
JUST WHAT DO I PAY YOU FOR, CLAYTON?
YOU'RE SUPPOSED TO BE MY HEAD OF SECURITY, WHICH IMPLIES THAT MY PROPERTY SHOULD BE--
WHAT'S THE WORD? OH YES...
--SECURE!

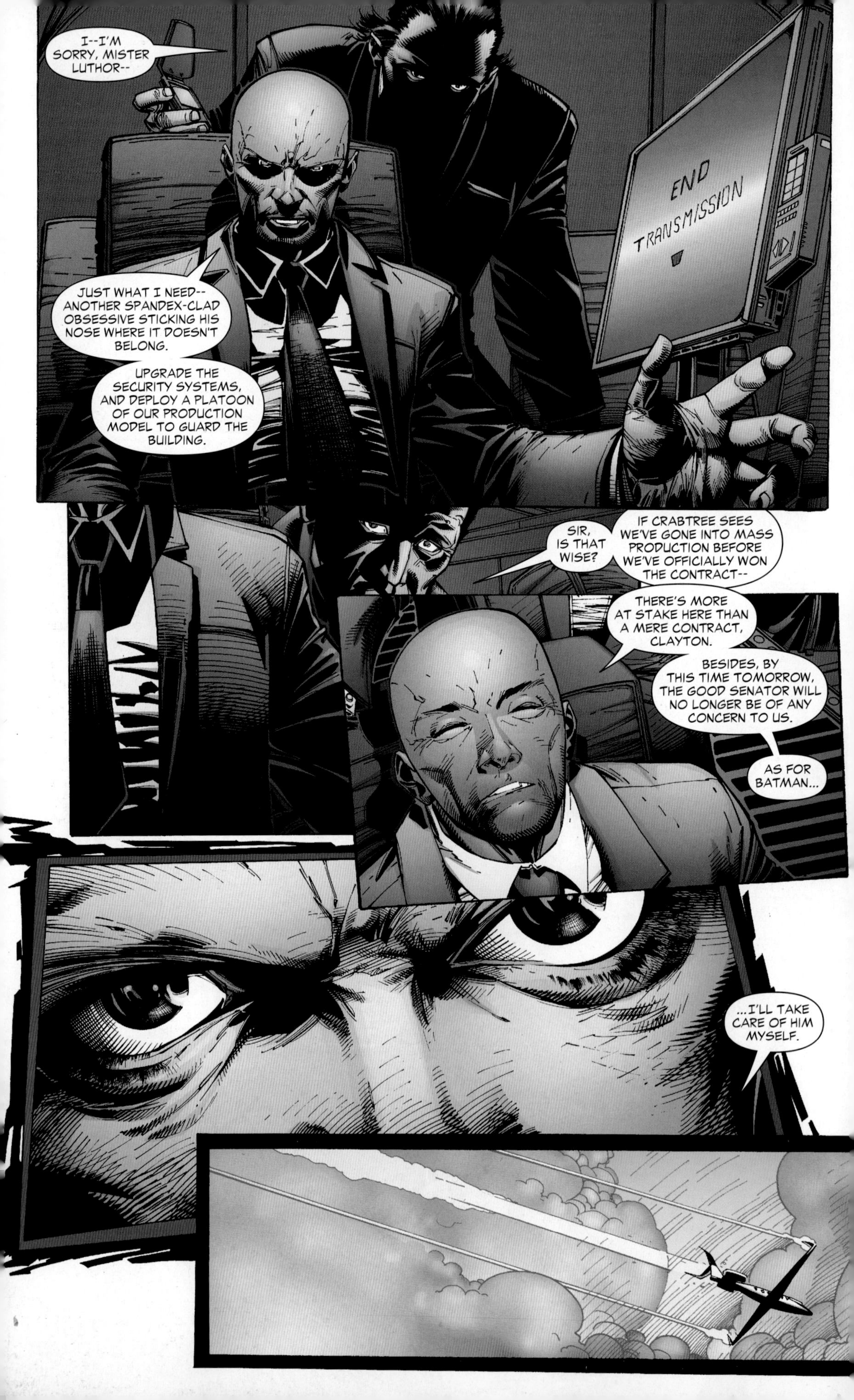
I--I'M SORRY, MISTER LUTHOR--
END TRANSMISSION
JUST WHAT I NEED-- ANOTHER SPANDEX-CLAD OBSESSIVE STICKING HIS NOSE WHERE IT DOESN'T BELONG.
UPGRADE THE SECURITY SYSTEMS, AND DEPLOY A PLATOON OF OUR PRODUCTION MODEL TO GUARD THE BUILDING.
SIR, IS THAT WISE?
IF CRABTREE SEES WE'VE GONE INTO MASS PRODUCTION BEFORE WE'VE OFFICIALLY WON THE CONTRACT--
THERE'S MORE AT STAKE HERE THAN A MERE CONTRACT, CLAYTON.
BESIDES, BY THIS TIME TOMORROW, THE GOOD SENATOR WILL NO LONGER BE OF ANY CONCERN TO US.
AS FOR BATMAN...
...I'LL TAKE CARE OF HIM MYSELF.

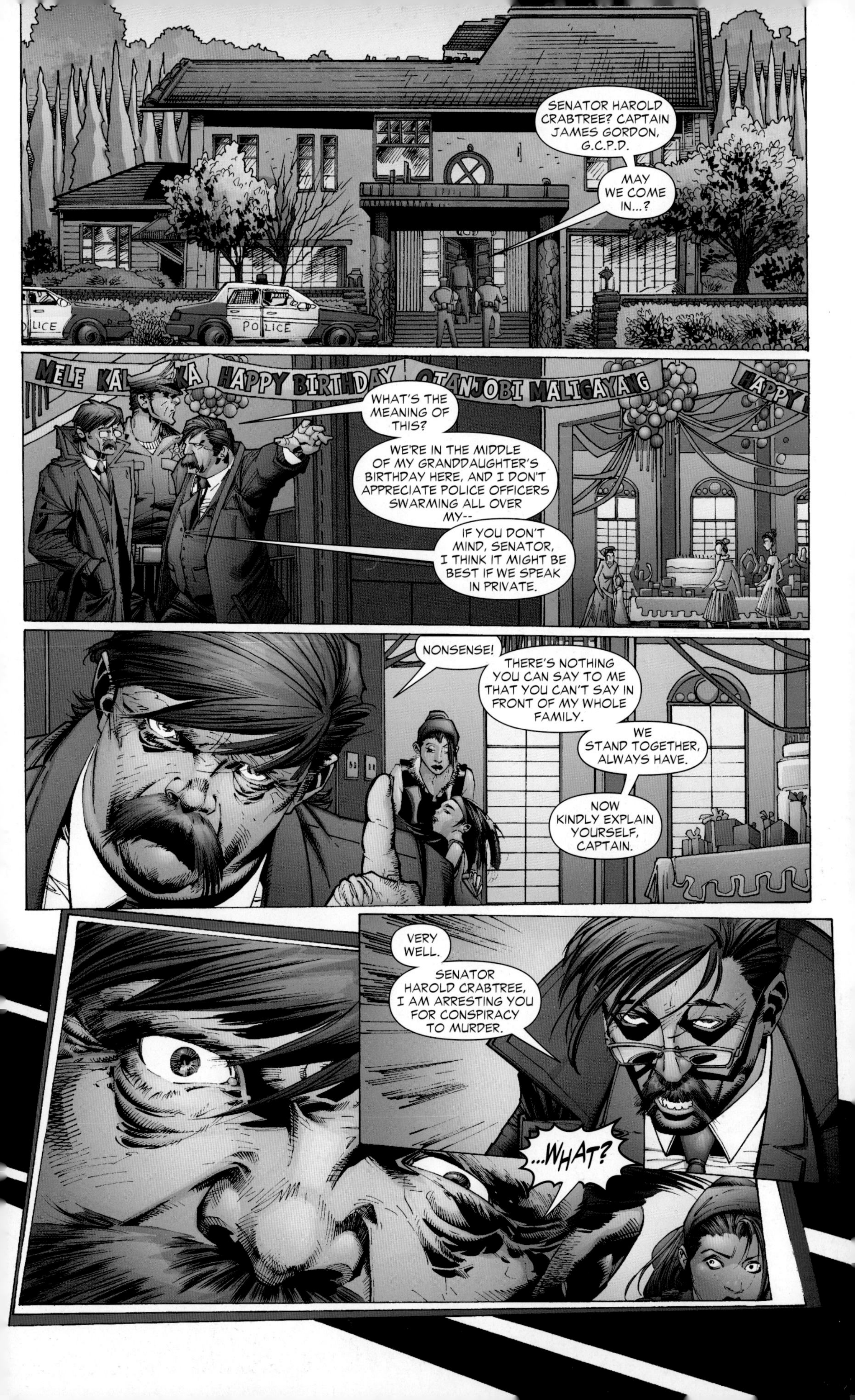
SENATOR HAROLD CRABTREE? CAPTAIN JAMES GORDON, G.C.P.D.
MAY WE COME IN...?
POLICE
POLICE
HAPPY BIRTHDAY
MALIGAYANG
WHAT'S THE MEANING OF THIS?
WE'RE IN THE MIDDLE OF MY GRANDDAUGHTER'S BIRTHDAY HERE, AND I DON'T APPRECIATE POLICE OFFICERS SWARMING ALL OVER MY--
IF YOU DON'T MIND, SENATOR, I THINK IT MIGHT BE BEST IF WE SPEAK IN PRIVATE.
NONSENSE!
THERE'S NOTHING YOU CAN SAY TO ME THAT YOU CAN'T SAY IN FRONT OF MY WHOLE FAMILY.
WE STAND TOGETHER, ALWAYS HAVE.
NOW KINDLY EXPLAIN YOURSELF, CAPTAIN.
VERY WELL.
SENATOR HAROLD CRABTREE, I AM ARRESTING YOU FOR CONSPIRACY TO MURDER.
...WHAT?

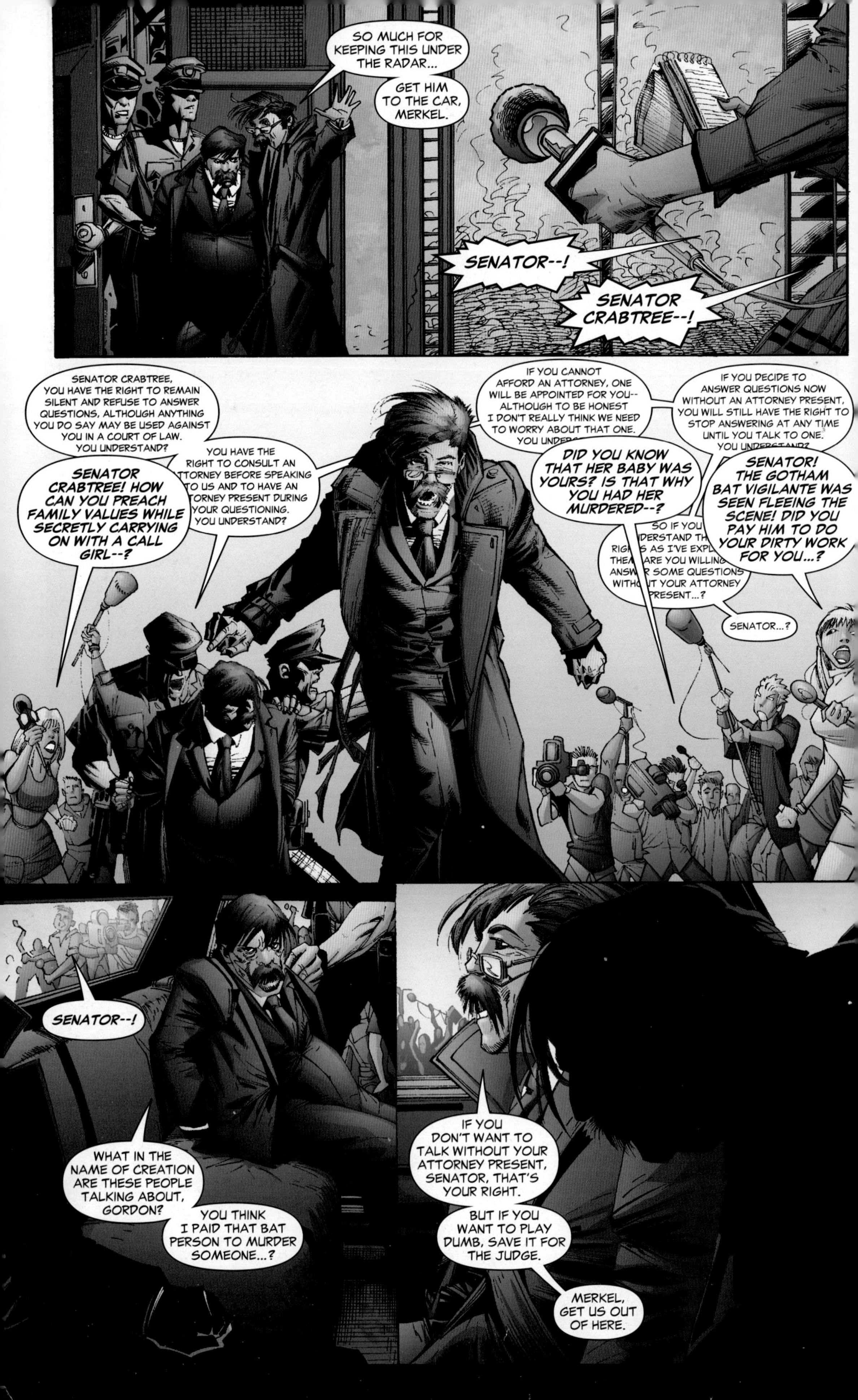
SO MUCH FOR KEEPING THIS UNDER THE RADAR...
GET HIM TO THE CAR, MERKEL.
SENATOR--!
SENATOR CRABTREE--!
SENATOR CRABTREE, YOU HAVE THE RIGHT TO REMAIN SILENT AND REFUSE TO ANSWER QUESTIONS, ALTHOUGH ANYTHING YOU DO SAY MAY BE USED AGAINST YOU IN A COURT OF LAW. YOU UNDERSTAND?
YOU HAVE THE RIGHT TO CONSULT AN ATTORNEY BEFORE SPEAKING TO US AND TO HAVE AN ATTORNEY PRESENT DURING YOUR QUESTIONING. YOU UNDERSTAND?
SENATOR CRABTREE! HOW CAN YOU PREACH FAMILY VALUES WHILE SECRETLY CARRYING ON WITH A CALL GIRL--?
IF YOU CANNOT AFFORD AN ATTORNEY, ONE WILL BE APPOINTED FOR YOU-- ALTHOUGH TO BE HONEST I DON'T REALLY THINK WE NEED TO WORRY ABOUT THAT ONE. YOU UNDER
IF YOU DECIDE TO ANSWER QUESTIONS NOW WITHOUT AN ATTORNEY PRESENT, YOU WILL STILL HAVE THE RIGHT TO STOP ANSWERING AT ANY TIME UNTIL YOU TALK TO ONE. YOU UNDERSTAND?
DID YOU KNOW THAT HER BABY WAS YOURS? IS THAT WHY YOU HAD HER MURDERED--?
SENATOR! THE GOTHAM BAT VIGILANTE WAS SEEN FLEEING THE SCENE! DID YOU PAY HIM TO DO YOUR DIRTY WORK FOR YOU...?
SO IF YOU DERSTAND TH RIG S AS I'VE EXPL THEM ARE YOU WILLIN ANSW R SOME QUESTIONS WITHO T YOUR ATTORNEY PRESENT...?
SENATOR...?
SENATOR--!
WHAT IN THE NAME OF CREATION ARE THESE PEOPLE TALKING ABOUT, GORDON?
YOU THINK I PAID THAT BAT PERSON TO MURDER SOMEONE...?
IF YOU DON'T WANT TO TALK WITHOUT YOUR ATTORNEY PRESENT, SENATOR, THAT'S YOUR RIGHT.
BUT IF YOU WANT TO PLAY DUMB, SAVE IT FOR THE JUDGE.
MERKEL, GET US OUT OF HERE.

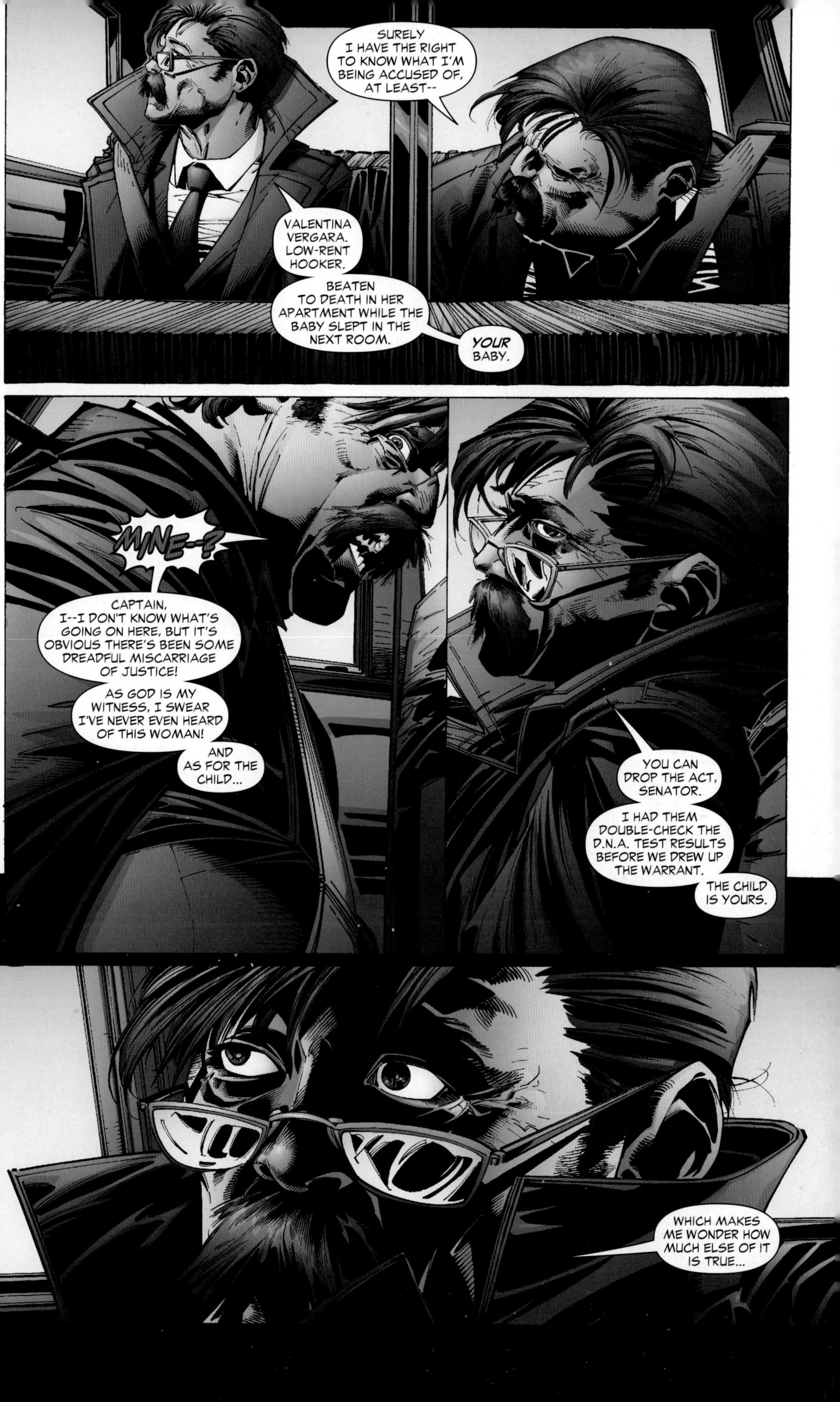

SURELY I HAVE THE RIGHT TO KNOW WHAT I'M BEING ACCUSED OF, AT LEAST--
VALENTINA VERGARA. LOW-RENT HOOKER.
BEATEN TO DEATH IN HER APARTMENT WHILE THE BABY SLEPT IN THE NEXT ROOM.
YOUR BABY.
MINE--?
CAPTAIN, I--I DON'T KNOW WHAT'S GOING ON HERE, BUT IT'S OBVIOUS THERE'S BEEN SOME DREADFUL MISCARRIAGE OF JUSTICE!
AS GOD IS MY WITNESS, I SWEAR I'VE NEVER EVEN HEARD OF THIS WOMAN!
AND AS FOR THE CHILD...
YOU CAN DROP THE ACT, SENATOR.
I HAD THEM DOUBLE-CHECK THE D.N.A. TEST RESULTS BEFORE WE DREW UP THE WARRANT.
THE CHILD IS YOURS.
WHICH MAKES ME WONDER HOW MUCH ELSE OF IT IS TRUE...

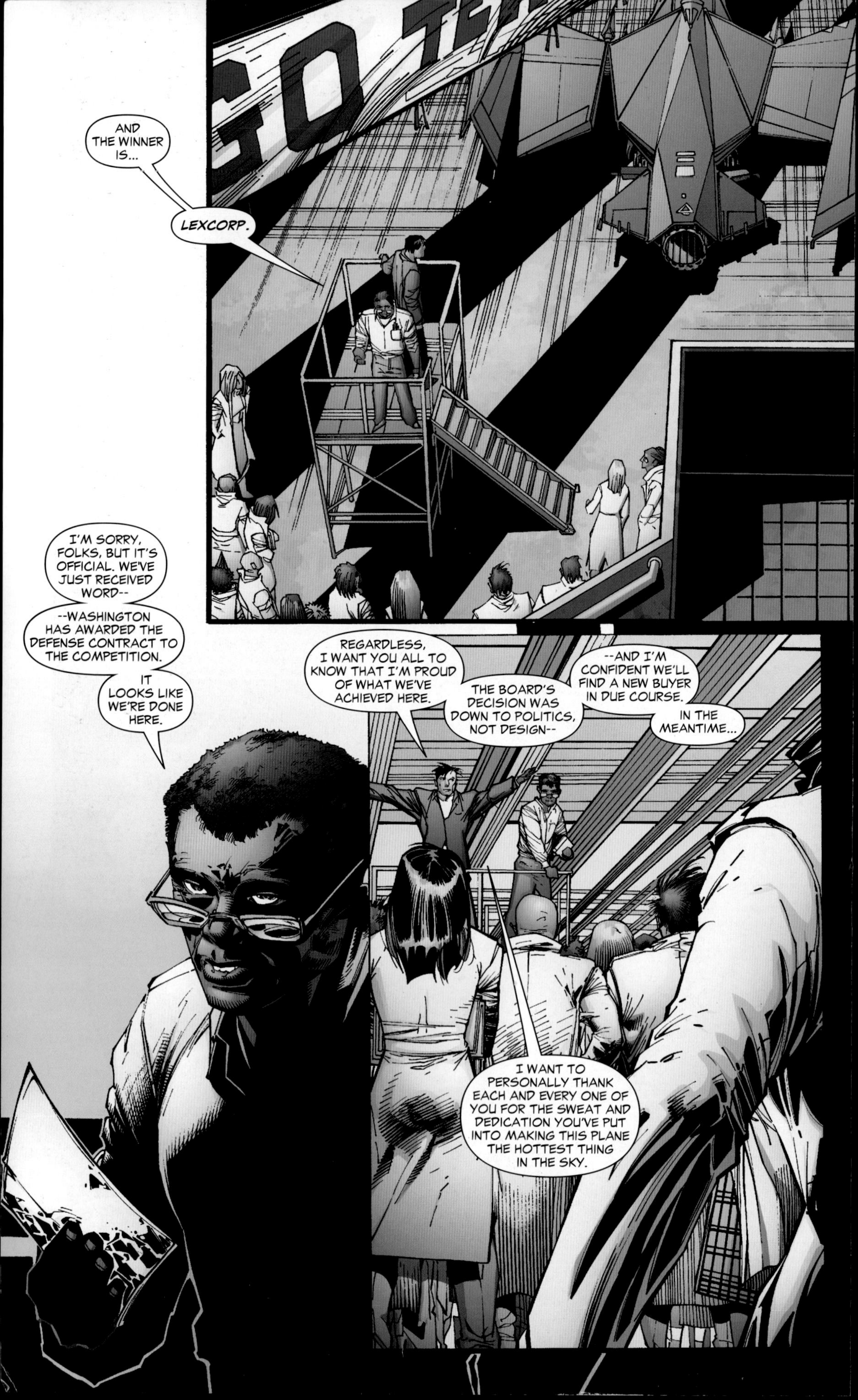
GO TE
AND THE WINNER IS...
LEXCORP.
I'M SORRY, FOLKS, BUT IT'S OFFICIAL. WE'VE JUST RECEIVED WORD--
--WASHINGTON HAS AWARDED THE DEFENSE CONTRACT TO THE COMPETITION.
IT LOOKS LIKE WE'RE DONE HERE.
REGARDLESS, I WANT YOU ALL TO KNOW THAT I'M PROUD OF WHAT WE'VE ACHIEVED HERE.
THE BOARD'S DECISION WAS DOWN TO POLITICS, NOT DESIGN--
--AND I'M CONFIDENT WE'LL FIND A NEW BUYER IN DUE COURSE.
IN THE MEANTIME...
I WANT TO PERSONALLY THANK EACH AND EVERY ONE OF YOU FOR THE SWEAT AND DEDICATION YOU'VE PUT INTO MAKING THIS PLANE THE HOTTEST THING IN THE SKY.

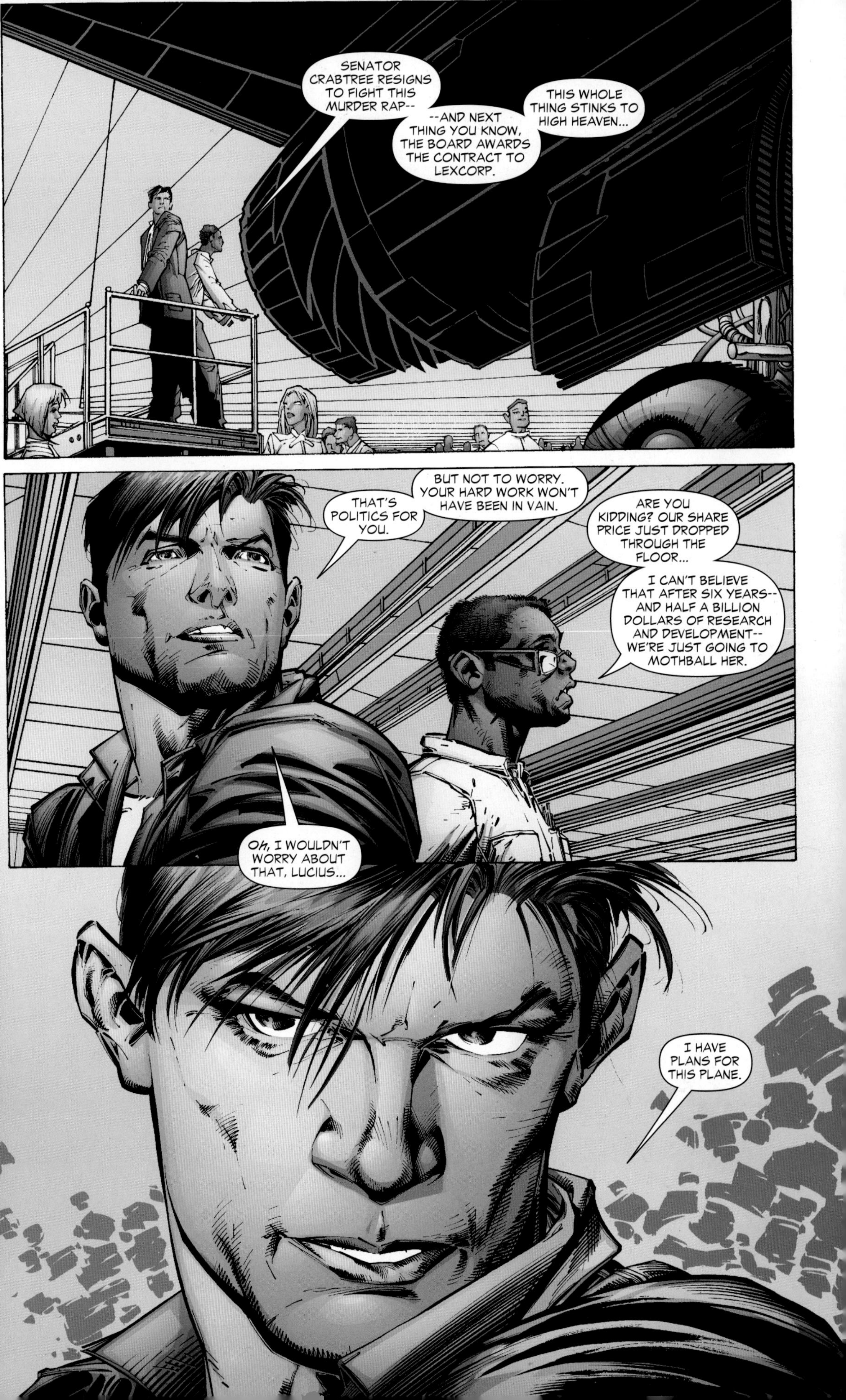
SENATOR CRABTREE RESIGNS TO FIGHT THIS MURDER RAP--
--AND NEXT THING YOU KNOW, THE BOARD AWARDS THE CONTRACT TO LEXCORP.
THIS WHOLE THING STINKS TO HIGH HEAVEN...
THAT'S POLITICS FOR YOU.
BUT NOT TO WORRY. YOUR HARD WORK WON'T HAVE BEEN IN VAIN.
ARE YOU KIDDING? OUR SHARE PRICE JUST DROPPED THROUGH THE FLOOR...
I CAN'T BELIEVE THAT AFTER SIX YEARS-- AND HALF A BILLION DOLLARS OF RESEARCH AND DEVELOPMENT-- WE'RE JUST GOING TO MOTHBALL HER.
Oh, I WOULDN'T WORRY ABOUT THAT, LUCIUS...
I HAVE PLANS FOR THIS PLANE.

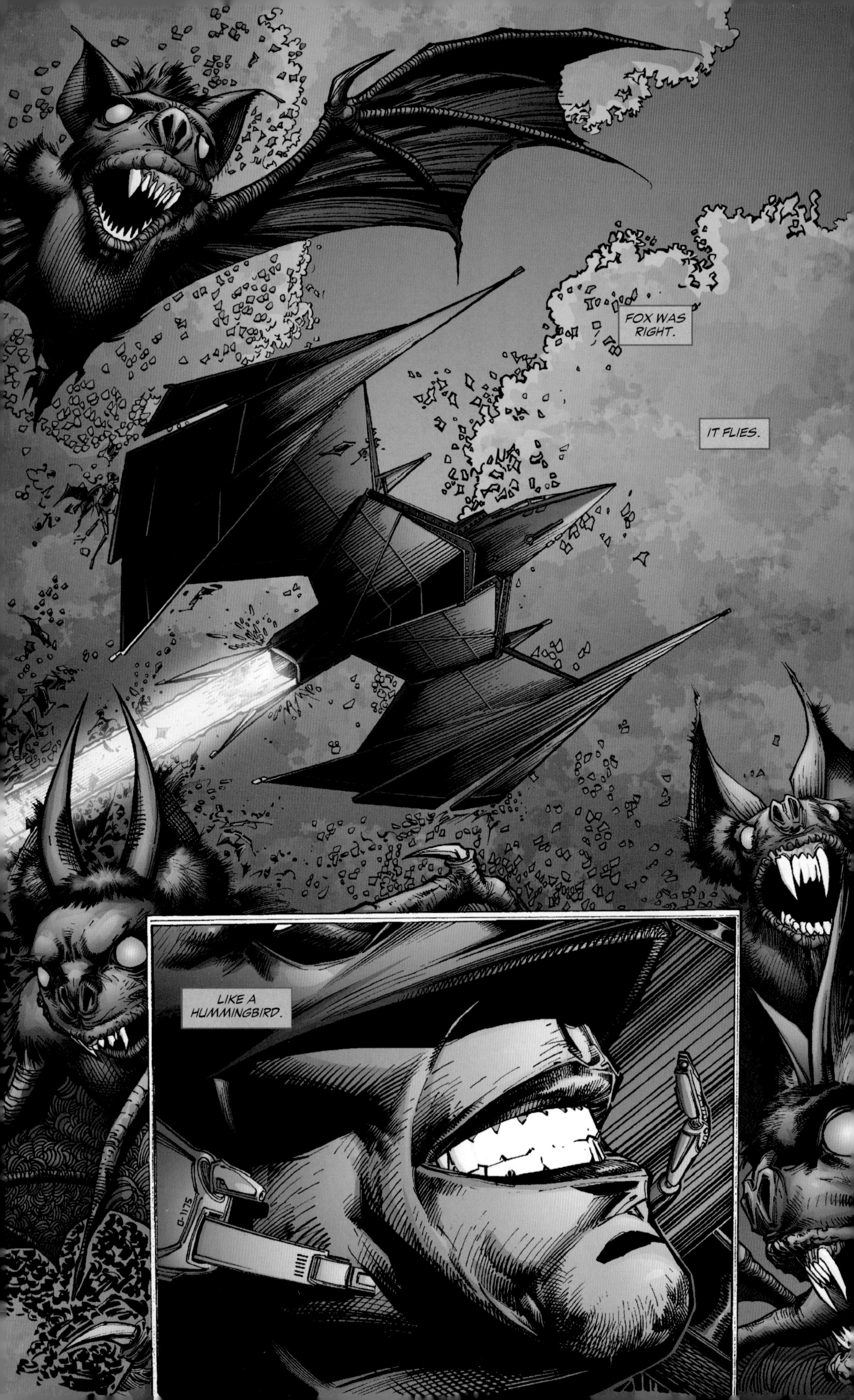
FOX WAS RIGHT.
IT FLIES.
LIKE A HUMMINGBIRD.

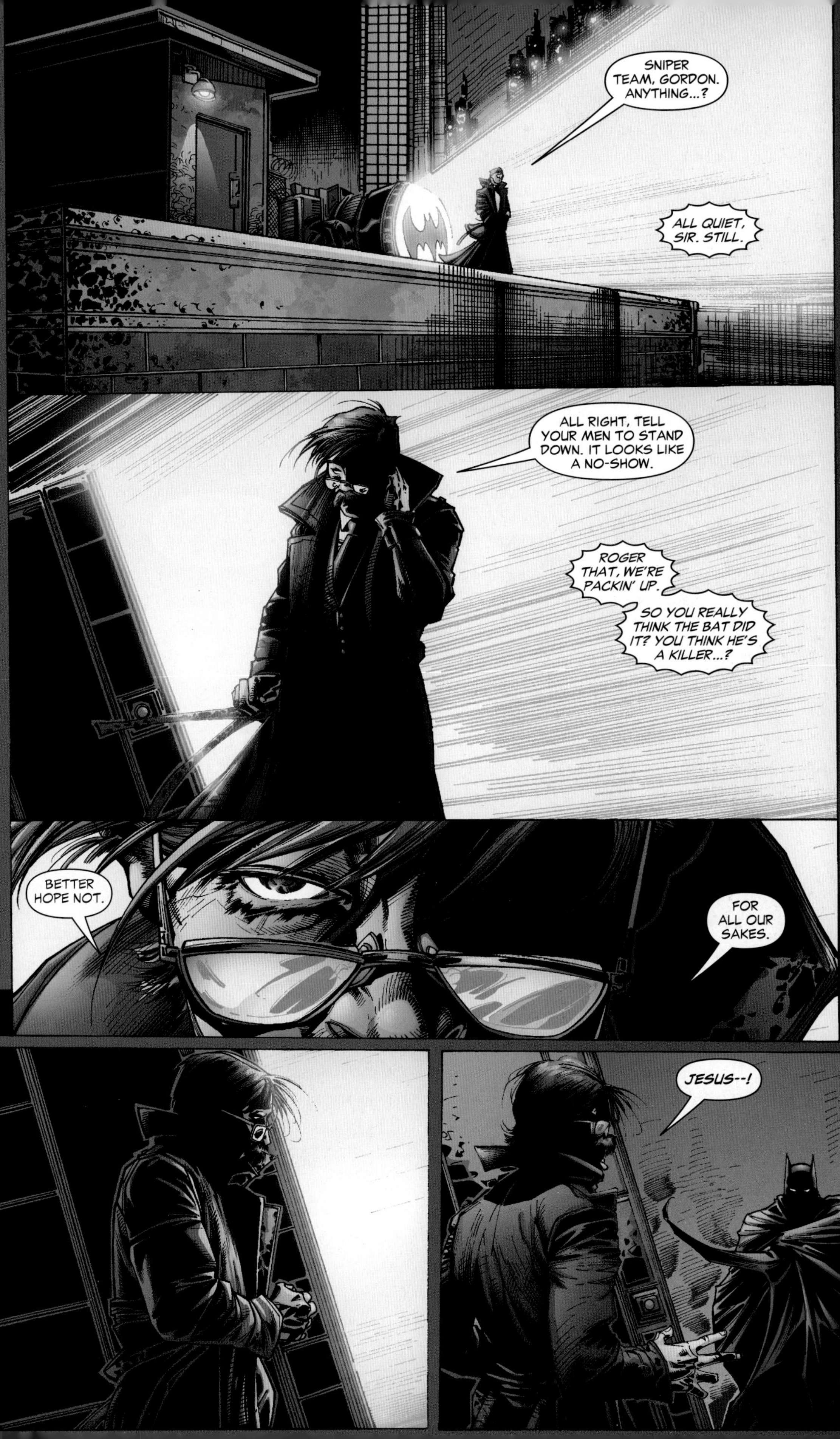
SNIPER TEAM, GORDON. ANYTHING...?
ALL QUIET, SIR. STILL.
ALL RIGHT, TELL YOUR MEN TO STAND DOWN. IT LOOKS LIKE A NO-SHOW.
ROGER THAT, WE'RE PACKIN' UP.
SO YOU REALLY THINK THE BAT DID IT? YOU THINK HE'S A KILLER...?
BETTER HOPE NOT.
FOR ALL OUR SAKES.
JESUS--!

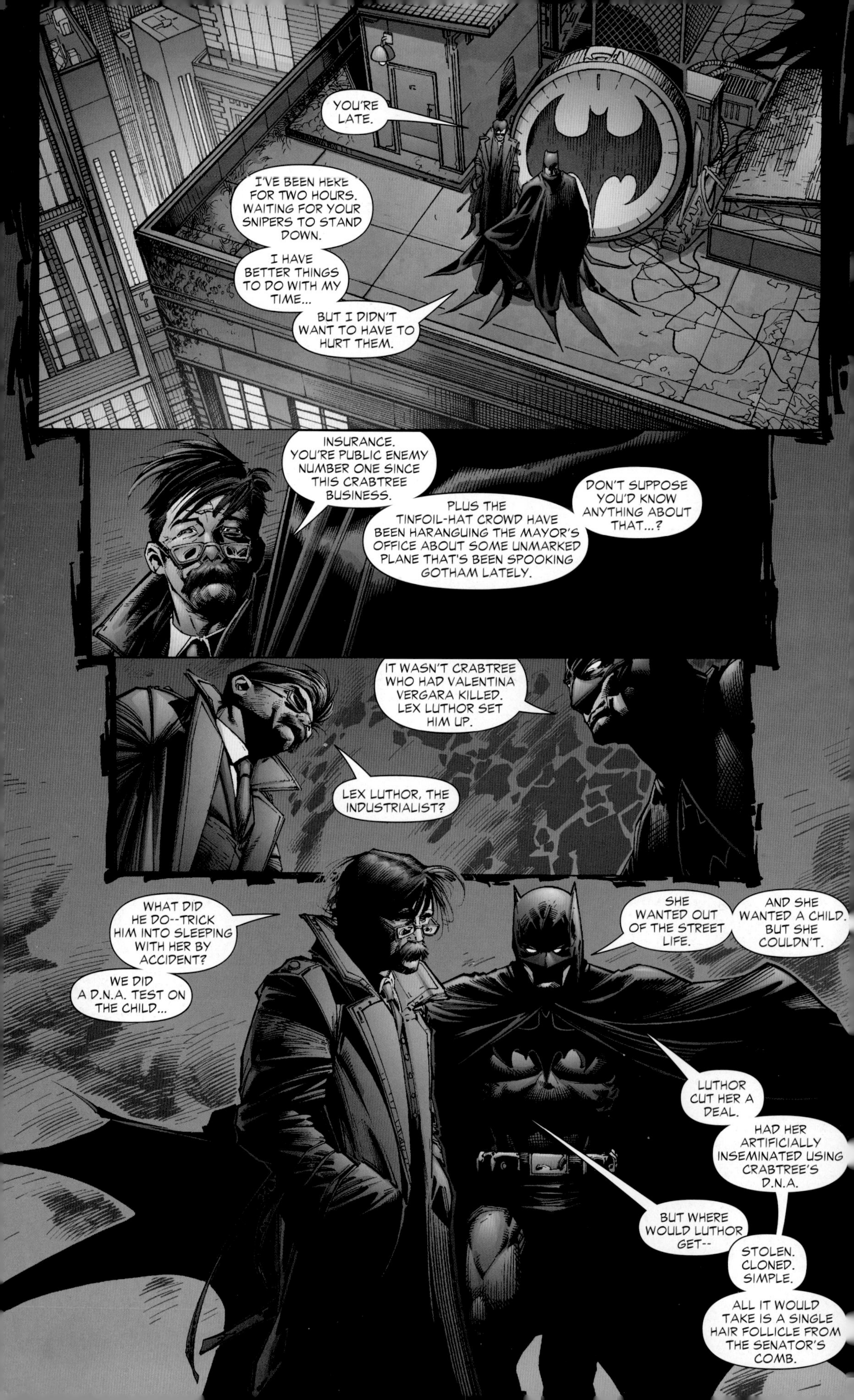
YOU'RE LATE.
I'VE BEEN HERE FOR TWO HOURS. WAITING FOR YOUR SNIPERS TO STAND DOWN.
I HAVE BETTER THINGS TO DO WITH MY TIME...
BUT I DIDN'T WANT TO HAVE TO HURT THEM.
INSURANCE. YOU'RE PUBLIC ENEMY NUMBER ONE SINCE THIS CRABTREE BUSINESS.
PLUS THE TINFOIL-HAT CROWD HAVE BEEN HARANGUING THE MAYOR'S OFFICE ABOUT SOME UNMARKED PLANE THAT'S BEEN SPOOKING GOTHAM LATELY.
DON'T SUPPOSE YOU'D KNOW ANYTHING ABOUT THAT...?
IT WASN'T CRABTREE WHO HAD VALENTINA VERGARA KILLED. LEX LUTHOR SET HIM UP.
LEX LUTHOR, THE INDUSTRIALIST?
WHAT DID HE DO--TRICK HIM INTO SLEEPING WITH HER BY ACCIDENT?
WE DID A D.N.A. TEST ON THE CHILD...
SHE WANTED OUT OF THE STREET LIFE.
AND SHE WANTED A CHILD. BUT SHE COULDN'T.
LUTHOR CUT HER A DEAL.
HAD HER ARTIFICIALLY INSEMINATED USING CRABTREE'S D.N.A.
BUT WHERE WOULD LUTHOR GET--
STOLEN. CLONED. SIMPLE.
ALL IT WOULD TAKE IS A SINGLE HAIR FOLLICLE FROM THE SENATOR'S COMB.

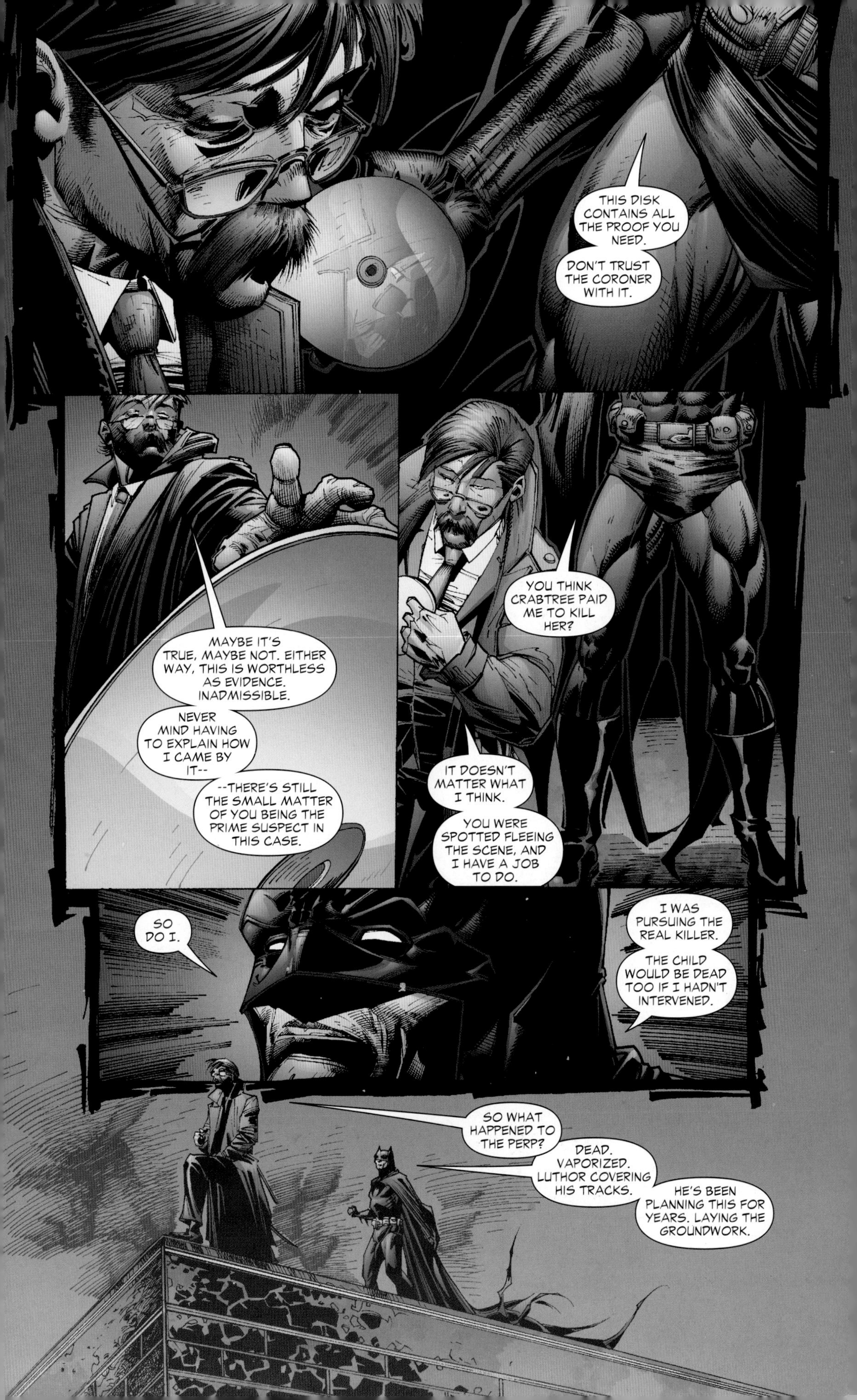
THIS DISK CONTAINS ALL THE PROOF YOU NEED.
DON'T TRUST THE CORONER WITH IT.
MAYBE IT'S TRUE, MAYBE NOT. EITHER WAY, THIS IS WORTHLESS AS EVIDENCE. INADMISSIBLE.
NEVER MIND HAVING TO EXPLAIN HOW I CAME BY IT--
--THERE'S STILL THE SMALL MATTER OF YOU BEING THE PRIME SUSPECT IN THIS CASE.
YOU THINK CRABTREE PAID ME TO KILL HER?
IT DOESN'T MATTER WHAT I THINK.
YOU WERE SPOTTED FLEEING THE SCENE, AND I HAVE A JOB TO DO.
SO DO I.
I WAS PURSUING THE REAL KILLER.
THE CHILD WOULD BE DEAD TOO IF I HADN'T INTERVENED.
SO WHAT HAPPENED TO THE PERP?
DEAD. VAPORIZED. LUTHOR COVERING HIS TRACKS.
HE'S BEEN PLANNING THIS FOR YEARS. LAYING THE GROUNDWORK.

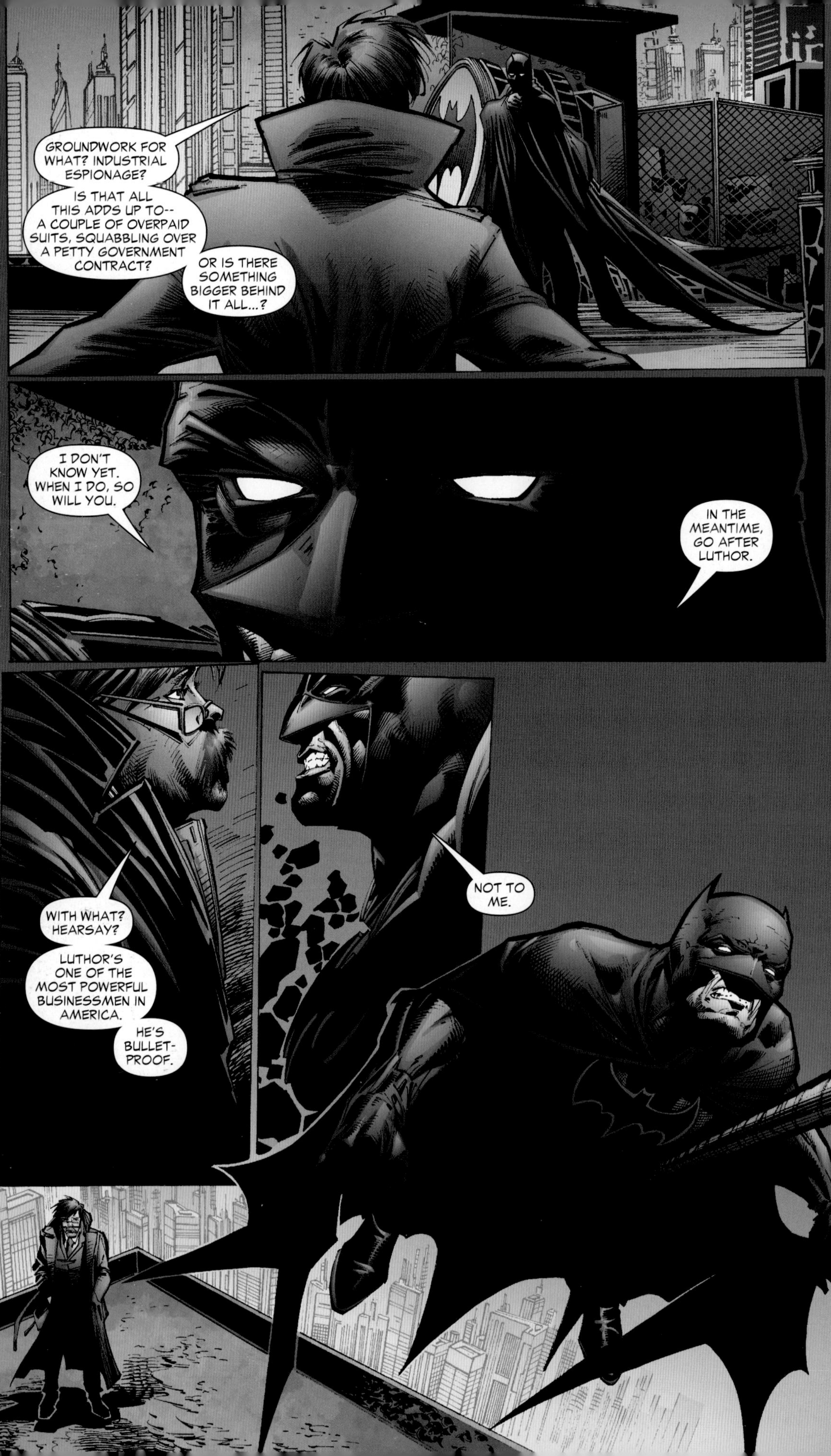
GROUNDWORK FOR WHAT? INDUSTRIAL ESPIONAGE?
IS THAT ALL THIS ADDS UP TO-- A COUPLE OF OVERPAID SUITS, SQUABBLING OVER A PETTY GOVERNMENT CONTRACT?
OR IS THERE SOMETHING BIGGER BEHIND IT ALL...?
I DON'T KNOW YET. WHEN I DO, SO WILL YOU.
IN THE MEANTIME, GO AFTER LUTHOR.
WITH WHAT? HEARSAY?
LUTHOR'S ONE OF THE MOST POWERFUL BUSINESSMEN IN AMERICA.
HE'S BULLET-PROOF.
NOT TO ME.

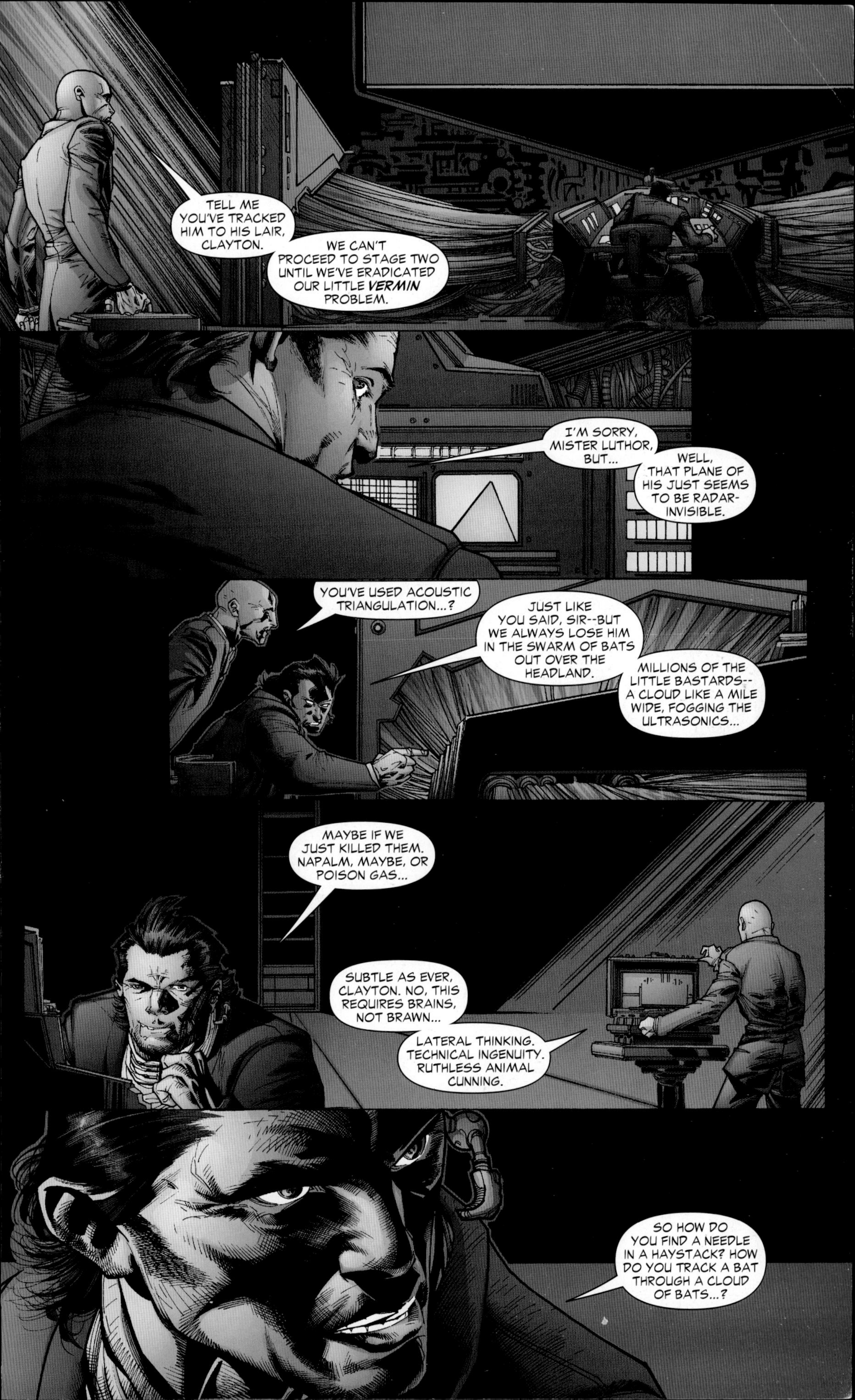
TELL ME YOU'VE TRACKED HIM TO HIS LAIR, CLAYTON.
WE CAN'T PROCEED TO STAGE TWO UNTIL WE'VE ERADICATED OUR LITTLE VERMIN PROBLEM.
I'M SORRY, MISTER LUTHOR, BUT...
WELL, THAT PLANE OF HIS JUST SEEMS TO BE RADAR-INVISIBLE.
YOU'VE USED ACOUSTIC TRIANGULATION...?
JUST LIKE YOU SAID, SIR--BUT WE ALWAYS LOSE HIM IN THE SWARM OF BATS OUT OVER THE HEADLAND.
MILLIONS OF THE LITTLE BASTARDS--A CLOUD LIKE A MILE WIDE, FOGGING THE ULTRASONICS...
MAYBE IF WE JUST KILLED THEM. NAPALM, MAYBE, OR POISON GAS...
SUBTLE AS EVER, CLAYTON. NO, THIS REQUIRES BRAINS, NOT BRAWN...
LATERAL THINKING. TECHNICAL INGENUITY. RUTHLESS ANIMAL CUNNING.
SO HOW DO YOU FIND A NEEDLE IN A HAYSTACK? HOW DO YOU TRACK A BAT THROUGH A CLOUD OF BATS...?

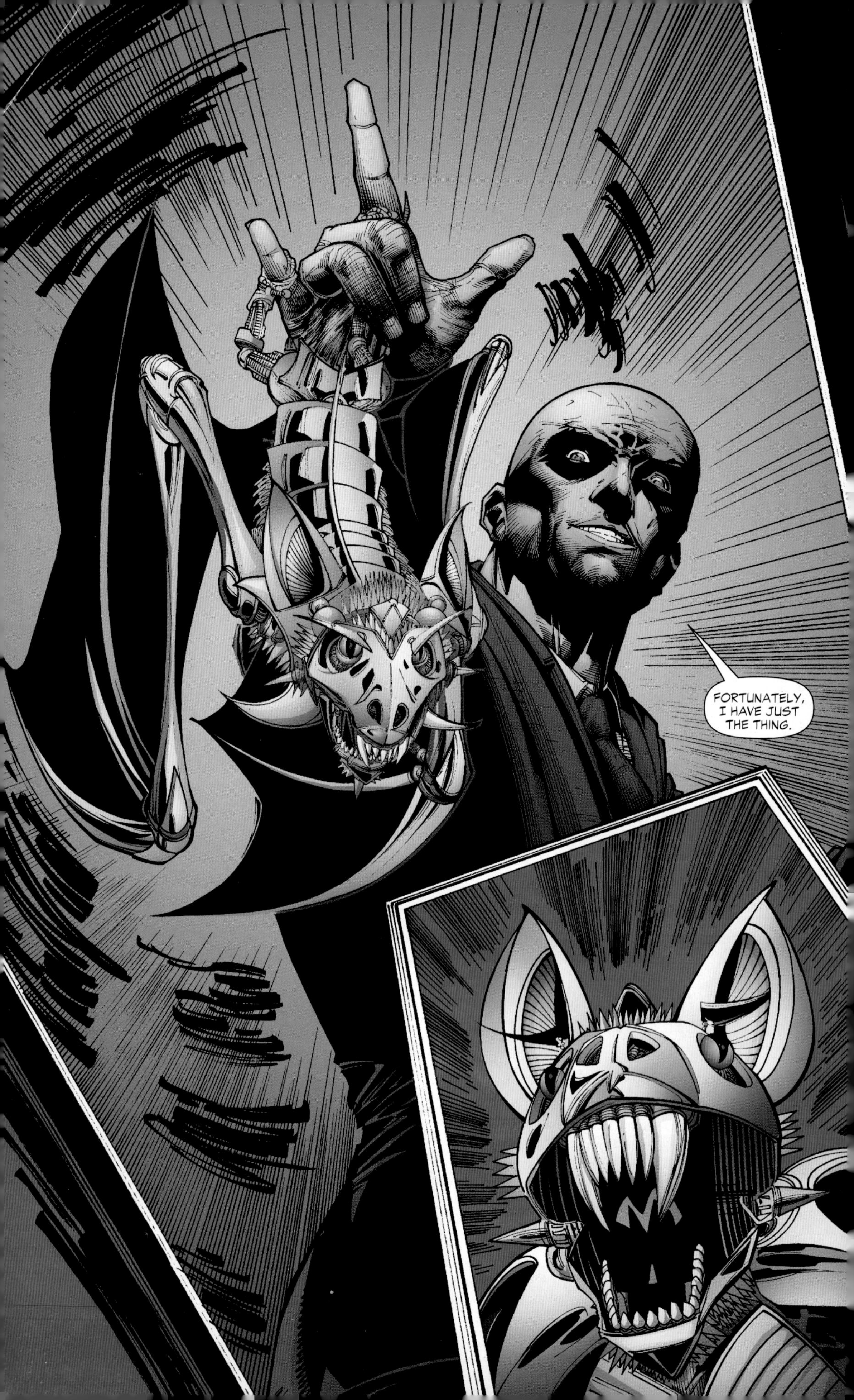
FORTUNATELY, I HAVE JUST THE THING.

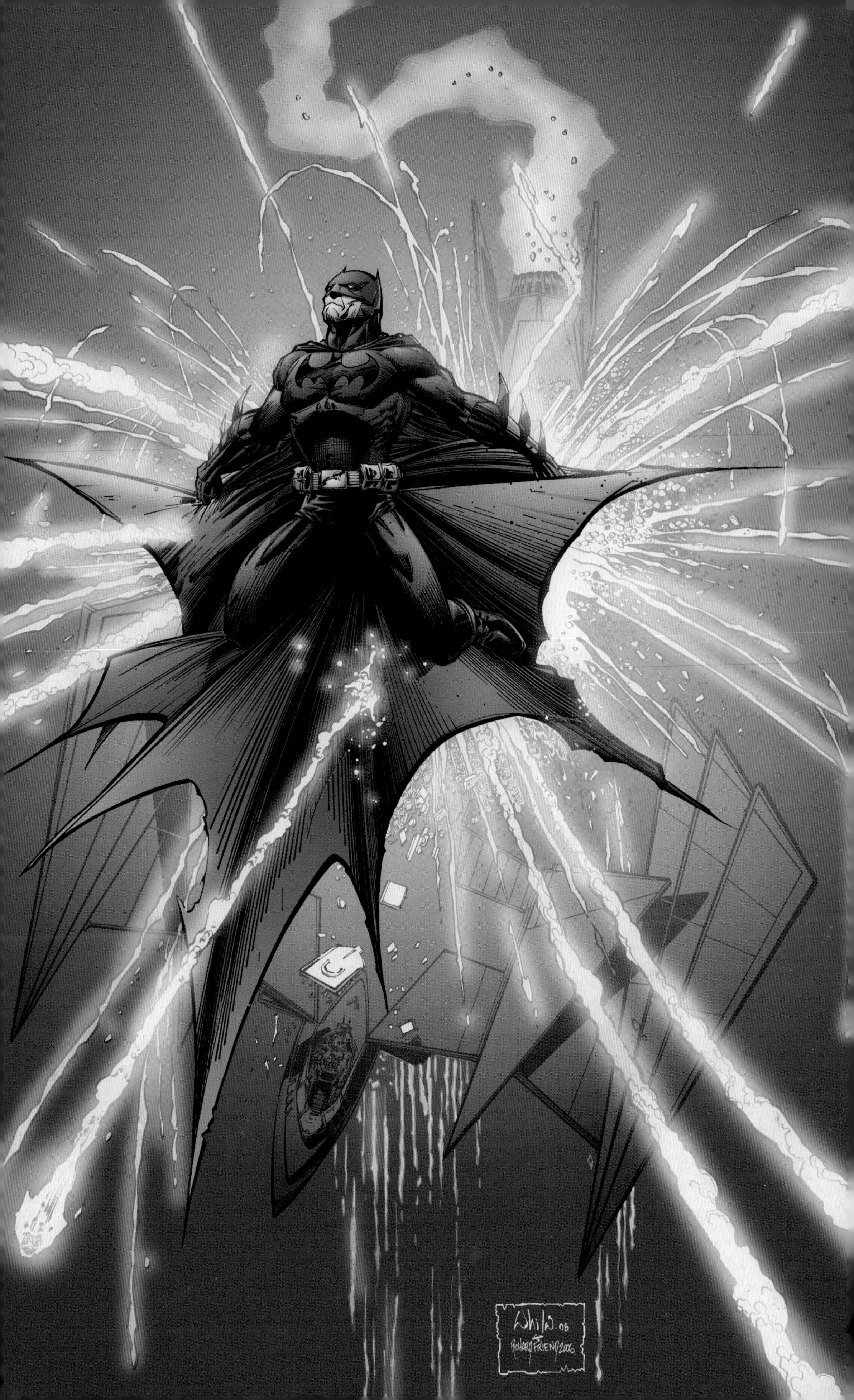

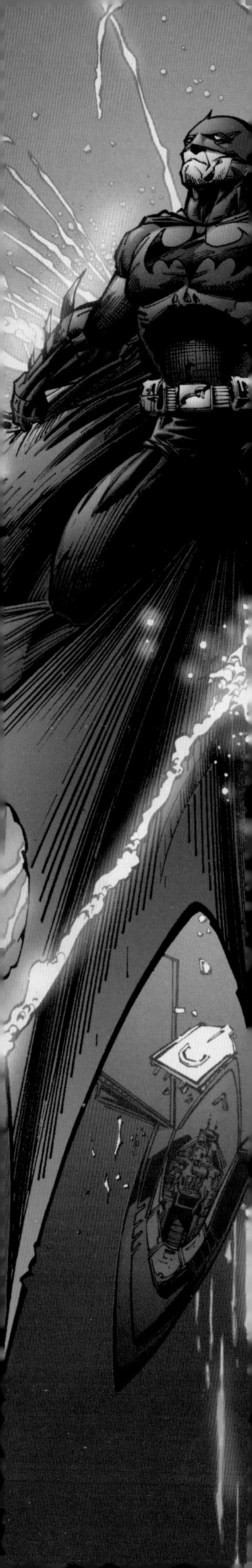

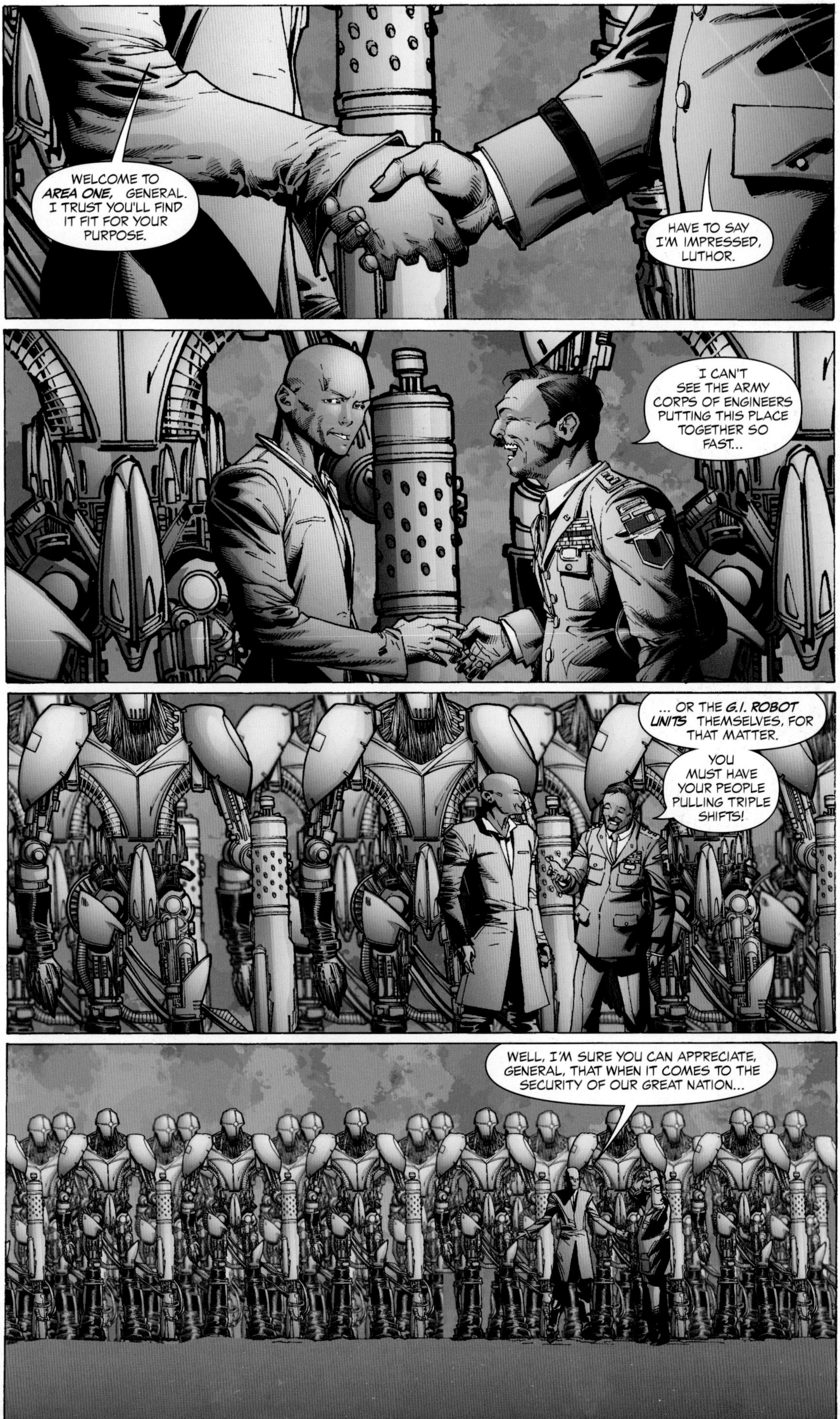
WELCOME TO AREA ONE, GENERAL. I TRUST YOU'LL FIND IT FIT FOR YOUR PURPOSE.
HAVE TO SAY I'M IMPRESSED, LUTHOR.
I CAN'T SEE THE ARMY CORPS OF ENGINEERS PUTTING THIS PLACE TOGETHER SO FAST...
... OR THE G.I. ROBOT UNITS THEMSELVES, FOR THAT MATTER.
YOU MUST HAVE YOUR PEOPLE PULLING TRIPLE SHIFTS!
WELL, I'M SURE YOU CAN APPRECIATE, GENERAL, THAT WHEN IT COMES TO THE SECURITY OF OUR GREAT NATION...

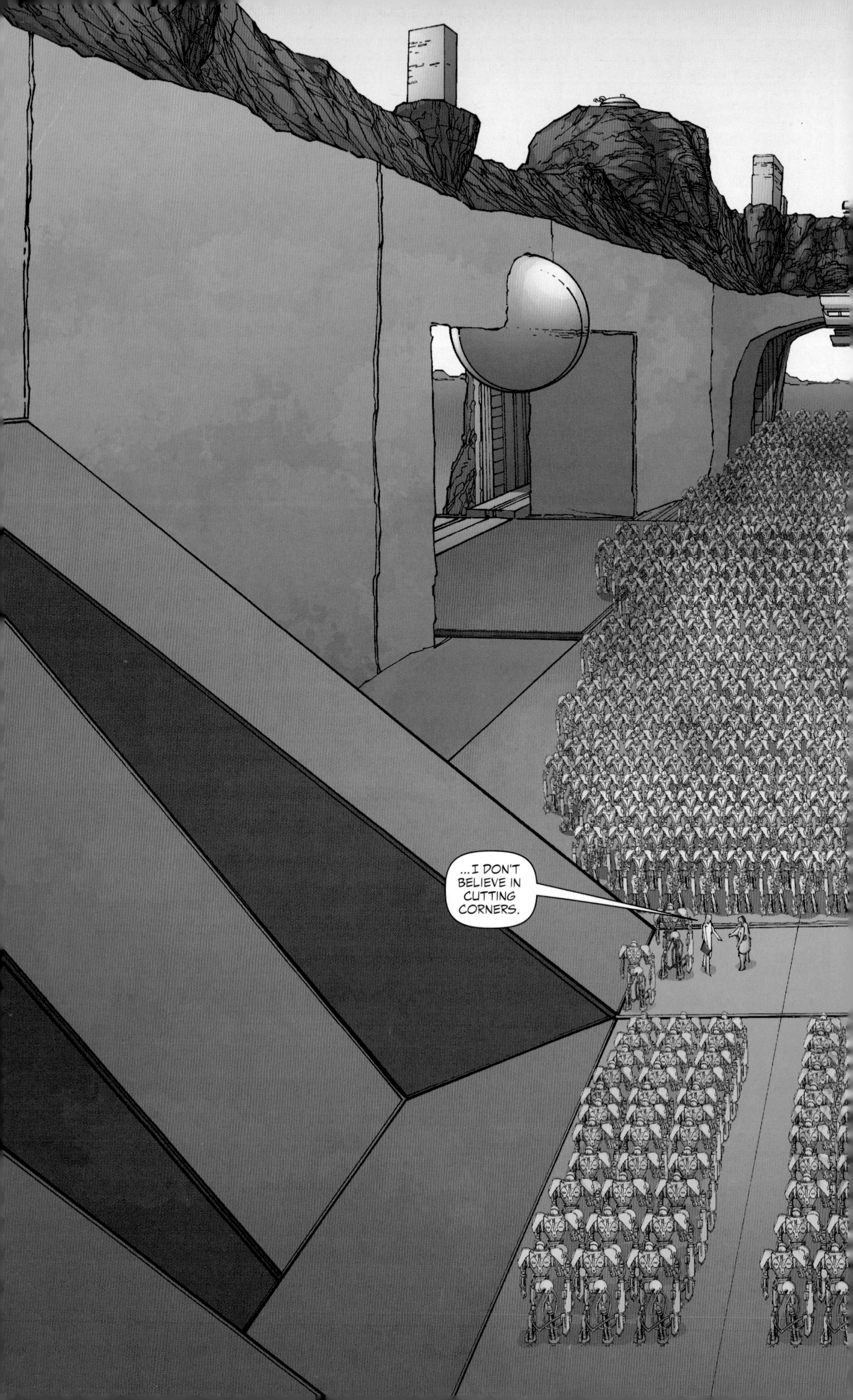
...I DON'T BELIEVE IN CUTTING CORNERS.

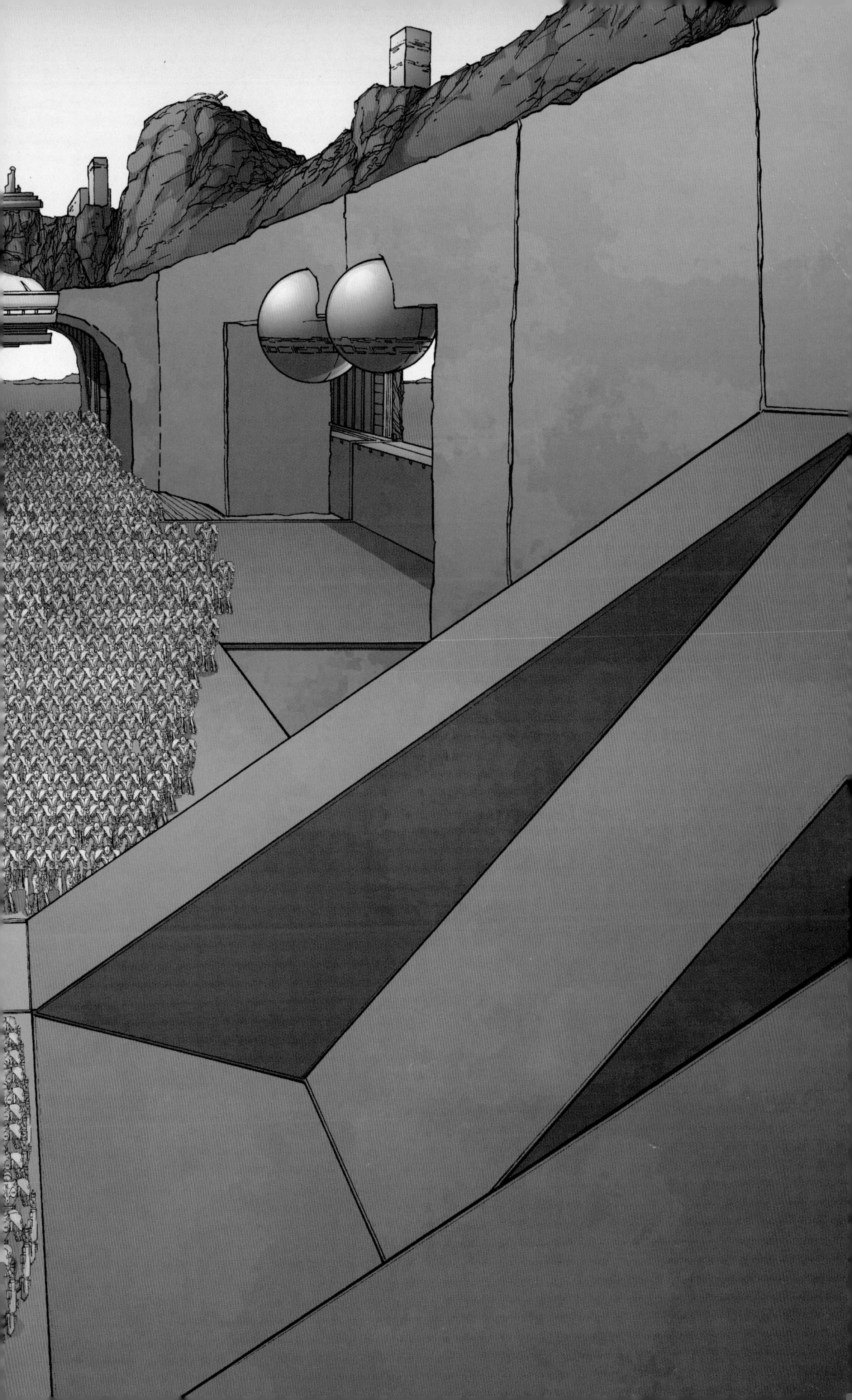

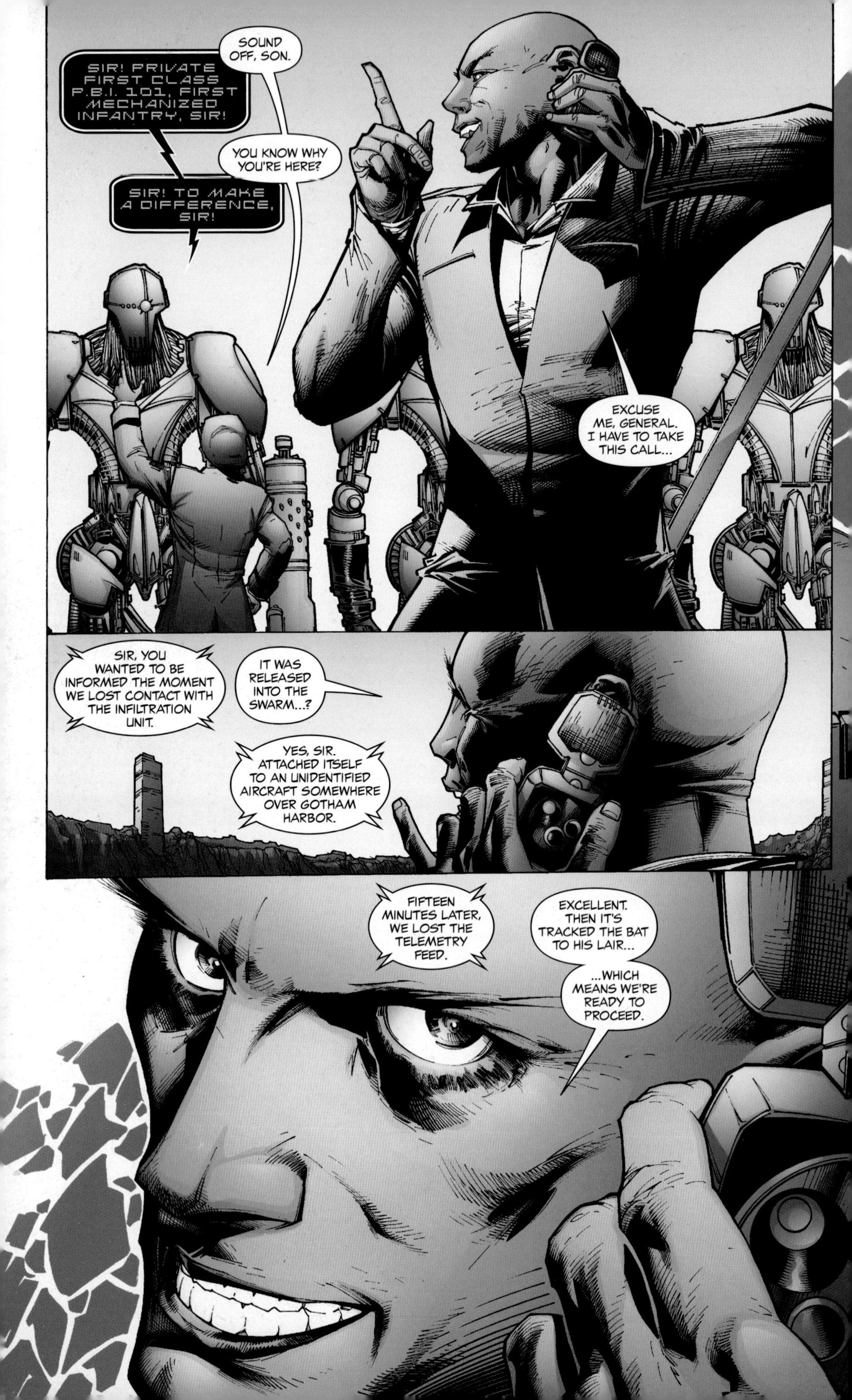
SIR! PRIVATE FIRST CLASS P.B.I. 101, FIRST MECHANIZED INFANTRY, SIR!
SOUND OFF, SON.
YOU KNOW WHY YOU'RE HERE?
SIR! TO MAKE A DIFFERENCE, SIR!
EXCUSE ME, GENERAL. I HAVE TO TAKE THIS CALL...
SIR, YOU WANTED TO BE INFORMED THE MOMENT WE LOST CONTACT WITH THE INFILTRATION UNIT.
IT WAS RELEASED INTO THE SWARM...?
YES, SIR. ATTACHED ITSELF TO AN UNIDENTIFIED AIRCRAFT SOMEWHERE OVER GOTHAM HARBOR.
FIFTEEN MINUTES LATER, WE LOST THE TELEMETRY FEED.
EXCELLENT. THEN IT'S TRACKED THE BAT TO HIS LAIR...
...WHICH MEANS WE'RE READY TO PROCEED.

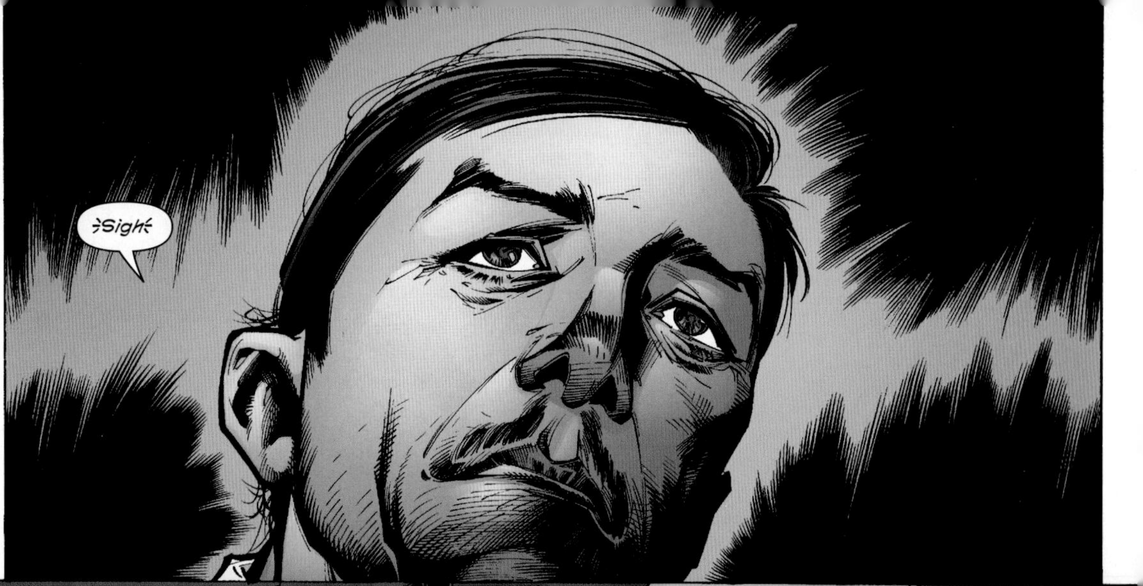
Sigh

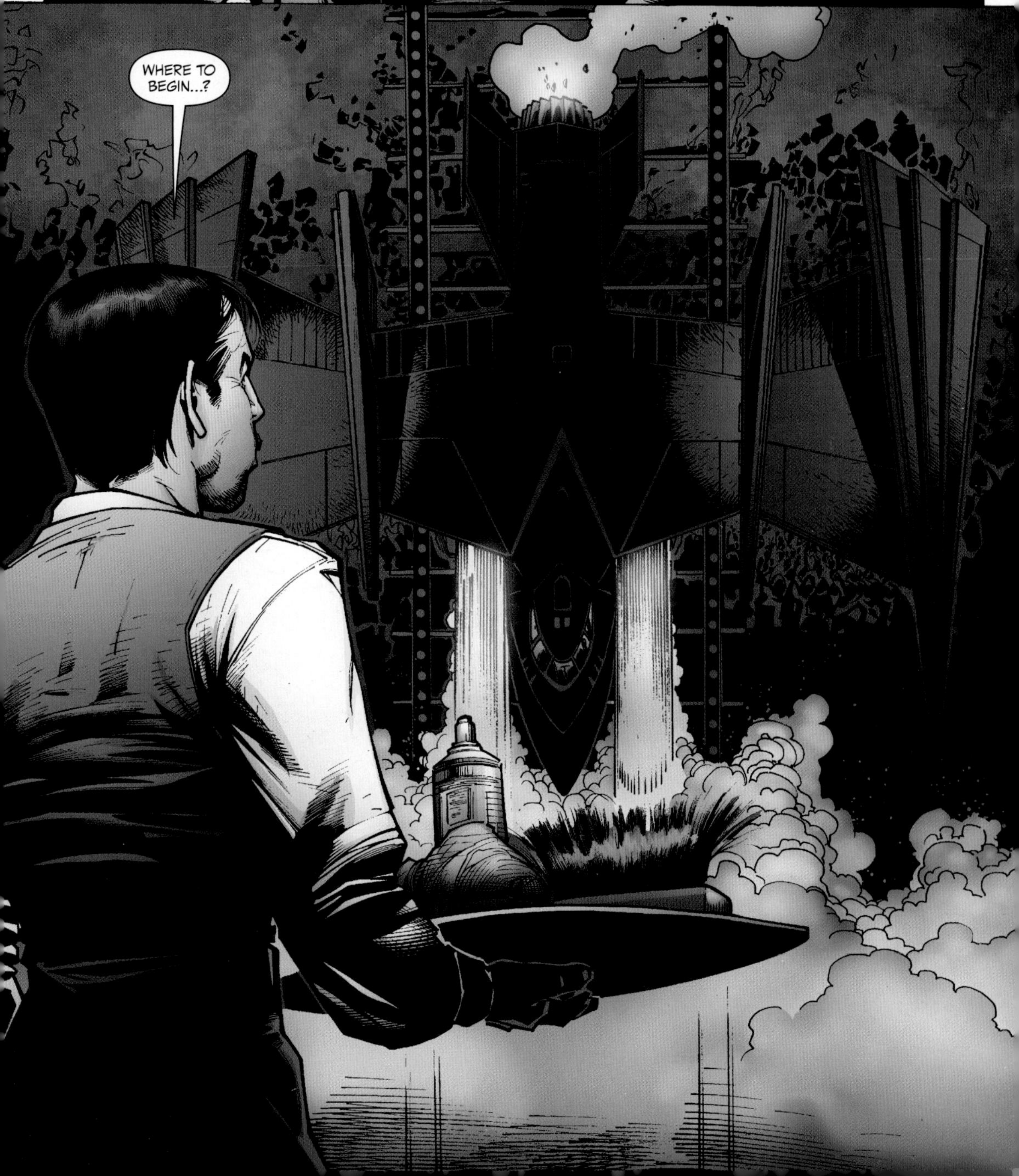
WHERE TO BEGIN...?

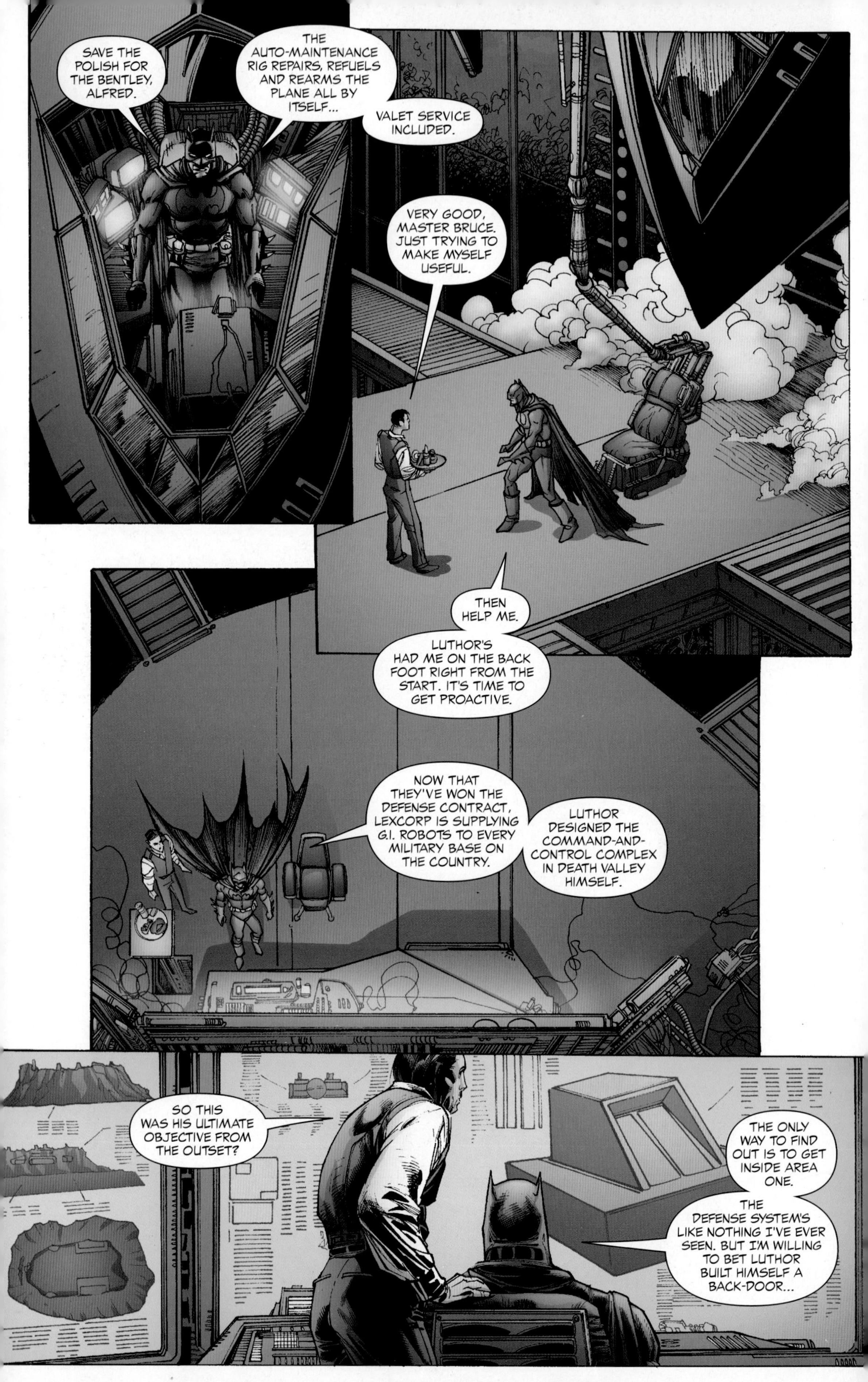
SAVE THE POLISH FOR THE BENTLEY, ALFRED.
THE AUTO-MAINTENANCE RIG REPAIRS, REFUELS AND REARMS THE PLANE ALL BY ITSELF...
VALET SERVICE INCLUDED.
VERY GOOD, MASTER BRUCE. JUST TRYING TO MAKE MYSELF USEFUL.
THEN HELP ME.
LUTHOR'S HAD ME ON THE BACK FOOT RIGHT FROM THE START. IT'S TIME TO GET PROACTIVE.
NOW THAT THEY'VE WON THE DEFENSE CONTRACT, LEXCORP IS SUPPLYING G.I. ROBOTS TO EVERY MILITARY BASE ON THE COUNTRY.
LUTHOR DESIGNED THE COMMAND-AND-CONTROL COMPLEX IN DEATH VALLEY HIMSELF.
SO THIS WAS HIS ULTIMATE OBJECTIVE FROM THE OUTSET?
THE ONLY WAY TO FIND OUT IS TO GET INSIDE AREA ONE.
THE DEFENSE SYSTEM'S LIKE NOTHING I'VE EVER SEEN. BUT I'M WILLING TO BET LUTHOR BUILT HIMSELF A BACK-DOOR...

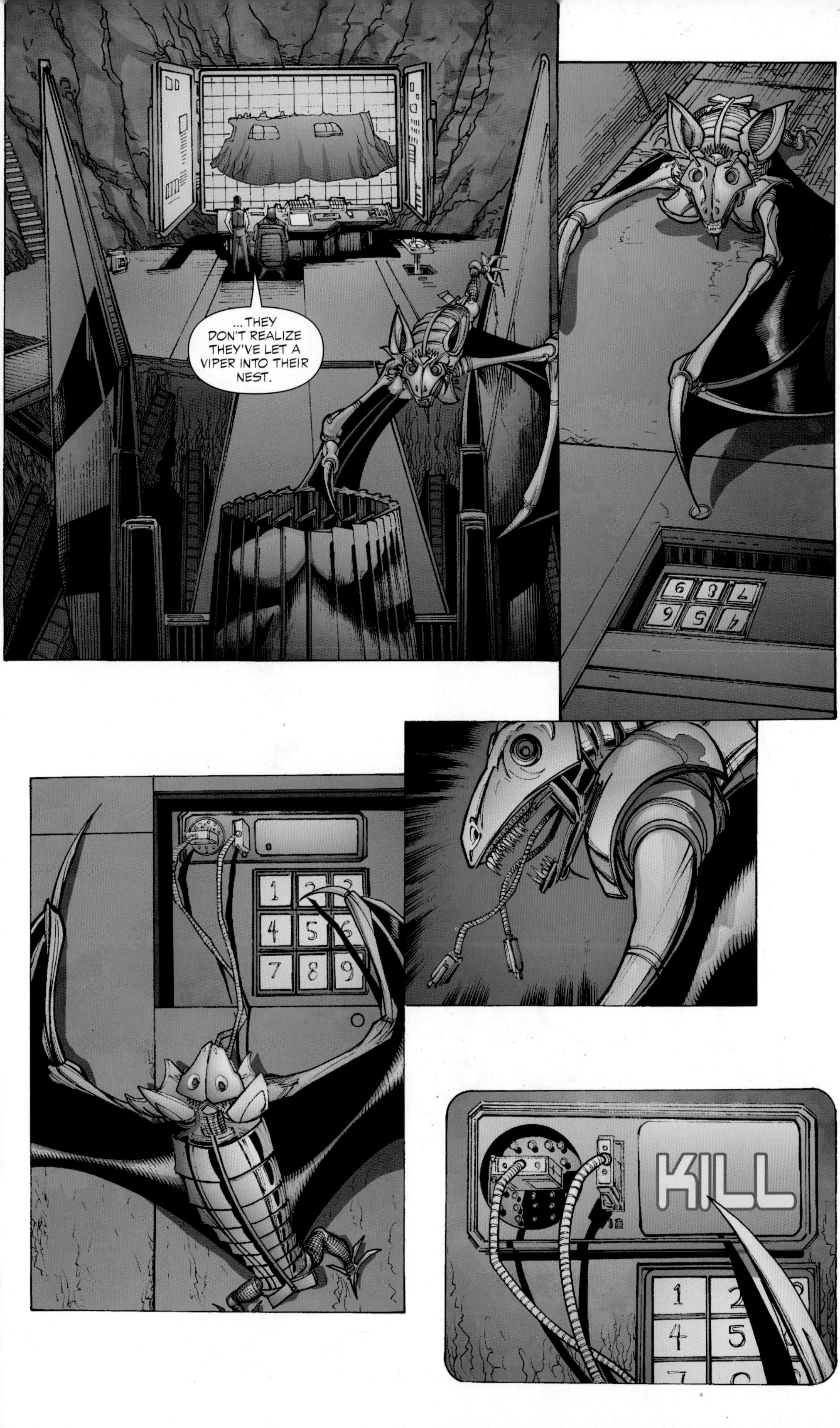
...THEY DON'T REALIZE THEY'VE LET A VIPER INTO THEIR NEST.
KILL

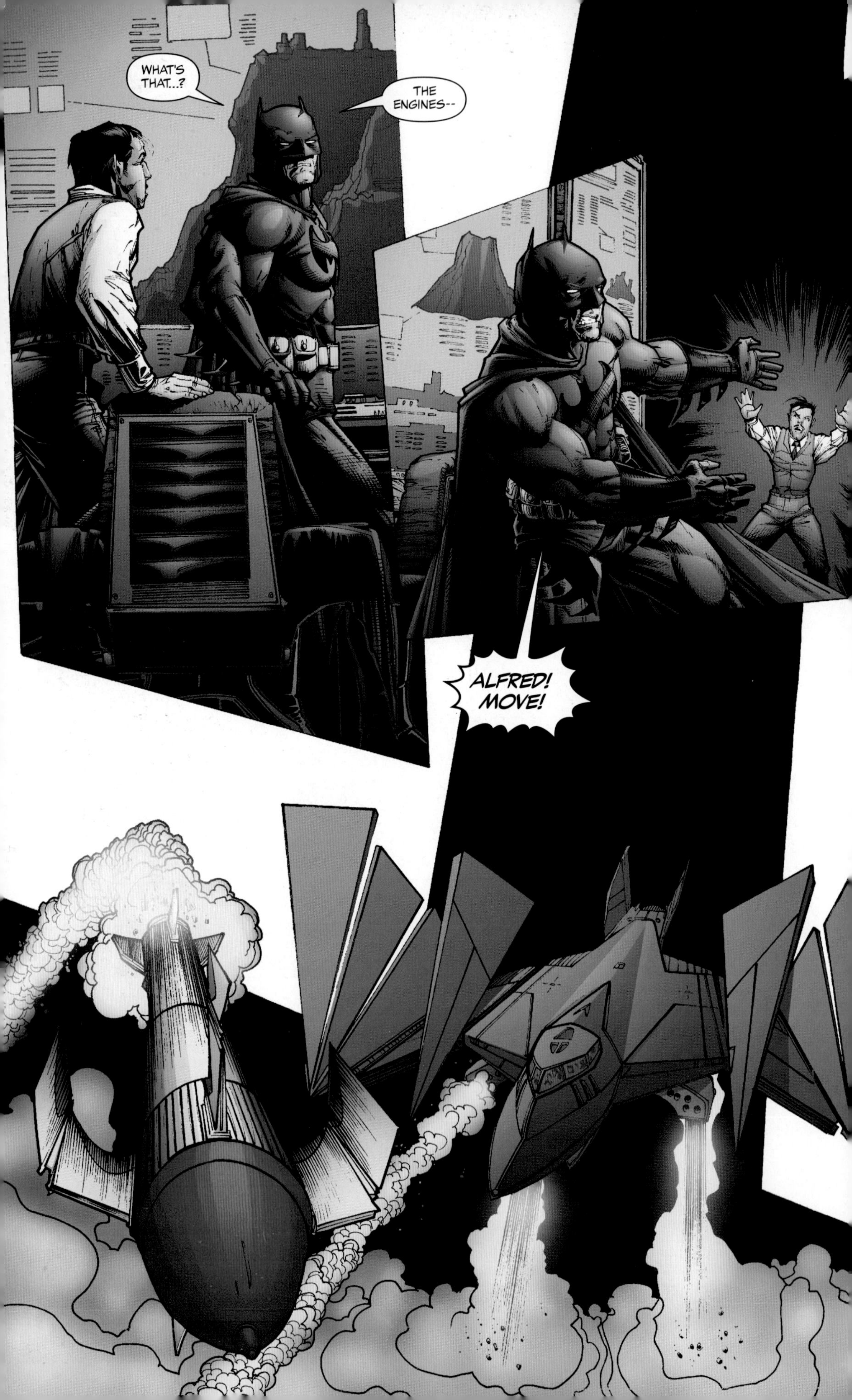
WHAT'S THAT...?
THE ENGINES--
ALFRED! MOVE!

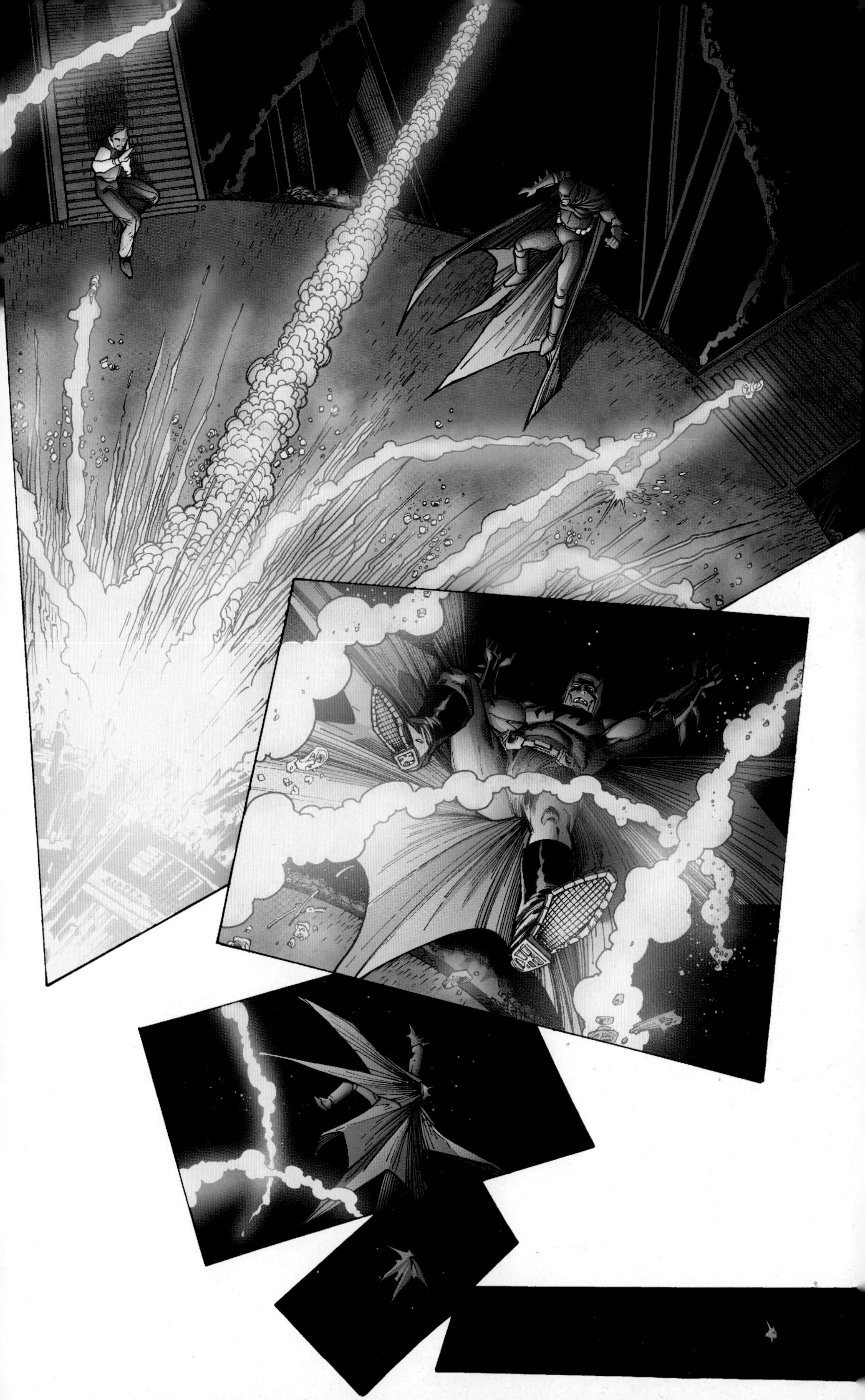

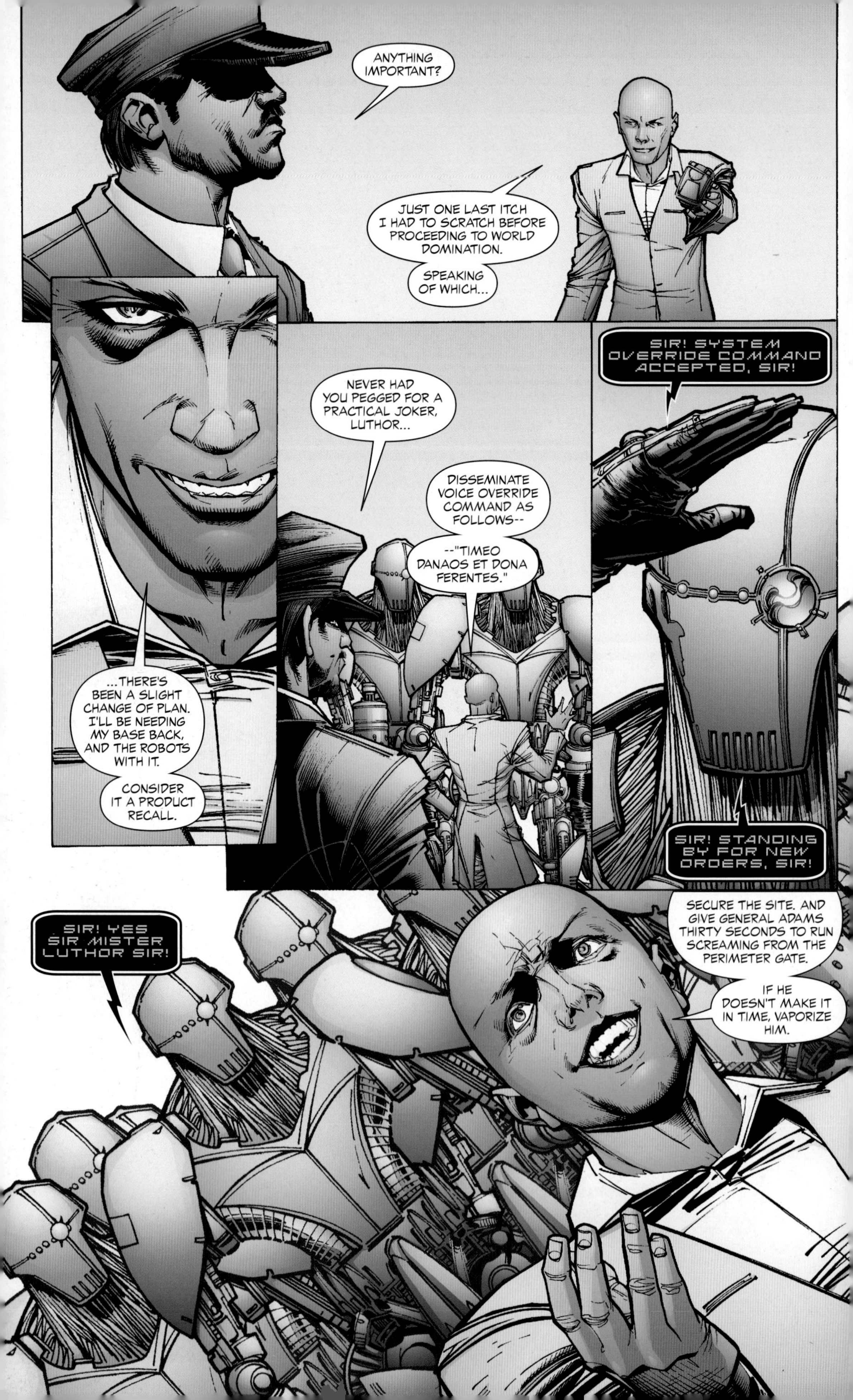
ANYTHING IMPORTANT?
JUST ONE LAST ITCH I HAD TO SCRATCH BEFORE PROCEEDING TO WORLD DOMINATION.
SPEAKING OF WHICH...
...THERE'S BEEN A SLIGHT CHANGE OF PLAN. I'LL BE NEEDING MY BASE BACK, AND THE ROBOTS WITH IT.
CONSIDER IT A PRODUCT RECALL.
NEVER HAD YOU PEGGED FOR A PRACTICAL JOKER, LUTHOR...
DISSEMINATE VOICE OVERRIDE COMMAND AS FOLLOWS--
--"TIMEO DANAOS ET DONA FERENTES."
SIR! SYSTEM OVERRIDE COMMAND ACCEPTED, SIR!
SIR! STANDING BY FOR NEW ORDERS, SIR!
SECURE THE SITE. AND GIVE GENERAL ADAMS THIRTY SECONDS TO RUN SCREAMING FROM THE PERIMETER GATE.
IF HE DOESN'T MAKE IT IN TIME, VAPORIZE HIM.
SIR! YES SIR MISTER LUTHOR SIR!

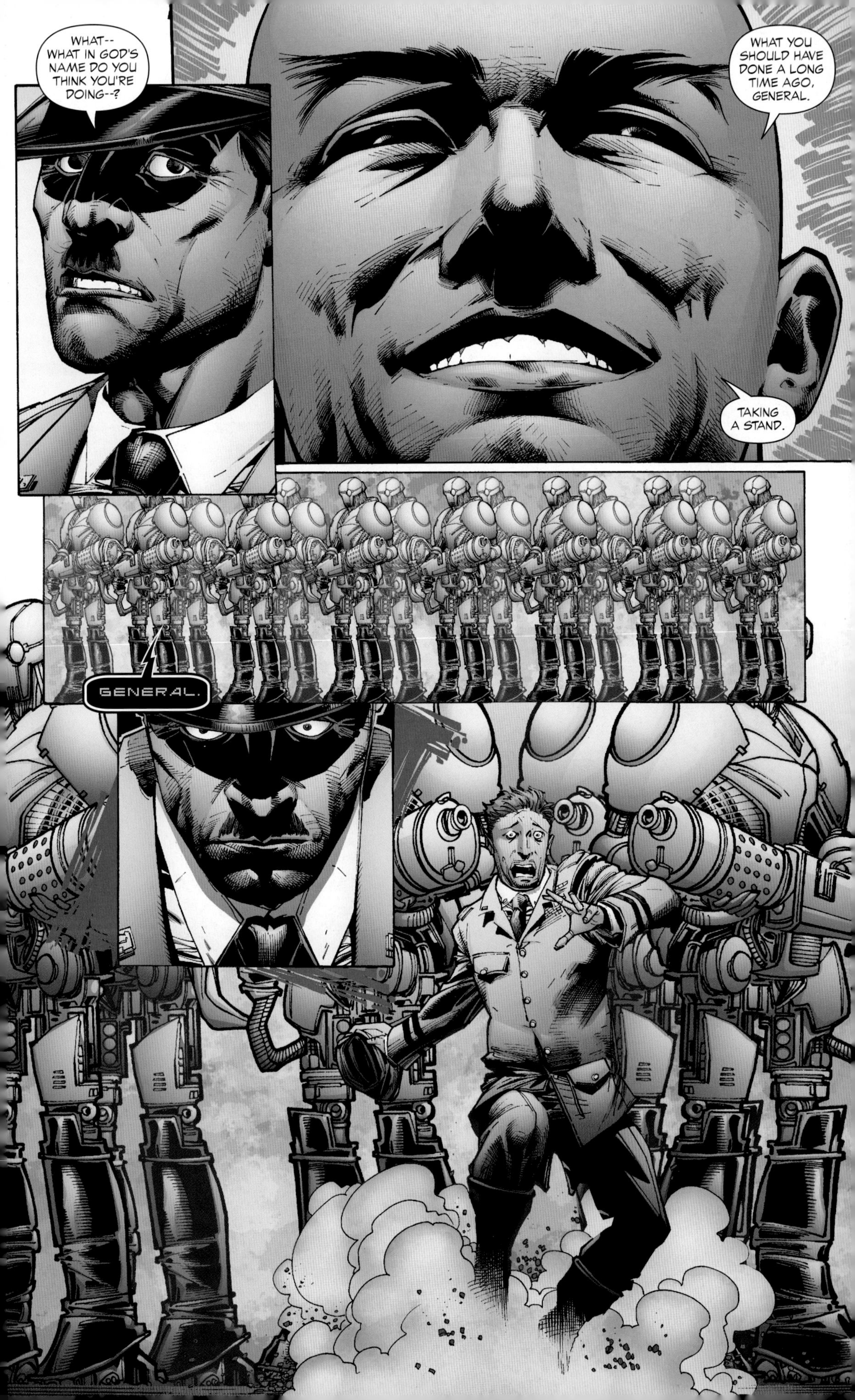
WHAT-- WHAT IN GOD'S NAME DO YOU THINK YOU'RE DOING--?
WHAT YOU SHOULD HAVE DONE A LONG TIME AGO, GENERAL.
TAKING A STAND.
GENERAL.

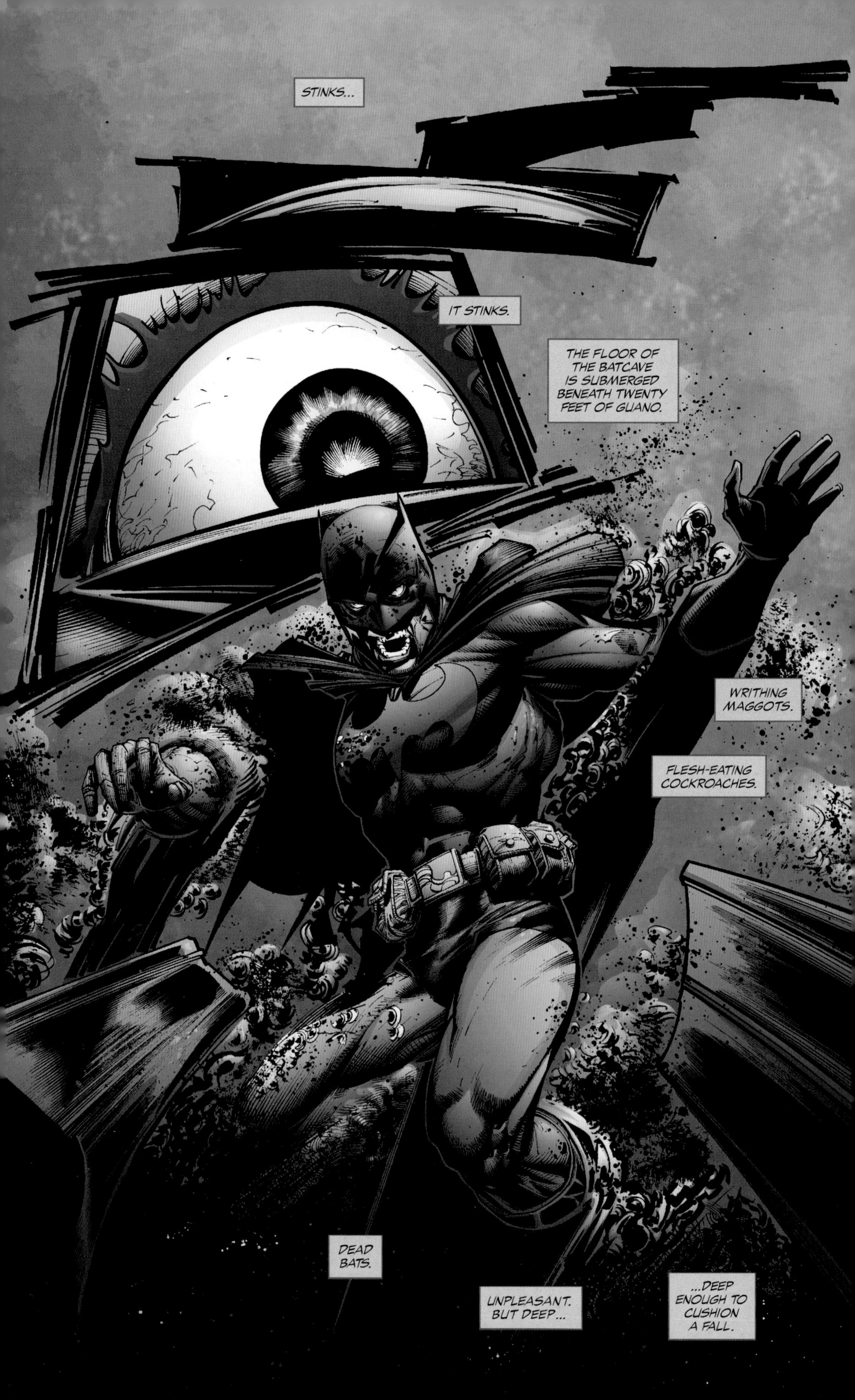
STINKS...
IT STINKS.
THE FLOOR OF THE BATCAVE IS SUBMERGED BENEATH TWENTY FEET OF GUANO.
WRITHING MAGGOTS.
FLESH-EATING COCKROACHES.
DEAD BATS.
UNPLEASANT. BUT DEEP...
...DEEP ENOUGH TO CUSHION A FALL.

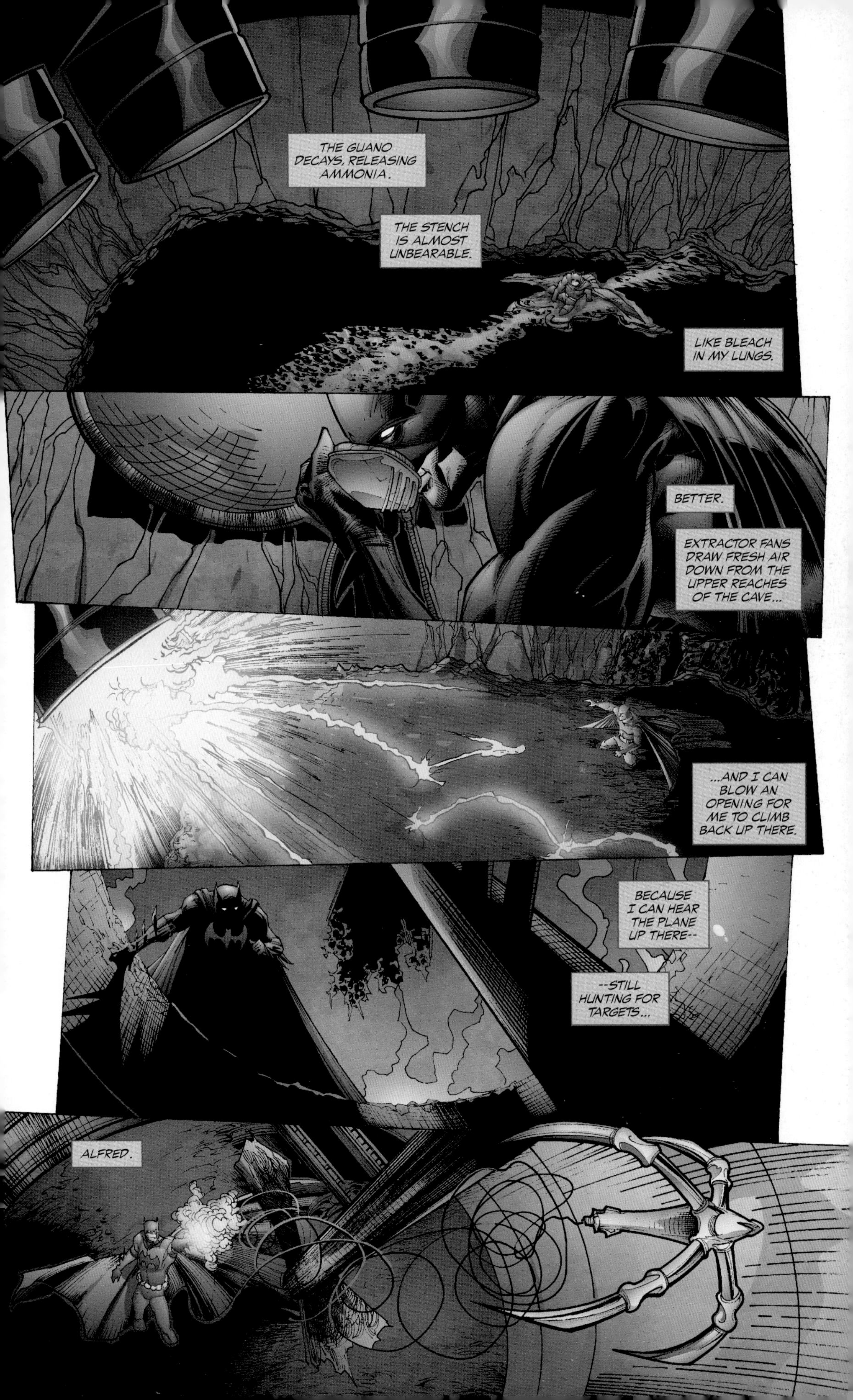
THE GUANO DECAYS, RELEASING AMMONIA.
THE STENCH IS ALMOST UNBEARABLE.
LIKE BLEACH IN MY LUNGS.
BETTER.
EXTRACTOR FANS DRAW FRESH AIR DOWN FROM THE UPPER REACHES OF THE CAVE...
...AND I CAN BLOW AN OPENING FOR ME TO CLIMB BACK UP THERE.
BECAUSE I CAN HEAR THE PLANE UP THERE--
--STILL HUNTING FOR TARGETS...
ALFRED.

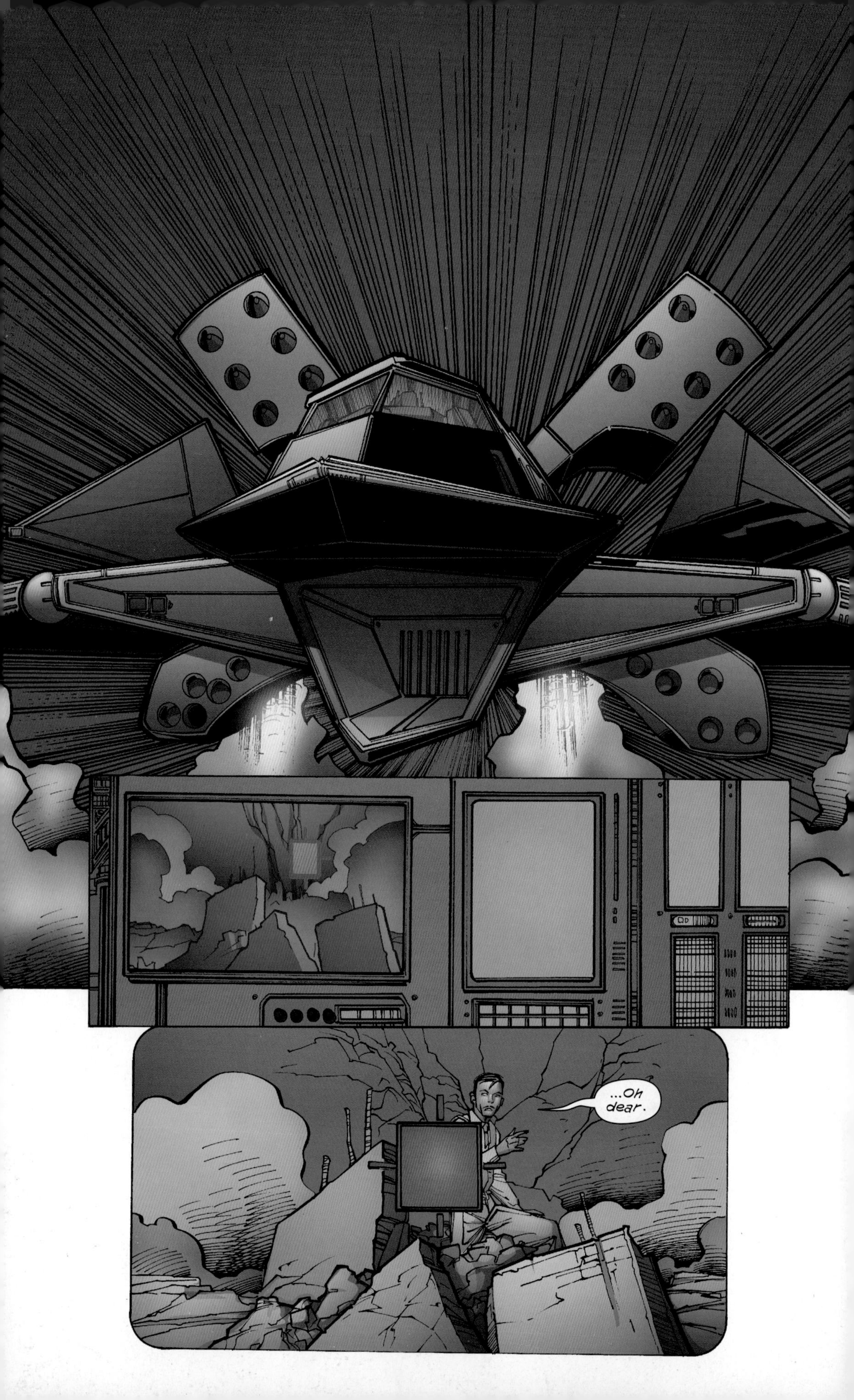
...Oh dear.

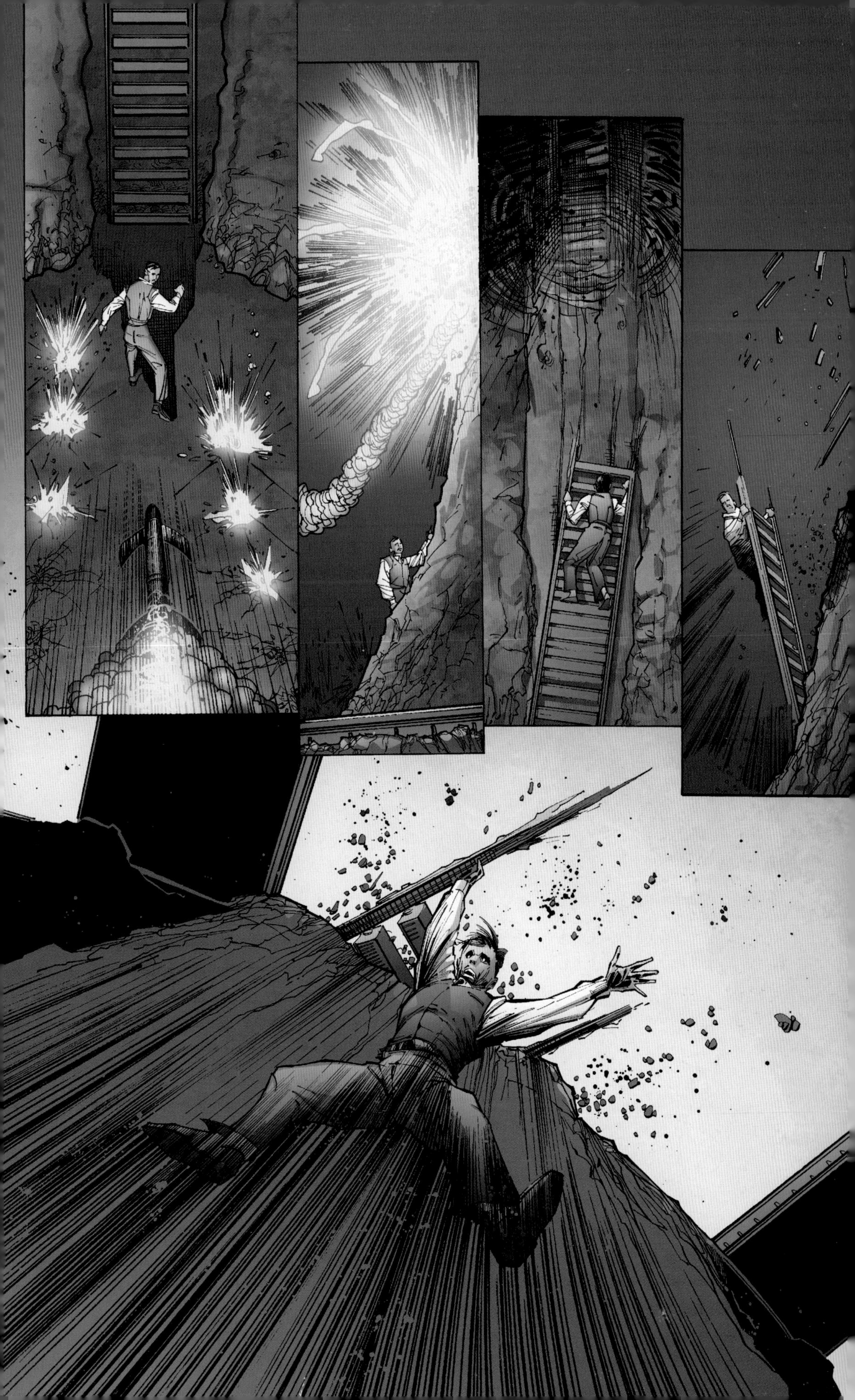

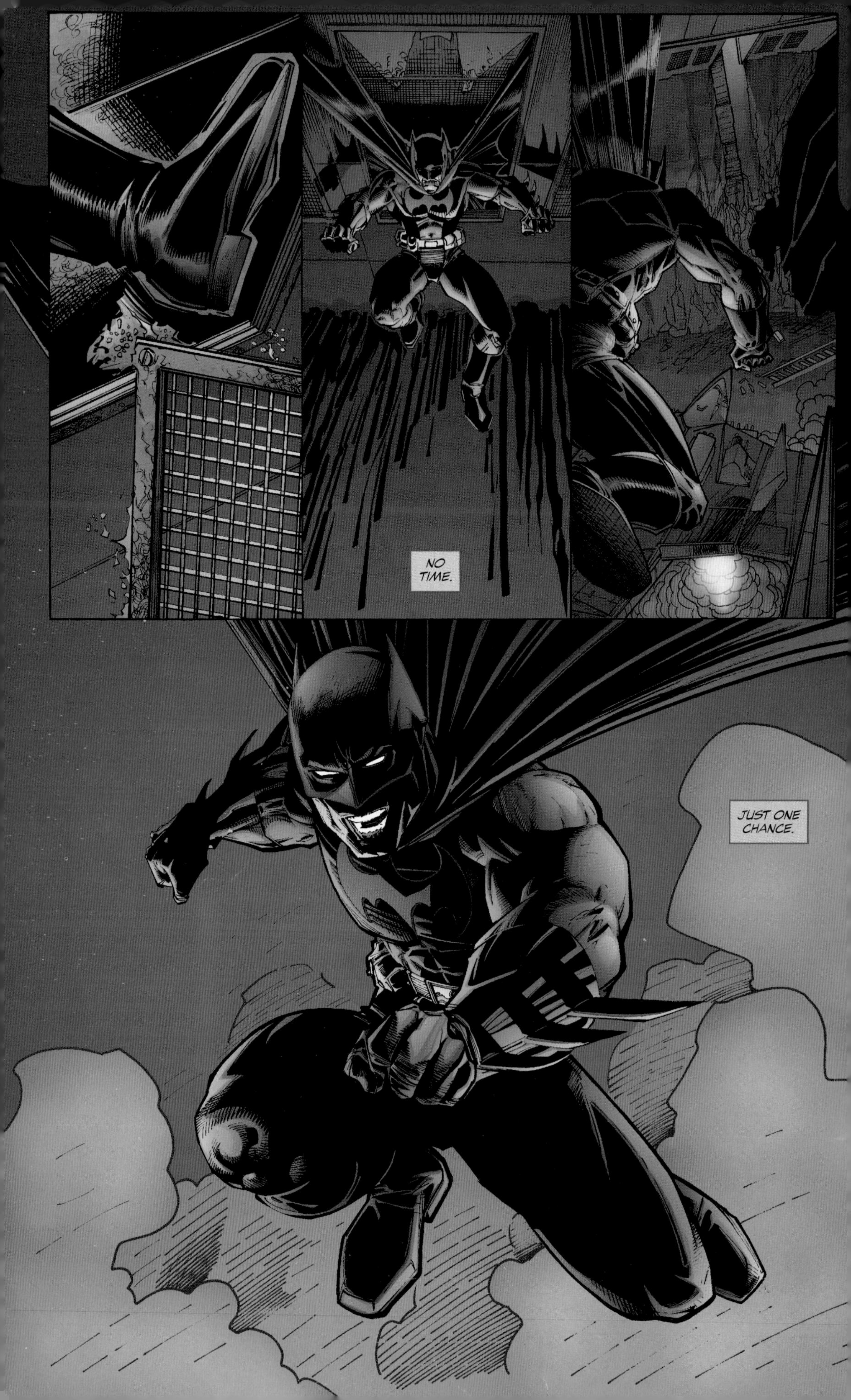
NO TIME.
JUST ONE CHANCE.

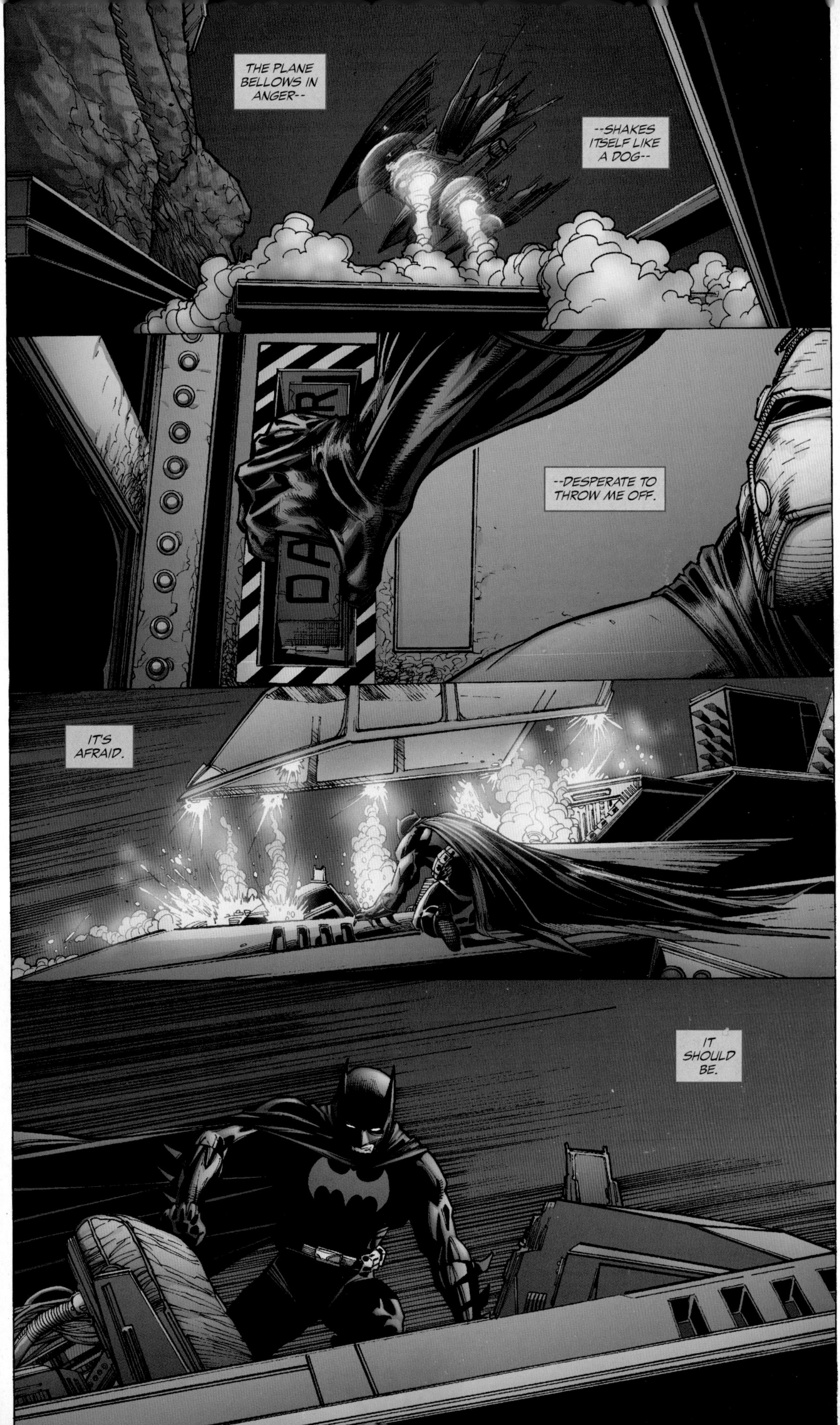
THE PLANE BELLOWS IN ANGER--
--SHAKES ITSELF LIKE A DOG--
--DESPERATE TO THROW ME OFF.
IT'S AFRAID.
IT SHOULD BE.

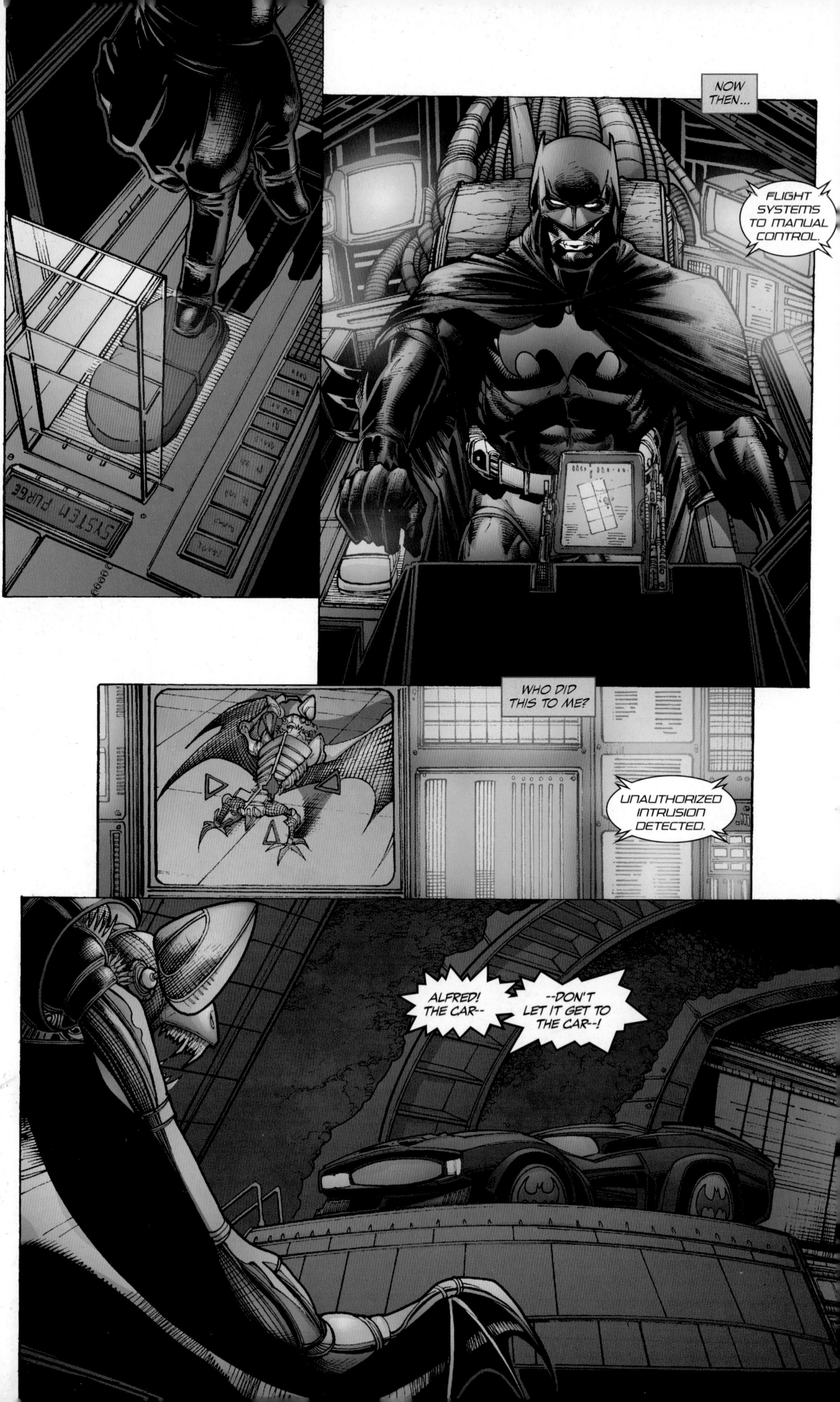

SYSTEM PURGE
NOW THEN...
FLIGHT SYSTEMS TO MANUAL CONTROL.
WHO DID THIS TO ME?
UNAUTHORIZED INTRUSION DETECTED.
ALFRED! THE CAR--
--DON'T LET IT GET TO THE CAR--!

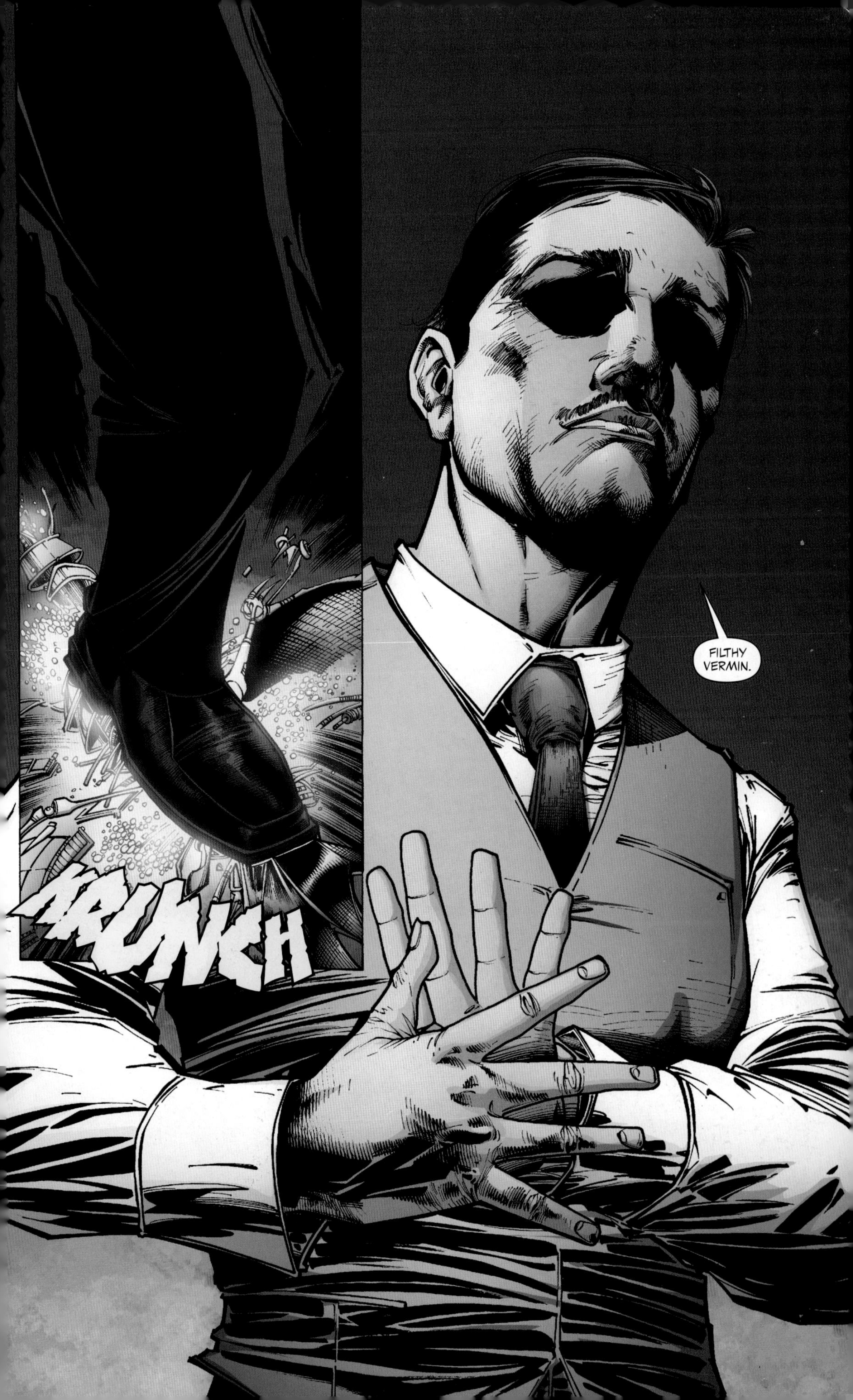
KRUNCH
FILTHY VERMIN.

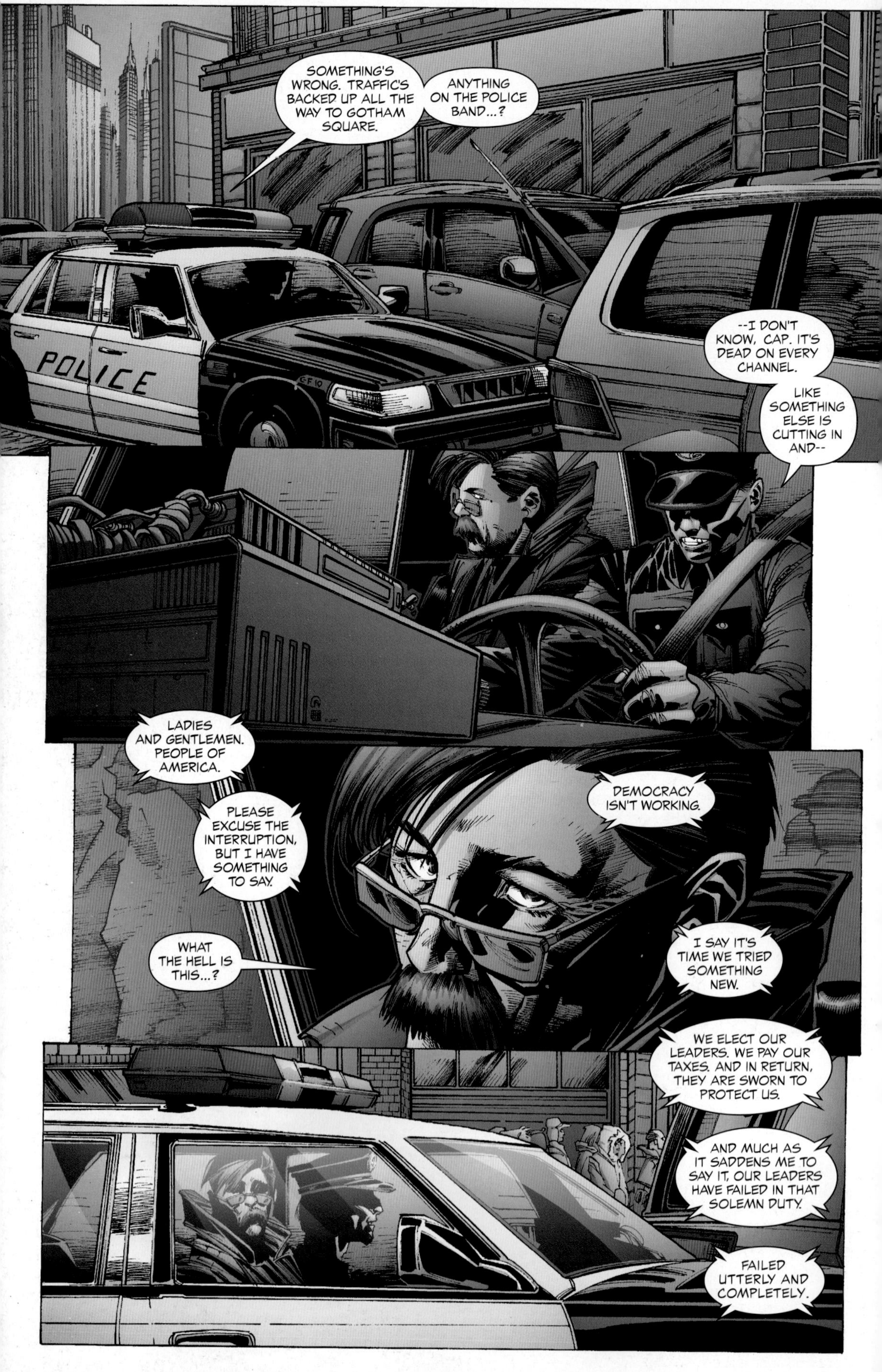
SOMETHING'S WRONG. TRAFFIC'S BACKED UP ALL THE WAY TO GOTHAM SQUARE.
ANYTHING ON THE POLICE BAND...?
POLICE
--I DON'T KNOW, CAP. IT'S DEAD ON EVERY CHANNEL.
LIKE SOMETHING ELSE IS CUTTING IN AND--
LADIES AND GENTLEMEN. PEOPLE OF AMERICA.
PLEASE EXCUSE THE INTERRUPTION, BUT I HAVE SOMETHING TO SAY.
DEMOCRACY ISN'T WORKING.
WHAT THE HELL IS THIS...?
I SAY IT'S TIME WE TRIED SOMETHING NEW.
WE ELECT OUR LEADERS. WE PAY OUR TAXES. AND IN RETURN, THEY ARE SWORN TO PROTECT US.
AND MUCH AS IT SADDENS ME TO SAY IT, OUR LEADERS HAVE FAILED IN THAT SOLEMN DUTY.
FAILED UTTERLY AND COMPLETELY.

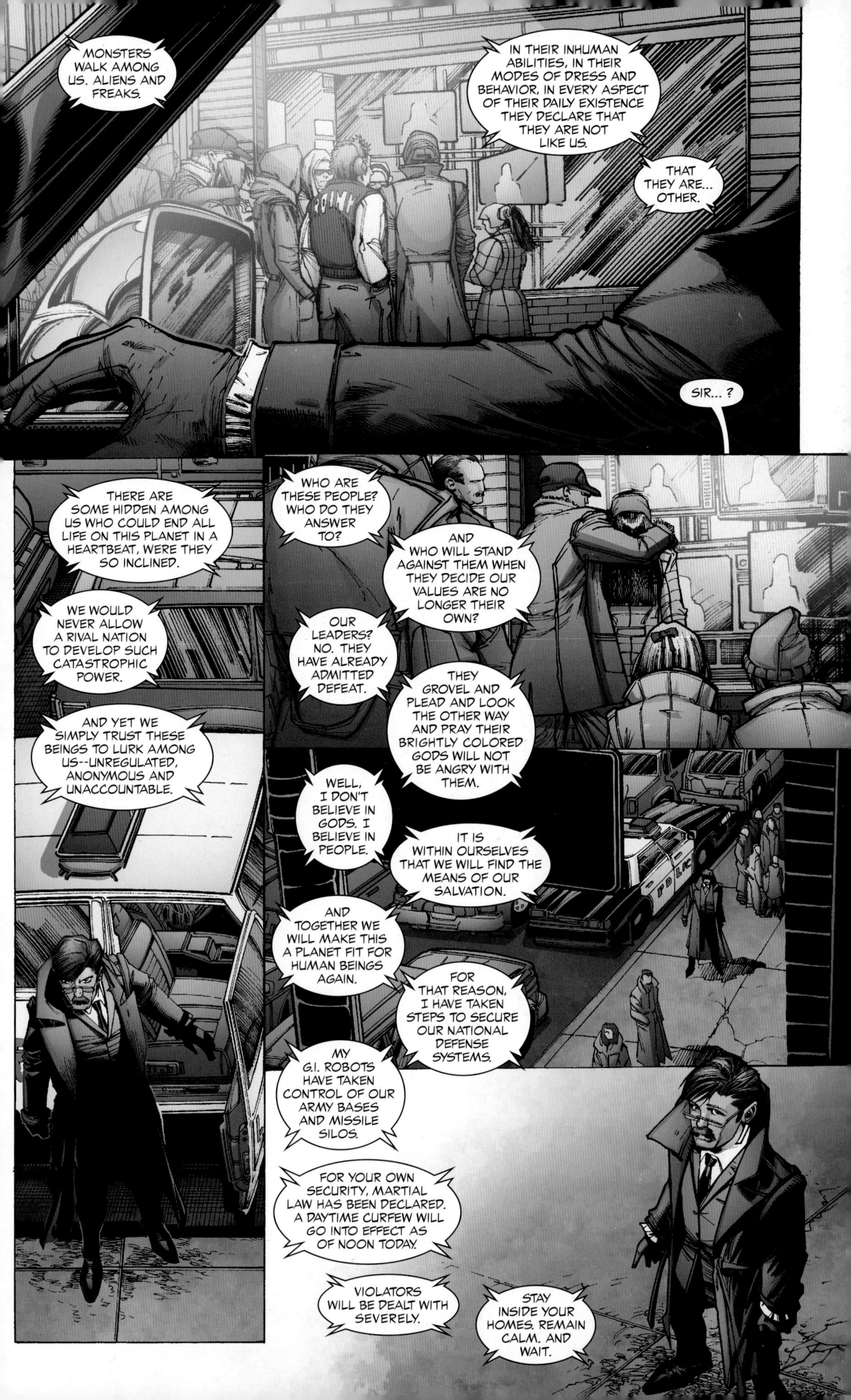
MONSTERS WALK AMONG US. ALIENS AND FREAKS.
IN THEIR INHUMAN ABILITIES, IN THEIR MODES OF DRESS AND BEHAVIOR, IN EVERY ASPECT OF THEIR DAILY EXISTENCE THEY DECLARE THAT THEY ARE NOT LIKE US.
THAT THEY ARE... OTHER.
SIR... ?
THERE ARE SOME HIDDEN AMONG US WHO COULD END ALL LIFE ON THIS PLANET IN A HEARTBEAT, WERE THEY SO INCLINED.
WE WOULD NEVER ALLOW A RIVAL NATION TO DEVELOP SUCH CATASTROPHIC POWER.
AND YET WE SIMPLY TRUST THESE BEINGS TO LURK AMONG US--UNREGULATED, ANONYMOUS AND UNACCOUNTABLE.
WHO ARE THESE PEOPLE? WHO DO THEY ANSWER TO?
AND WHO WILL STAND AGAINST THEM WHEN THEY DECIDE OUR VALUES ARE NO LONGER THEIR OWN?
OUR LEADERS? NO. THEY HAVE ALREADY ADMITTED DEFEAT.
THEY GROVEL AND PLEAD AND LOOK THE OTHER WAY AND PRAY THEIR BRIGHTLY COLORED GODS WILL NOT BE ANGRY WITH THEM.
WELL, I DON'T BELIEVE IN GODS. I BELIEVE IN PEOPLE.
IT IS WITHIN OURSELVES THAT WE WILL FIND THE MEANS OF OUR SALVATION.
AND TOGETHER WE WILL MAKE THIS A PLANET FIT FOR HUMAN BEINGS AGAIN.
FOR THAT REASON, I HAVE TAKEN STEPS TO SECURE OUR NATIONAL DEFENSE SYSTEMS.
MY G.I. ROBOTS HAVE TAKEN CONTROL OF OUR ARMY BASES AND MISSILE SILOS.
FOR YOUR OWN SECURITY, MARTIAL LAW HAS BEEN DECLARED. A DAYTIME CURFEW WILL GO INTO EFFECT AS OF NOON TODAY.
VIOLATORS WILL BE DEALT WITH SEVERELY.
STAY INSIDE YOUR HOMES. REMAIN CALM. AND WAIT.

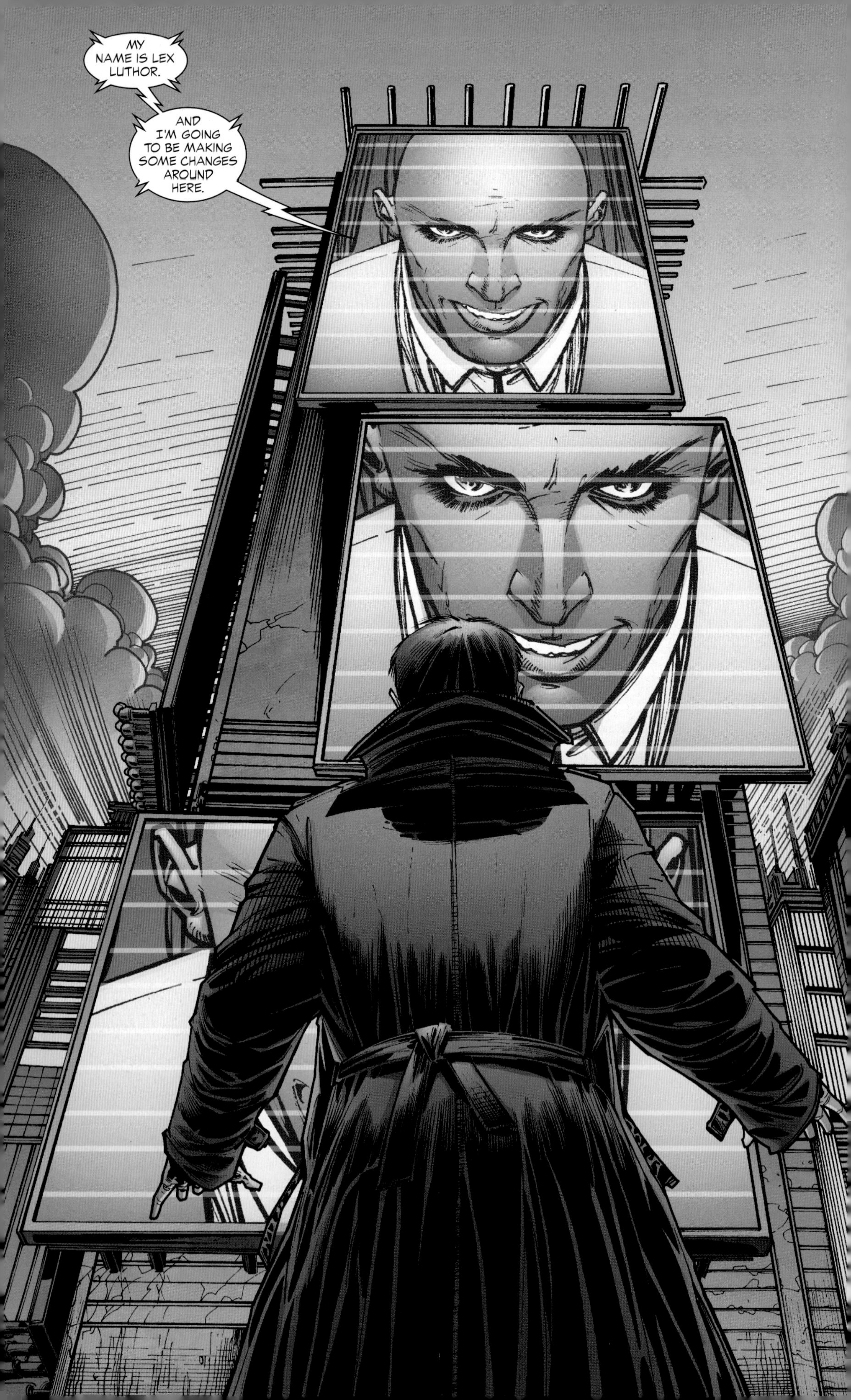
MY NAME IS LEX LUTHOR.
AND I'M GOING TO BE MAKING SOME CHANGES AROUND HERE.

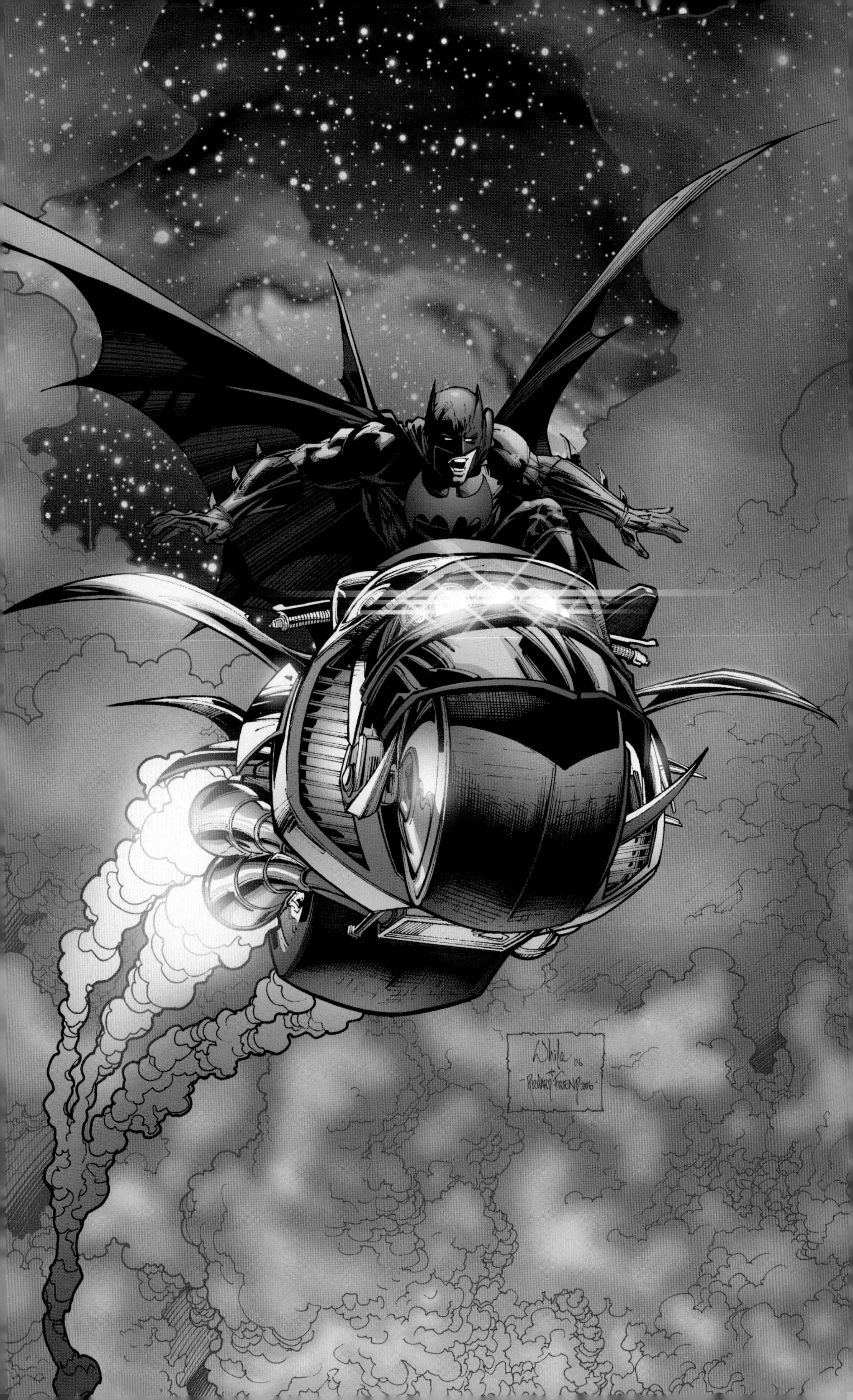

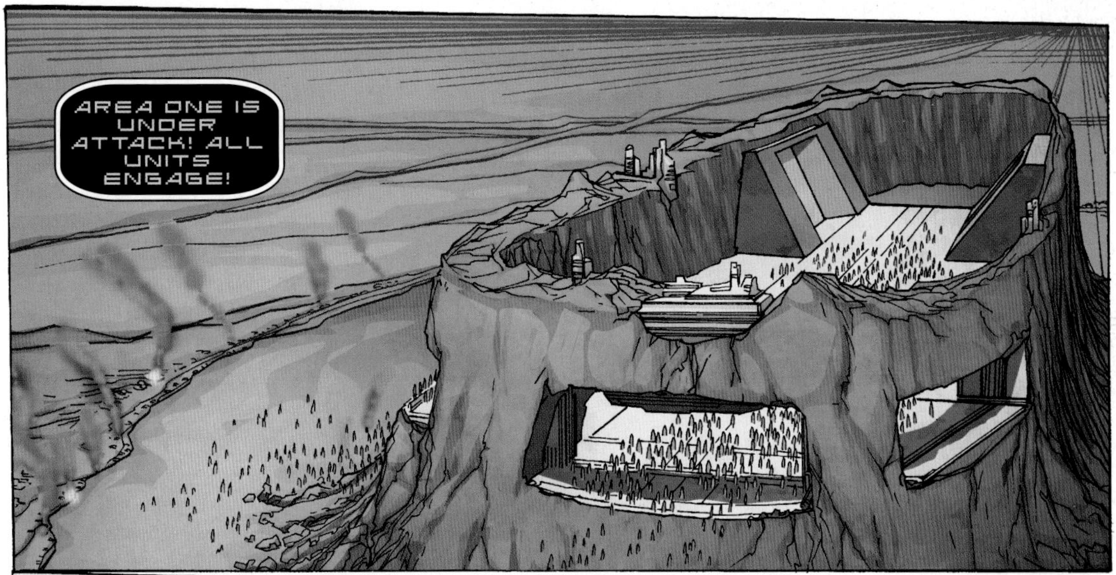
AREA ONE IS UNDER ATTACK! ALL UNITS ENGAGE!

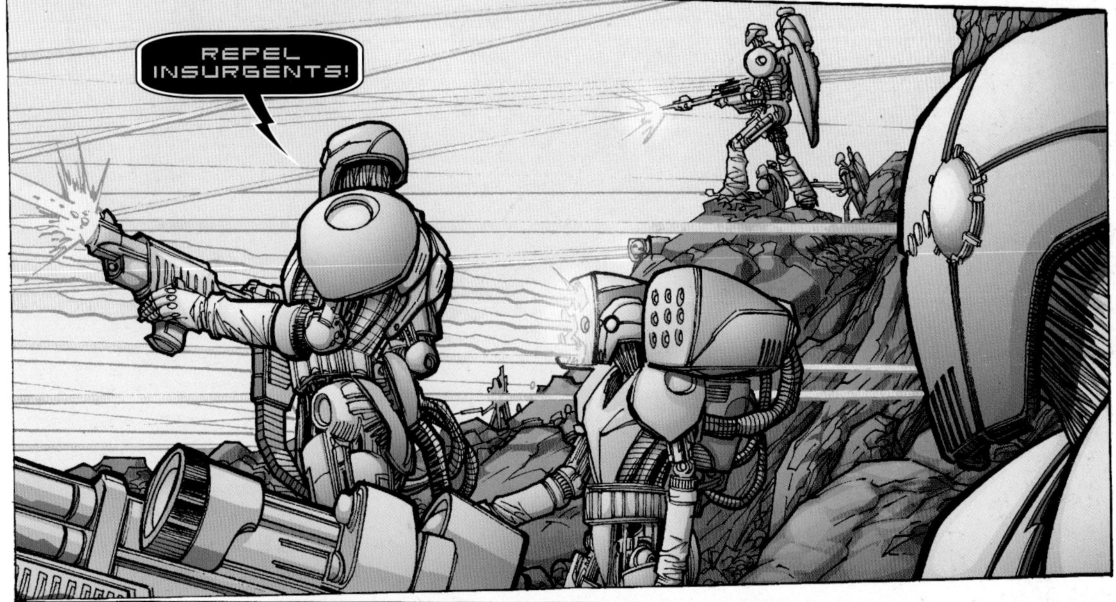
REPEL INSURGENTS!

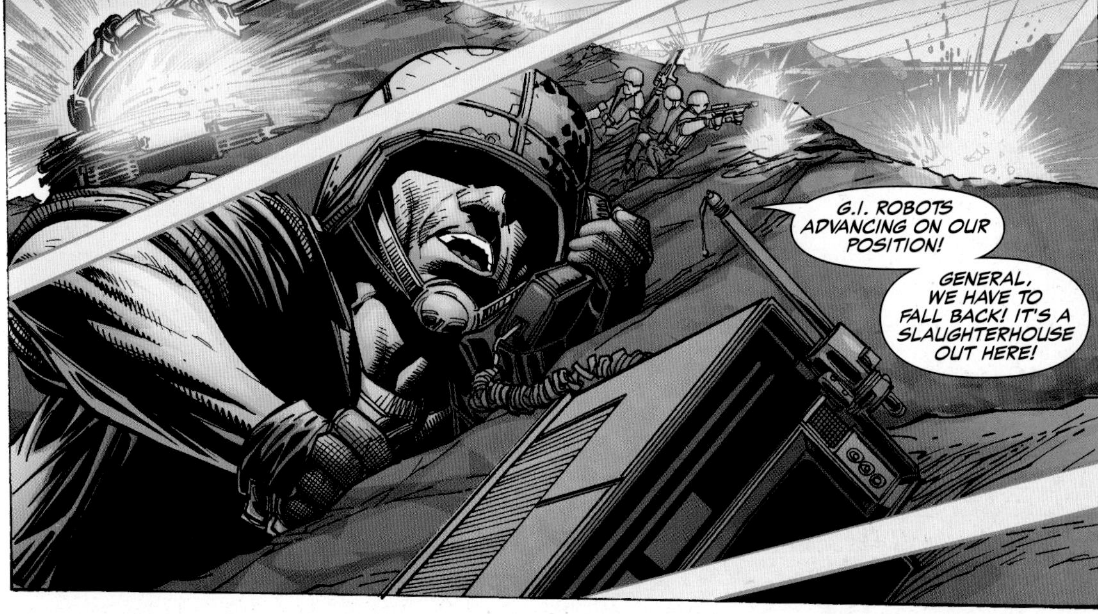
G.I. ROBOTS ADVANCING ON OUR POSITION!
GENERAL, WE HAVE TO FALL BACK! IT'S A SLAUGHTERHOUSE OUT HERE!

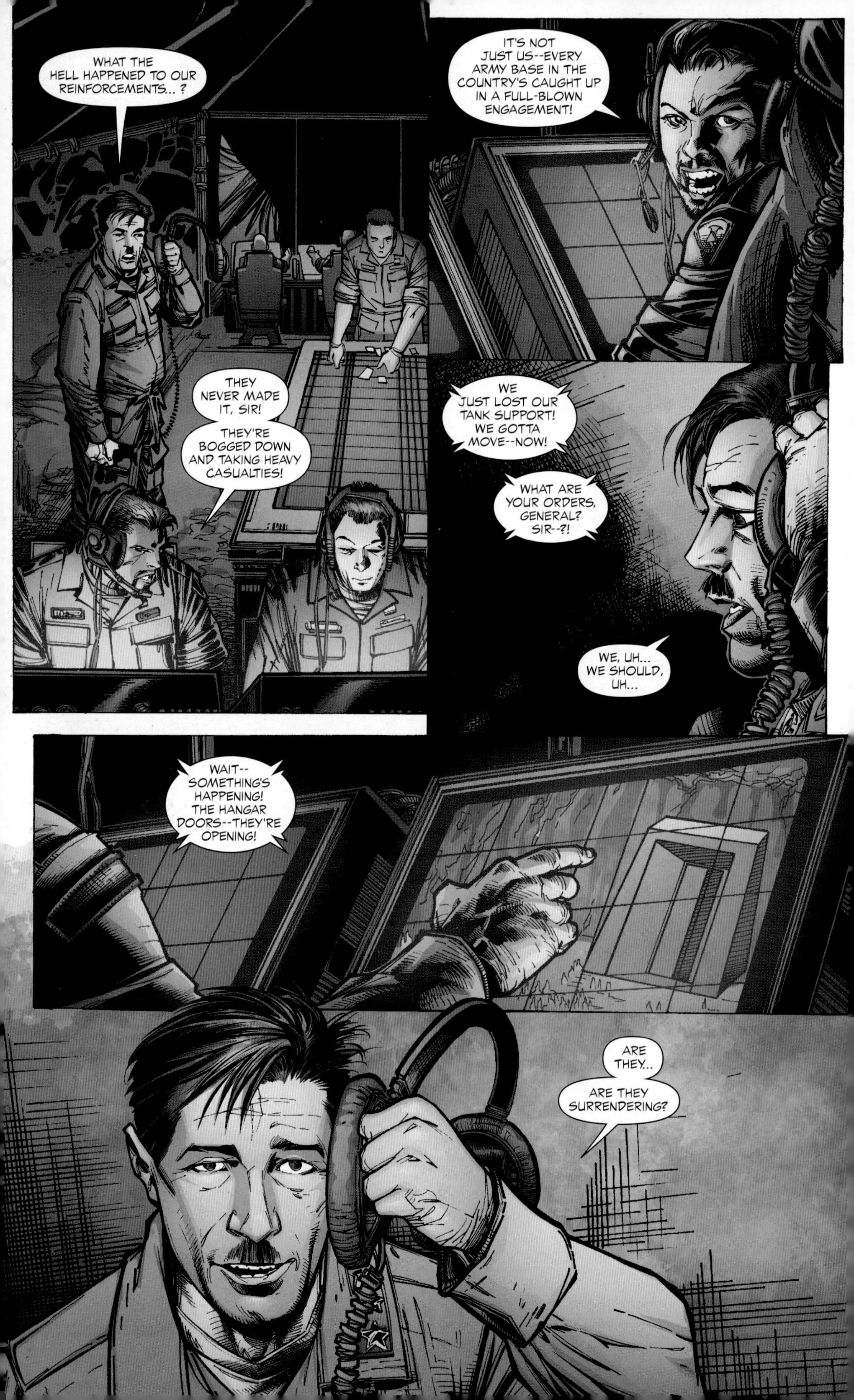
WHAT THE HELL HAPPENED TO OUR REINFORCEMENTS... ?
THEY NEVER MADE IT, SIR!
THEY'RE BOGGED DOWN AND TAKING HEAVY CASUALTIES!
IT'S NOT JUST US--EVERY ARMY BASE IN THE COUNTRY'S CAUGHT UP IN A FULL-BLOWN ENGAGEMENT!
WE JUST LOST OUR TANK SUPPORT! WE GOTTA MOVE--NOW!
WHAT ARE YOUR ORDERS, GENERAL? SIR--?!
WE, UH... WE SHOULD, UH...
WAIT--SOMETHING'S HAPPENING! THE HANGAR DOORS--THEY'RE OPENING!
ARE THEY...
ARE THEY SURRENDERING?

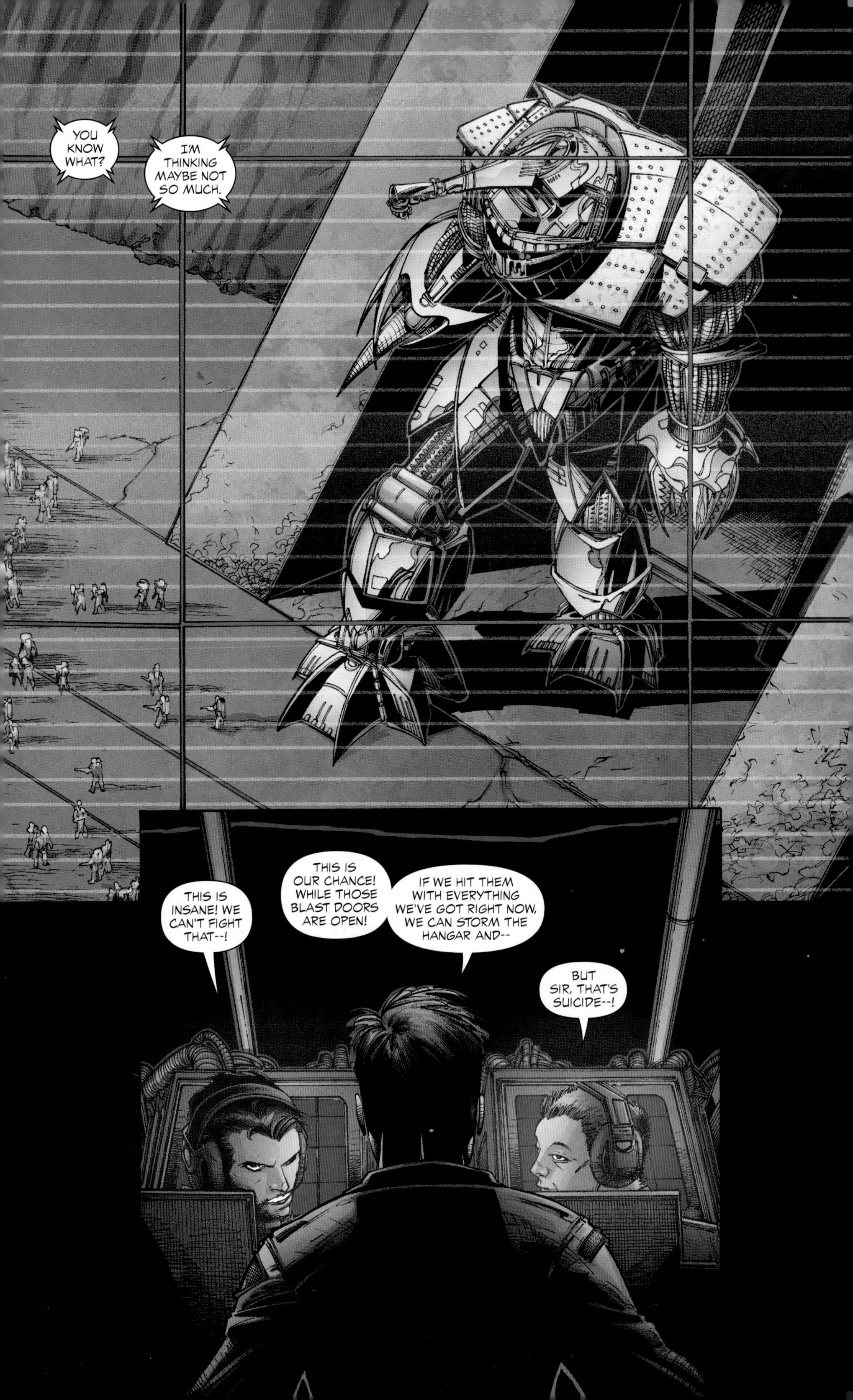
YOU KNOW WHAT?
I'M THINKING MAYBE NOT SO MUCH.
THIS IS INSANE! WE CAN'T FIGHT THAT--!
THIS IS OUR CHANCE! WHILE THOSE BLAST DOORS ARE OPEN!
IF WE HIT THEM WITH EVERYTHING WE'VE GOT RIGHT NOW, WE CAN STORM THE HANGAR AND--
BUT SIR, THAT'S SUICIDE--!

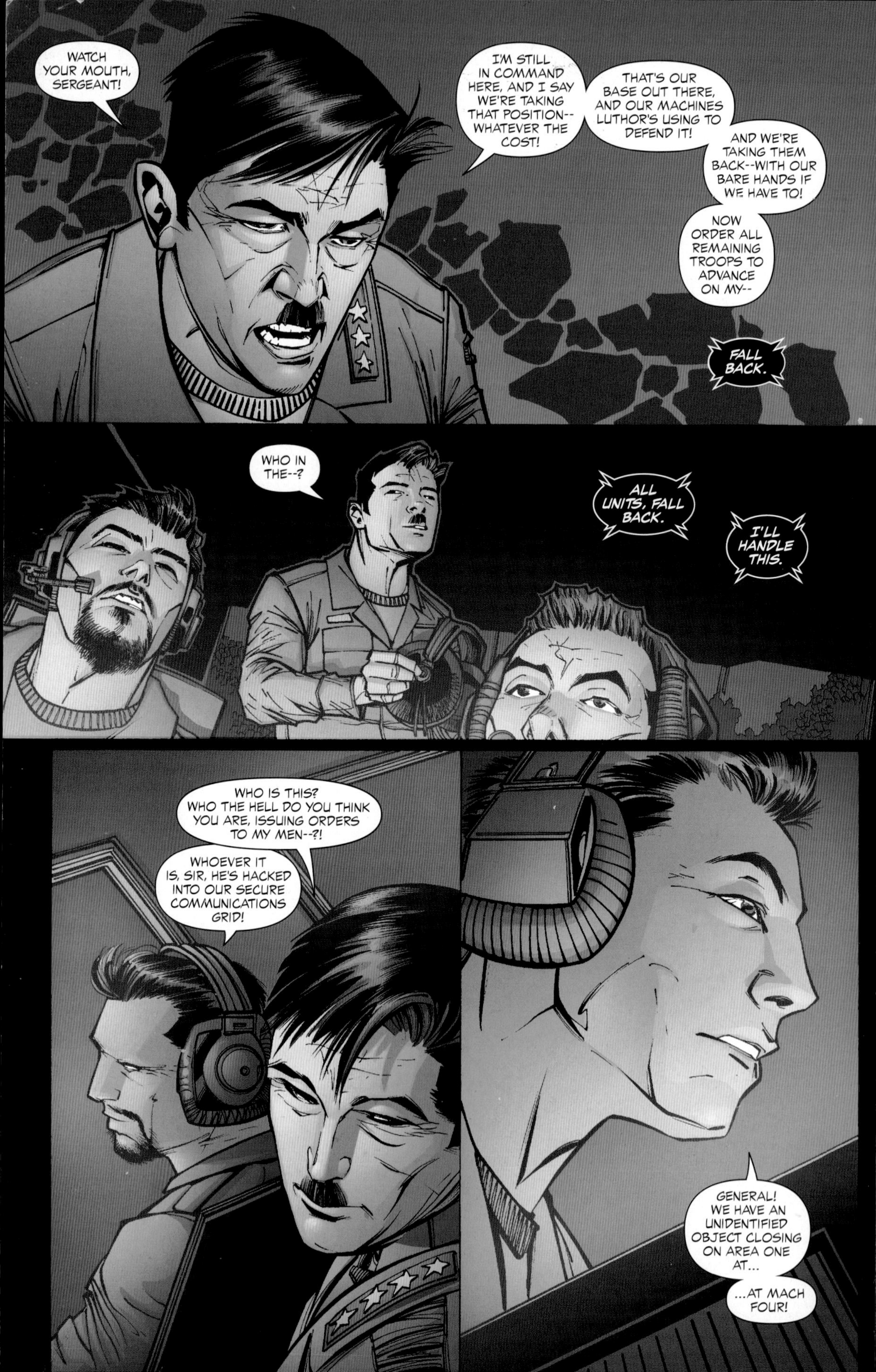
WATCH YOUR MOUTH, SERGEANT!
I'M STILL IN COMMAND HERE, AND I SAY WE'RE TAKING THAT POSITION--WHATEVER THE COST!
THAT'S OUR BASE OUT THERE, AND OUR MACHINES LUTHOR'S USING TO DEFEND IT!
AND WE'RE TAKING THEM BACK--WITH OUR BARE HANDS IF WE HAVE TO!
NOW ORDER ALL REMAINING TROOPS TO ADVANCE ON MY--
FALL BACK.
WHO IN THE--?
ALL UNITS, FALL BACK.
I'LL HANDLE THIS.
WHO IS THIS? WHO THE HELL DO YOU THINK YOU ARE, ISSUING ORDERS TO MY MEN--?!
WHOEVER IT IS, SIR, HE'S HACKED INTO OUR SECURE COMMUNICATIONS GRID!
GENERAL! WE HAVE AN UNIDENTIFIED OBJECT CLOSING ON AREA ONE AT...
...AT MACH FOUR!

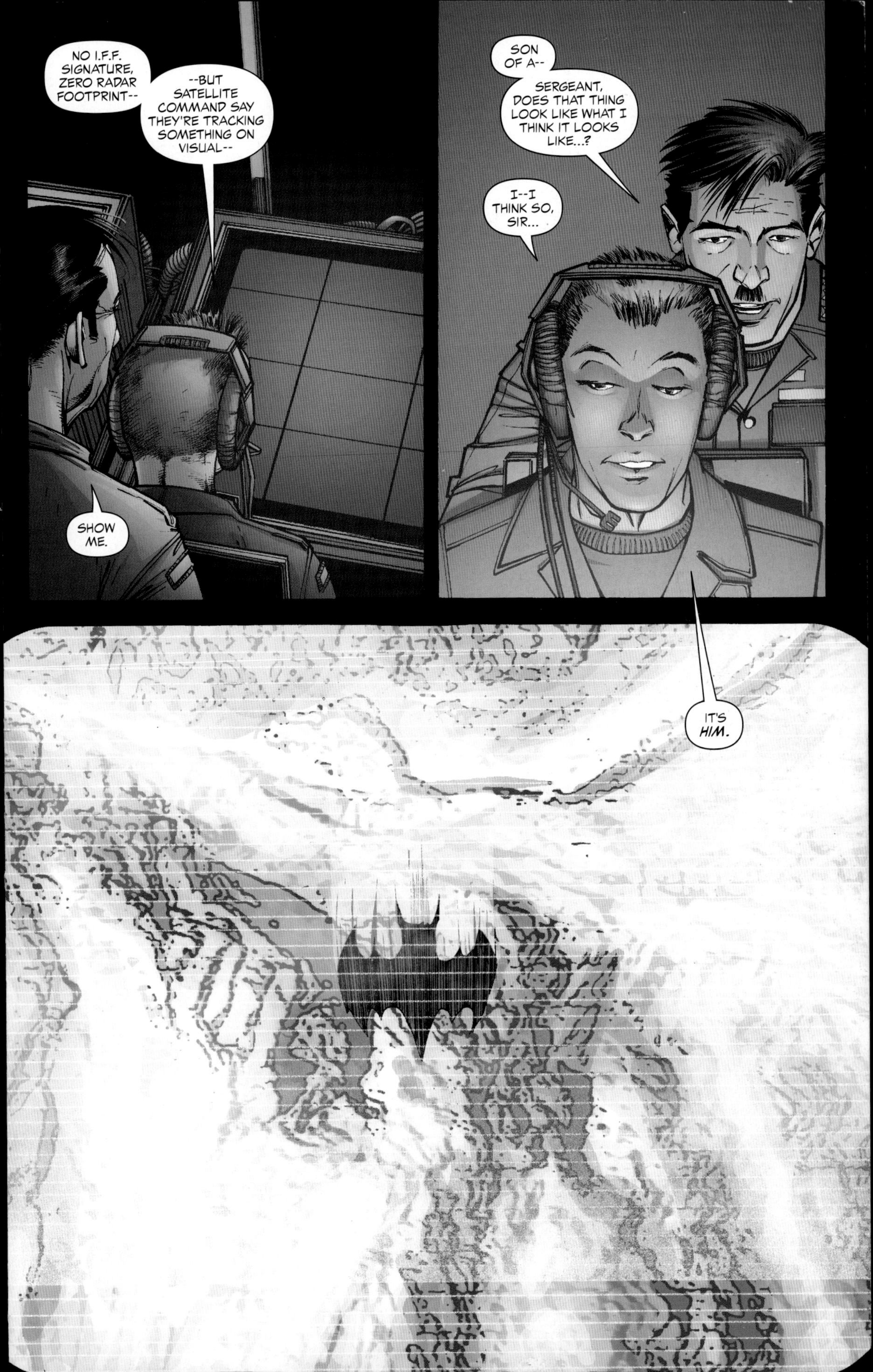
NO I.F.F. SIGNATURE, ZERO RADAR FOOTPRINT--
--BUT SATELLITE COMMAND SAY THEY'RE TRACKING SOMETHING ON VISUAL--
SHOW ME.
SON OF A--
SERGEANT, DOES THAT THING LOOK LIKE WHAT I THINK IT LOOKS LIKE...?
I--I THINK SO, SIR...
IT'S *HIM*.

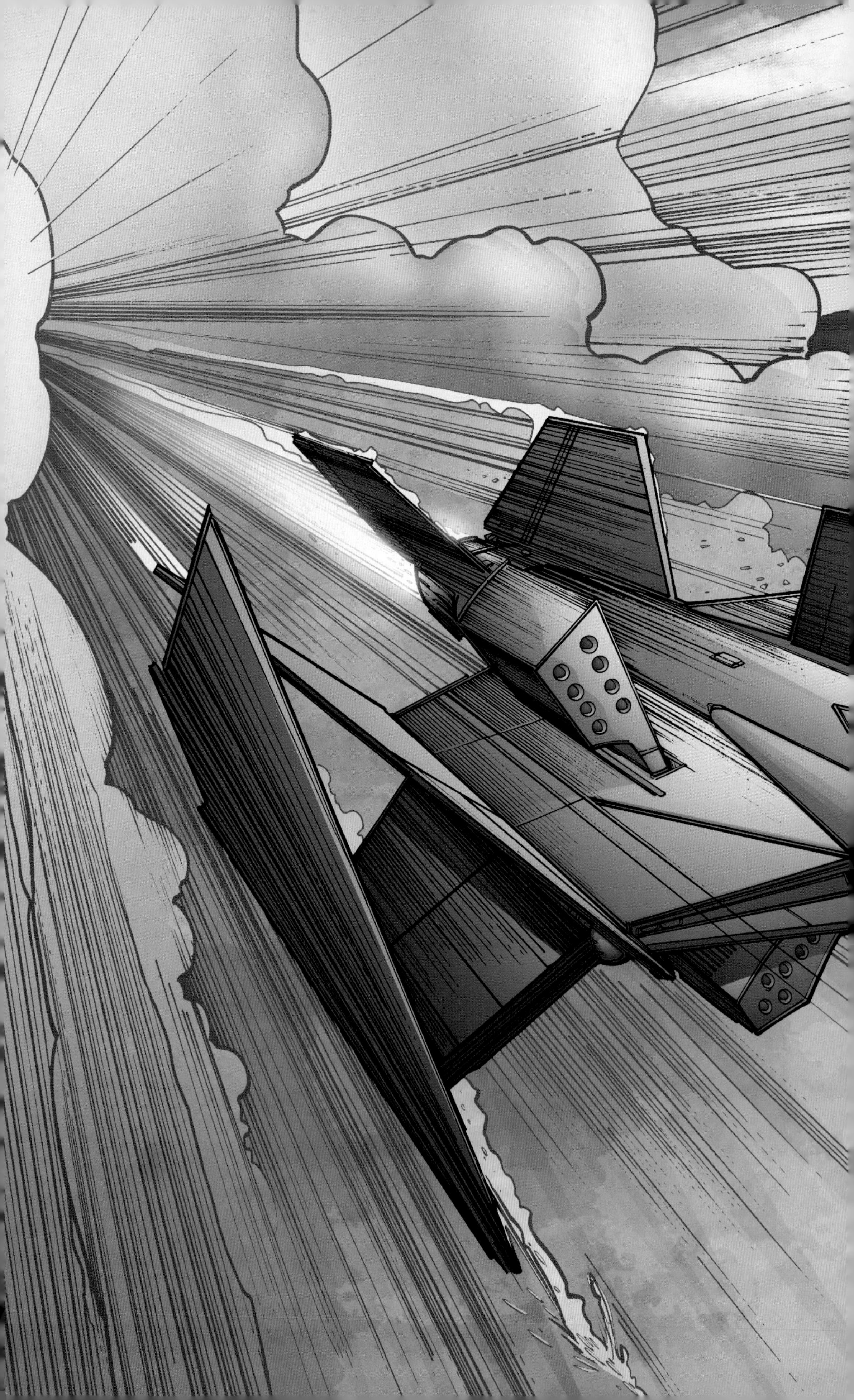

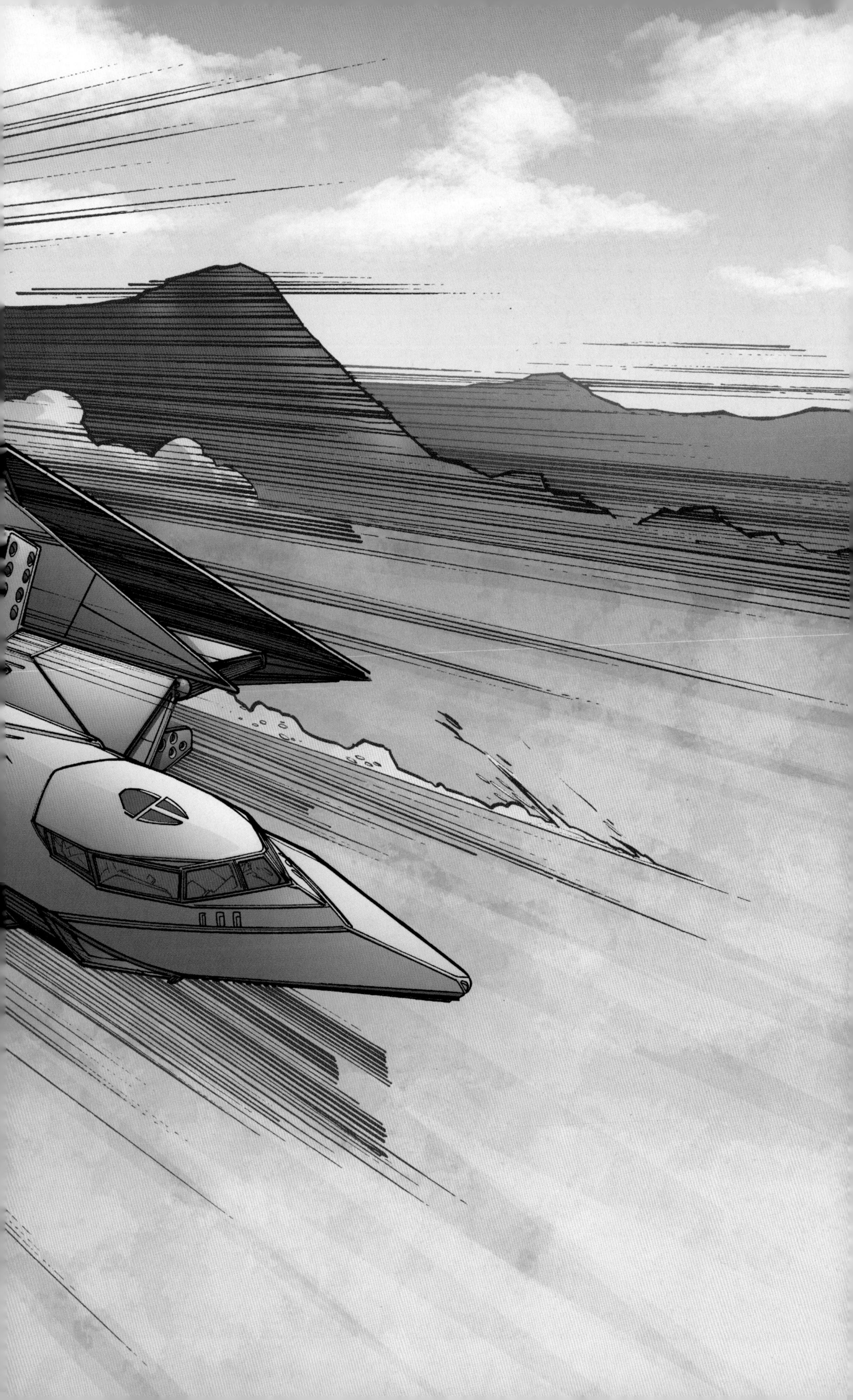

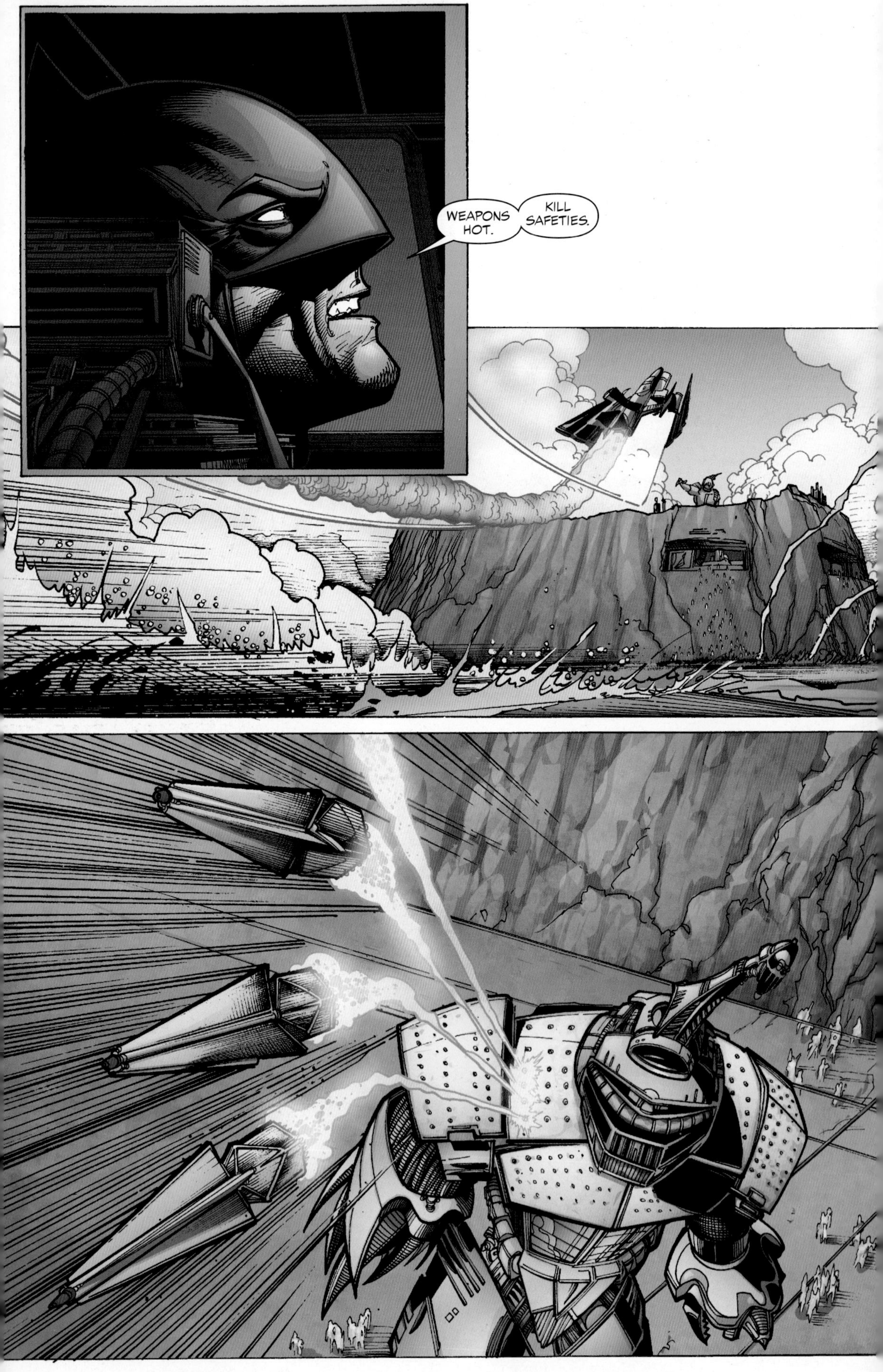
WEAPONS HOT.
KILL SAFETIES.

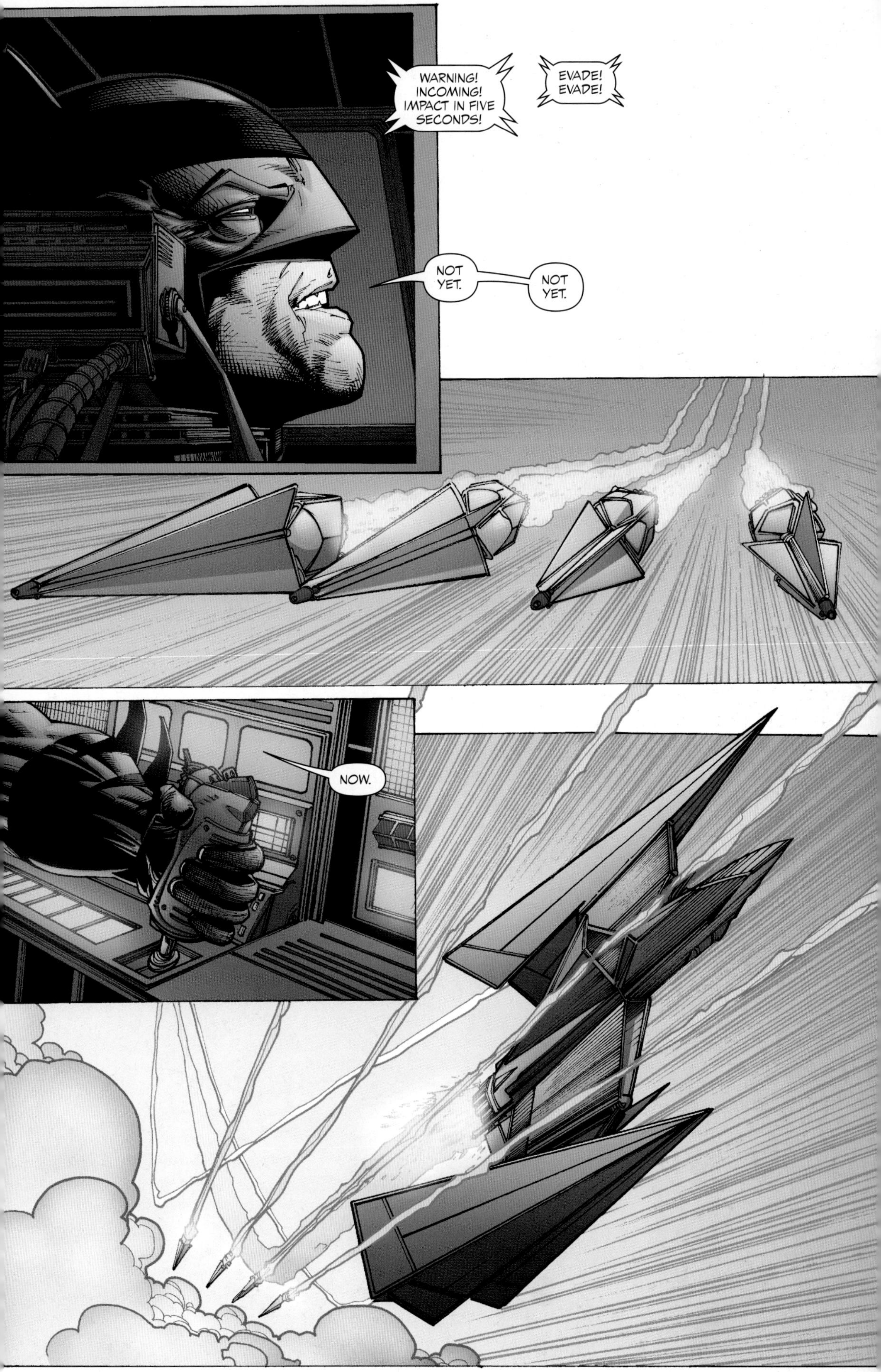
WARNING! INCOMING! IMPACT IN FIVE SECONDS!
EVADE! EVADE!
NOT YET.
NOT YET.
NOW.

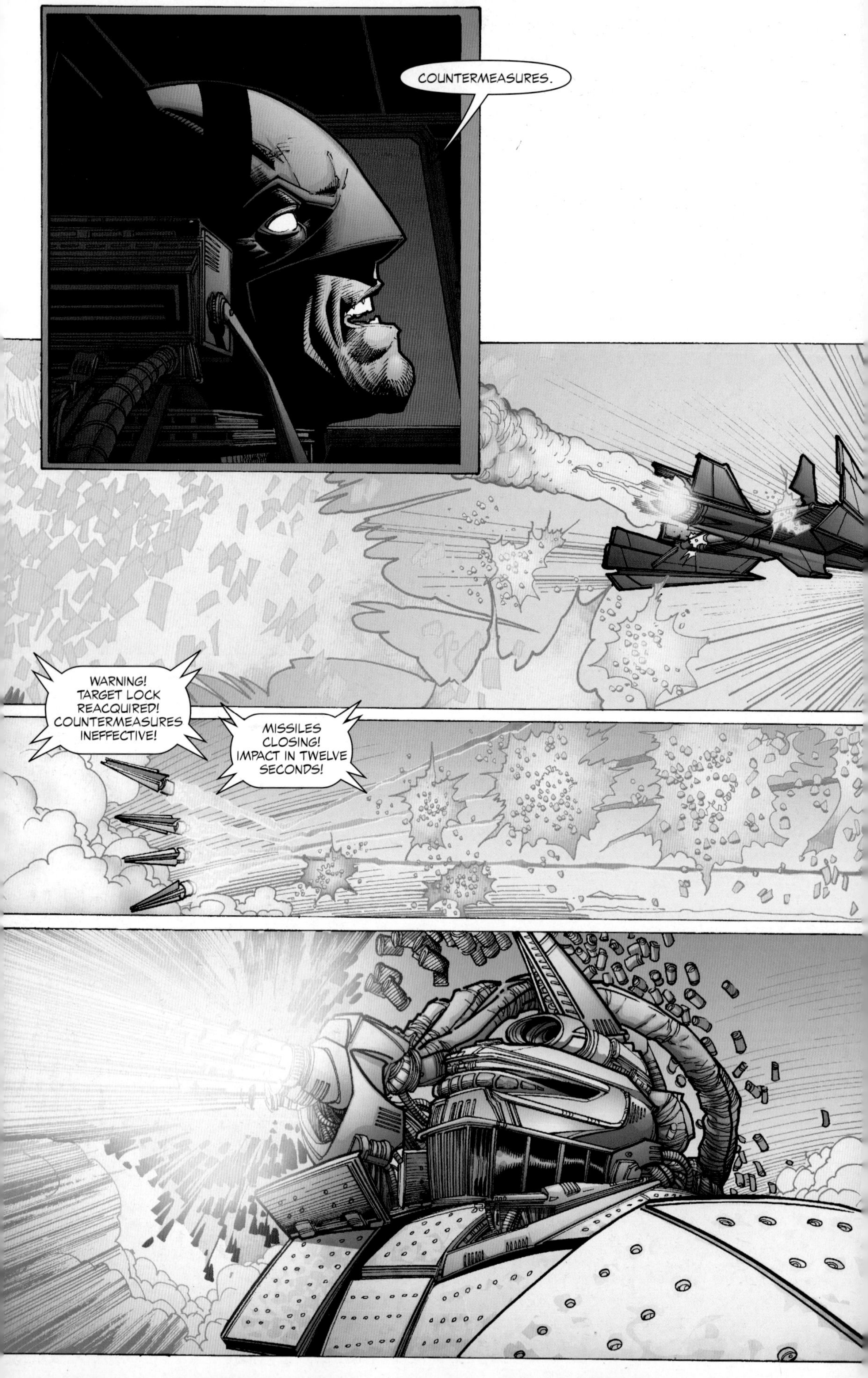
COUNTERMEASURES.
WARNING! TARGET LOCK REACQUIRED! COUNTERMEASURES INEFFECTIVE!
MISSILES CLOSING! IMPACT IN TWELVE SECONDS!

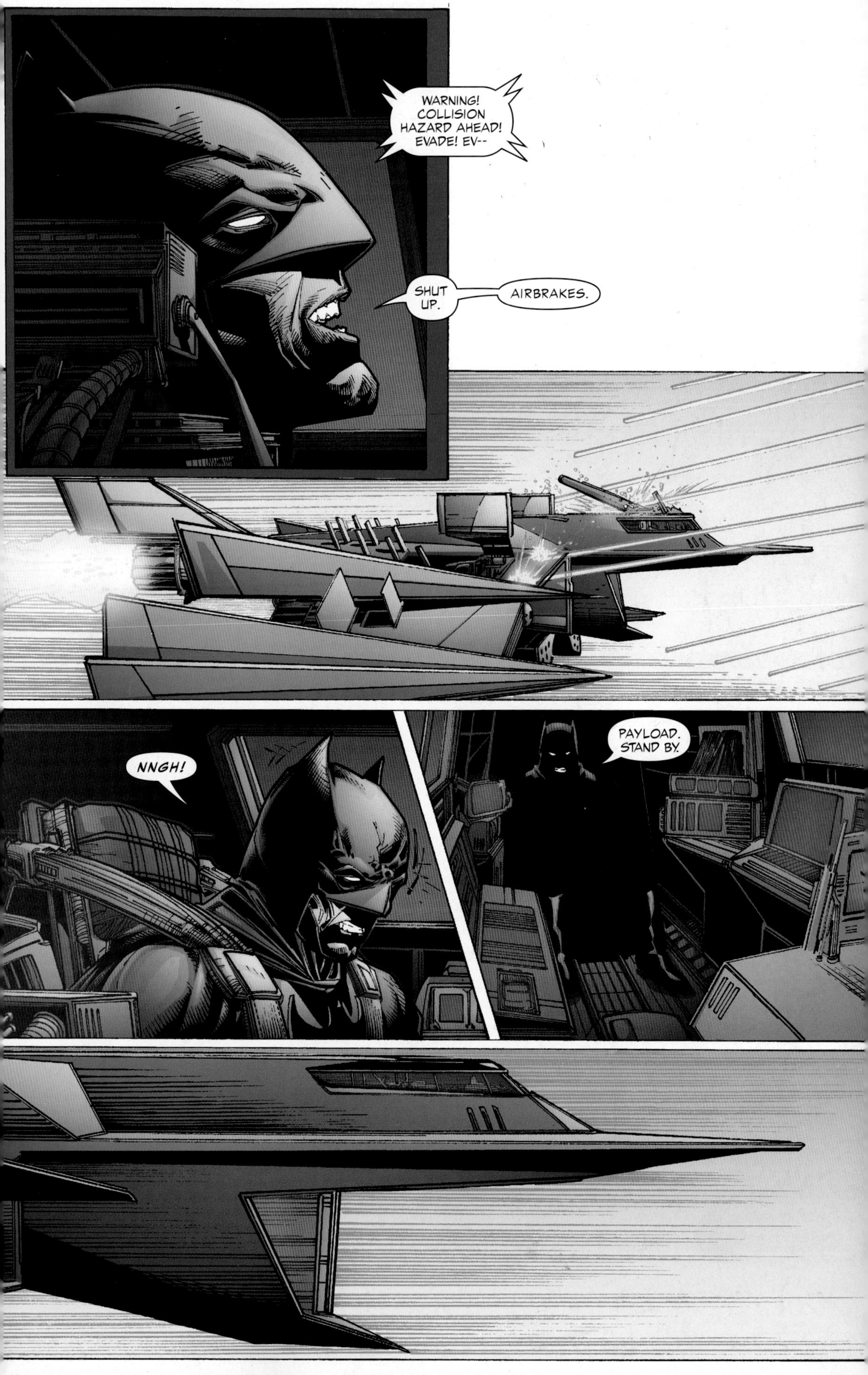
WARNING! COLLISION HAZARD AHEAD! EVADE! EV--
SHUT UP.
AIRBRAKES.
NNGH!
PAYLOAD. STAND BY.

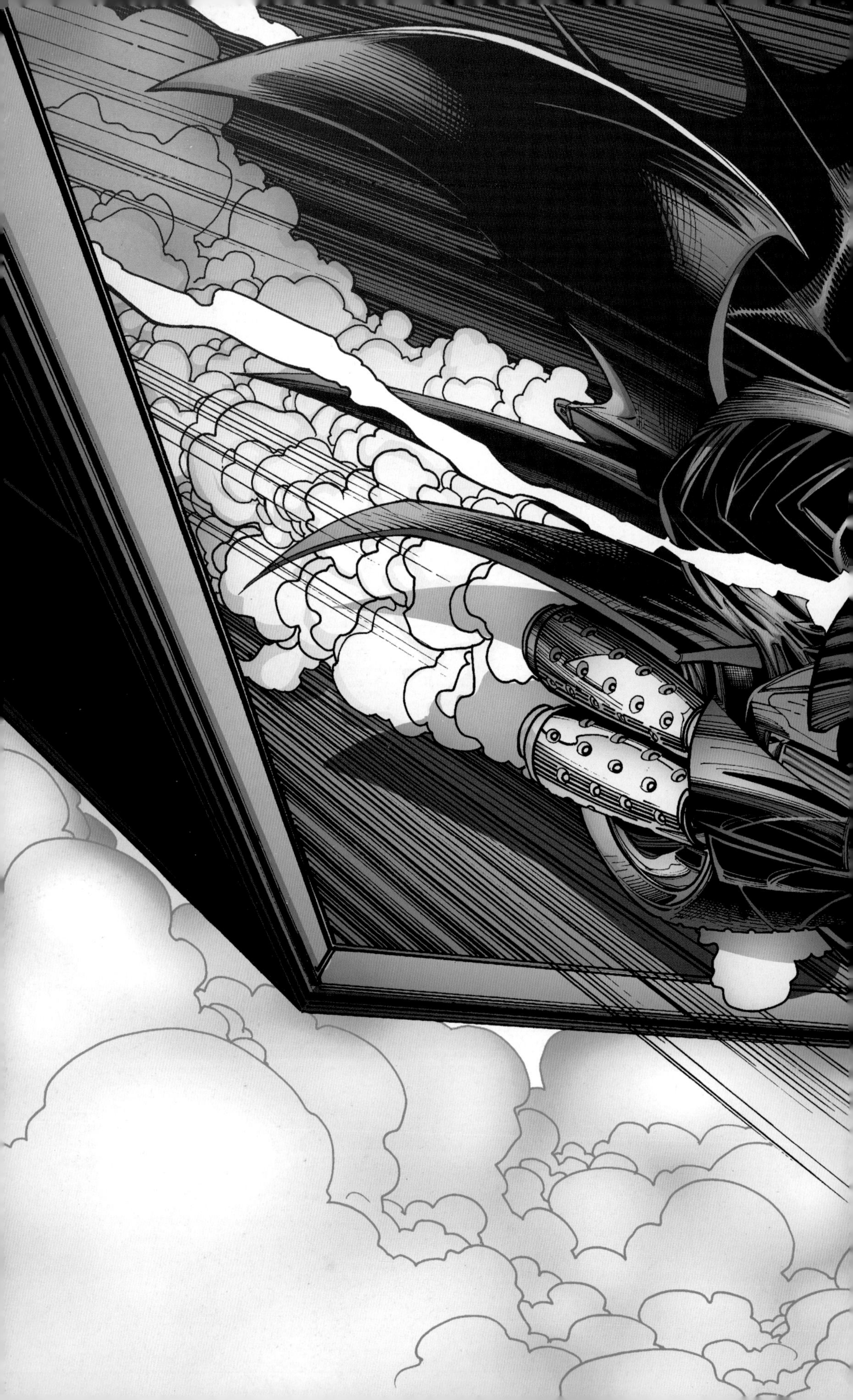

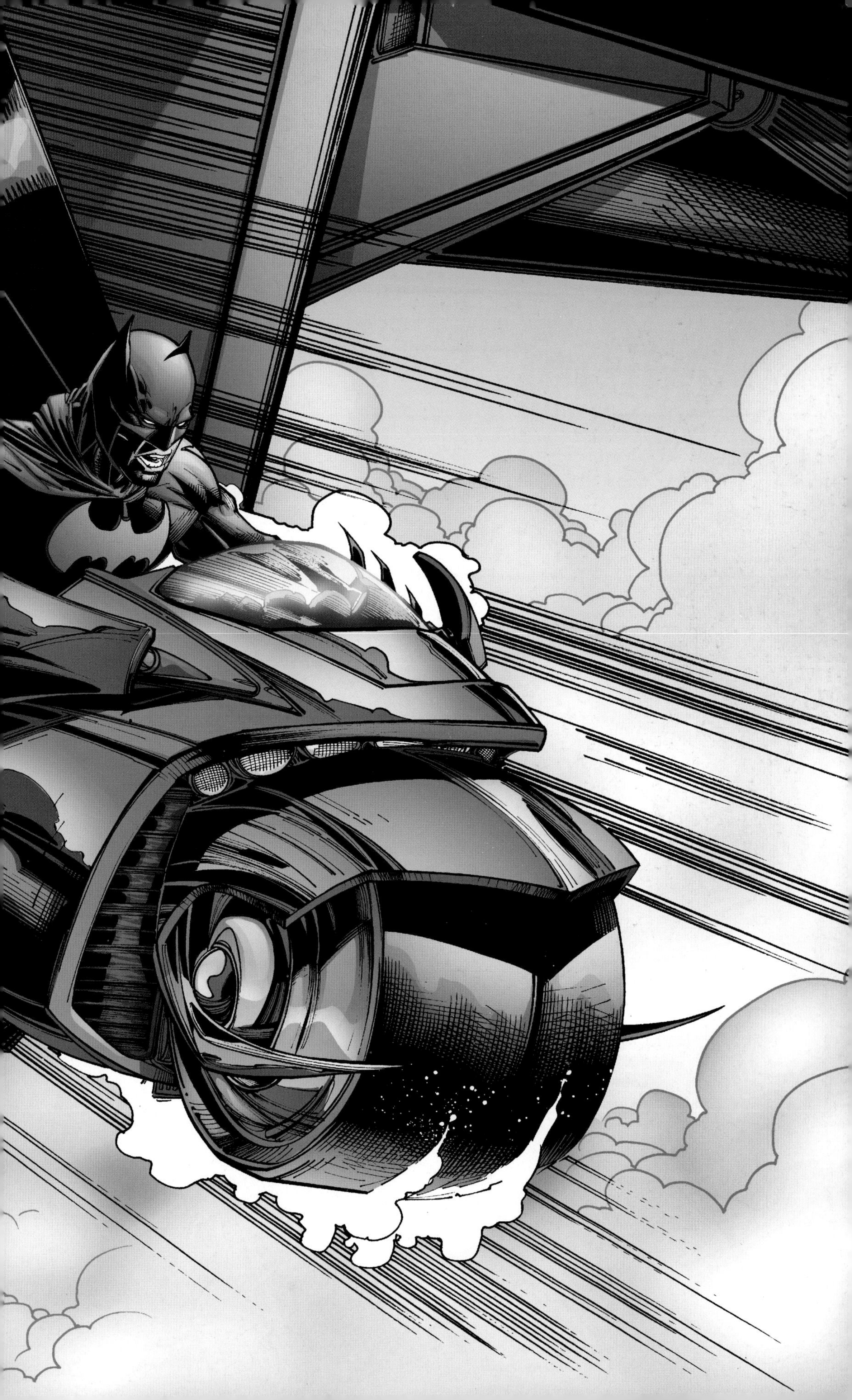

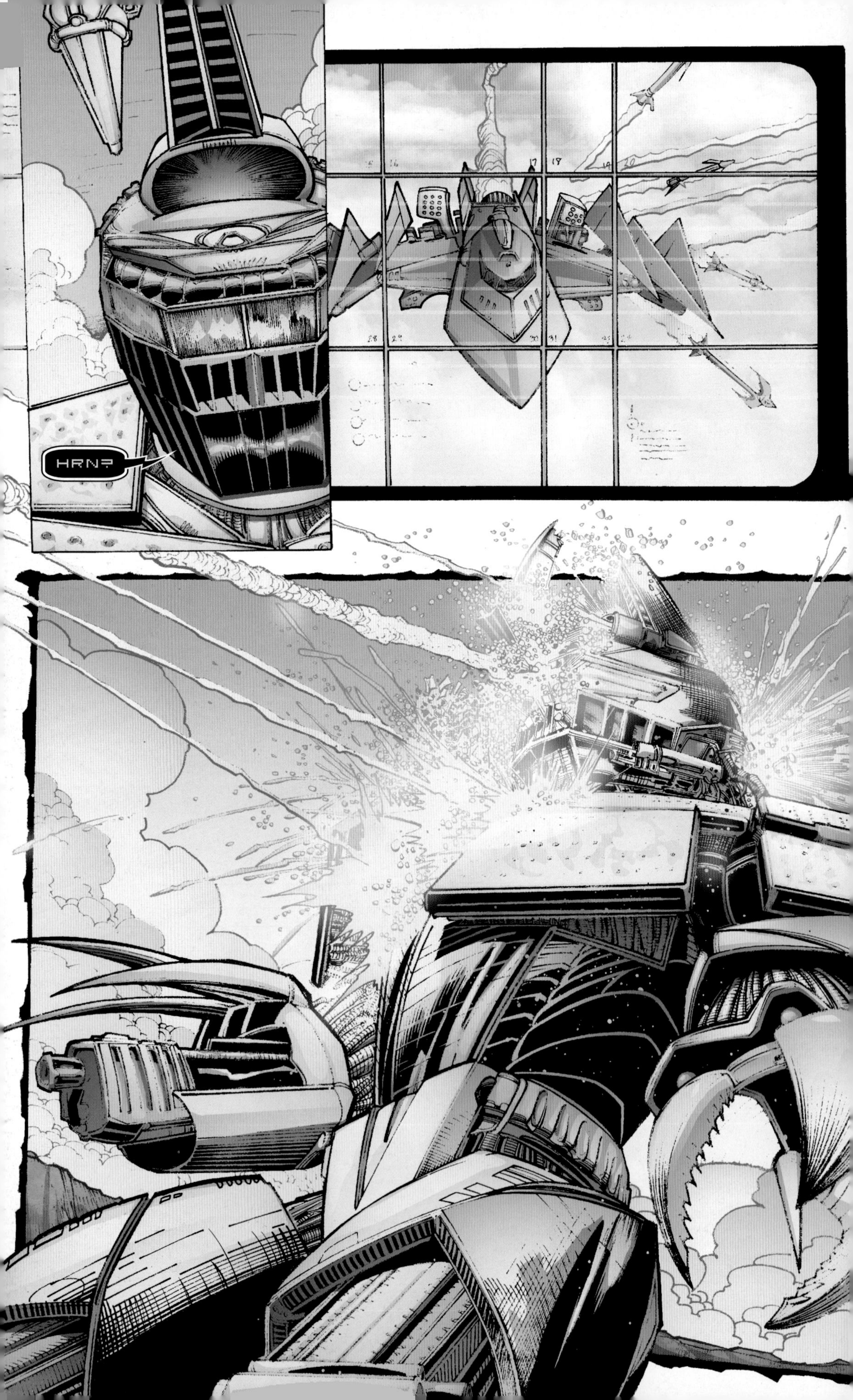
HRN?

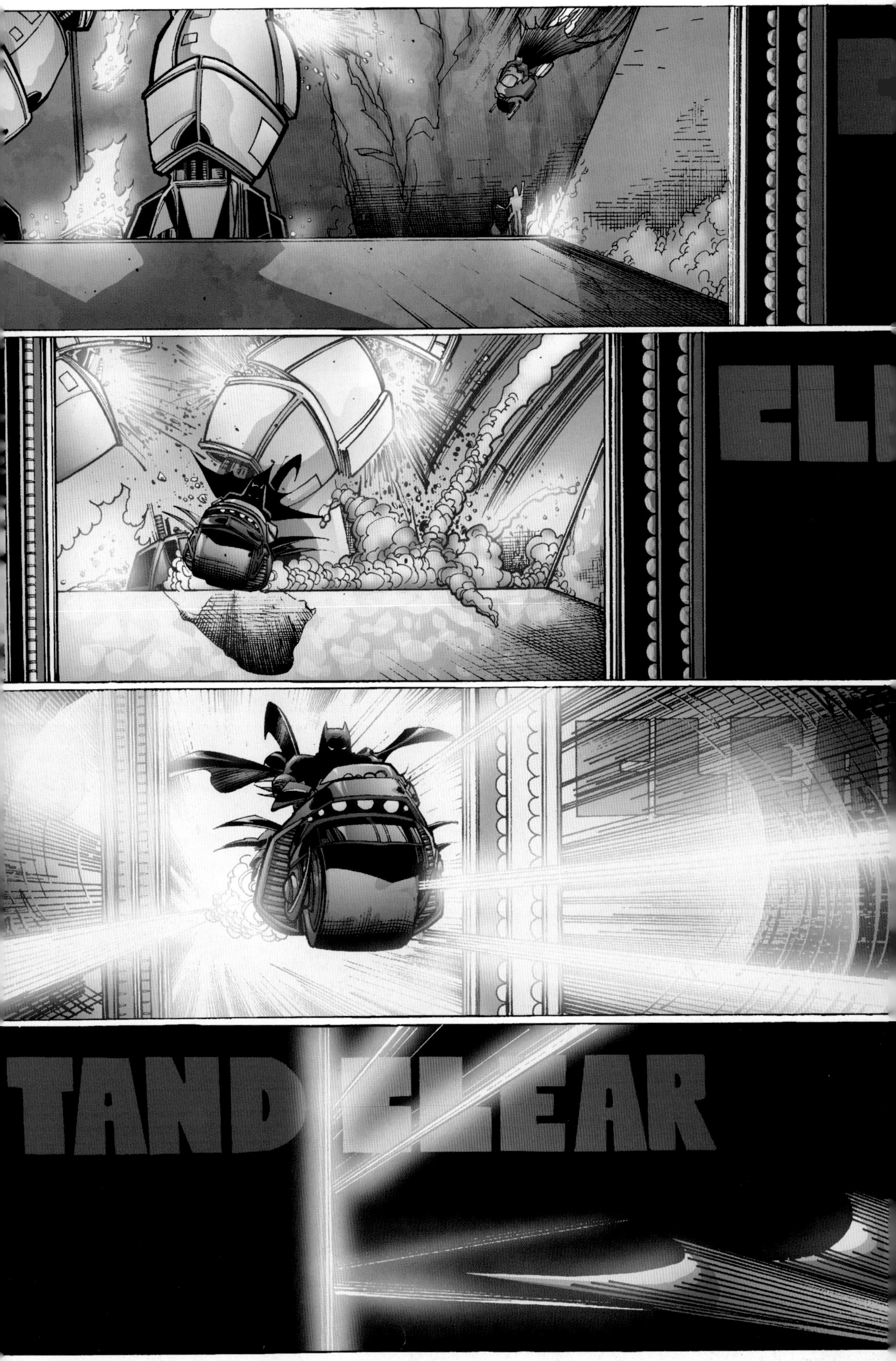
TAND LEAR

AUTO-DESTRUCT.

FIVE SECOND COUNTDOWN.

ON MY MARK.

MARK.

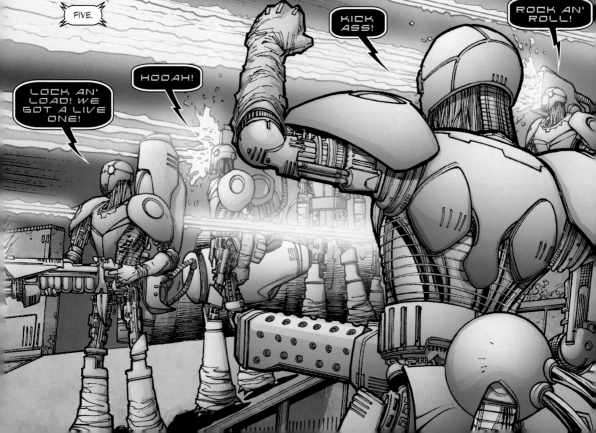

FIVE.

LOCK AN' LOAD! WE GOT A LIVE ONE!

HOOAH!

KICK ASS!

ROCK AN' ROLL!

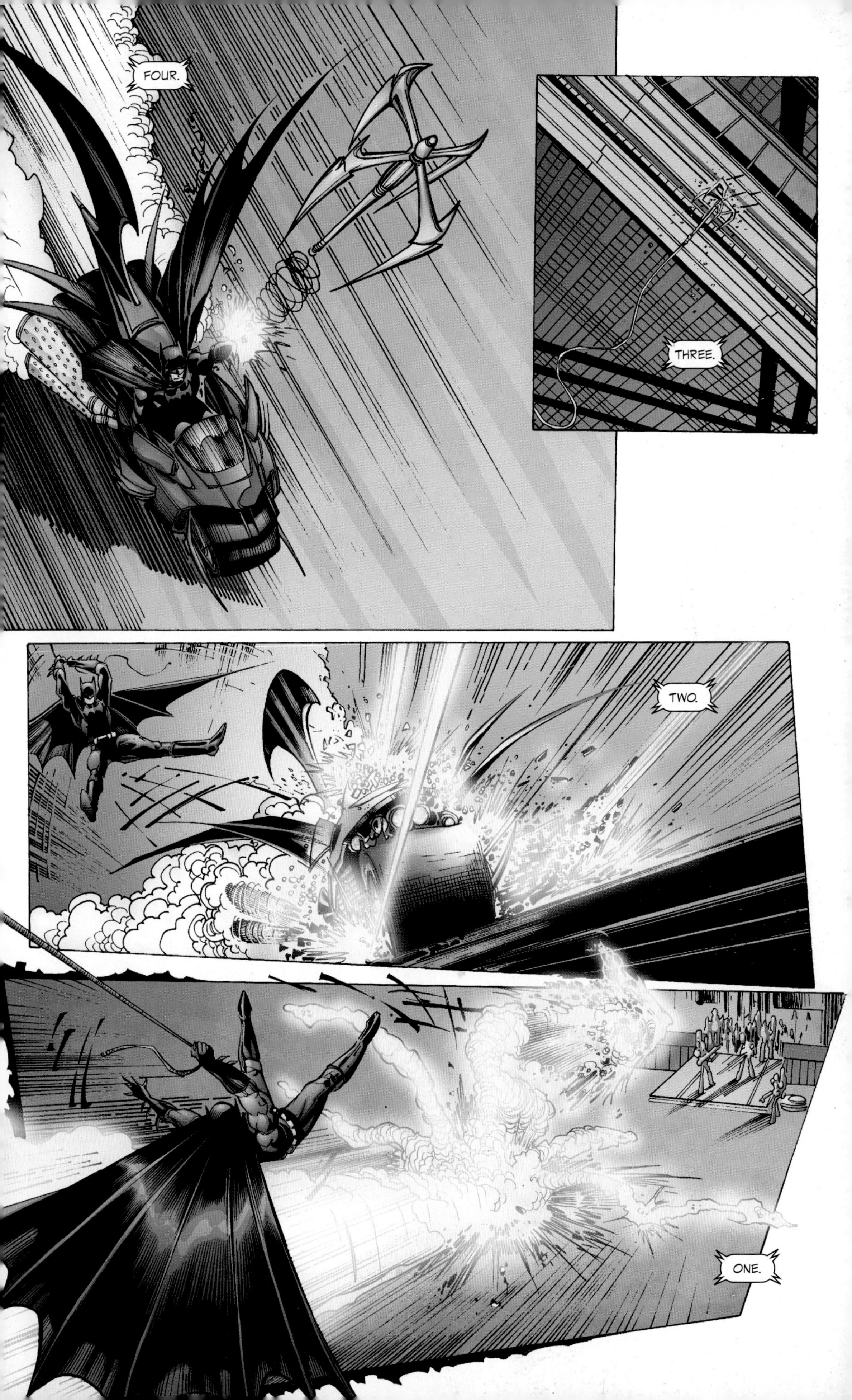
FOUR.
THREE.
TWO.
ONE.

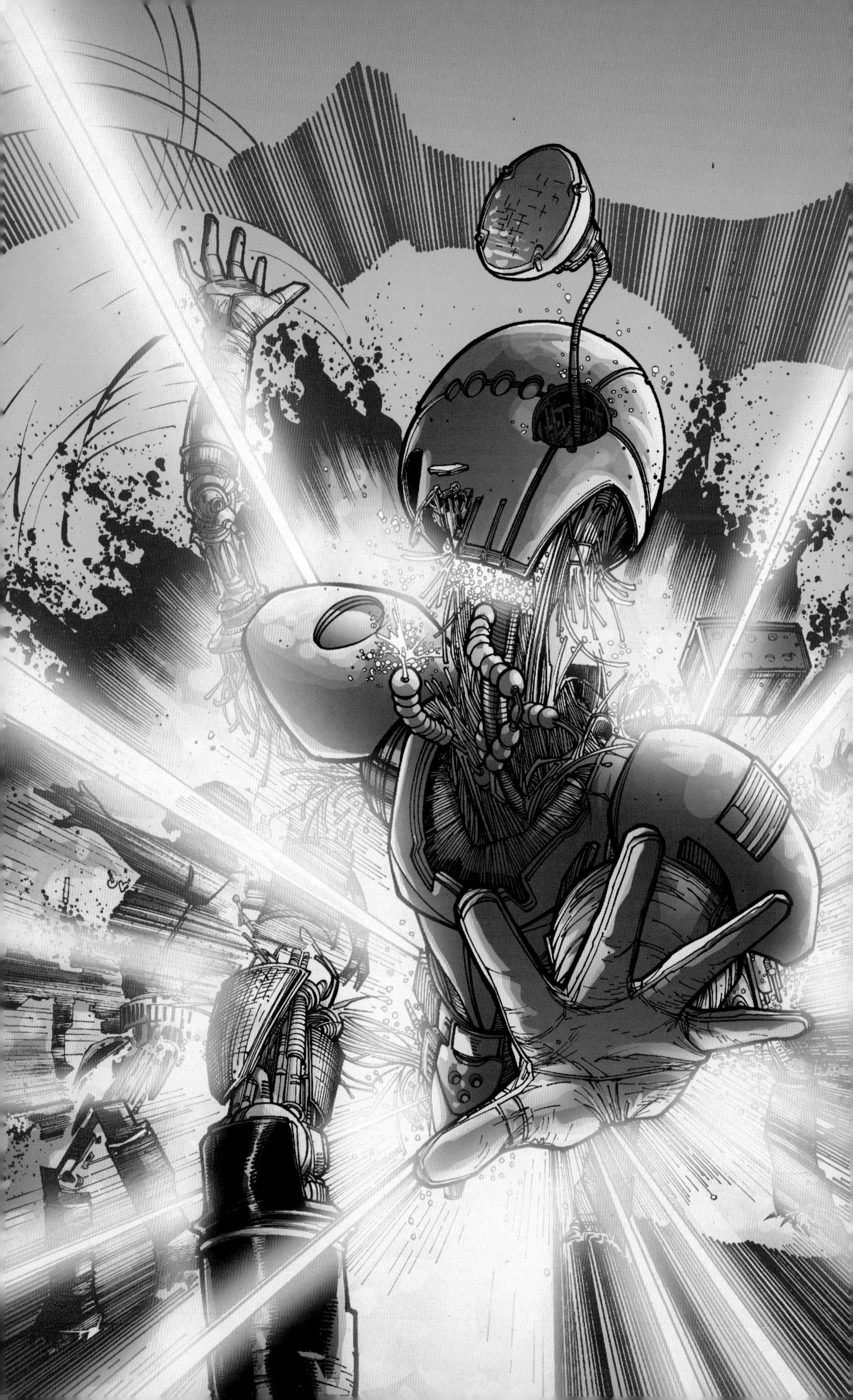

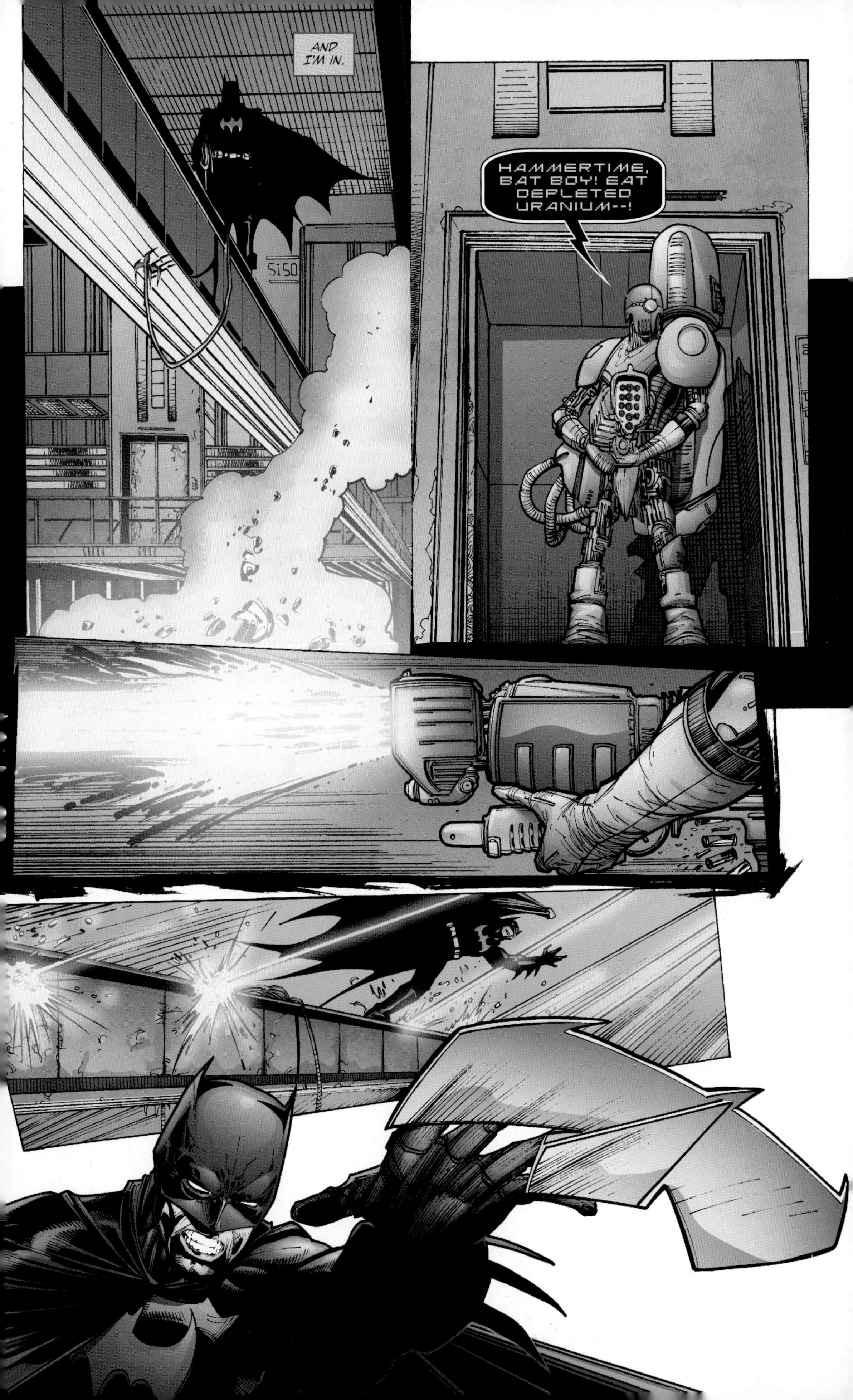
AND I'M IN.
HAMMERTIME, BAT BOY! EAT DEPLETED URANIUM--!

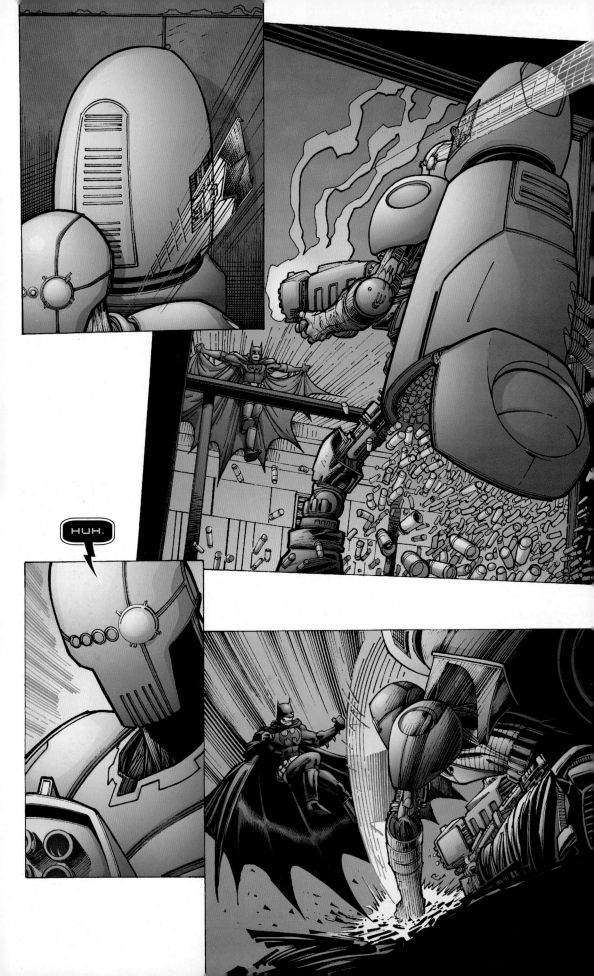

HUH.

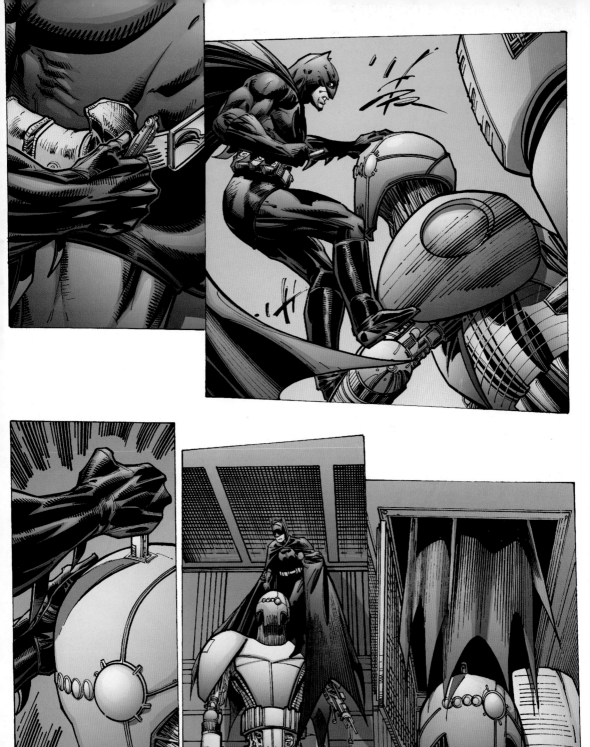

COMMAND INPUT UPDATED. STANDING BY.

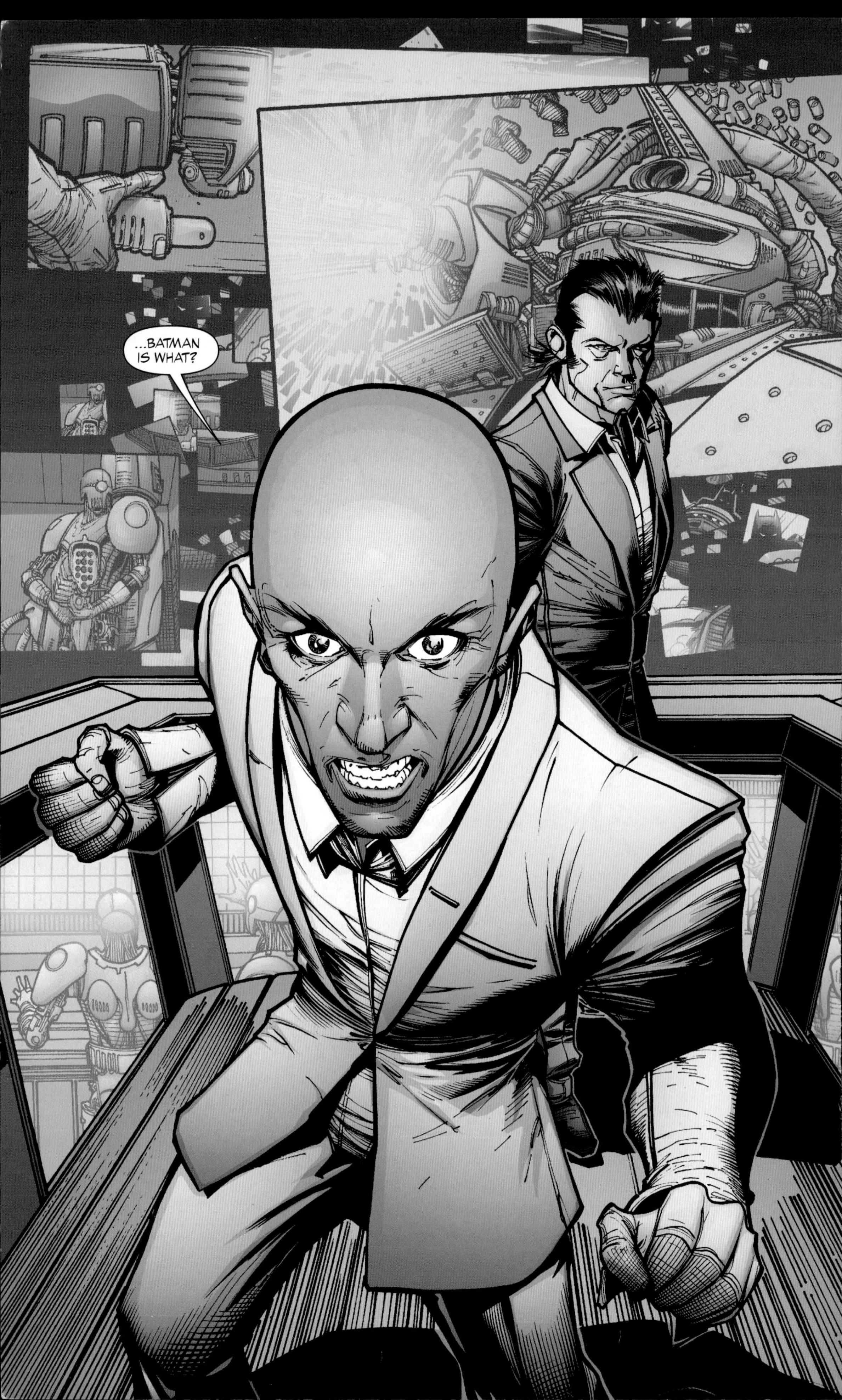
...BATMAN IS WHAT?

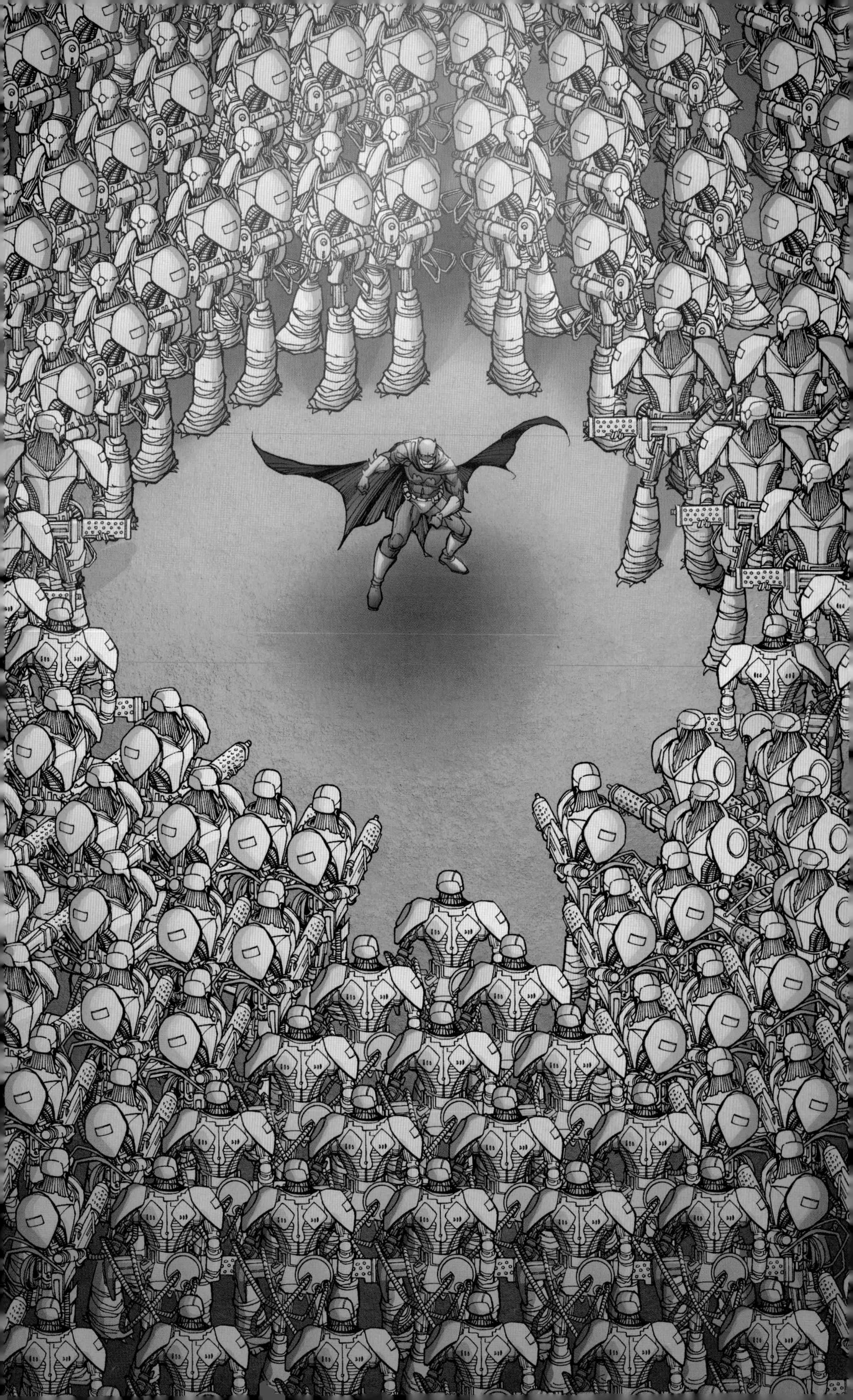

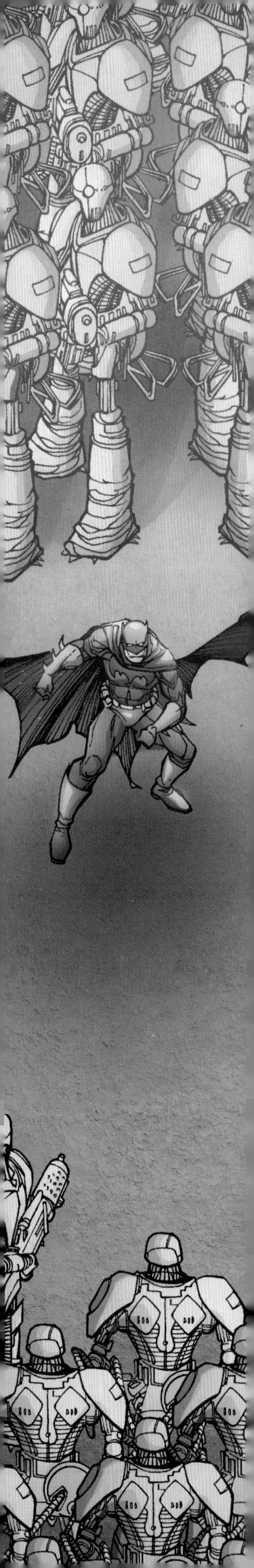

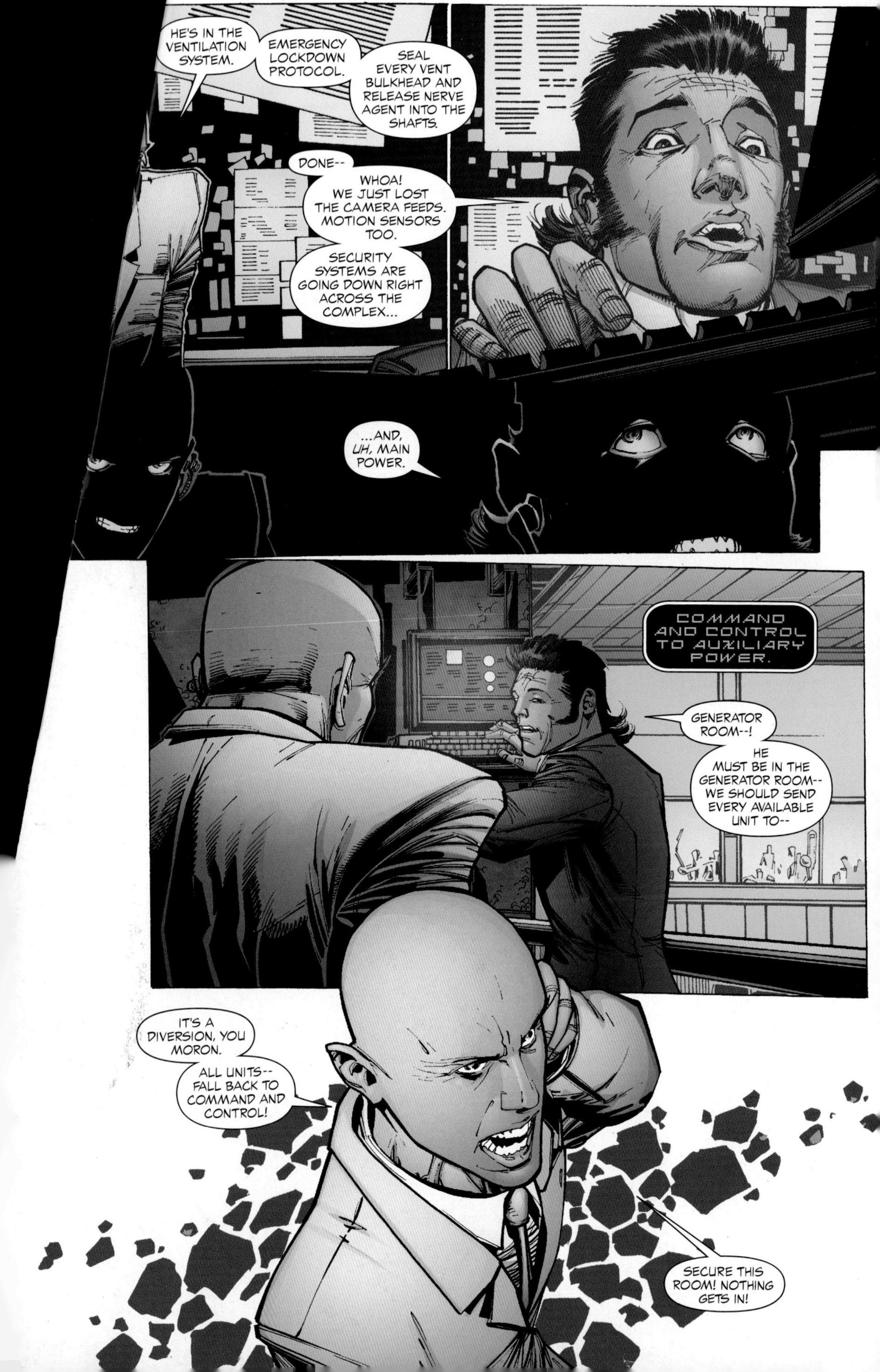
HE'S IN THE VENTILATION SYSTEM.
EMERGENCY LOCKDOWN PROTOCOL.
SEAL EVERY VENT BULKHEAD AND RELEASE NERVE AGENT INTO THE SHAFTS.
DONE--
WHOA! WE JUST LOST THE CAMERA FEEDS. MOTION SENSORS TOO.
SECURITY SYSTEMS ARE GOING DOWN RIGHT ACROSS THE COMPLEX...
...AND, *UH,* MAIN POWER.
COMMAND AND CONTROL TO AUXILIARY POWER.
GENERATOR ROOM--!
HE MUST BE IN THE GENERATOR ROOM-- WE SHOULD SEND EVERY AVAILABLE UNIT TO--
IT'S A DIVERSION, YOU MORON.
ALL UNITS-- FALL BACK TO COMMAND AND CONTROL!
SECURE THIS ROOM! NOTHING GETS IN!

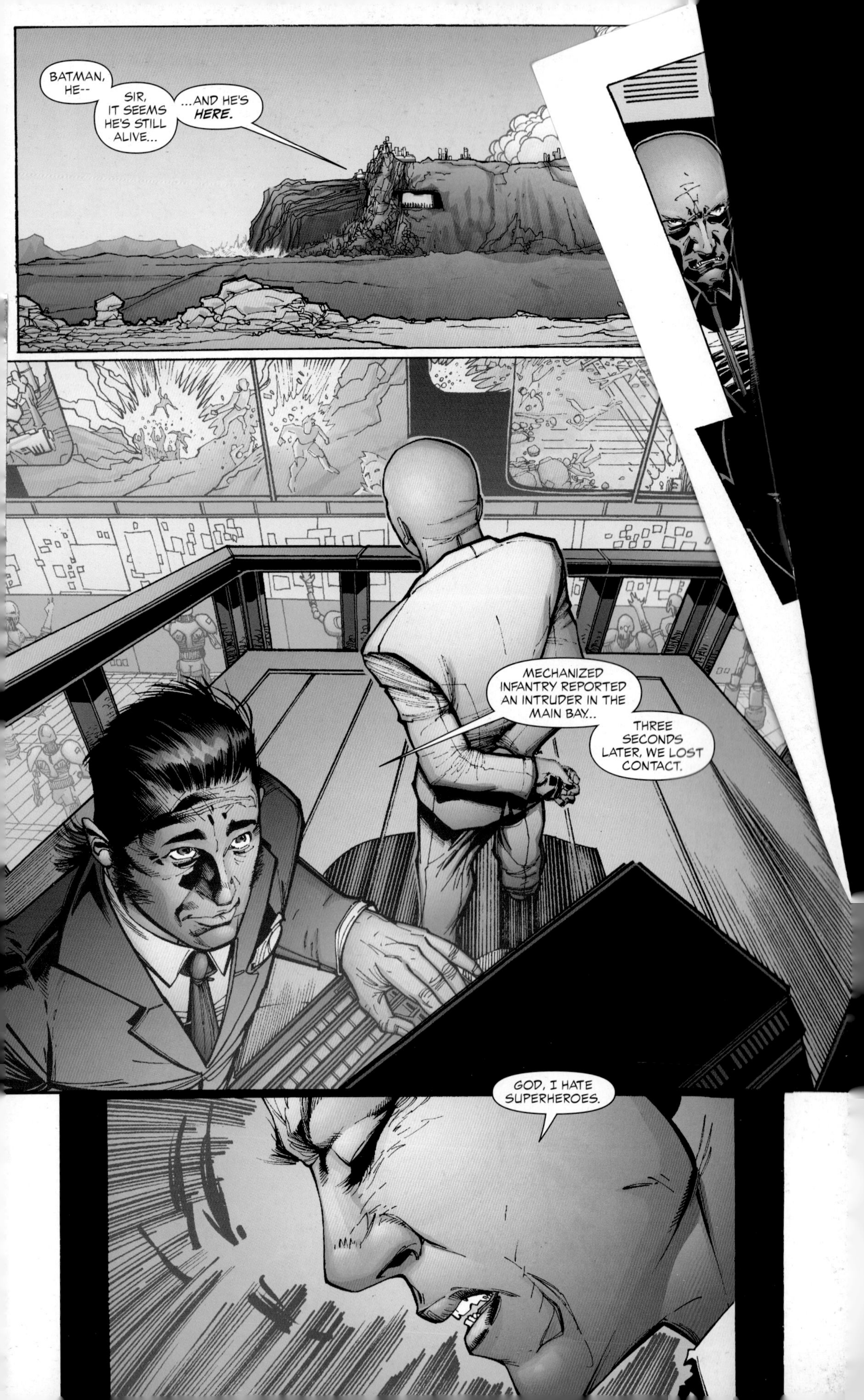
BATMAN, HE--
SIR, IT SEEMS HE'S STILL ALIVE...
...AND HE'S *HERE.*
MECHANIZED INFANTRY REPORTED AN INTRUDER IN THE MAIN BAY...
THREE SECONDS LATER, WE LOST CONTACT.
GOD, I HATE SUPERHEROES.

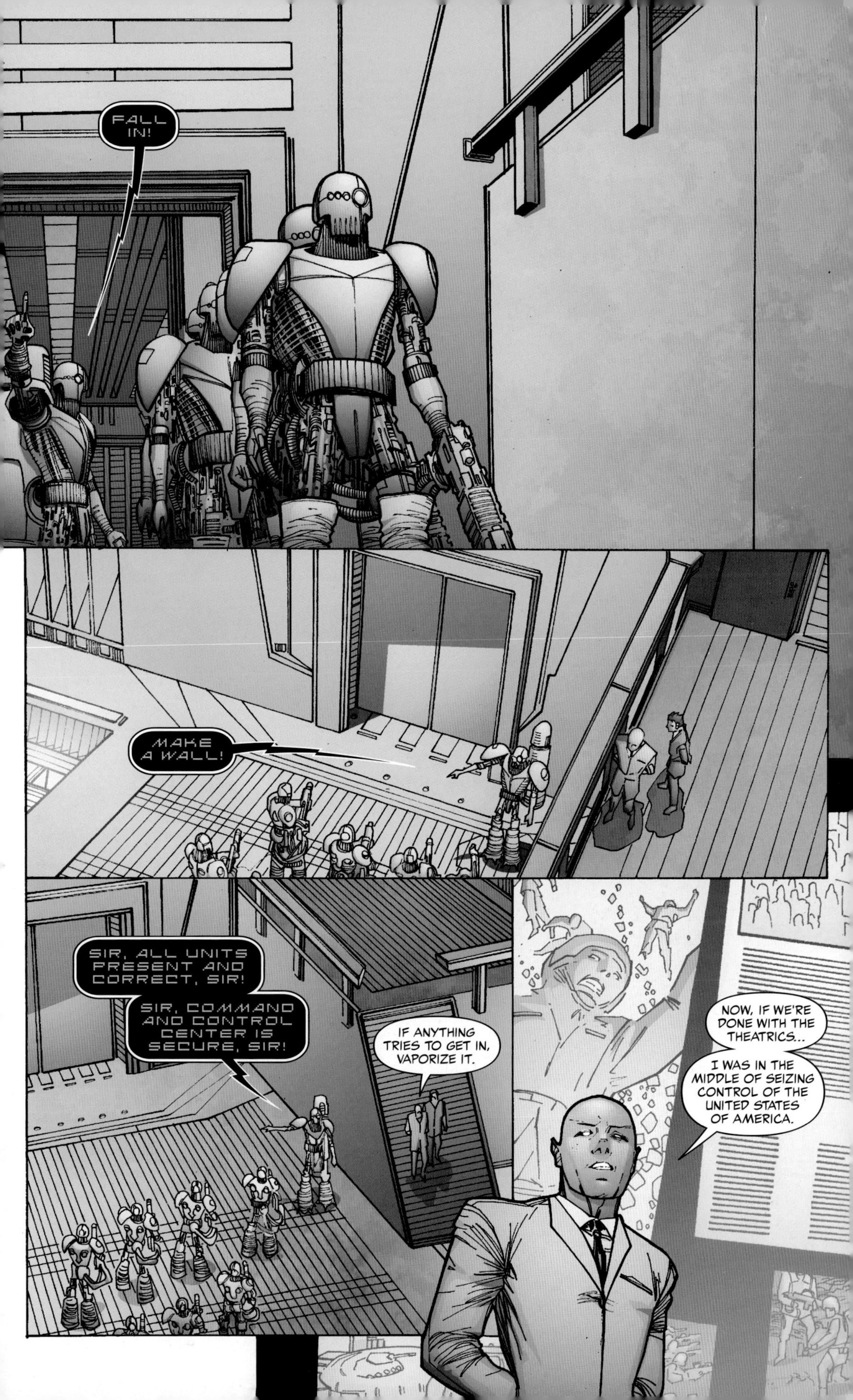
FALL IN!
MAKE A WALL!
SIR, ALL UNITS PRESENT AND CORRECT, SIR!
SIR, COMMAND AND CONTROL CENTER IS SECURE, SIR!
IF ANYTHING TRIES TO GET IN, VAPORIZE IT.
NOW, IF WE'RE DONE WITH THE THEATRICS...
I WAS IN THE MIDDLE OF SEIZING CONTROL OF THE UNITED STATES OF AMERICA.

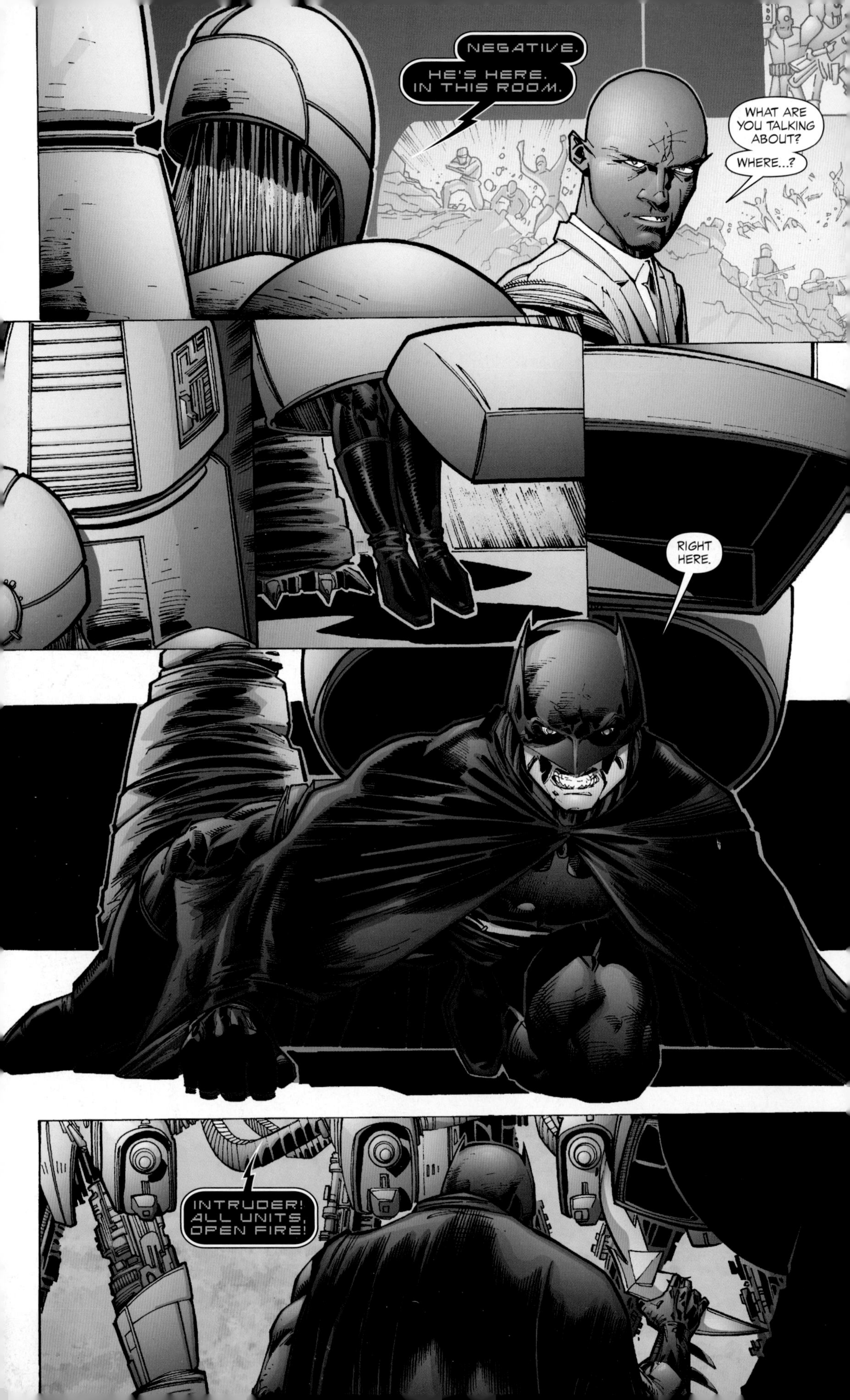
NEGATIVE.
HE'S HERE. IN THIS ROOM.
WHAT ARE YOU TALKING ABOUT?
WHERE...?
RIGHT HERE.
INTRUDER! ALL UNITS, OPEN FIRE!

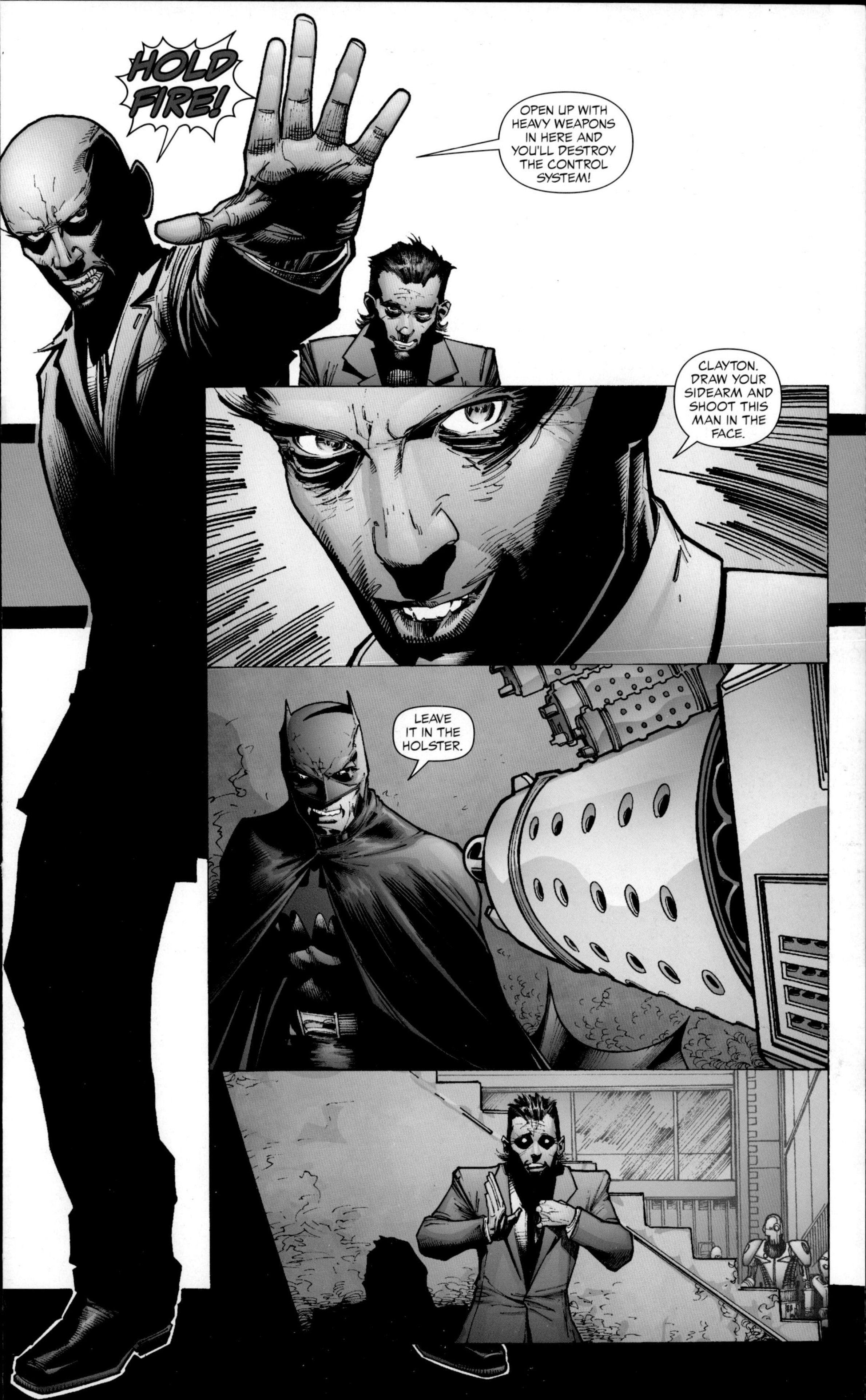
HOLD FIRE!
OPEN UP WITH HEAVY WEAPONS IN HERE AND YOU'LL DESTROY THE CONTROL SYSTEM!
CLAYTON. DRAW YOUR SIDEARM AND SHOOT THIS MAN IN THE FACE.
LEAVE IT IN THE HOLSTER.

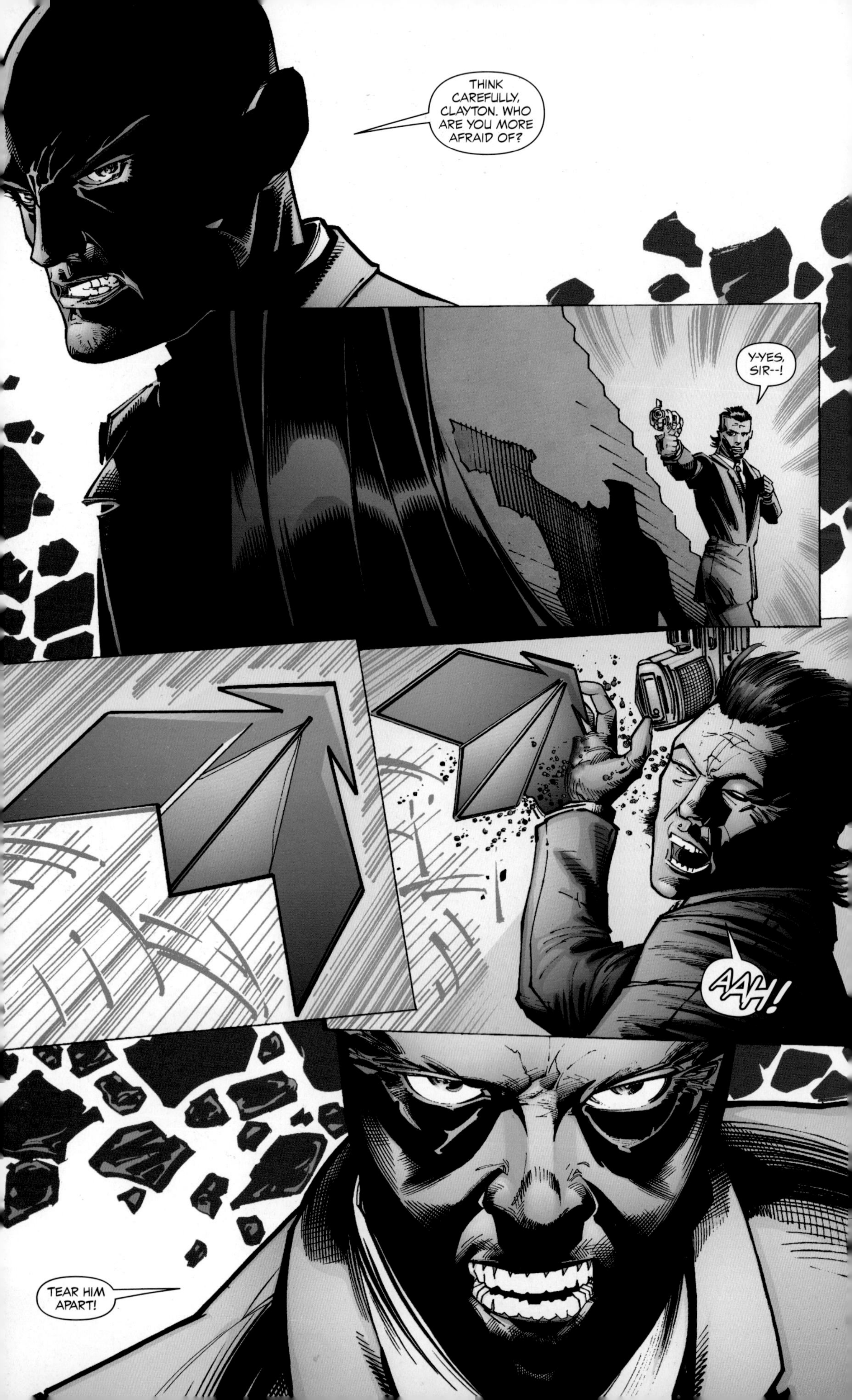
THINK CAREFULLY, CLAYTON. WHO ARE YOU MORE AFRAID OF?
Y-YES, SIR--!
AAH!
TEAR HIM APART!

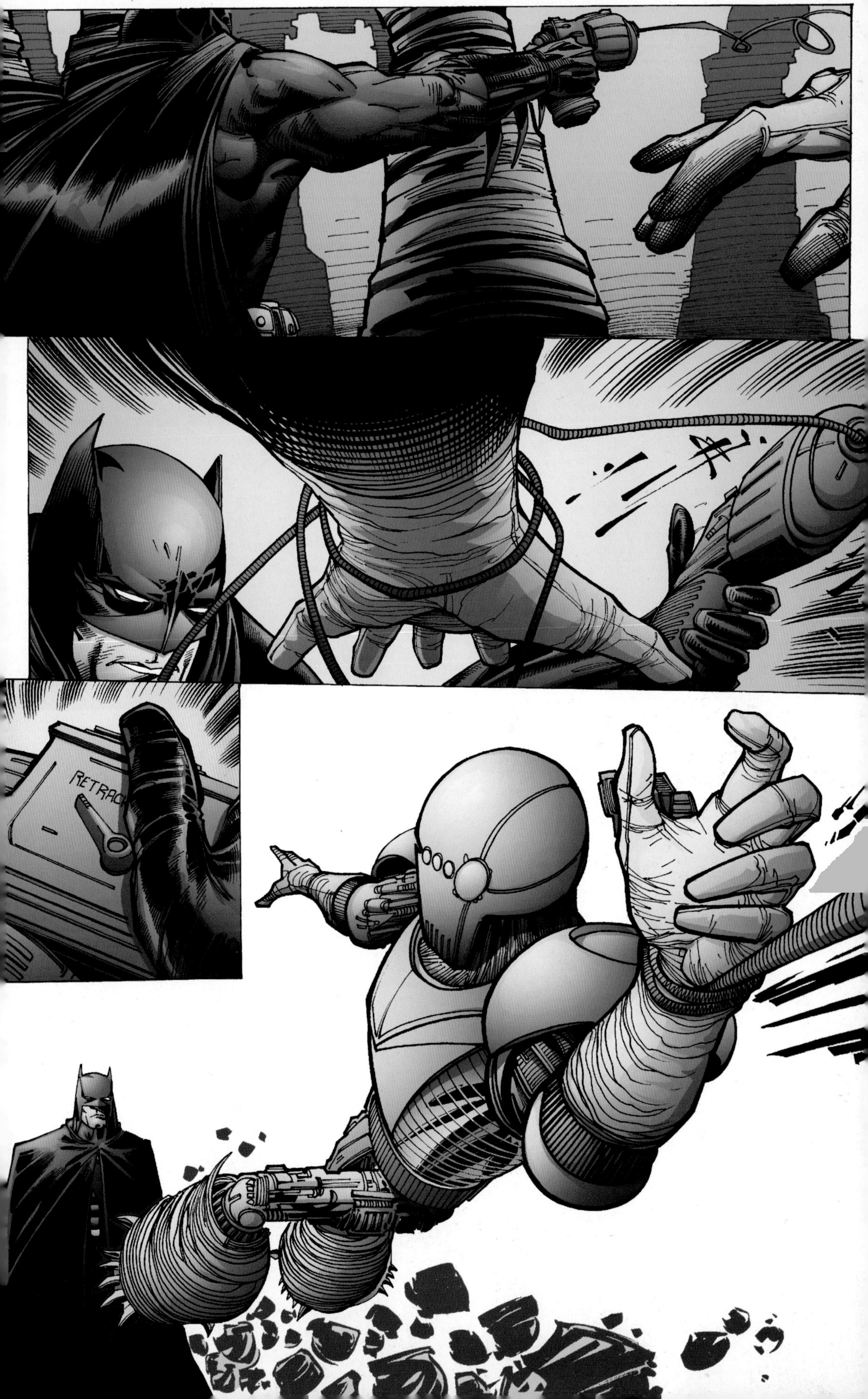
RETRAC

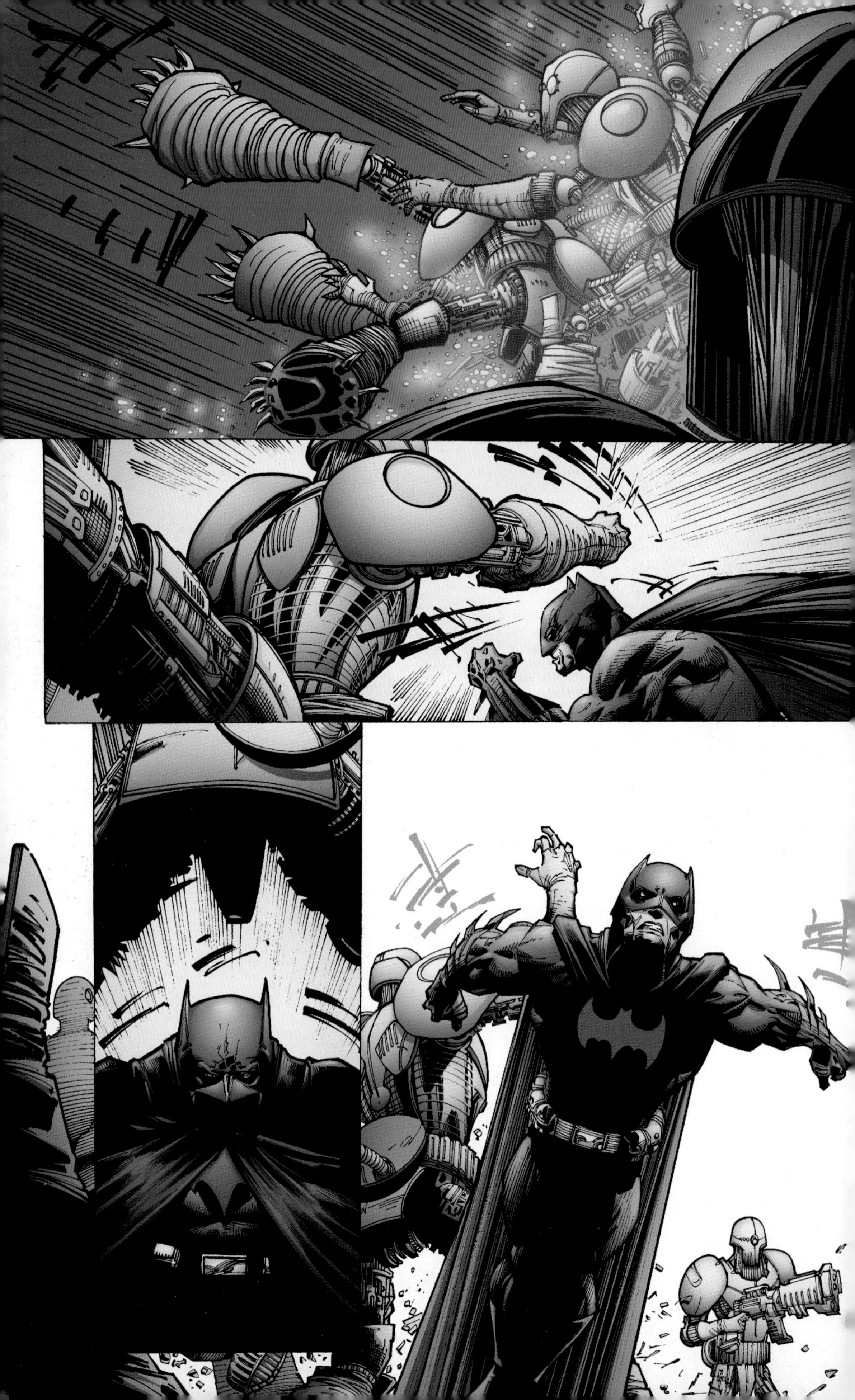

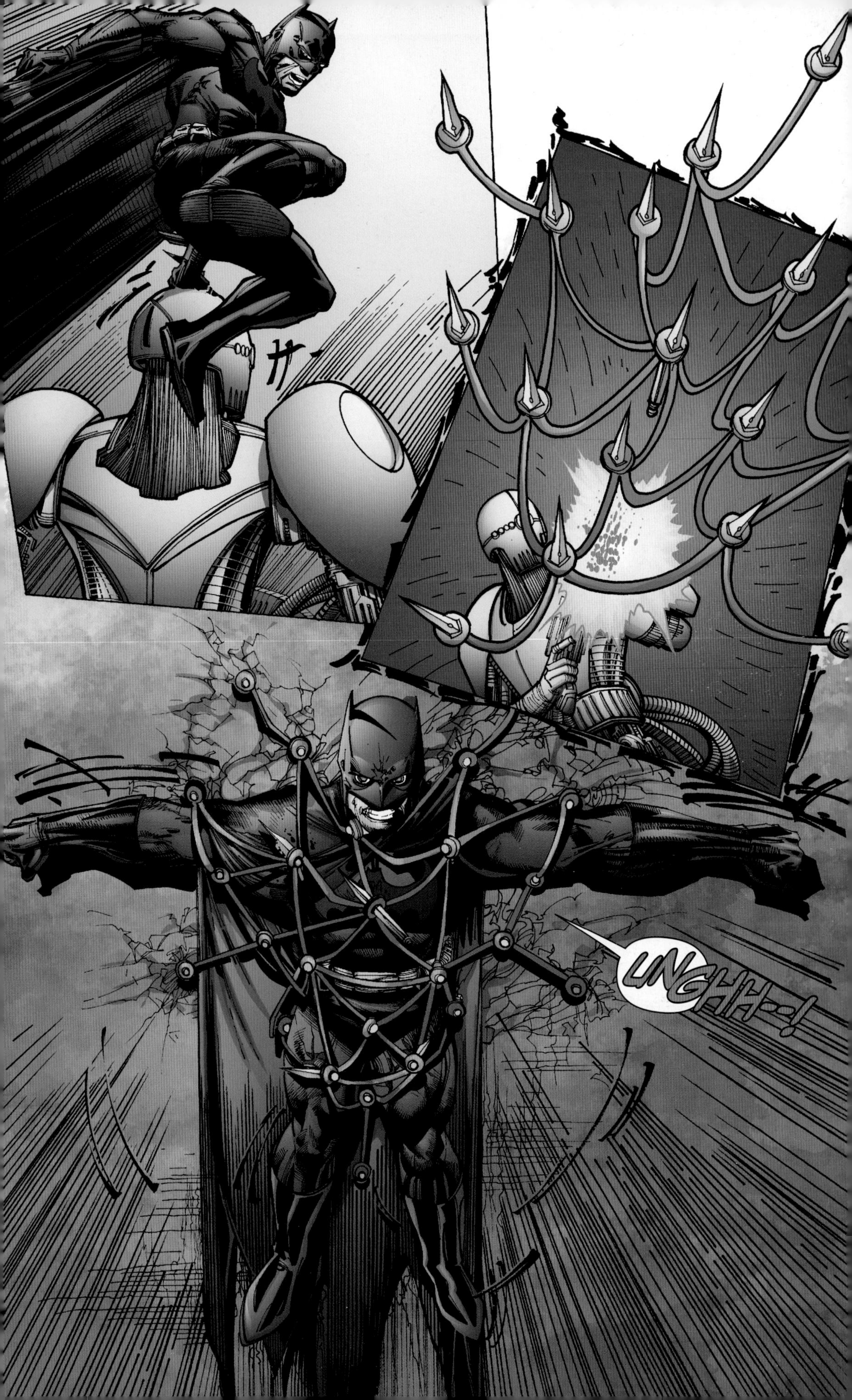
ガー
UNGHH--!

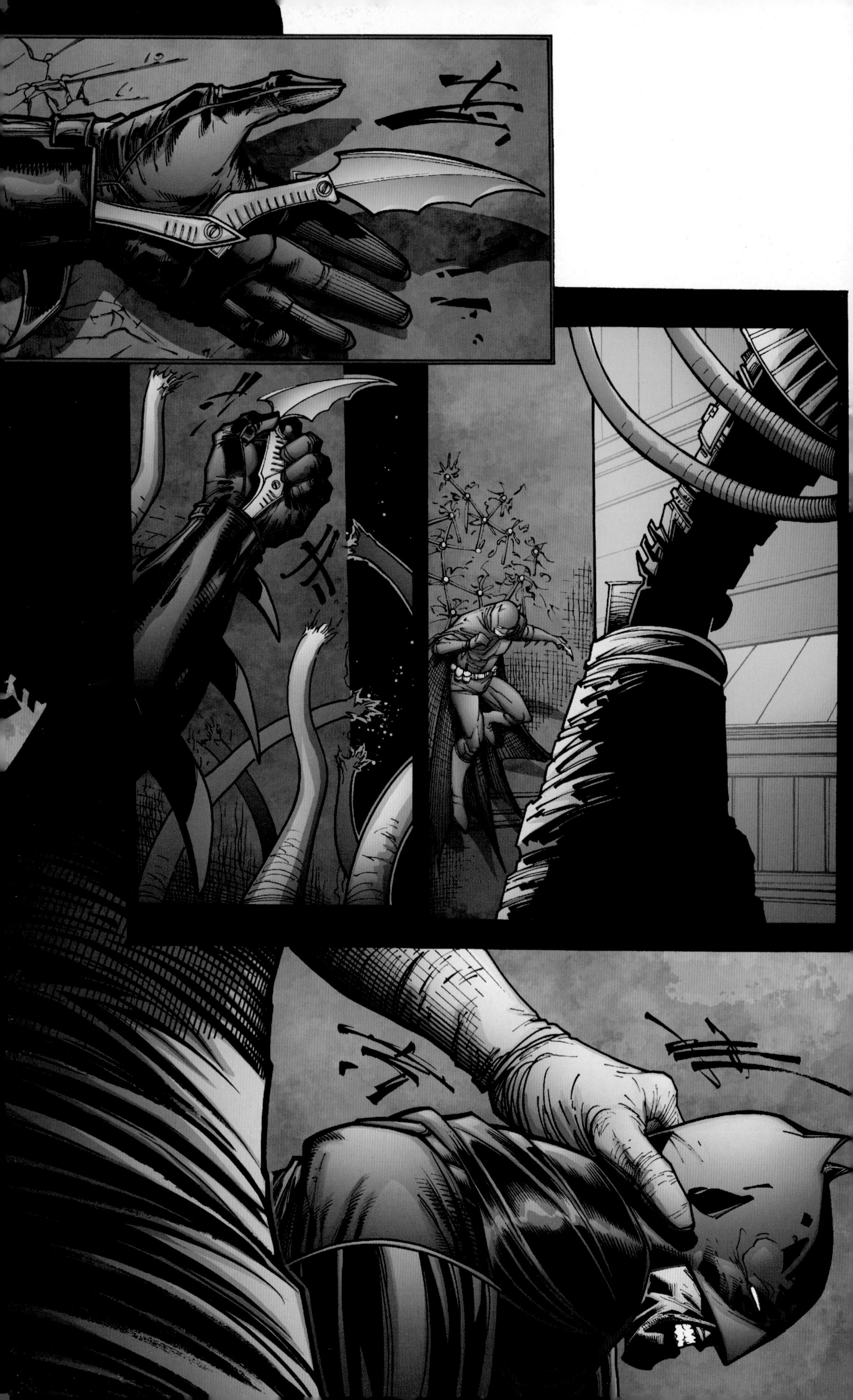

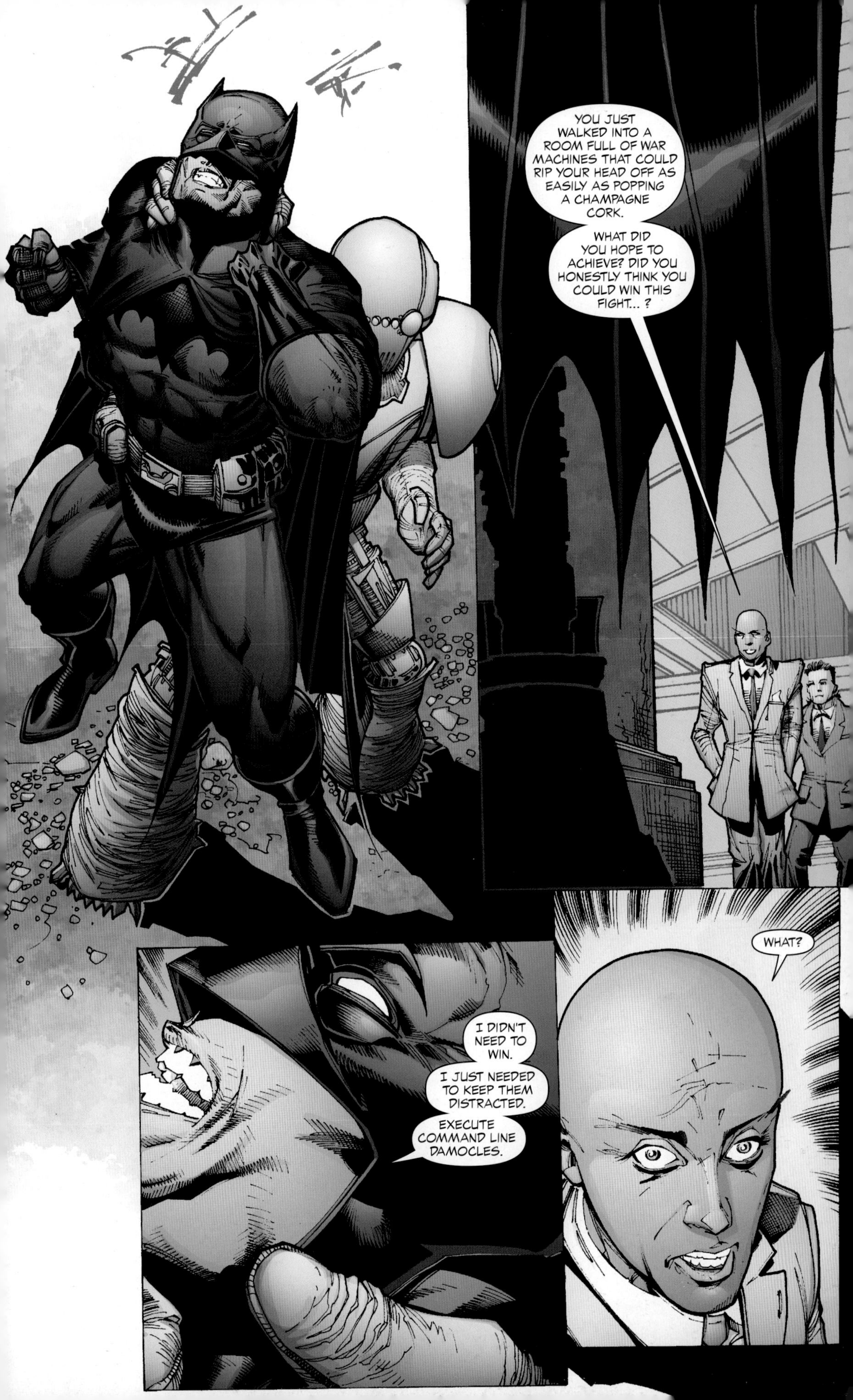
YOU JUST WALKED INTO A ROOM FULL OF WAR MACHINES THAT COULD RIP YOUR HEAD OFF AS EASILY AS POPPING A CHAMPAGNE CORK.
WHAT DID YOU HOPE TO ACHIEVE? DID YOU HONESTLY THINK YOU COULD WIN THIS FIGHT... ?
I DIDN'T NEED TO WIN.
I JUST NEEDED TO KEEP THEM DISTRACTED.
EXECUTE COMMAND LINE DAMOCLES.
WHAT?

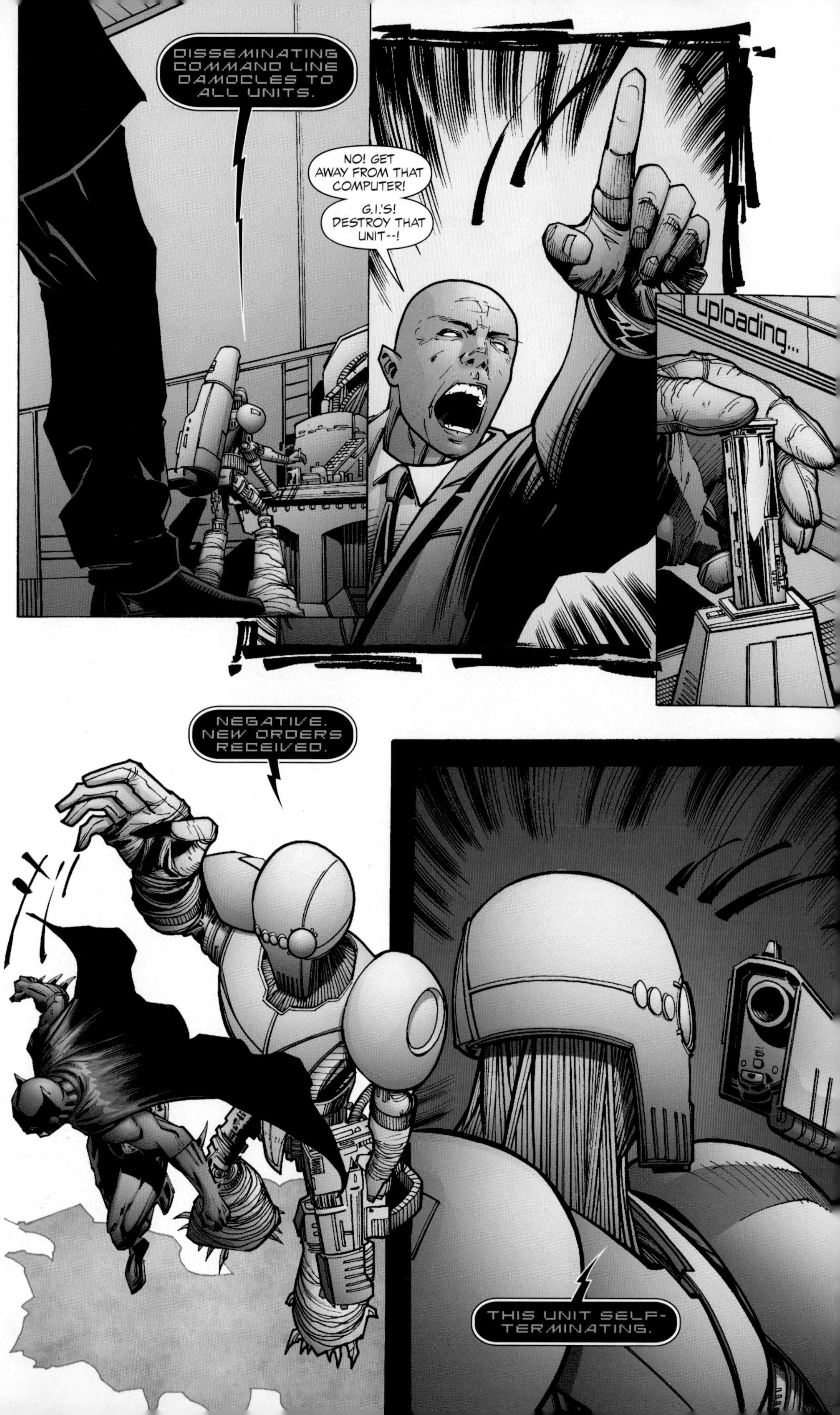
DISSEMINATING COMMAND LINE DAMOCLES TO ALL UNITS.
NO! GET AWAY FROM THAT COMPUTER!
G.I.'S! DESTROY THAT UNIT--!
uploading...
NEGATIVE. NEW ORDERS RECEIVED.
THIS UNIT SELF-TERMINATING.

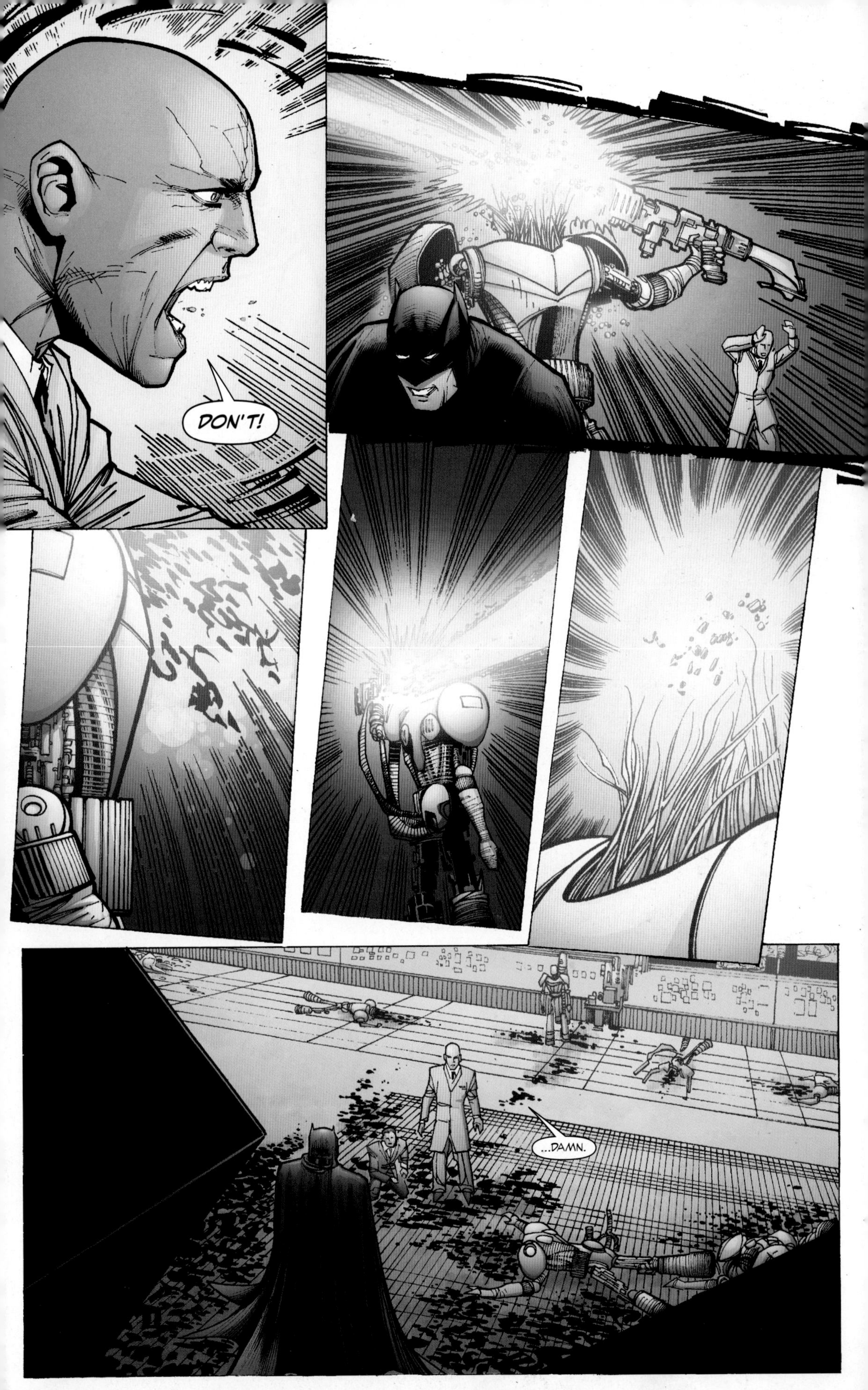
DON'T!
...DAMN.

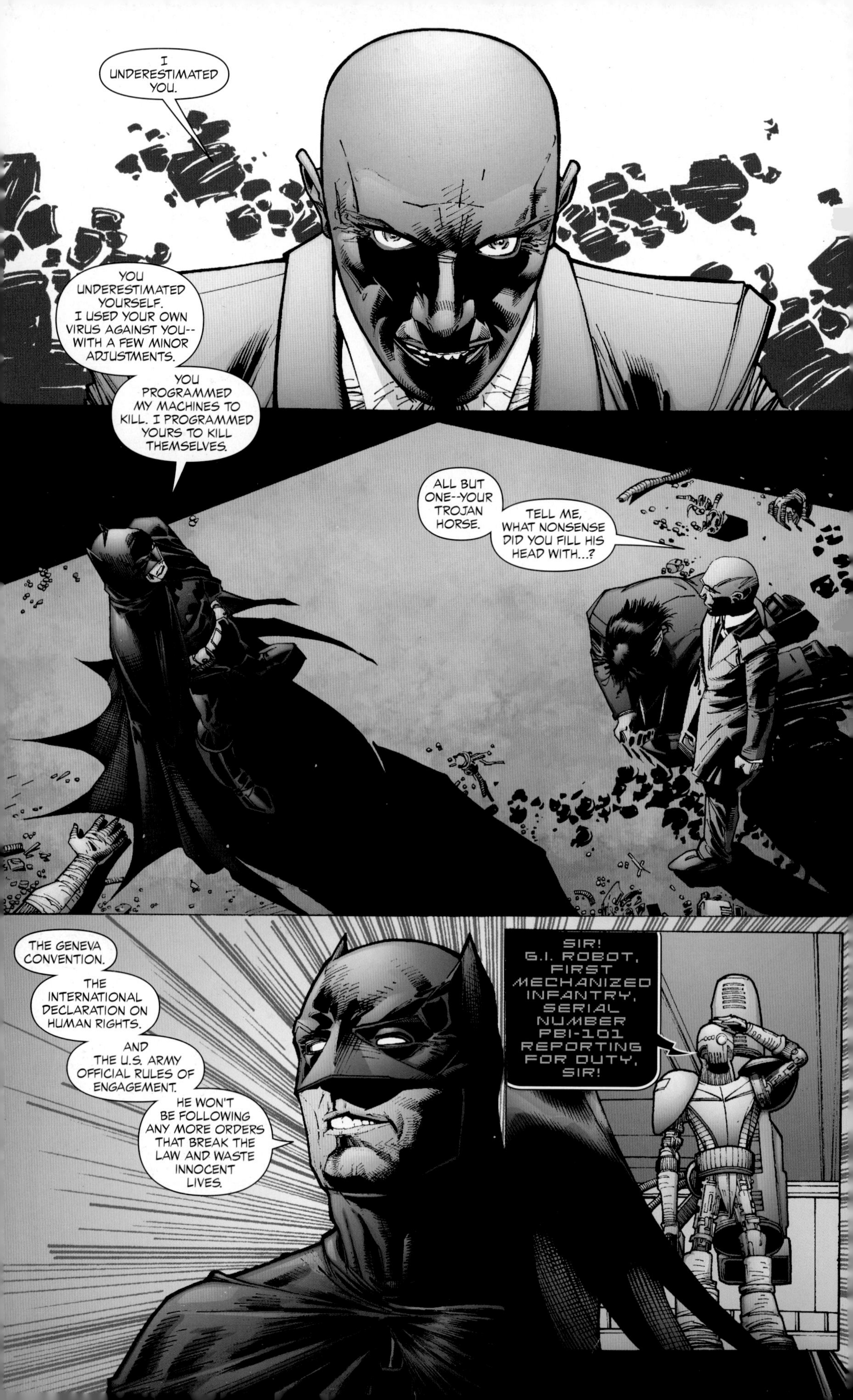
I UNDERESTIMATED YOU.
YOU UNDERESTIMATED YOURSELF. I USED YOUR OWN VIRUS AGAINST YOU-- WITH A FEW MINOR ADJUSTMENTS.
YOU PROGRAMMED MY MACHINES TO KILL. I PROGRAMMED YOURS TO KILL THEMSELVES.
ALL BUT ONE--YOUR TROJAN HORSE.
TELL ME, WHAT NONSENSE DID YOU FILL HIS HEAD WITH...?
THE GENEVA CONVENTION.
THE INTERNATIONAL DECLARATION ON HUMAN RIGHTS.
AND THE U.S. ARMY OFFICIAL RULES OF ENGAGEMENT.
HE WON'T BE FOLLOWING ANY MORE ORDERS THAT BREAK THE LAW AND WASTE INNOCENT LIVES.
SIR! G.I. ROBOT, FIRST MECHANIZED INFANTRY, SERIAL NUMBER PBI-101 REPORTING FOR DUTY, SIR!

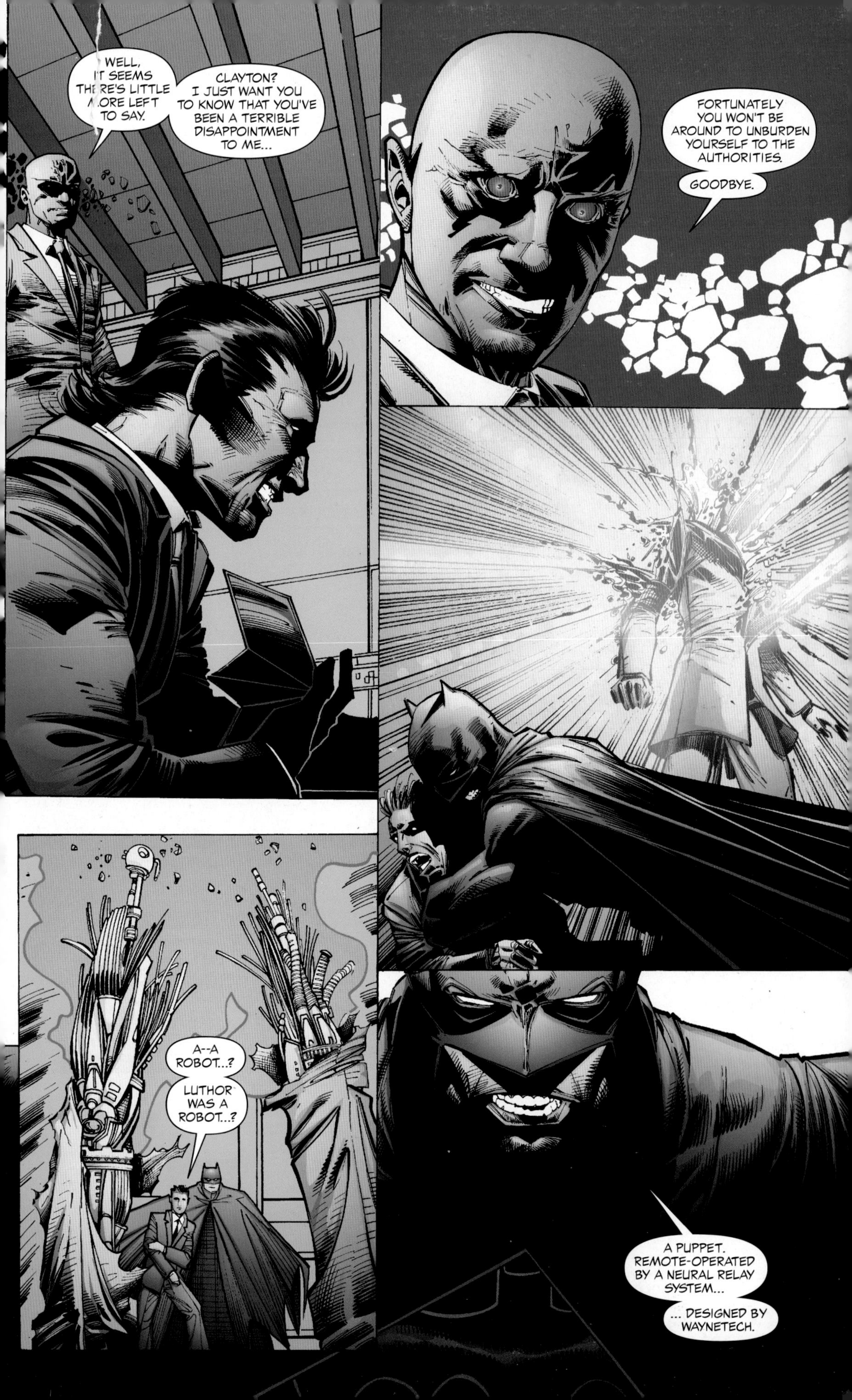
WELL, IT SEEMS THERE'S LITTLE MORE LEFT TO SAY.
CLAYTON? I JUST WANT YOU TO KNOW THAT YOU'VE BEEN A TERRIBLE DISAPPOINTMENT TO ME...
FORTUNATELY YOU WON'T BE AROUND TO UNBURDEN YOURSELF TO THE AUTHORITIES.
GOODBYE.
A--A ROBOT...?
LUTHOR WAS A ROBOT...?
A PUPPET. REMOTE-OPERATED BY A NEURAL RELAY SYSTEM...
... DESIGNED BY WAYNETECH.

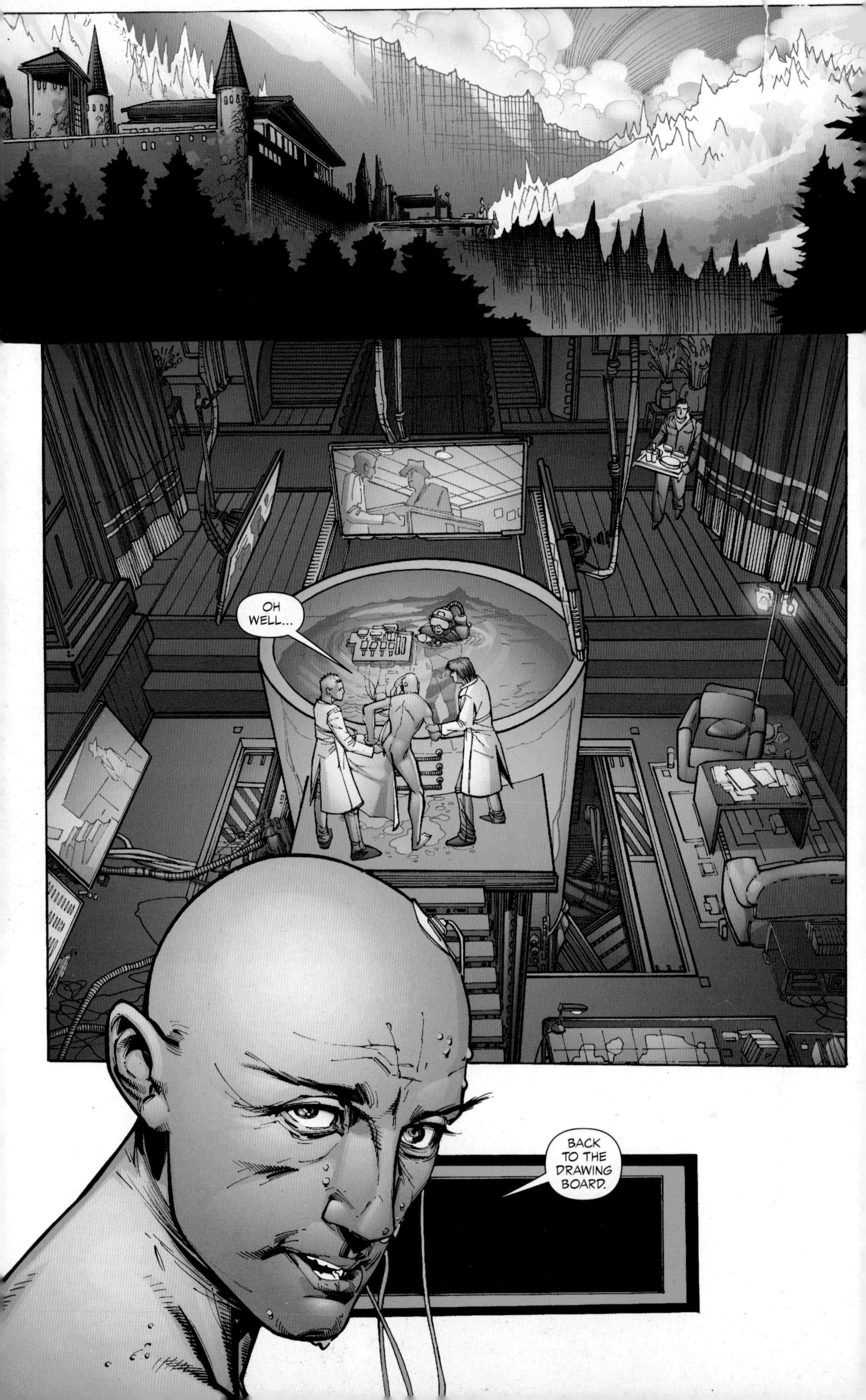
OH WELL...
BACK TO THE DRAWING BOARD.

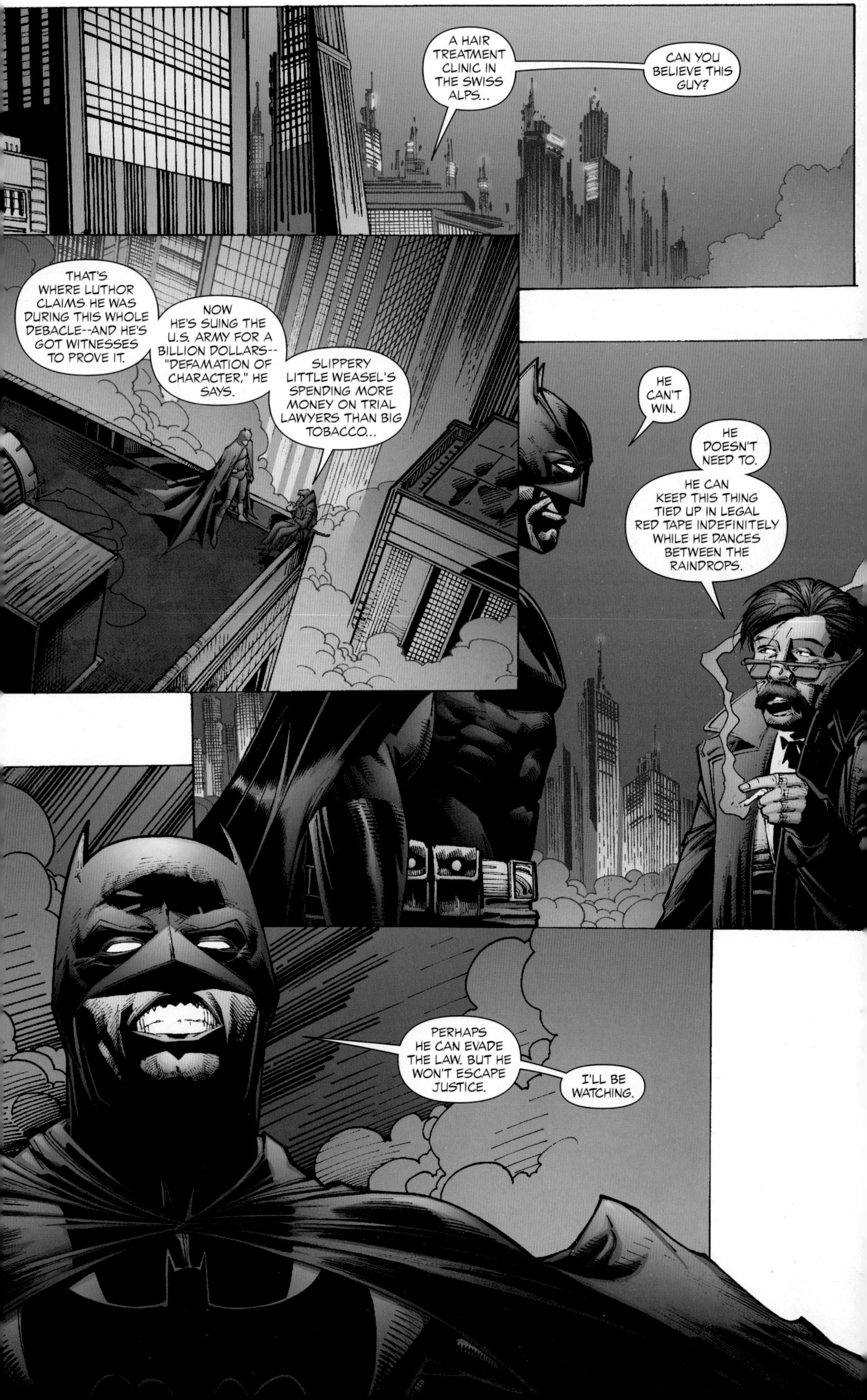
A HAIR TREATMENT CLINIC IN THE SWISS ALPS...
CAN YOU BELIEVE THIS GUY?
THAT'S WHERE LUTHOR CLAIMS HE WAS DURING THIS WHOLE DEBACLE--AND HE'S GOT WITNESSES TO PROVE IT.
NOW HE'S SUING THE U.S. ARMY FOR A BILLION DOLLARS-- "DEFAMATION OF CHARACTER," HE SAYS.
SLIPPERY LITTLE WEASEL'S SPENDING MORE MONEY ON TRIAL LAWYERS THAN BIG TOBACCO...
HE CAN'T WIN.
HE DOESN'T NEED TO.
HE CAN KEEP THIS THING TIED UP IN LEGAL RED TAPE INDEFINITELY WHILE HE DANCES BETWEEN THE RAINDROPS.
PERHAPS HE CAN EVADE THE LAW. BUT HE WON'T ESCAPE JUSTICE.
I'LL BE WATCHING.

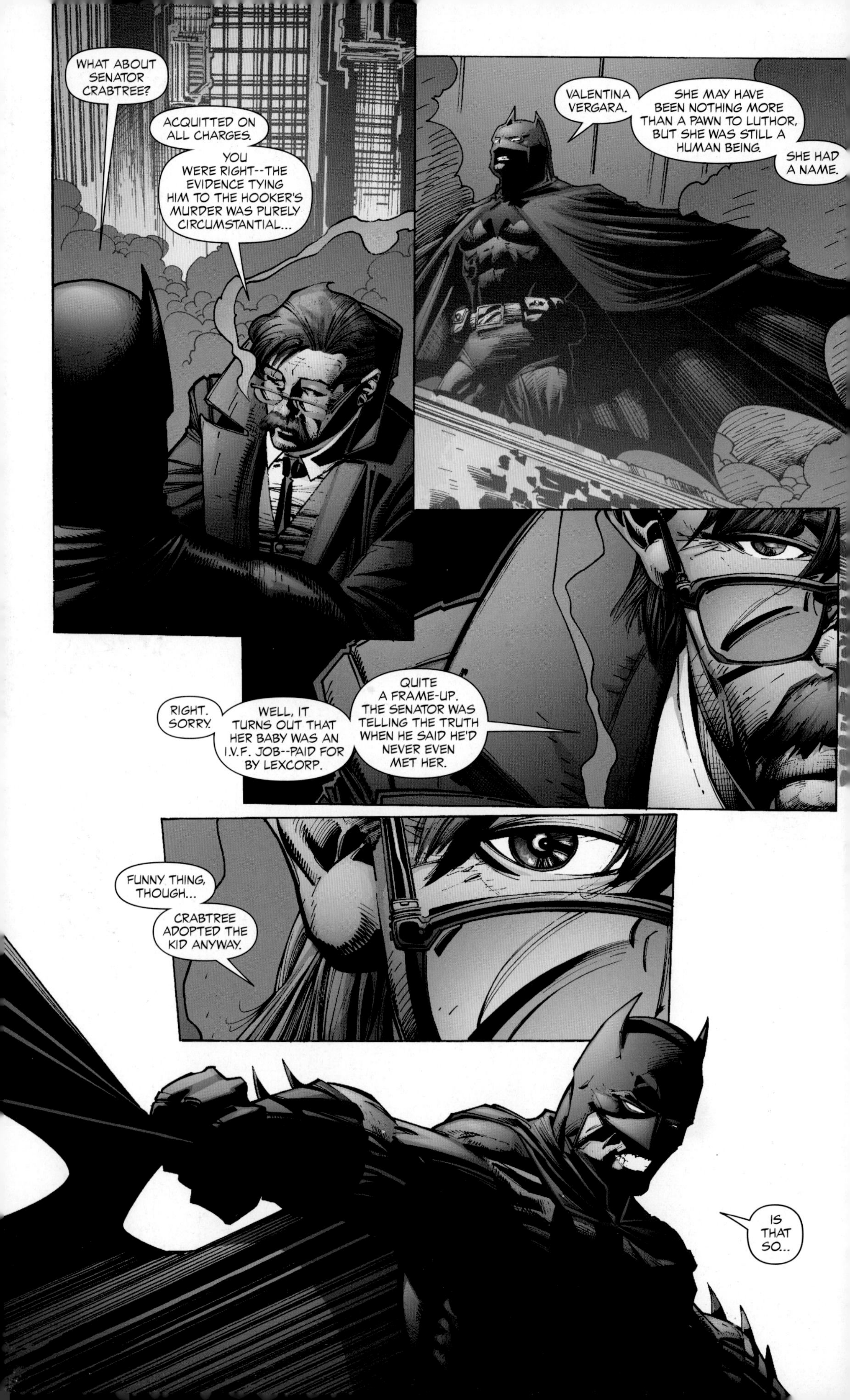

WHAT ABOUT SENATOR CRABTREE?
ACQUITTED ON ALL CHARGES.
YOU WERE RIGHT--THE EVIDENCE TYING HIM TO THE HOOKER'S MURDER WAS PURELY CIRCUMSTANTIAL...
VALENTINA VERGARA.
SHE MAY HAVE BEEN NOTHING MORE THAN A PAWN TO LUTHOR, BUT SHE WAS STILL A HUMAN BEING.
SHE HAD A NAME.
RIGHT. SORRY.
WELL, IT TURNS OUT THAT HER BABY WAS AN I.V.F. JOB--PAID FOR BY LEXCORP.
QUITE A FRAME-UP. THE SENATOR WAS TELLING THE TRUTH WHEN HE SAID HE'D NEVER EVEN MET HER.
FUNNY THING, THOUGH...
CRABTREE ADOPTED THE KID ANYWAY.
IS THAT SO...

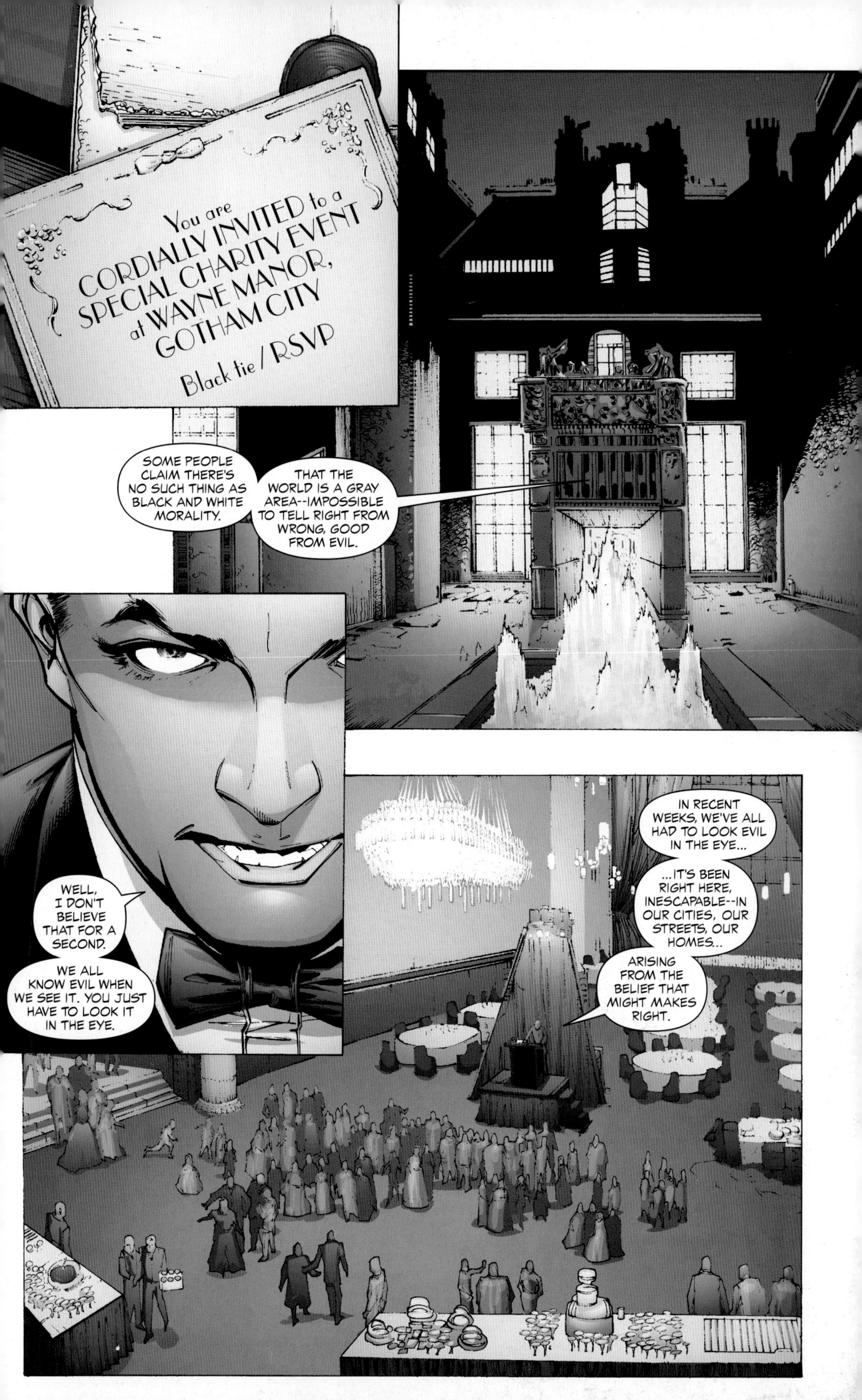
You are CORDIALLY INVITED to a SPECIAL CHARITY EVENT at WAYNE MANOR, GOTHAM CITY
Black tie / RSVP
SOME PEOPLE CLAIM THERE'S NO SUCH THING AS BLACK AND WHITE MORALITY.
THAT THE WORLD IS A GRAY AREA--IMPOSSIBLE TO TELL RIGHT FROM WRONG, GOOD FROM EVIL.
WELL, I DON'T BELIEVE THAT FOR A SECOND.
WE ALL KNOW EVIL WHEN WE SEE IT. YOU JUST HAVE TO LOOK IT IN THE EYE.
IN RECENT WEEKS, WE'VE ALL HAD TO LOOK EVIL IN THE EYE...
...IT'S BEEN RIGHT HERE, INESCAPABLE--IN OUR CITIES, OUR STREETS, OUR HOMES...
ARISING FROM THE BELIEF THAT MIGHT MAKES RIGHT.

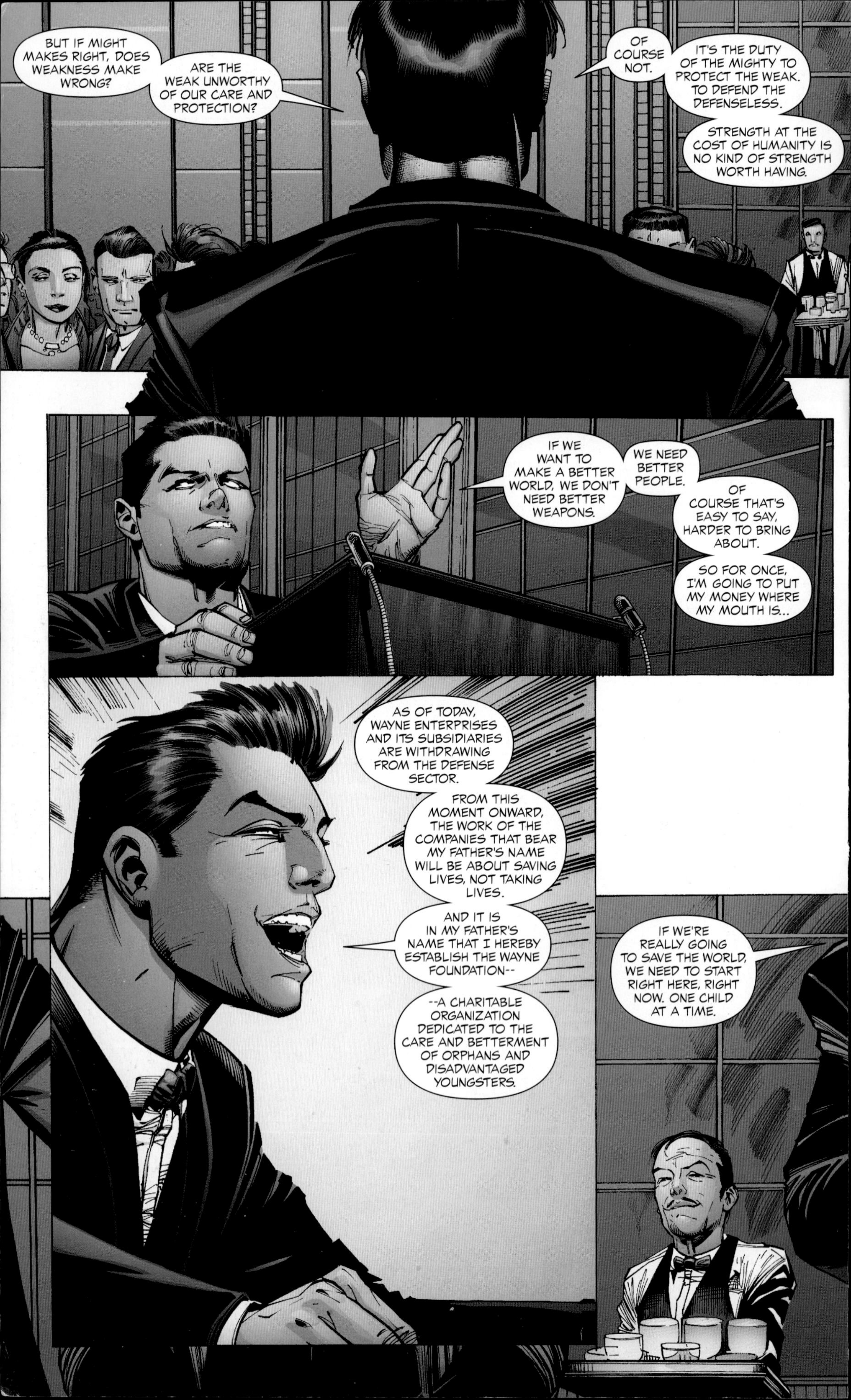
BUT IF MIGHT MAKES RIGHT, DOES WEAKNESS MAKE WRONG?
ARE THE WEAK UNWORTHY OF OUR CARE AND PROTECTION?
OF COURSE NOT.
IT'S THE DUTY OF THE MIGHTY TO PROTECT THE WEAK. TO DEFEND THE DEFENSELESS.
STRENGTH AT THE COST OF HUMANITY IS NO KIND OF STRENGTH WORTH HAVING.
IF WE WANT TO MAKE A BETTER WORLD, WE DON'T NEED BETTER WEAPONS.
WE NEED BETTER PEOPLE.
OF COURSE THAT'S EASY TO SAY, HARDER TO BRING ABOUT.
SO FOR ONCE, I'M GOING TO PUT MY MONEY WHERE MY MOUTH IS...
AS OF TODAY, WAYNE ENTERPRISES AND ITS SUBSIDIARIES ARE WITHDRAWING FROM THE DEFENSE SECTOR.
FROM THIS MOMENT ONWARD, THE WORK OF THE COMPANIES THAT BEAR MY FATHER'S NAME WILL BE ABOUT SAVING LIVES, NOT TAKING LIVES.
AND IT IS IN MY FATHER'S NAME THAT I HEREBY ESTABLISH THE WAYNE FOUNDATION--
--A CHARITABLE ORGANIZATION DEDICATED TO THE CARE AND BETTERMENT OF ORPHANS AND DISADVANTAGED YOUNGSTERS.
IF WE'RE REALLY GOING TO SAVE THE WORLD, WE NEED TO START RIGHT HERE, RIGHT NOW. ONE CHILD AT A TIME.

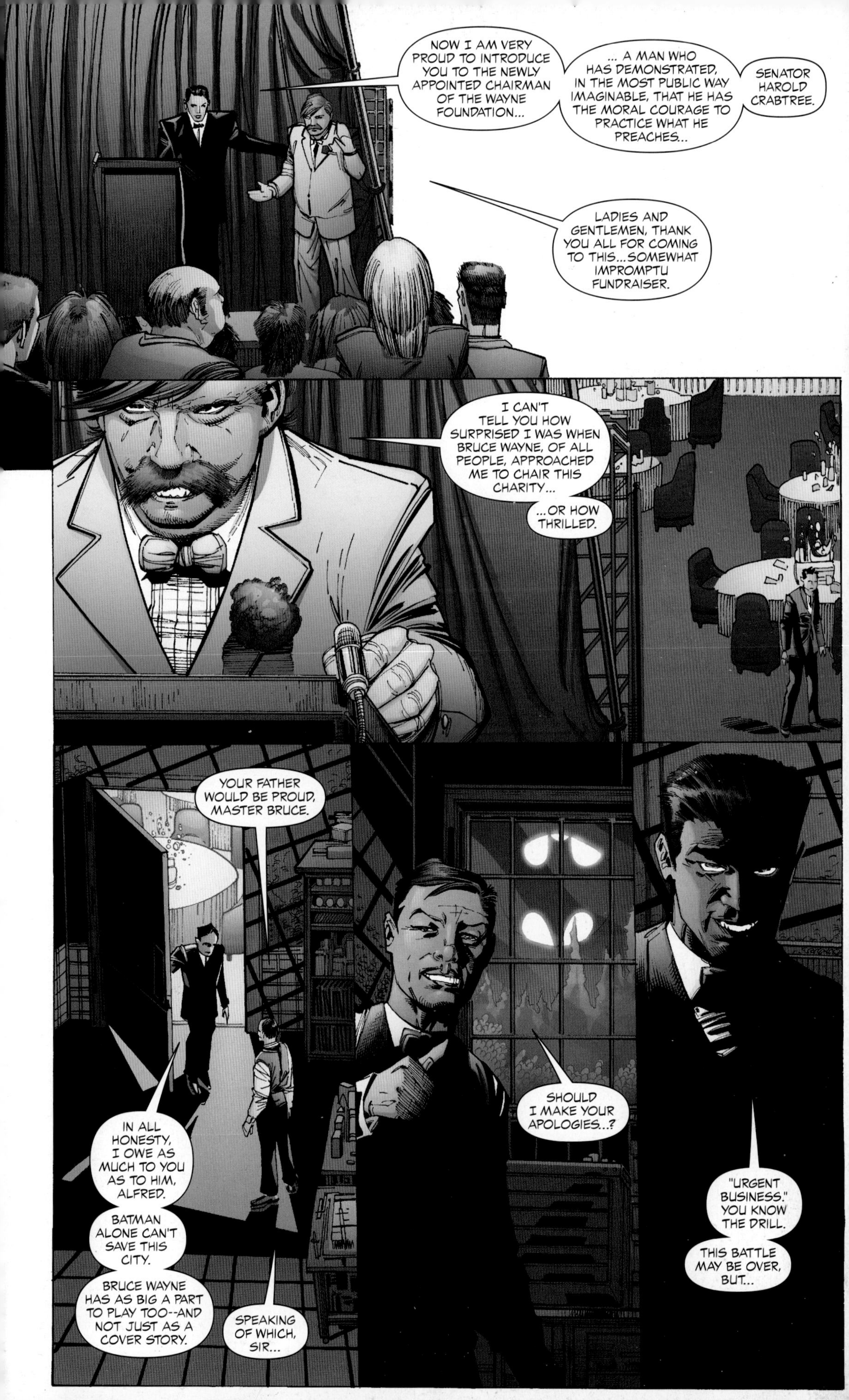
NOW I AM VERY PROUD TO INTRODUCE YOU TO THE NEWLY APPOINTED CHAIRMAN OF THE WAYNE FOUNDATION...
... A MAN WHO HAS DEMONSTRATED, IN THE MOST PUBLIC WAY IMAGINABLE, THAT HE HAS THE MORAL COURAGE TO PRACTICE WHAT HE PREACHES...
SENATOR HAROLD CRABTREE.
LADIES AND GENTLEMEN, THANK YOU ALL FOR COMING TO THIS...SOMEWHAT IMPROMPTU FUNDRAISER.
I CAN'T TELL YOU HOW SURPRISED I WAS WHEN BRUCE WAYNE, OF ALL PEOPLE, APPROACHED ME TO CHAIR THIS CHARITY...
...OR HOW THRILLED.
YOUR FATHER WOULD BE PROUD, MASTER BRUCE.
IN ALL HONESTY, I OWE AS MUCH TO YOU AS TO HIM, ALFRED.
BATMAN ALONE CAN'T SAVE THIS CITY.
BRUCE WAYNE HAS AS BIG A PART TO PLAY TOO--AND NOT JUST AS A COVER STORY.
SPEAKING OF WHICH, SIR...
SHOULD I MAKE YOUR APOLOGIES...?
"URGENT BUSINESS." YOU KNOW THE DRILL.
THIS BATTLE MAY BE OVER, BUT...

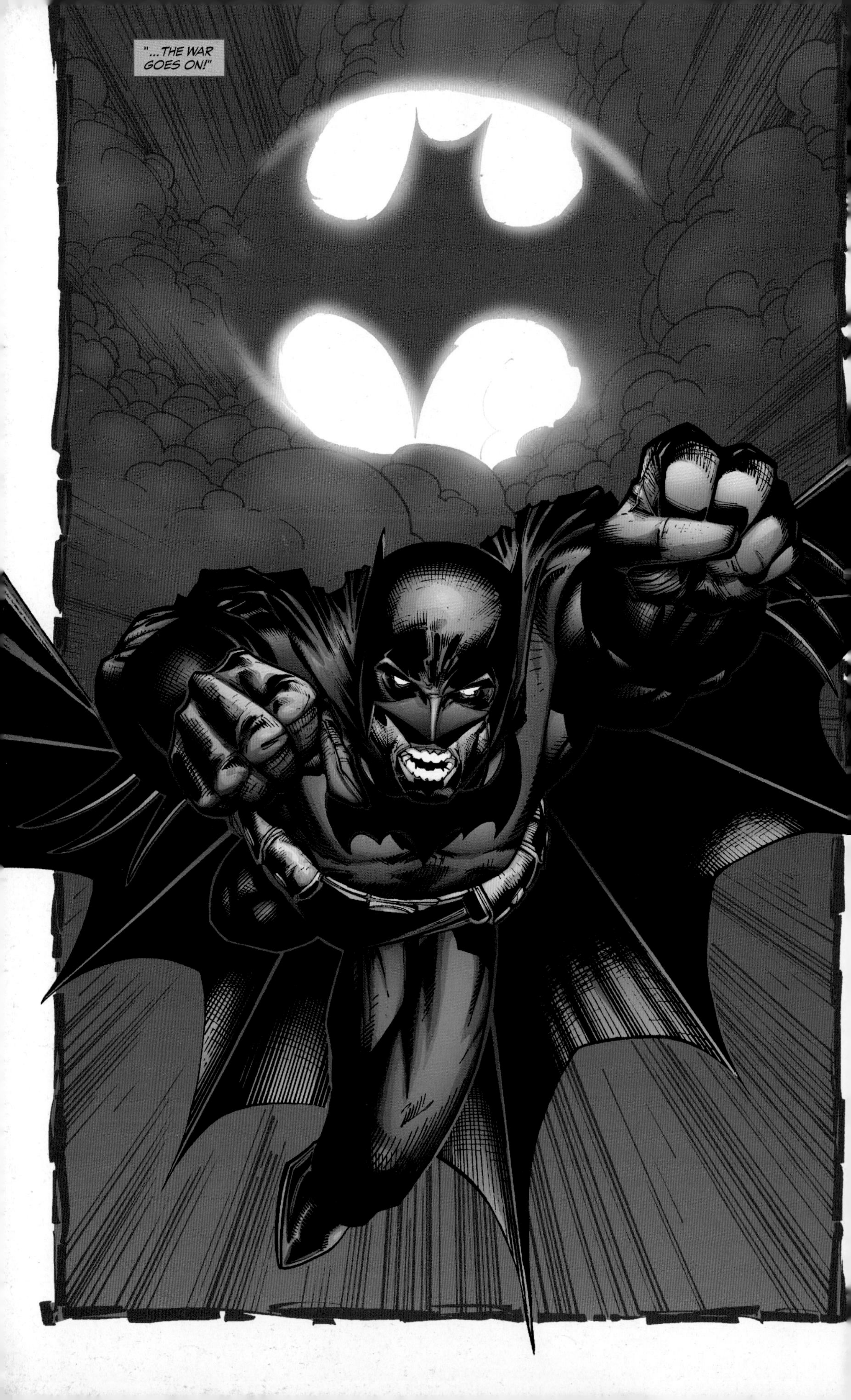
"...THE WAR GOES ON!"

SKETCHES BY WHILCE PORTACIO

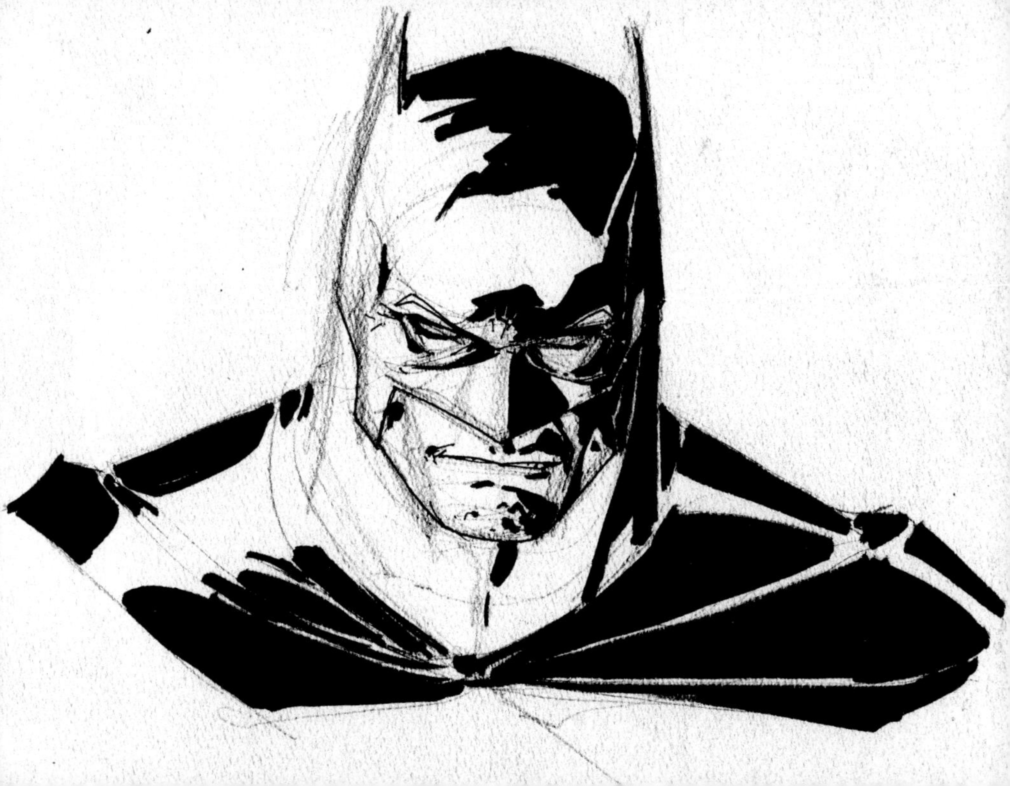

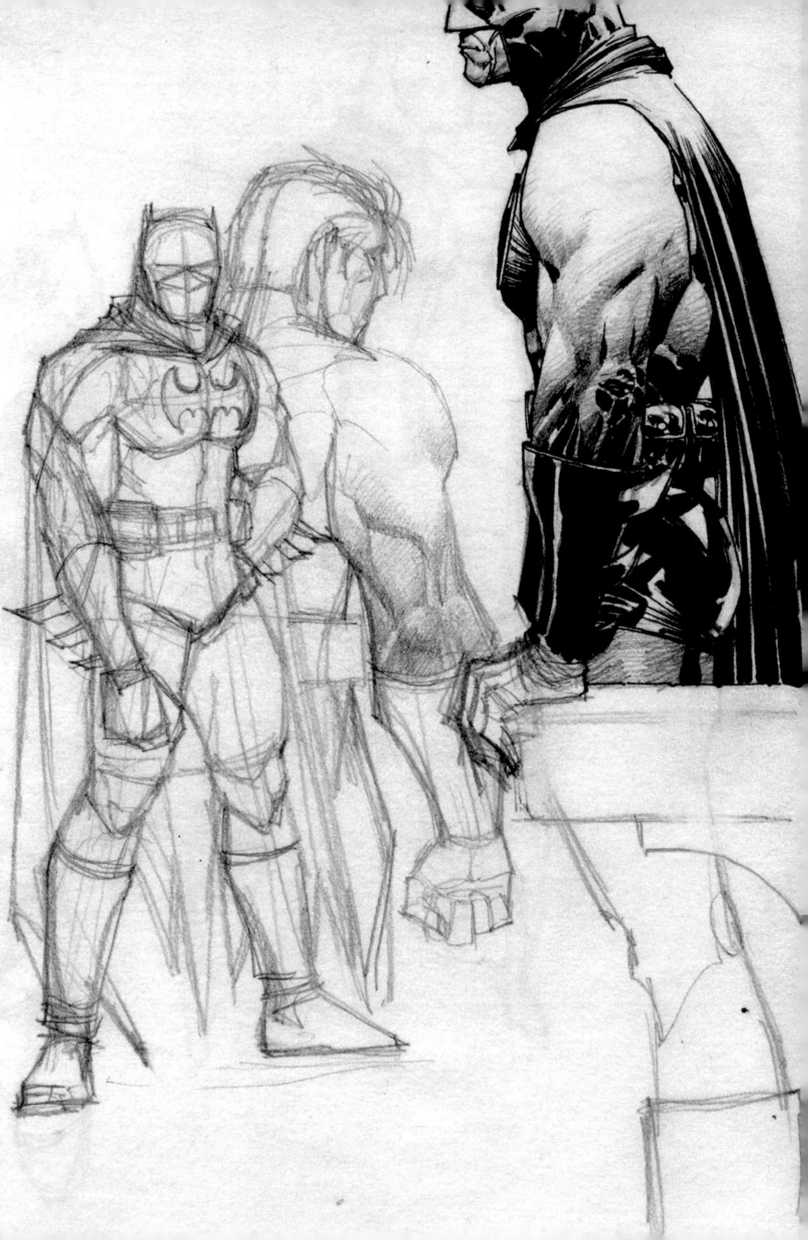

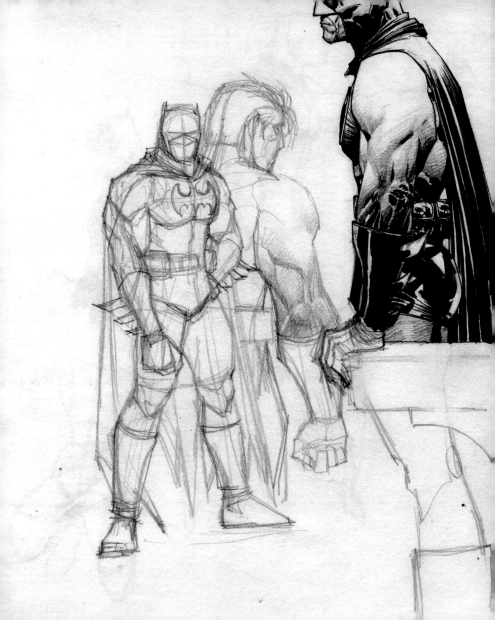

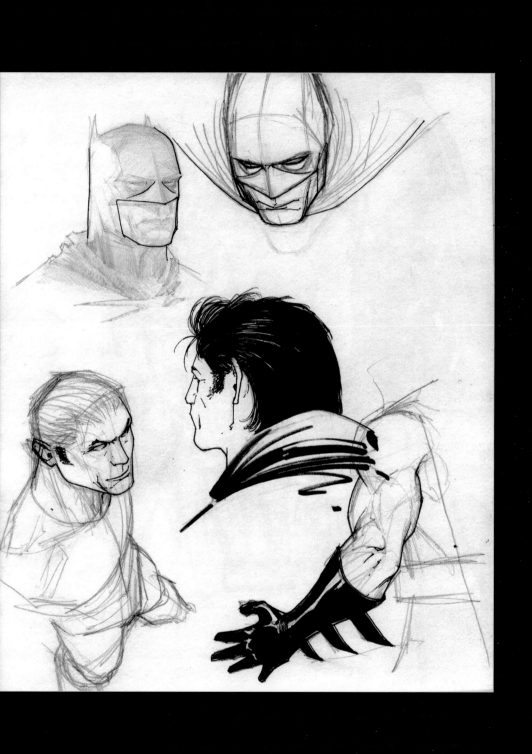

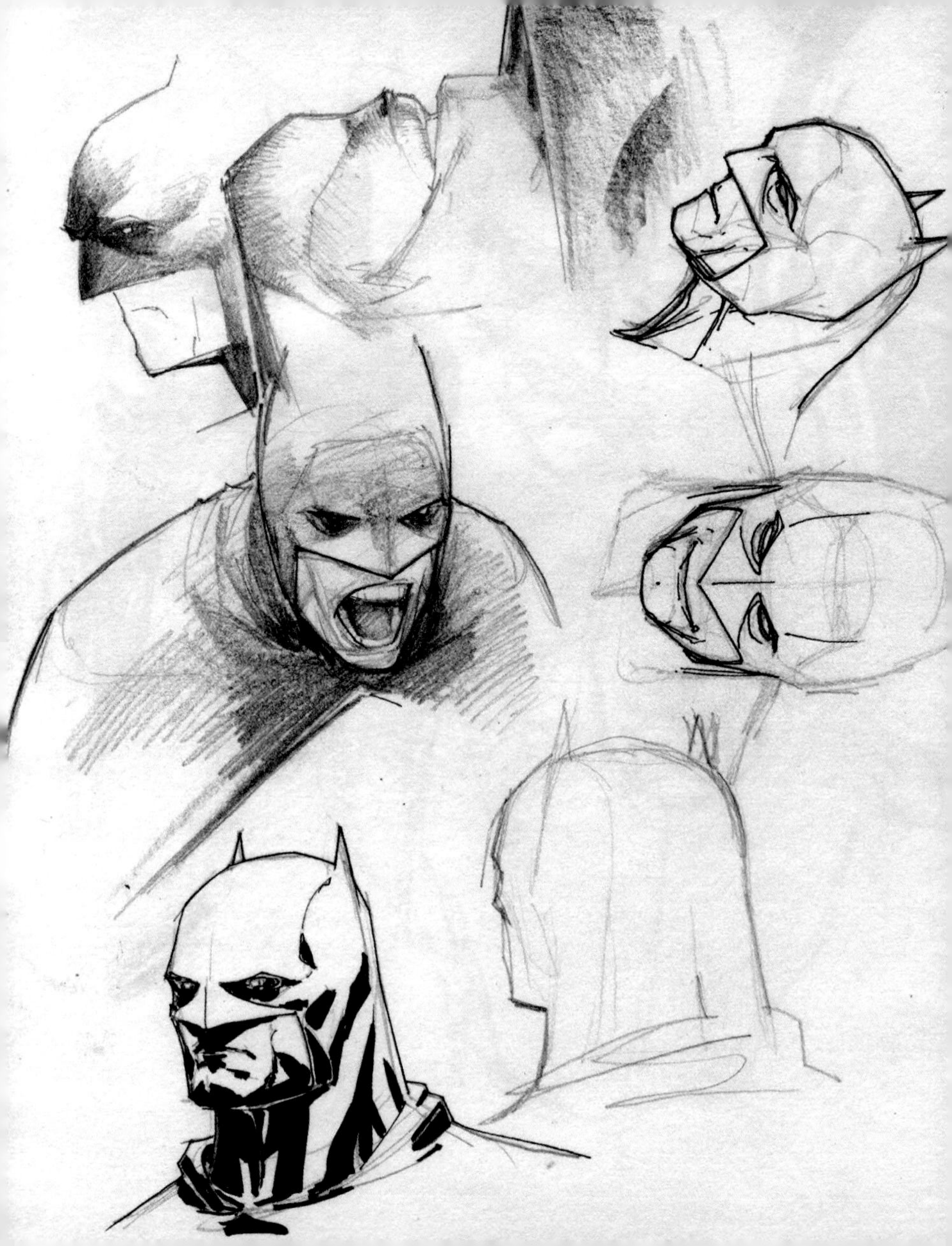

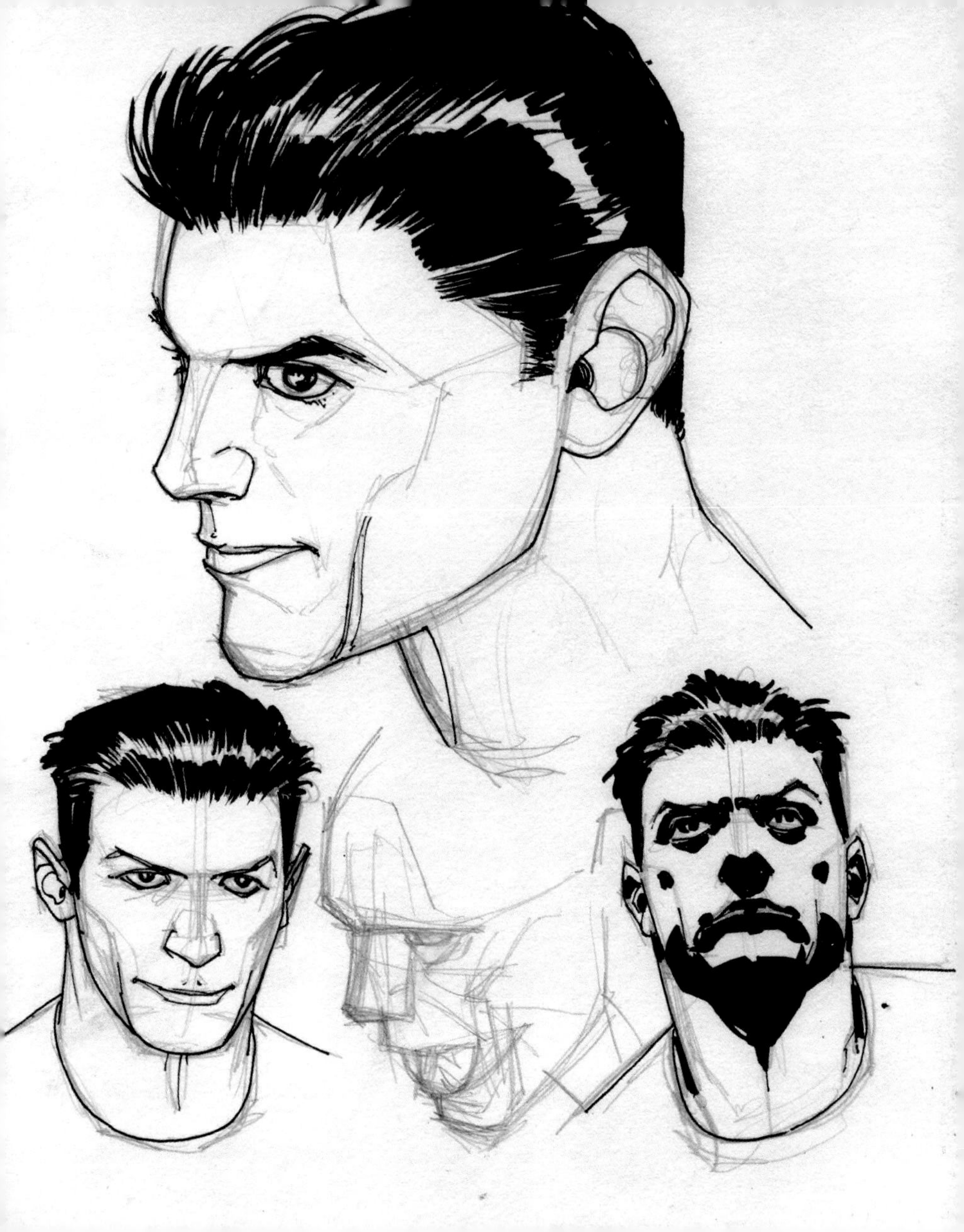

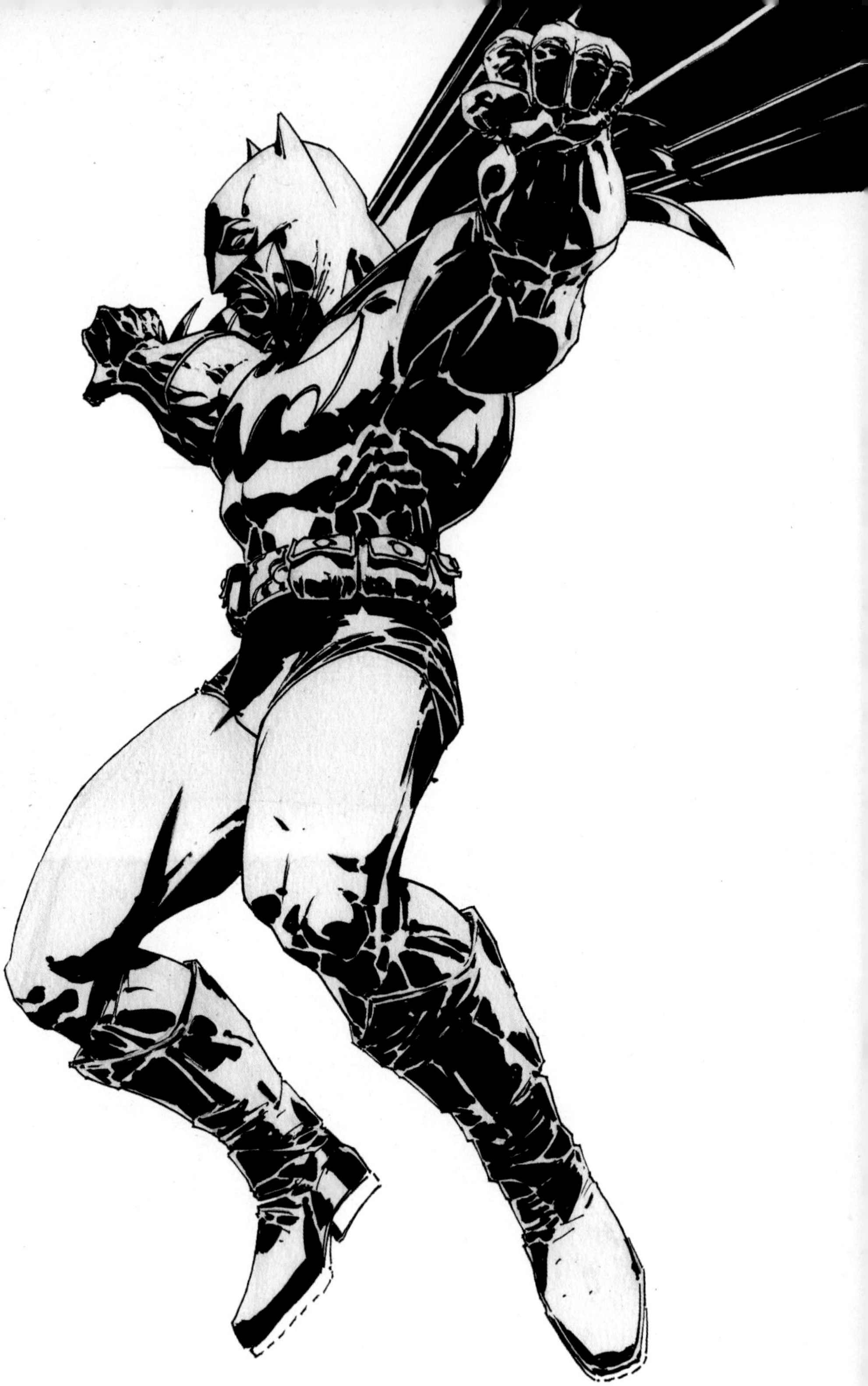

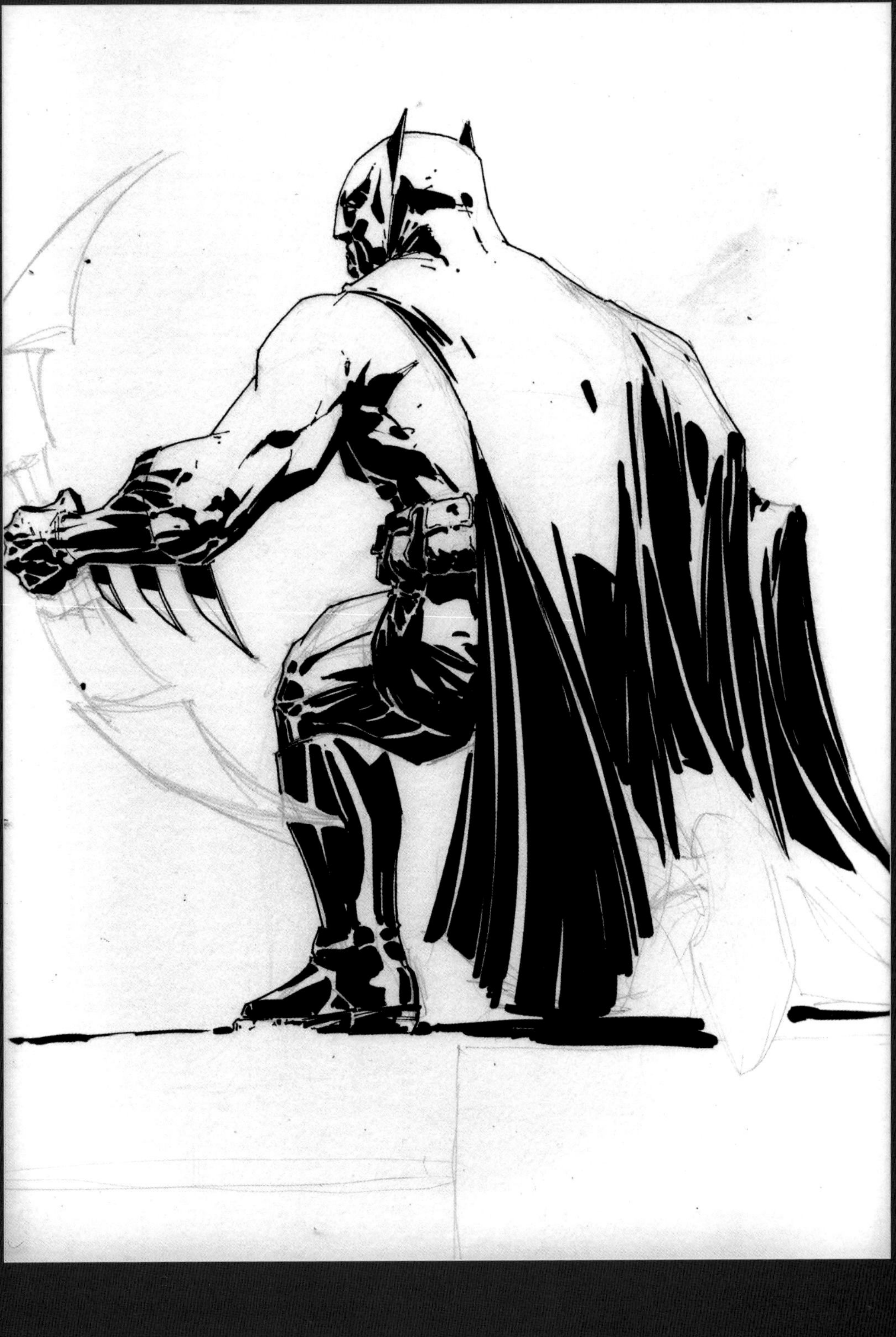

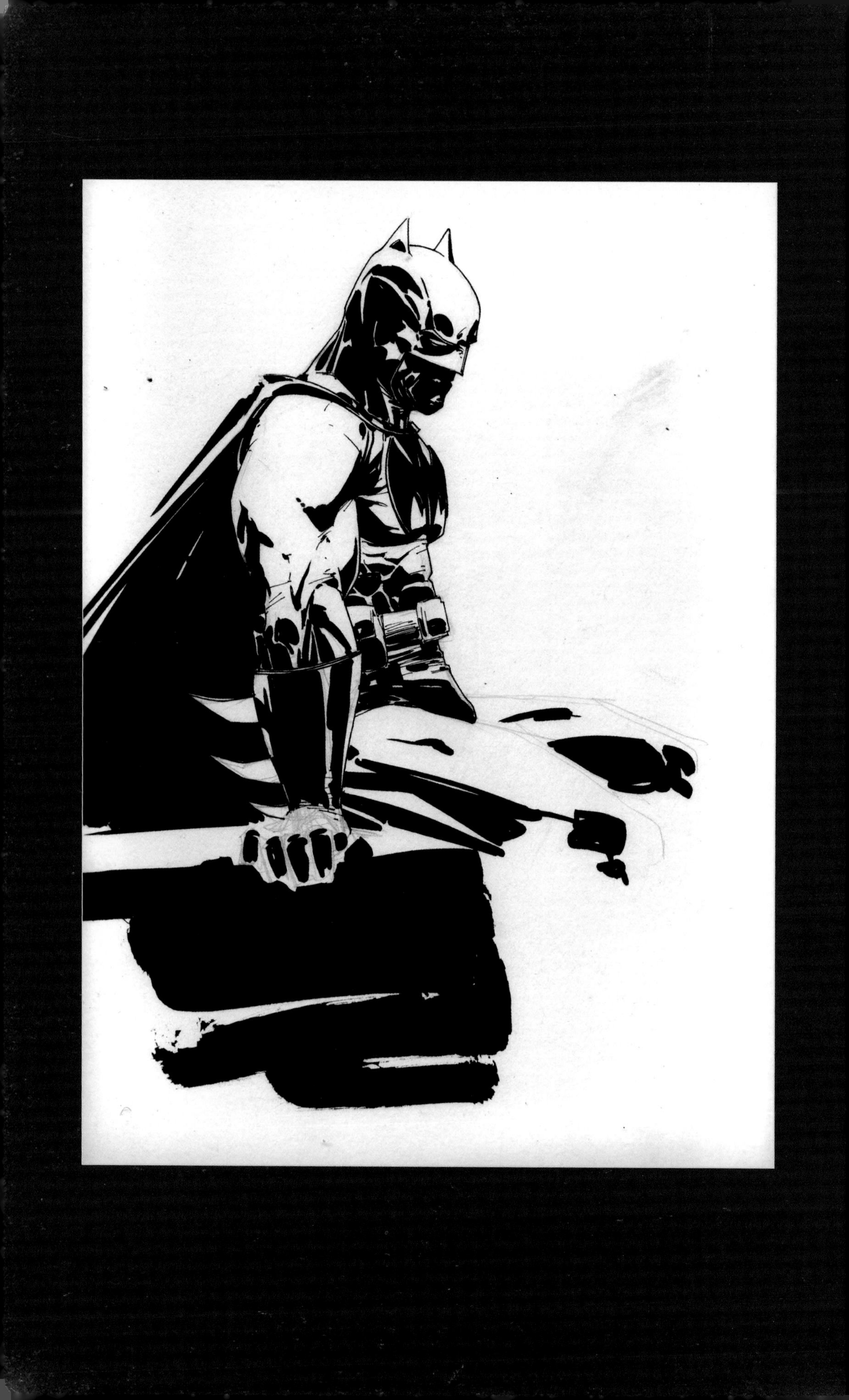

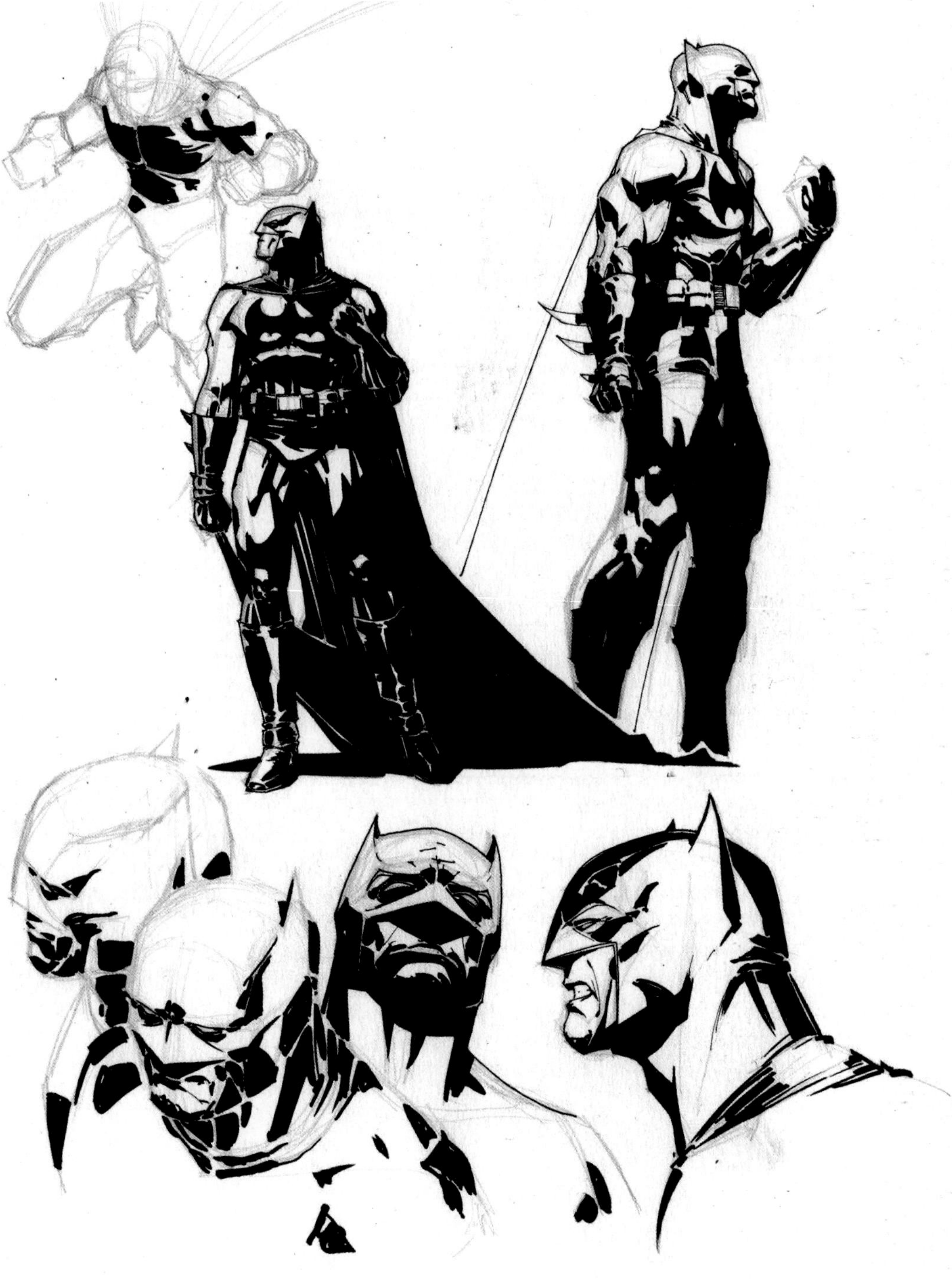

ANDY DIGGLE's comics career began somewhat inauspiciously, running the comics section of the Sherratt & Hughes bookshop in Croydon. His university dissertation on comics technique led to his teaching an undergraduate course on graphic narrative the following year. He became the editor of the seminal British sci-fi comic 2000 AD in the year 2000, before moving on to become a full-time writer. Since then he has co-created Vertigo's THE LOSERS — soon to be a major motion picture from Warner Bros. — as well as writing GREEN ARROW: YEAR ONE, HELLBLAZER, ADAM STRANGE, SWAMP THING, SILENT DRAGON, Lenny Zero, Judge Dredd vs. Aliens (with John Wagner), The Punisher and Guy Ritchie's Gamekeeper, also in development in Hollywood. He currently divides his time between comics and screenwriting. Born and bred in London, he currently lives in northwest England... but can't wait to get back.

WHILCE PORTACIO was born in the Philippines and grew up in and around the Pacific rim and West Coast of the United States. He started in comics as an inker in the late 1980s, inking such comics greats as Art Adams and Jim Lee. He was quickly promoted to penciller on titles such as *Punisher, X-Factor* and *Uncanny X-Men*. Along with a group of the industry's top artists, Whilce went on to create the comics company Image, where he created the popular book WETWORKS. As part of WildStorm Studios, he was in the forefront of bringing in computers as a tool to produce and color comics. Whilce moved on to teach the art and creation of comic books back in his native Philippines, where he helped develop some of today's top talent. Whilce recently made a return to comics, illustrating BATMAN CONFIDENTIAL and the long-awaited return of WETWORKS. He happily resides in the peaceful "Inland Empire" of Southern California with his wife Jo and his beautiful children Kevin, Kamilla Faye, and Kaira Meg.

RICHARD FRIEND was born in San Diego, California, and began drawing at an early age. At age 11 he started playing guitar, singing, and writing music, and art was put on the back burner until age 24. Starting to collect comics at that late stage and getting his first pro work in less than a year, Richard rose up the ranks, inking artists including Travis Charest, Chris Bachalo, and J. Scott Campbell. Nominated for an Eisner Award in 1999 for best penciller/inker team on WildCats 2.0 and with goals to pencil and illustrate his own work this upcoming year...hopefully things will continue to be exciting and challenging.

READ MORE OF THE DARK KNIGHT DETECTIVE'S ADVENTURES IN THESE COLLECTIONS FROM DC COMICS:

BATMAN

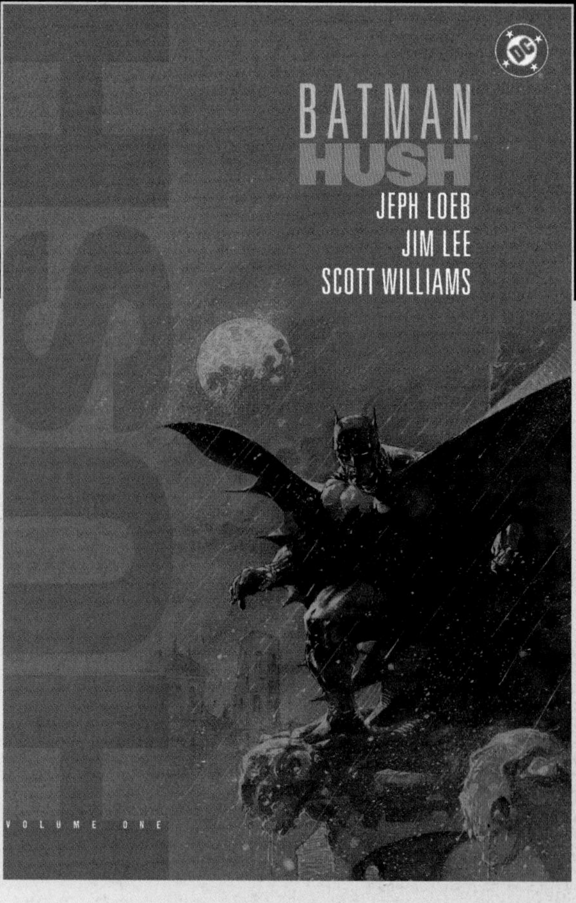
BATMAN
HUSH
JEPH LOEB
JIM LEE
SCOTT WILLIAMS
VOLUME ONE

BATMAN: HUSH VOLUME 1

Jeph Loeb, Jim Lee and **Scott Williams** tell an epic tale of friendship, trust and betrayal, in the first volume of a tale that spans a lifetime of the Dark Knight.

"*THE ACTION IS EXCITING AND THE DETAIL IS METICULOUS.*"
— CRITIQUES ON INFINITE EARTHS

BATMAN: THE DARK KNIGHT RETURNS

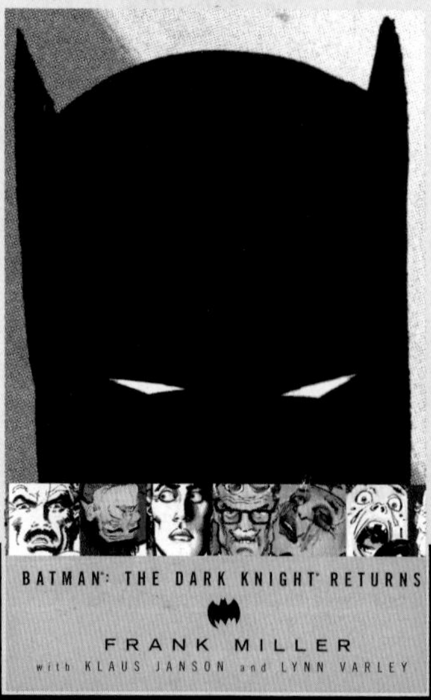
BATMAN: THE DARK KNIGHT RETURNS
FRANK MILLER
with KLAUS JANSON and LYNN VARLEY

FRANK MILLER
KLAUS JANSON
LYNN VARLEY

BATMAN: THE LONG HALLOWEEN

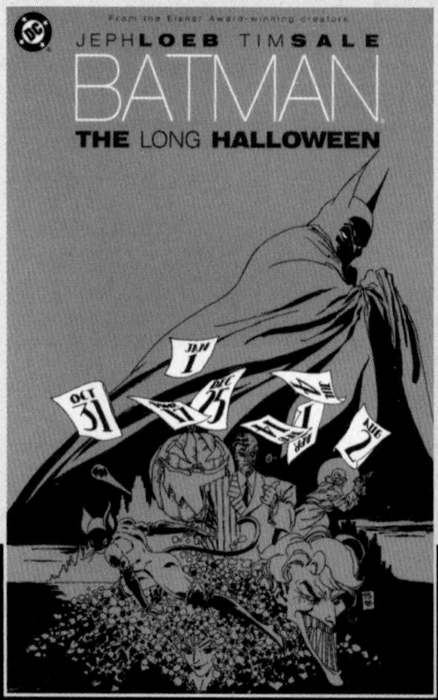
JEPH LOEB TIM SALE
BATMAN
THE LONG HALLOWEEN

JEPH LOEB
TIM SALE

BATMAN: YEAR ONE

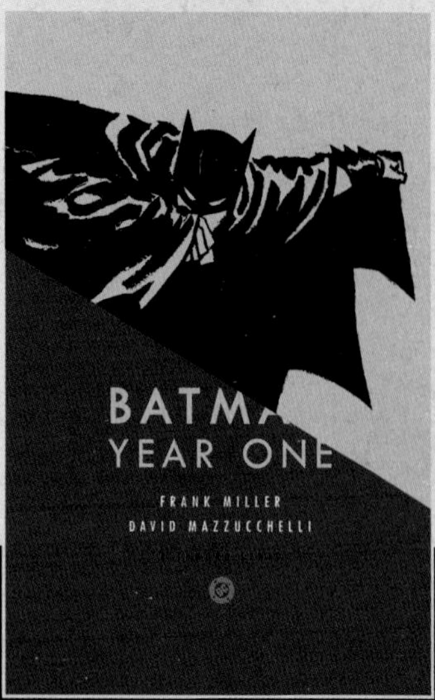
YEAR ONE
FRANK MILLER
DAVID MAZZUCCHELLI

FRANK MILLER
DAVID MAZZUCCHELLI